STANDING
YOUR GROUND

THE PERSECUTION OF THE SAINTS
AND HOW TO OVERCOME IT

A BIBLICAL HANDBOOK

DONALD E. JONES, PHD

J & A Book Publishers
www.jabookpublishers.com

(C) 2020 Donald E. Jones, PhD

Printed in the United States of America

All rights reserved. No part of this book may be reproduced in any form without permission in writing from the author, except in the case of brief quotations embodied in critical articles or reviews.

All Scripture quotations are from the World English Bible. This version was selected, because it is in the public domain and can be quoted without limit. A personal translation of a verse or passage will be designated with (DEJ).

ISBN-13:978-1946368140
ISBN-10: 1946368148

DEDICATION

I dedicate this book to my Savior and Lord Jesus Christ. He has been with me every step of my journey upon the Earth, and I so look forward to being in His presence forever and ever.

Contents

Introduction	1
Chapter - 1. Let Your Lights Shine	11
Chapter - 2. Prepare for Global Oppression	31
Chapter - 3. Expect A Contentious Opposition	133
Chapter - 4. Keep the Divine Perspective	211
Chapter - 5. Beware of Satan's Schemes	239
Chapter - 6. Counter with a Holy Action	253
Chapter - 7. Submit in Human Affairs	293
Chapter - 8. Restrain with Deliberate Actions	337
Chapter - 9. Apply with A Judicial Response	377
Chapter - 10. Defy to Obey A Divine Command	393
Chapter - 11. Mislead to Prevent Harm	435
Chapter - 12. Avoid to Protect the Saints	493
Chapter - 13. Evade with a Careful Rhetoric	527
Chapter - 14. Answer with a Strong Presentation	555
Chapter - 15. Defend as God Directs	577
Chapter - 16. Persist in Watchful Prayer	579
Chapter - 17. Respond with a Courageous Persistence	609
Conclusion	631

ACKNOWLEDGMENTS

I want to thank my wonderful and gracious wife Carol who has supported me in this ministry with sacrifice, enthusiasm, encouragement, and accountability. Most of all, she has been a constant blessing because of her willingness to listen. I was always sharing with her the truths God had been teaching me as I studied His word and wrote this book. It consumed many hours. Thank you, Carol and I deeply love you.

I want to thank my children, Krista, Matt, Greg, and Kara for their constant support of my ministries, love for Christ and His Word, and their willingness to live for Him. I love you all.

Introduction

On the Island of Patmos in the Mediterranean lived the oldest and last apostle of Jesus Christ. He had been banished there by the Roman emperor. Since John would die on this island, this would be his final days of persecution for his faith. Deliverance would come through his death. Before he went home to be with his Savior and Lord, Jesus revealed to him through a vision all that would happen in the end of man's days upon the earth.

This final revelation was given to John to encourage the persecuted Christians throughout the ages that they would ultimately overcome any burden, trial, or pain inflicted upon them due to His Holy Name. Jesus Christ, Lord of Lords and King of Kings will return. Then, at His second coming, He will take back the earth and judge the living and the dead. Those who had persecuted the saints of God will be fully judged for every thought, word, or action against the saints and then thrown into the eternal fire. At this point all the believers they persecuted will be fully avenged. Of course, persecutors who had received Jesus Christ as Savior and Lord before their death will be fully forgiven. Together with them, all Christians will be welcomed joyfully into heaven and rewarded for their many good deeds upon the earth which includes whatever persecution they had to endure. These overcomers will find victory in Christ Jesus.

All throughout the New Testament and into the end of the age Christians have been and will be persecuted for their faith. How are believers in Christ to respond to this constant and continual onslaught? The answer is found in the title of this book. We should "stand our ground." We are to accept the persecution as a part of living in God's kingdom on earth and then become "overcomers." No matter what comes our way, we are to persist in our faith. We are to never give up on Christ, must stand our ground and endure the suffering that may come for His name's sake. In Revelation chapter 2, the Spirit of Jesus speaks to Christians as "overcomers." This term refers to believers who have overcome persecution and the difficulties that life brings to test their faith. He tells us that we will be rewarded for our willingness to stand our ground.

Revelation 2:7
Whoever has ears, let them hear what the Spirit says to the churches. To the one who overcomes... (DEJ).

Revelation 2:11
Whoever has ears, let them hear what the Spirit says to the churches. The one who overcomes... (DEJ).

Revelation 2:17
Whoever has ears, let them hear what the Spirit says to the churches. To the one who overcomes... (DEJ).

Revelation 3:5
The one who overcomes... (DEJ).

Revelation 3:12
The one who overcomes... (DEJ).

Revelation 3:21
To the one who overcomes... (DEJ).

These words were not written for future Christians, they were written for those in the first century and all Christians throughout the ages. This includes us.

In Matthew 13, Jesus described three seeds sown that did not grow into the full plant of faith. One seed was thrown on the rocky road and the persecution for their faith caused them to fall away. The seeds are the ones who claim to be Christians but cannot endure persecution. They fall away before their faith has taken hold. They cannot handle the trials and pressures of those who hate Christ. The seeds that endure and produce fruit. These are the "overcomers" of Revelation. These are the real Christians. This is a critical distinction. True believers overcome and false believers fall away and abandon their faith. Authentic saints will endure whatever comes on behalf of their Savior and Lord.

By no means is this a passive endurance but an active one. They will stand their ground against the forces of evil and not fall away from the faith. As we will see, standing our ground against persecution is not a passive suffering and simple trusting of God while the forces of evil surround and consume us. Instead, it is an active battle sometimes legal, at times physical, certainly social, and always spiritual against the forces of human wickedness instigated and empowered by demons. When Paul said our battle is not against flesh and blood, he meant ultimately not against flesh and blood. But as we will see, the "principalities and powers" work through people. People crucified Christ. People hounded the apostles. People kill mock, humiliate, and restrict Christians. And people have persecuted the church from its inception. Therefore, to stand our ground in persecution, we will have at times take a stand against people and the demons behind them.

This persecution culminates in the dragon and his angelic and human minions attempting to blast Christ, His angels, and Holy Ones (us) out of the sky at Armageddon. He fails as the King of Kings and Lord of Lords defeats them. He is bound for a thousand years, and it finally ends when this Serpent of Old, is unleashed and gathers an army to destroy Christ and His people once and for all. In Revelation 20, we see that evil will not and cannot succeed. The gates of hell will not prevail. John describes it powerfully, vividly, and clearly in verses 7-10.

Revelation 20:7-10
When the thousand years are over, Satan will be released from his prison and will go out to deceive the nations in the four corners of the Earth – Gog and Magog – and to gather them for battle. In number they are like the sand on the seashore. They marched across the breadth of the earth and surrounded the camp of God's people, the city he loves. But fire came down from heaven and devoured them. And the devil, who deceived them, was thrown into the lake of burning sulfur, where the beast and the false prophet had been thrown. They will be tormented day and night forever....

Unfortunately for them and fortunately for us, the Lord God is more powerful than any human or demonic force in the universe and all evil beings will be defeated, judged, and condemned for all eternity.

In fact, much of the content of the Bible encompasses the constant persecution of God's people. The Almighty spends many pages of His Holy Book describing how the world and the fallen Lucifer and his evil legions come after believers. He attacked Cain and Job, those after them, the nation of Israel and their prophets, then Christ, and His apostles. He continues his attacks on Christ's church, those who will be saved during the Tribulation, and finally the believers at the end of the final thousand years on earth (millennium).

Often, we will take notice of the harshness or horrific nature of the persecutions but fail to note how the believers actually responded in the name of Jesus Christ. They did not cower in fear before their persecutors but "overcame" these persecutions by standing their ground. They battled as great warriors to defend their faith.

Today, we actually ignore much of the persecution which is described in the Bible and turn our attention toward the "practical principles" in which we can live prosperously in our daily lives. We treat the Bible as a book of inspirational sayings. Yet, the Bible is not written in this way. It is written as a history of real-life circumstances and how His believers reacted to them as God directed. Much of this history has to do with persecution. This becomes a difficult subject because Christians do not like to consider the possibility that they may be persecuted until it occurs. Well, it is here and will become world-wide.

Though some may go about their daily lives as if this will never happen, the bible's numerous examples of it indicate that it is a common part of believers' lives who are sharing the gospel and living righteous lives. If some Christians live in a region of the world where there is little or no direct physical persecution, this should be seen as the exception to the rule. Of course, in many regions where there is no direct physical persecution there is often intolerance, verbal and legal attacks, and numerous less obvious ways of showing disapproval. We must not be silenced and take our stand for Jesus. We cannot be concerned with "political correctness" or anything else that would keep us from glorifying our Lord every day.

This silence occurred in Rome. The church there had been muted and Paul had made them bold again as he proclaimed his faith as a prisoner. In Philippians 1:12-15, Paul explains to the Philippian believers what God had done to further the good news through his persecution and imprisonment and trial before the emperor.

Philippians 1:12-15
Now I want you to know, brothers and sisters, that what has happened to me has actually served to advance the gospel. As a

result, it has become clear throughout the whole palace guard and to everyone else that I am in chains for Christ. And because of my chains, most of the brothers and sisters have become confident in the Lord and dare all the more to proclaim the gospel without fear. It is true that some preach Christ out of envy and rivalry, but others out of goodwill.

As the apostle boldly proclaimed the gospel, the church in Rome awakened from their slumber and, most likely, their "political correctness" to also boldly stand their ground for the faith. As the capitol of the Roman Empire, there were many good reasons to remain silent, but this has never been the way of "overcomers." We cannot remain silent about Christ, nor can we stop living out our faith in Him.

In other parts of the world, persecution is the rule and not the exception. Throughout human history up to this very moment, there are Christians suffering untold violence for their faith. The purpose of this book is to provide a complete picture of what the Bible says concerning persecution. This book is a book of action. It is designed to answer all of the questions one might have on the subject and explain exactly what Christians may and may not do. There are few, if any, books that deal with this important subject in great detail as I have done. When books address this critical subject, they either disagree with each other or only concern themselves with one or two issues. Often, the most controversial aspects of the topic or the Bible passages involved are not discussed. This leaves saints in the church with a woefully incomplete picture of this all too important topic. A biblical handbook must be written; this is what I have endeavored to do.

I attempted to stay away from the typical study cycle of some in Christianity. Often, when Christians desire to study a topic, they simply read a book about the topic. The book they read is usually based on a book or books that someone wrote, whose foundation is on a book or books someone else wrote. This continues until all the information passed from book to book becomes extremely limited and incomplete. I have ventured away from this typical approach to broaden the church's understanding of this important doctrine.

This was no small task to research and study. I did not read any books on persecution until after the initial study. I basically read through the entire Bible verse by verse. Then, I identified and categorized every individual verse or passage which addressed persecution in some way. These categories were built from the individual verses, rather than a set of preconceived beliefs and notions. Each category became a chapter or section heading. All the Scriptural passages were carefully studied in their many contexts, including historical, grammatical, and scriptural.

Once my interpretations were complete, I compared them to the interpretation of other commentators both past and present. Finally, I compared my personal interpretation of the all the biblical passages to the historical interpretation of the evangelical church. Also, when I read, I attempted to let the Bible define and explain itself by itself. I studied the many words, concepts, ideas, and principles in the Bible and compared them to other Bible passages to define, elucidate, describe, or explain a truth. At every moment, I labored in my attempt to remove my biased cultural, language, and past biblical frameworks that I would impose upon the texts in order to study them afresh. This was especially important with the use of my English terminology which sometimes cannot provide a word that is precise enough to properly translate the Hebrew or Greek word in a passage.

I paid attention to analogies, metaphors, and similes used by both the inspired authors and the biblical characters that addressed the topic in some way for insight. Once the study was finished and the biblical framework was completed, I compared what I had discovered to books and articles on the subject to determine discrepancies, differences of opinion, and what might be missing. Once these further studies were finished, this book was written.

Why must doctrinal study require such labor? I think the answer is found in the way God composed the Scriptures. The Lord did not write the Bible in consecutive narratives, a list of commands, or even an organized outline of doctrines. Instead, it was written as God's people journeyed through life. To understand a subject fully, often we must pull out fragments of truth from many different places to discover the complete truth about a given topic. There are numerous treasures and gold nuggets buried within the pages of God's Word and the faithful must find it. Only those willing to labor in sound doctrine will be able to discover its riches.

Then, those who have found them are required to teach it to others. This is what I have done, and others like me. As a result, this book will be no small task to read. Since I cross reference so many verses, I have put the full texts in the book because it would be an impossible task to read even one paragraph without having to remember or to look up every verse and passage referenced. I utilized the World English Translation because it is the only English translation which can be quoted without limits. Though some of the translation is rough, I have pointed out the times when this happened. I am so incredibly grateful for this copyright free translation. This book is sort of a hybrid between an outline and a series of doctrinal statements.

Every aspect of this study touched on so many theological truths, that they could not possibly be incorporated into this book. As a result, I often left a particular truth with a few proof texts that could be filled in with a simple concordance study. Other truths were explained and left for the readers to research on their own. Also, I have repeated many passages over and over viewing them from many different angles. Though this might be tedious at times to read, it is crucial to discovering every truth concerning this topic.

In 1 Corinthians 14:20, the apostle commands all believers to be mature in their thinking. He writes, "Brothers, don't be children in thoughts, yet in malice be babies, but in thoughts be mature." This book is for those who want the deeper truths in God's Word concerning the doctrine of persecution. It is for those who desire to discover the depth and breadth of God's thinking on this topic or as Paul calls it "the mind of Christ" on this doctrine (1 Corinthians 2:16). Therefore, the reading of this book will require much time, a commitment, and thought. Passages might need to be referenced in their scriptural context and studied to confirm their truths. If you are capable, please do not skip this step in your growth.

In 1 John 4:4, John discloses to his readers that they are to test the spirits. Here is my challenge to all my readers and a method by which God desires us to test truth. I want the readers to test the Spirit in me by the Spirit in them in order to verify the truths that I disclose based on my careful study. In 1 Thessalonians 5:21, those in the church are exhorted to examine everything with care. I exhort my readers to do the same with this book. In Acts 17:11, the Bereans are described as nobler because they closely examined the Holy Scriptures even though Paul was presenting the truth. I encourage you to be nobler and examine the Scriptures I present to support my doctrinal statements, if needed. This scrutiny is critical, since Christians share a message that brings not only eternal life but unveils the Triune God and His divine truth.

Readers will notice that the book is written in a simple, straightforward style. This framework is not presented with a vast number of theological terms, complex philosophical thoughts, obscure vocabulary, or my personal opinions. This design is intended to focus all of the reader's attention on the Bible and what it teaches concerning the subject. I am truly interested in allowing God to fully speak from His Word. The words the Lord Almighty chooses to use through His inspired writers are the words that should teach us, as much as possible, before we add other terms for comprehension or clarification. It is my way of remaining true to God and His words to us.

I leave you with Paul's final words to the elders in the city of Ephesus. In Acts 20:32, He says, "Now, brothers, I entrust you to God, and to the word of his grace [Bible], which is able to build up, and to give you the inheritance among all those who are sanctified." Here, he commended the elders to the Lord and His Word. He was leaving them and would never return. He knew that they would have to commit themselves to the study of His Word and trust His guidance through the Holy Spirit. In the same way, I leave you to the Lord's guidance and the careful study of His Word. Read the book. Study the Scriptures contained within it. Share the truths with others. Be prepared to be used by God. Watch for the fruits of your labor. Trust in His Spirit to lead you (2 Timothy 2:7). This will take much faith on your part and the journey down this path is worth it.

Chapter 1

Let Your Lights Shine

In order to be persecuted, we must share the gospel. As long as we are silent, we will never be in harm's way. Yet, as we saw in the introduction, this is not God's way. The gospel must be shared, and people must be saved. Why? This is the task Jesus gave to us as His followers. To put it another way, He is the light of the world and has given that light to us, and we must shine our light to all mankind. Personally, it means to shine our lights to our family, friends, and others.

The apostle John opens his gospel with this very truth. In John 1:1-5, John takes us back to eternity past and explains who Christ was in relationship to the Father. He describes how Jesus came into the world to be a light in the darkness.

John 1:1-5
In the beginning was the Word, and the Word was with God, and the Word was God. The same was in the beginning with God. All things were made through him. Without him was not anything made that has been made. In him was life, and the life was the light of men. The light shines in the darkness, and the darkness hasn't overcome it.

The word "light" has two aspects to it. One is doctrinal contrasting the light of spiritual truth with the darkness of spiritual error. The second aspect is moral and contrasts the light of righteousness and holiness with the darkness of sin, evil, and wickedness. So, John is saying that Christ came to reveal in Himself what truth and righteousness is in the midst of a world filled with lies and falsehoods, sin and wickedness. This is what Jesus Himself claimed.

John 12:46
I have come as a light into the world, that whoever believes in me may not remain in the darkness.

This is the true gospel uttered in the simplest of terms. This light is the truth of who God is. It reveals that Christ had come to die for mankind and people must receive Him as Savior and Lord. Why? The Lord God is righteous, and man simply is not. Man lives in the darkness of thinking that he can find God, deny God, or create a god on his own. He is basically good, and all things will work out in the end. God's Son came to explain that this was not the case at all; instead, judgment for sin will damn all mankind forever and ever.

Man must take on the righteousness of Christ by grace through faith. Paul described this saving good news in this way.

Ephesians 2:4-5
But God, being rich in mercy, for his great love with which he [God] loved us, even when we were [spiritually] dead through our trespasses, made us alive together with Christ (by grace you have been saved).

How is this accomplished exactly in our lives?

Ephesians 2:8-9
For by grace you have been saved through faith, and that not of yourselves; it is the gift of God, not of works, that no one would boast.

God's grace is poured out upon man in his wickedness and sin as a gift which he receives by faith. Then Paul adds our immediate purpose. You see, receiving Christ as Savior and Lord is not the end but the beginning of our time on Earth. Then, we are to do good works. This is our purpose.

Ephesians 2:10
For we are his workmanship, created in Christ Jesus for good works, which God prepared before [the beginning of the world] that we would walk in them.

This is not just any "good works" of our choosing but specific thoughts, words, and actions which honor God based on His commandments in the Scriptures. One of those commands is to share this good news with others.

This is the reason Jesus told His disciples and thereby all generations of Christians that they too are lights.

Matthew 5:14-15
You are the light of the world. A city located on a hill can't be hidden. Neither do you light a lamp, and put it under a measuring basket, but on a stand; and it shines to all who are in the house.

Jesus is saying that we must shine our lights as lamps and never cover over and hide what we believe and who we are individually. As a city of saints, we must be on top of a hill shining our lights in the same way together as a local church.

Our Personal Witness

There are two ways we personally shine our lights to the world, which are sharing the gospel and living a righteous life before all those around us. The first is evangelism.

First, we share the light of the truth. Jesus passed this on to His disciples.

Matthew 10:27
What I tell you in the darkness, speak in the light; and what you hear whispered in the ear, proclaim on the housetops.

When Paul entered Pisidian Antioch to preach the gospel, he told them that he had this mission to preach the good news to all.

Acts 13:47
For so has the Lord commanded us, saying, "I have set you as a light for the Gentiles, that you should bring salvation to the uttermost parts of the Earth."

He saw himself as a light shining into their dark city of error and sin. The Lord could have selected a wide variety of ways in which He could have revealed His plan of redemption to a dying world; instead, He chose for His people to proclaim it as lights shining in the darkness.

How is this accomplished? In Romans 10:14, Paul answers this through by utilizing a series of rhetorical questions.

Romans 10:14-15
How then will they [those in darkness] call on him in whom they have not believed? How will they believe in him whom [Jesus Christ] they have not heard? How will they hear [the gospel] without a preacher [someone to present it]? And how will they preach unless they are sent? As it is written: "How beautiful are the feet of those who preach the Good News of peace, who bring glad tidings of good things!"

Paul is not describing a preacher by profession but anyone who proclaims the gospel. He portrays those who let their light shine in this way as having "beautiful feet!" Christians must use their feet to spread the good news with their lips. If we try and live the gospel without sharing it, how will they connect our actions to the gospel and receive Christ?

The Roman saints had put a basket over every lamp in the church. Paul alludes to this when he wrote his letter to the

Philippians describing how his boldness in shining the light even in chains had emboldened the Romans to shine theirs.

Philippians 1:14
And that most of the brothers in the Lord, being confident through my bonds, are more abundantly bold to speak the word of God....

Paul was in the midst of persecution and still shining his light. He was a prisoner awaiting a trial before the emperor and was sharing the good news of Christ with the servants of his household who came to care for him and the guards who were watching him.

Philippians 1:13
Now I desire to have you know, brothers, that the things which happened to me [persecution] have turned out...to the progress of the Good News; so that it became evident to the whole palace guard, and to all the rest, that my bonds are in Christ.

Later, the apostle mentions the household of the ruler of the Roman Empire.

Philippians 4:22
All the saints greet you, especially those who are of Caesar's household.

What a blessing it would be to say after shining our lights all day, "The Lord made my feet beautiful today!" These are the beautiful feet of saints who shine their lights by sharing the gospel! We cannot be fearful of persecution and become dim lights with baskets over our heads and mute saints hidden in the darkness of man's error and sin. They need our lights.

After Jesus resurrected, His final words encompassed the speaking of the truth of the gospel.

Matthew 28:18-20
Jesus came to them and spoke to them, saying, "All authority has been given to me in heaven and on Earth. Go, and make disciples of all nations, baptizing them in the name of the Father and of the Son and of the Holy Spirit, teaching them to observe all things that I commanded you. Behold, I [Jesus] am with you always, even to the end of the age. Amen.

Here, the Lord mandates His eleven disciples to make other disciples of Him. How? They were to go, baptize, and teach. This simply means that they were to go and shine their lights. When people responded by receiving Christ as Savior and Lord, they were to baptize them. Then, they were to be taught the Holy Scriptures. We are to follow this pattern in our Christian lives also.

Luke speaks of a second incident before Christ leaves the earth where once again, He tells His disciples to shine their lights.

Acts 1:8
But you will receive power when the...Spirit has come upon you. You will be witnesses to me in Jerusalem, in all Judea and Samaria, and to the uttermost parts of the Earth.

This refers to all Christians. All of us are to shine our lights by sharing the gospel.

We saw this occur when the saints ran for their lives from Saul's persecution.

Acts 8:3-4
But Saul ravaged the assembly, entering into every house, and dragged both men and women off to prison. Therefore those who were scattered abroad went around preaching the good news of Jesus Christ, the Savior and Lord.

Though they were persecuted, they shined their lights by "preaching the Word" everywhere they went.

Secondly, we are to shine our lights by living righteously before the world. The sharing of the good news is His truth displayed rather than error and living in a holy way is His righteousness displayed rather than wickedness. In Matthew 5, the Lord explained that to shine their lights Christians must also live righteous lives.

Matthew 5:16
Even so, let your light shine before men; that they may see your good works, and glorify your Father who is in heaven.

In Philippians 2, the apostle declared that the saints were to appear as lights in the world and were to be holding forth the Word of Truth.

Philippians 2:14-15
Do all things without murmurings and disputes, that you may become blameless [no fault found] and harmless, children of God without blemish in the midst of a crooked and perverse [opposed to God] generation, among whom you are seen as lights in the world.

We, as believers, are to be lights in our evil, dark world. We should live in harmony, without disputes or grumbling, and with holy habits in the midst of people who are living in the darkness of sin and opposition to God.

Paul discusses this very same concept again in his letter to the Ephesians. Again, the apostle utilizes the terms of light and darkness.

Ephesians 5:8
For you were once darkness, but are now light in the Lord. Walk as children of light.

We must walk (meaning walk about living our lives) as children of light. Our words and actions must be the words and actions as those in the light. We must be steadfast.

To the Colossian Christians, the apostle commands that they walk (live their lives) moment by moment in a manner that was worthy of the Lord.

Colossians 2:6
Therefore as you have received Christ Jesus the Lord, so walk in Him.

Paul also states that they were to live to please Him in every area of their lives (in all respects). They were to bear fruit as they did many good works and increase in their knowledge of Him.

Colossians 1:10
So that you will walk in a manner worthy of the Lord, to please Him in all respects, bearing fruit in every…work and increasing in the knowledge of God.

We are to do the same.

In Ephesians, the apostle entreats his readers to live for Christ by walking worthy of His call.

Ephesians 4:1
I therefore, the prisoner in the Lord, beg you to walk worthily of the calling with which you were called.

We were called out of the world into eternal life and out of the darkness to walk worthy of that calling. Again, Paul was in prison waiting for his trial because he walked worthy. If he had not been living righteously and also proclaiming the gospel, he would have still been free.

In 1 Thessalonians 2:12, he instructs the new believers to live worthy of their Father God when he writes.

1 Thessalonians 2:12
To the end that you should walk worthily of God, who calls you into his own Kingdom and glory.

We are members of the kingdom of God and recipients of His glory manifested in all His blessings and must always walk worthy of this great honor. This is not the earning of our salvation but the display of it. Later in the letter, Paul adds these words.

1 Thessalonians 4:1
Finally then, brothers, we beg and exhort you in the Lord Jesus, that as you received from us how you ought to walk and to please God, that you abound more and more.

Their goal was to grow more and more in righteous living.

In the letter of 1 John, the beloved disciple John calls this "walking in the light." This holy lifestyle is a great testimony of the Lord Jesus Christ.

1 John 1:7-9
But if we walk in the light, as he [Christ] is in the light, we have fellowship with one another, and the blood of Jesus Christ, his Son, cleanses us from all sin. If we say that we have no sin, we deceive ourselves, and the truth is not in us. If we confess our sins, he is faithful and righteous to forgive us the sins, and to cleanse us from all unrighteousness.

As we walk in the light by living righteous lives before the world, we evidence the fact that the blood of Jesus Christ is cleansing us from our sins. Here John implies a pattern: we walk in the light, we stumble, we confess, we are forgiven, we walk again. Notice, these lead to "fellowship" with one another. The word "fellowship" speaks of "partnership" on the Greek. We join together in partnership with one another. We partner to carry out our purpose upon this Earth which is to shine as a city of people upon the hill. This brings us to the corporate aspect of shining our lights. Not only are we individual lights but lights shining together.

Our Corporate Testimony

Not only are we to have a personal testimony to the world as lights but also a corporate witness as well. In 1 Peter 2, the apostle Paul explains that Christians are to be a joint witness together.

1 Peter 2:9
But you are a chosen race...royal priesthood...holy nation, a people for God's own possession, that you may proclaim the excellence of him who called you out of darkness into his marvelous light.

What is a chosen race, royal priests, a holy nation, and God's possession to do? According to Peter, we are to proclaim all that is excellent about the Lord God who called us out of the darkness of error and sin and into the light of His truth and holiness. Then, we should share together that holiness and truth so all may see.

In Colossians 1, Paul alludes to this group witness when he calls the church the "saints in light." We are not just individual lights but saints "in the light." Here, the church is seen a one true light.

Colossians 1:12
Giving thanks to the Father, who made us fit to be partakers of the inheritance of the saints in light.

What are we to do as we walk together in the light? How do we portray the light of Christ as churches to a dark world? It is not so much the sharing of the good news in words but the demonstration of the gospel in actions. These primarily involve behaviors toward those inside the church for those outside to view.

Our corporate witness is our fellowship as saints in Christ together. It is displayed in how we treat one another in love and grace. Christians portray Christ to the world by the way they interact with each other. This is our true testimony, and it is a powerful one.

The Lord has placed Christians into a unique relationship with each other. Besides "saints in light," many analogies are used of our oneness. We are one holy kingdom, one flock, one vine, one family and household, one spiritual body, one bride, and one temple.

Colossians 1:13
Who delivered us [Christians] out of the power of darkness, and translated us into the kingdom of the Son of his love.

John 10:16
I have other sheep, which are not of this fold. I must bring them also, and they will hear my voice. They will become one flock with one shepherd.

John 15:5
I am the vine. You are the branches. He who remains in me, and I in him, the same bears much fruit, for apart from me you can do nothing.

Ephesians 2:19-22
So then you are no longer strangers and sojourners, but you are fellow citizens with the saints, and of the household of God, being

built on the foundation of...apostles and prophets, Christ Jesus himself being the chief cornerstone; in whom the whole building, fitted together, grows into a holy temple in the Lord...also are built together for a habitation of God in the Spirit.

1 Corinthians 12:12
For...the body is one, and has many members, and all the members of the body, being many, are one body; so also is Christ.

Revelation 19:7-8
Let us rejoice and be exceedingly glad, and let us give the glory to him. For the marriage of the Lamb has come, and his wife has made herself ready." It was given to her that she would array herself in bright, pure, fine linen: for the fine linen is the righteous acts of the saints.

Ephesians 2:20-22
Being built on the foundation of the apostles and prophets, Christ Jesus himself being the chief cornerstone; in whom the whole building, fitted together, grows into a holy temple in the Lord; in whom you also are built together for a habitation of God in the Spirit.

Regardless of our gender, ethnicities, backgrounds, social status, and or any other human factors, we are called into oneness by one Spirit. Paul explains that all Christians are baptized into and made to drink of one Spirit. As a result, we must behave as "one body."

1 Corinthians 12:13
For in one [Holy] Spirit were we all baptized into one body, whether Jews or Greeks, whether bond or free; and were all made to drink into one Spirit.

This important witness of the early church involved the interaction of Christians in spiritual activities.

THE PERSECUTION OF THE SAINTS AND HOW TO OVERCOME IT

Acts 2:42-46
They continued steadfastly in the apostles' teaching...fellowship, in the breaking of bread, and prayer. Fear came on every soul, and many wonders and signs were done through the apostles. All who believed were together, and had all things in common. They sold their possessions and goods, and distributed them to all, according as anyone had need. Day by day, continuing steadfastly with one accord in the temple, and breaking bread at home, they took their food with gladness and singleness of heart.

They were fellowshipping, participating in communion by breaking bread, praying, and devoting themselves to the teaching given by the apostles. Every day they were meeting in the temple and each other's homes with joy and sincerity. They took care of each other's needs first, not the world's. This is an important and often misunderstood distinction.

This was all done in view of the public. And what was the impact? Luke portrays the reaction upon the world.

Acts 2:47
Praising God, and having favor with all the people. The Lord added to the assembly [church] day by day those who were being saved.

They were having favor with all the people. What was the result from this "favor?" The Lord Jesus was adding to their number.

This is seen again in Acts 4.

Acts 4:32-36
The multitude of those who believed were of one heart and soul. Not one of them claimed that anything of the things which he possessed was his own, but they had all things common. With great power, the apostles [the twelve] gave their testimony of the resurrection of the Lord Jesus. Great grace was on them all. For

neither was there among them any who lacked, for as many as were owners of lands or houses sold them, and brought the prices of the things that were sold, and laid them at the apostles' [the twelve] feet, and distribution was made to each, according as anyone had need. Joses, who by the apostles was surnamed Barnabas (which is, being interpreted, Son of Exhortation...Levite, a man of Cyprus....

Notice that after Peter had completed his second sermon, about 5,000 were saved. This brought the size of the church to over 10,000 counting the woman and children who were baptized. The people were of one heart and soul. They met the needs of each other by having all things in common.

Another way our light as one body can shine in the world is through the Lord's discipline of His church in order to protect the purity of His people. When the world sees these actions whether directly by the Lord or by its leaders, they know the Lord God is present among them. When they see God's people seeking righteousness and judging sin among themselves, they will come to understand this is how the true God is. Then, this right God will come to judge them. This will bring fear and conviction leading to repentance and faith.

This is exactly what happened in the church in Jerusalem. The apostles were collecting donations to give to the poor among its new believers. Why? Many had come to Christ and had never left the city because they would have been disowned by their Jewish families, shunned by the Jews, and lost their jobs. In fact, they remained until Saul's persecution broke out. Many of these people would have to begin their new lives in Christ with nothing. Who would care for them? The church would.

Ananias and Sapphira sold a piece of land and tried to gain favor from the other believers by lying about how much they had given from the proceeds to the poor saints among them. They told Peter that they had given all of it to the assembly when they hadn't. Luke describes what happened.

Acts 5:1-6
But a certain man named Ananias, with Sapphira, his wife, sold a possession, and kept back part of the price, his wife also being aware of it, and brought a certain part, and laid it at the apostles' feet. But Peter said, "Ananias, why has Satan filled your heart to lie to the Holy Spirit, and to keep back part of the price of the land? While you kept it, didn't it remain your own? After it was sold, wasn't it in your power? How is it that you have conceived this thing in your heart? You haven't lied to men, but...God. Ananias, hearing these words, fell down and died. Great fear came on all who heard these things. The young men arose and wrapped him up, and they carried him out and buried him.

After Ananias arrived, lied, and was struck dead, his wife came upon the scene not knowing what had just occurred. Unfortunately, his wife would receive the same fate. Though it appears harsh from man's standpoint, it is not from God's. Luke continues his narrative.

Acts 5:7-10
About three hours later, his wife, not knowing what had happened, came in. Peter answered her, "Tell me whether you sold the land for so much." She said, "Yes, for so much." But Peter asked her [Sapphira], "How is it that you have agreed together to tempt the Spirit of the Lord? Behold, the feet of those who have buried your husband are at the door, and they will carry you out." She fell down immediately at his feet, and died. The young men came in and found her dead, and they [members of the church] carried her out and buried her by her husband.

Now, Sapphira was struck dead. Why would God deal so harshly? Notice, the description of what occurs next.

STANDING YOUR GROUND

Acts 5:11-14
Great fear came on the whole assembly, and on all who heard these things. By the hands of the apostles many signs and wonders were done among the people. They were all with one accord.... None of the rest dared to join them, however the people honored them. More believers were added to the Lord, multitudes of both men and women.

The people saw the discipline of the Lord and how He had kept His church pure. It scared them but also brought the church honor. Next, it brought them souls. Salvation is all about judgment for sin. It begins there.

People must see their sin in order to know that judgment is coming, and they must be delivered from that judgment through the Savior Jesus Christ. In Acts 2, near the end of Peter's sermon on the day of Pentecost, the people cried out for salvation. What did they ask and how did Peter respond?

Acts 2:37-41
Now when they heard this, they were cut to the heart, and said to Peter and the rest of the apostles, "Brothers, what shall we do?" Peter said to them, "Repent, and be baptized, every one of you [all were under judgment], in the name of Jesus Christ for the forgiveness of sins, and you will receive the gift of the Holy Spirit. For the promise is to you, and to your children, and to all who are far off, even as many as the Lord...will call to himself." With many other words he testified...exhorted them, saying, "Save yourselves from this crooked [evil] generation!" Then those who gladly received his word were baptized. There were added that day about three thousand souls.

Here, Peter had been speaking about their evil, wicked ways and the judgment to come. As a result, they entreated him to please tell them what they must do. He begins with repentance for their sin to find forgiveness from God.

How do they then discover that they are sinners? They hear this fact presented. Also, they can see this fact lived out when they encounter believers who live a righteous example in front of them. The contrast is utterly convicting. We can live righteously as individuals before the world but also as a corporate body for all to see. Our purity and our desire to keep the church pure will shine our lights before the people.

In Pauls' first letter to the Corinthians, he discusses the proper utilization of their many spiritual gifts. Regarding the speaking gifts, he appeals to the result they should have, which is not a warm feeling from God's love and grace, but the deep conviction of their sin and God's judgment. This sense of conviction produces the need to find God's love and grace through faith in Christ. If they think God's love and grace will come to them apart from Christ's death on the cross for their sins, they will never be saved.

1 Corinthians 14:23-25
If therefore the whole assembly is assembled together and all speak with other languages, and unlearned or unbelieving people come in, won't they say that you are crazy? But if all prophesy, and someone unbelieving or unlearned comes in, he is reproved by all, and he is judged by all. And thus the secrets of his heart are revealed. So he will fall down on his face and worship the Lord, declaring that God is definitely among you indeed.

What secrets of the heart are revealed? It was their sin and wretchedness. So, what must they have heard? The gifted ones had to have been speaking about living righteously and holy before God to the believers. They must have been dealing with putting away the sin of their old unsaved lives and putting on the righteous behavior of their new lives.

Let's take this one step further. What if the unbeliever had come into their midst and saw a group of people whom they knew were sinning as much as they were and demonstrated no conviction? Why would he then fall on his face? What if he knew many of them were living as he was and had never demonstrated the transformation of the Holy Spirit? Why would he want to? Instead, he sees the repentance for sin and the slow but sure transformation of the Spirit as they also preach these truths. Our purity becomes a beacon of light to the world as our words and lives demonstrate this powerful conviction.

Though the individual and corporate shining of our lights can bring conviction of sin producing repentance, it can also bring persecution instead. Why? The world lives in darkness and loves their sin and wickedness. This causes them to hate the light. When our lights reveal the Lord God's existence and character, it will lead to the exposing of their sin and its resultant judgment. This is supposed to drive them to the brightest light which is Jesus Christ, and it does for some. Yet, for many it will drive them to attempt to shut our lights off as they did to Jesus Christ by crucifying Him. This is so important to understand. Our lights are shining all the time, and the darkness of sin is being revealed over and over again. Unbelievers who are not interested will stop us.

The very words of Jesus confirm this truth as recorded in the third chapter of John.

John 3:19
This is the judgment, that the light [referring to Himself] has come into the world, and men loved the darkness rather than the light; for their works were evil.

When people are in darkness in the physical world and we bring a light, we would expect them to allow us to shine the light and lead them out of the dark. Instead, they love it and persecute us for shining it in the first place.

Also, they must shut our light off because it constantly exposes their sin and wickedness. Jesus continues with this thought.

John 3:20
For everyone who does evil hates the light, and doesn't come to the light, lest his works would be exposed.

Believers must be prepared for persecution from those in the darkness. So, what is this darkness like?

The World's Darkness

Over and over, the Lord and His apostles mentioned that the world exists in utter darkness. Obviously, it does not mean physical darkness but instead spiritual darkness. Since we will discuss this condition at length in another chapter, we will introduce the concept here. To better understand what lights we are, it is necessary to comprehend exactly what the darkness is that we are illuminating. This spiritual darkness cannot be perceived and is accepted by faith.

John records the words of Jesus which provides one of the aspects of this darkness in his gospel.

John 12:35
Jesus therefore said to them, "Yet a little while the light is with you. Walk while you have the light, that darkness doesn't overtake you.... who walks in...darkness doesn't know where he is going."

In verse 46 of the same chapter, Jesus teaches.

John 12:46
I have come as a light into the world, that whoever believes in me may not remain in the darkness.

The implication in these two verses is that those who do not believe in Jesus "remain in darkness" and "the darkness has overtaken them." How does this show itself spiritually in real life? Jesus again provides the answer.

John 11:10
But if a man walks in the night [in unbelief], he stumbles, because the light isn't in him.

The Lord states that this darkness causes those enmeshed in it to stumble around. Unbelievers are "stumbling around" in their false beliefs about the world and their wickedness. They have no light in them, so they are filled with error and wickedness. This is not a literal and physical stumbling but a spiritual, intellectual, and moral one, because they have no idea really where they are going. It is like walking in total darkness. Then, we turn on the light and expose their sin which they know brings judgment and so they will either come to the light or attempt to turn off our light. When this happens, we must stand our ground and keep the lights on. Again, this must be accepted by faith.

Chapter 2

Prepare for Global Oppression

As Christians, we understand the deep darkness of the human condition in sin. Therefore, we must explore the evil characteristics that are spawned from this predicament. Our light exposes their sins and coming judgment. Those who desire to escape the judgment will find salvation in Christ. Those who desire to continue in their sins will do anything to turn their bright lights off. They did this to Jesus and will do it to His followers.

John 1:19-21
This is the judgment, that the light has come into the world, and men loved the darkness rather than the light; for their works were evil. For everyone who does evil hates the light, and doesn't come to the light [truth and holiness revealed], lest his works would be exposed. But he who does the truth comes to the light, that his works may be revealed, that they have been done in God.

Our lights cause great problems for the unsaved who reject Christ. They don't like the message because they love being who they are. They love the darkness and the constant expression of their wicked attributes. As we have seen, it is not simply that they are ignorant because the lights were on in creation. It is due to the fact that they loved their sin and then rejected the God who condemned them for it.

This love of this darkness will increase until the whole world is consumed in it. Then the opposition to Christians will become global. Persecution will increase from region to region until it consumes the whole world. This enables the rise of the final world government upon the Earth.

Revelation 13:6-8
He [the beast] opened his mouth for blasphemy against God, to blaspheme his name, and his dwelling, those who dwell in heaven. It was given to him to make war with the saints, and to overcome them. Authority over every tribe, people, language, and nation was given to him. All who dwell on the Earth will worship him, everyone whose name has not been written from the foundation of the world in the book of life of the Lamb who has been killed.

Behind this beast filling him and empowering him is Satan. The Devil loses his access to the heavenly places and is thrown down and confined to the Earth.

Revelation 12:7-9
There was war in the sky. Michael and his angels made war on the dragon. The dragon and his angels made war. They didn't prevail, neither was a place found for him any more in heaven. The great dragon was thrown down, the old serpent, he who is called the devil and Satan, the deceiver of the whole world. He was thrown down to the Earth, and his angels were thrown down with him.

So, the serpent turns his attention from the angelic armies to the saints of God. Rather than warring with those stronger than him, he determines to war directly against the saints that the angelic forces protect.

Revelation 12:17
The dragon grew angry with the woman, and went away to make war with the rest of her offspring [saints], who keep God's commandments and hold Jesus' testimony.

What is our response as believers to this ever-increasing opposition as it continues to permeate the entire planet? It is to stand our ground. We do not have to stand silent and take whatever evil men may decide to do to us due to our belief and trust in Christ as Savior and Lord.

THE PERSECUTION OF THE SAINTS AND HOW TO OVERCOME IT

Revelation 13:9-10
If anyone has an ear, let him hear. If anyone is to go into captivity, he will go into captivity. If anyone is to be killed with the sword, he must be killed. Here is the endurance and the faith of the saints.

Whatever happens we will never deny our Savior and Lord Jesus Christ even unto death.

In 2 Timothy 3:1-17, Paul explains this very process. Here the apostle describes the evil qualities of people on the Earth how they will increase. This will result in a persecution that is widespread and dangerous as the world becomes less and less tolerant of our Bible, our Savior, and our beliefs. Of course, we know that it ends in a world-wide persecution. Rather than taking the passage phrase by phrase, we will begin with several general descriptions then move on to a verse-by-verse explanation.

The Specific Time

Paul provides the time period of this growing opposition.

2 Timothy 3:1
But realize [know] this, that in the last days difficult times will come.

Notice, Paul calls this period in which evil will grow the "last days." Though it appears as if he is speaking about the end of the world, he is actually referring to the period from the birth of the church to the Second Coming of Christ.

The last days have been going on for a long time. They are going on now and will continue until His return. This time period is also referred to by other inspired New Testament authors with various terms.

In Hebrews 1:2, the author describes how the Lord God has revealed Himself first through the fathers and prophets and then in these "last days" through His Son.

Hebrews 1:2
Has in these last days spoken to us by his Son, whom he appointed heir of all things, through whom also he made the worlds (DEJ).

Then Peter mentions this time period in his letter.

2 Peter 3:3
Knowing this first, that in the last days mockers will come, walking after their own lusts.

So, we are in the midst of the last days. They began at the first coming of Christ and will end at His second. They will bring both salvation and opposition.

The Dangerous Season

These last days will be dangerous for those willing to shine their lights in the darkness. As the blackness of error and sin grows in the hearts of men, their hostility will increase.

2 Timothy 3:3
But know this, that in the last days, grievous times will come.

The word translated "grievous" means "difficult, dangerous, or violent." The Greek word "times" means a "time period, a season, or an era." So, Paul refers to these "last days" as a dangerous season, an era of trouble, and a time of violence.

The word is used in Matthew 8:28 to portray the two demonically possessed men who lived among the tombs and were "exceedingly fierce." They were such horribly violent men that no one was able to pass by the cemetery. While they lived among the tombs, it became a dangerous season for those walking past.

Matthew 8:28
When he [Jesus] came to the other side, into the country of the Gergesenes, two people possessed with demons met him there, coming forth out of the tombs, exceedingly fierce, so that no man could pass by that way.

Then the Lord came and healed them. The demons left and great calm and serenity settled upon their lives.

Luke 8:35
People went out to see what had happened. They came to Jesus, and found the man from whom the demons had gone out, sitting at Jesus' feet, clothed and in his right mind; and they were afraid [This is the exact same incident though Luke only mentions the main demoniac].

Like those men, we will encounter similar opposition for a different reason. Though the demoniacs were crazed from possession, those who oppose us will be crazed out of hate and rejection of our Savior and Lord. Within the period of the last days, there have been, are, and will continue to be violent seasons against the church in different areas of the Earth until the persecution becomes world-wide. Then Jesus will come and bring peace throughout the world.

Its Absolute Certainty

Persecution and its continued increase are an absolute certainty. Nothing can stop its movement throughout the entire Earth. The Lord may slow it down or speed it up according to His will, but it is guaranteed to increase.

2 Timothy 3:1
But realize [know] this, that in the last days grievous times will come."

Notice, he says, "will come." The verb translated "will come" speaks of the certainty of a threatening or impending doom in the future. Persecution and its increase are guaranteed.

When the apostle Paul explains that Christians can never be separated from the love of Jesus Christ, he gives examples of the many difficulties we will encounter. This included persecution. Paul saw this as inevitable.

Romans 8:35
Who shall separate [a follower, saint, Christian] from the love of Christ? Could oppression, or anguish, or persecution, or famine, or nakedness, or peril, or sword?

Jesus warned his disciples that if they persecuted Him, then they would do the same to His followers.

John 15:20
Remember the word that I [Jesus] said to you: "A servant is not greater than his lord." If they persecuted me, they will also persecute you. If they kept my [the Lord's] word, they will keep yours also.

Persecution is coming if it has not yet arrived in our lives. Paul guaranteed it.

Their Increased Intolerance

When we look at verse 13, Paul indicates that there will be an increase in their evil. This increase will lead inevitably to more and more persecution of God's saints.

THE PERSECUTION OF THE SAINTS AND HOW TO OVERCOME IT

2 Timothy 3:13
But evil men and impostors [seducers] will grow worse and worse, deceiving and being deceived.

The phrase "will grow worse and worse" comes from two words in the Greek language. The first is the preposition meaning "before" and the second is a root word meaning, "to cut, strike, or smite." The root word is used literally for cutting by both Matthew and mark.

Matthew 21:8
A very great multitude spread their clothes on the road. Others cut branches from the trees, and spread them on the road.

Mark 11:8
Many spread their garments on the way, and others were cutting down branches from the trees, and spreading them on the road.

In the rest of the New Testament, we see the word used to portray the striking of the breast in deep grief, anguish, and mourning. So, it carries the idea of "striking or smiting."

Matthew 11:17-16
But to what shall I compare this generation [of those who oppose Him]? It is like children sitting in the marketplaces, who call to their companions and say, "We played the flute for you, and you didn't dance. We mourned for you, and you didn't lament."

Matthew 24:30
And then the sign of the Son of Man will appear in the sky. Then all the tribes of the Earth will mourn, and they will see the Son of Man coming on the clouds of the sky with power and great glory.

Luke 8:51-52
When he came to the house, he didn't allow anyone to enter in, except Peter, John, James, the father [Jairus] of the child, and her

mother. All were weeping and mourning her, but he said, "Don't weep. She isn't dead, but sleeping." All were weeping...mourning her, but he said, "Don't weep. She isn't dead, but sleeping."

Luke 23:27
A great multitude of the people followed him [Jesus on the way to the cross], including women who also mourned and lamented him.

Revelation 1:7
Behold, he is coming with the clouds, and every eye will see him, including those who pierced him. All the tribes of the Earth will mourn over him. Even so, Amen.

Revelation 18:9
The kings of the Earth, who committed sexual immorality and lived wantonly with her [Babylon], will weep and wail over her, when they look at the smoke of her burning.

When the preposition is added, it takes on the idea of "cutting or striking before" with the notion of advancing. The word was used in the secular Greek to speak of the Roman armies cutting their way across a wooded area and building a road to proceed or advance for battle.

Therefore, it means to "promote, advance, proceed, or make progress." Notice, it carries the sense of labor, work, effort. So, it means "a pushing forward to advance." With this idea in mind, let's look at how the word in utilized in other contexts.

It was used to describe the "continual pushing" forward of physical, intellectual, emotional, and social growth.

Luke 2:52
And Jesus increased in wisdom and stature, and in favor with God and men.

It was utilized to signify the pushing forward of time.

Romans 13:12
The night is far gone, and the day is near. Let's therefore throw off the deeds of darkness, and let's put on the armor of light.

Paul referred to his pushing forward in the Jewish religion before his encounter with Christ by using this word.

Galatians 1:14
I advanced in the Jews' religion beyond many of my own age among my countrymen, being more exceedingly zealous for the traditions of my fathers.

So, in 2 Timothy 3:13, the apostle is indicating that these evil men and imposters (these unbelievers) will "push to advance their wicked agenda" which in turn will produce more and more people with qualities like themselves. As they advance, their perversion, wickedness, and sin will increase. Therefore, these characteristics, which brings forth all kinds of sin, will grow individually, and in societies at large. This will eventually encompass the whole world.

After providing the list of sins that evil rejecters of God will commit, Paul indicates that they will applaud the same evil when others imitate them. Would this not encourage the evil and sin to increase?

Romans 1:32
Who, knowing the ordinance of God, that those who practice such things are worthy of death, not only do the same, but also consent [applaud, give hearty approval] with those who practice them.

We find an example in the tower of Babel when Nimrod led a rebellion in order to build their own tower (a religion), name (a national identity), and city (a capitol).

STANDING YOUR GROUND

Since the Lord God saw these unified actions increasing to impossible proportions, He determined to separate these people up. The Lord scattered all the people over the Earth and confused their languages. In this way, they were unable to communicate with one another.

Genesis 11:1-8
The whole Earth was of one language and of one speech. As they traveled east, they found a plain in the land of Shinar, and they lived there. They said to one another, "Come, let's make bricks, and burn them thoroughly." They had brick for stone, and they used tar for mortar. They said, "Come, let's build ourselves a city, and a tower whose top reaches to the sky, and let's make a name for ourselves, lest we be scattered abroad on the surface of the whole Earth." Yahweh came down to see the city and the tower, which the children of men built. Yahweh said, "Behold, they are one people, and they have all one language, and this is what they begin to do. Now nothing will be withheld from them, which they intend to do. Come, let's go down, and there confuse their language...they may not understand one another's speech." So Yahweh scattered them abroad...on the surface of...the Earth. They stopped building the city.

Peter denounced those who questioned whether the Lord was coming back because He had not yet returned as the Christians said He would. In this letter, Peter explained that the Lord God is actually stalling His judgment and allowing the progress of evil for a purpose. That purpose is to bring more people into His kingdom. He desires more to be saved.

2 Peter 3:8-9
But do not let this one fact escape your notice, beloved, that with the Lord [Christ] one day is like a thousand years, and a thousand years like one day. The Lord is not slow about His promise, as some count slowness, but is patient toward you, not wishing for any to perish...all to come to repentance.

As the Lord demonstrates His patience toward the world, wickedness will grow and grow. Christians should expect this outcome and become prepared to stand their ground.

The Godly Persecuted

Now Paul indicates what is instigating this opposition. It is the outward pursuit after godliness.

2 Timothy 3:12
Yes, and all who desire to live godly in Christ Jesus will suffer persecution.

The adverb translated "godly" refers to being "reverent" by doing the things which demonstrate our deep respect for and honor of the God we have in our hearts. Some of these demonstrations of reverence involve reading the Scriptures, praying, attending church services, fellowshipping with the saints, taking communion regularly, and even giving to poor saints. It refers to the ways that believers serve their God.

The Greek word conveys the idea of doing "religious or spiritual" things. This concept is different than righteousness (general good behavior) and holiness (being separate from the sinning of the world). It comes from two Greek words meaning "good worship or well-done reverence." The three words portray the various aspects of true spirituality.

This meaning can be seen clearly in its use as an adjective by Luke to describe Cornelius.

Acts 10:2
A devout man, and one who feared God with all his house, who gave gifts for the needy generously to the people...always prayed to God.

Here we see elements of his reverence (fear of God) which was displayed by his generous giving to the needy and his many prayers.

Due to Cornelius's devotion to God, it was determined that he would receive the gift of the Holy Spirit by Peter to demonstrate that God had brought the gospel to the Gentiles as He did the Jews. So, the Lord God told Cornelius to send his friends to Peter to request that Peter come and stay in his home. In Acts 10, Luke records the arrival of the friends and how they described Cornelius to Peter.

Acts 10:22
They said, "Cornelius, a centurion, a righteous man...one who fears God, and well-spoken of by all the nation of the Jews, was directed by a holy angel to invite you to his house, and to listen to what you say."

He was a righteous (did many good deeds and obeyed God's commandments) man. He was a fair and decent commander in the Roman army because the man was well-spoken of by all that knew him. When Peter arrived, Cornelius humbled himself before Peter and explained exactly God had done.

Acts 10:30
Cornelius said, "Four days ago, I was fasting until this hour, and at the ninth hour, I prayed in my house, and behold, a man stood before me in bright clothing [angel], and said, 'Cornelius, your prayer is heard, and your gifts to the needy are remembered in the sight of God. Send therefore to Joppa, and summon Simon, who is also called Peter. He lodges in the house of a tanner named Simon, by the seaside. When he comes, he will speak to you.'"

Cornelius was fasting and praying and giving. These are all the actions of a reverent, devout man. Cornelius was a God-fearing Jew and they respected him for his devotion to God.

When we show this same kind of godliness (reverence for God) to the unbelieving world, it will bother those in the darkness because there will be such a contrast. We do not even need to utter a word necessarily; instead, our behavior toward God will indict and incite them. The bright light of devotion shines brightly as they descend into the darkness.

Their Powerless Pretense

Since this same word "devout" is used in 2 Timothy 3:9 to contrast some of these increasingly evil individuals in the world, we will discuss it here.

2 Timothy 3:5
Holding a form of godliness, but having denied its power. Turn away from these, also.

This is the same word that was just discussed which has to do with participation in religious activities demonstrating an inner devotion and reverence of God. Here, Paul notes that they have only the "form" of it. The word "form" speaks of an "outward display or an appearance." They will do exactly the same things as the devout and godly but for evil goals.

An example of these "religious sounding" and "devout looking" people is found among the Pharisees. In Matthew 23, Jesus describes their fake religiosity and the motives that guided them. He uses harsh words for these evil people.

First, he describes their pride in that they love to be seen and admired by others.

Matthew 23:5-7
But all their works they do to be seen by men. They make their phylacteries broad, enlarge the fringes of their garments, and love

the place of honor at [their] feasts, the best seats in the synagogues, the salutations in the marketplaces, and to be called "Rabbi, Rabbi" by men.

Second, Jesus speaks of their desire for power.

Matthew 23:13-15
Woe to you, scribes [teachers and interpreters of God's law] and Pharisees, hypocrites! For you devour widows' houses, and as a pretense you make long prayers. Therefore you will receive greater condemnation. But woe to you, scribes and Pharisees, hypocrites! Because you shut up the Kingdom of Heaven against men...you don't enter in yourselves, neither do you allow those who are entering in to enter. Woe to you, scribes and Pharisees, hypocrites! For you travel around by sea and land to make one proselyte; and when he becomes one, you make him twice as much of a son of [Hell] Gehenna as yourselves.

Third, the Lord presents their blind and foolish hearts.

Matthew 23:16-20
Woe to you, you blind guides, who say, "Whoever swears by the temple, it is nothing; but whoever swears by the gold of the temple, he is obligated." You blind fools! For which is greater, the gold, or...temple that sanctifies the gold? [They say,] "Whoever swears by the altar, it is nothing...whoever swears by the gift that is on it, he is obligated?" You blind fools! For which is greater, the gift, or the altar that sanctifies the gift? He therefore who swears by the altar, swears by it, and by everything on it.

Fourth, the King of Kings calls them hypocrites (saying one thing and doing another).

Matthew 23:23-24
Woe to you, scribes and Pharisees, hypocrites! For you tithe mint, dill, and cumin, and have left undone the weightier matters of the

law: justice, mercy, and faith. But you ought to have done these, and not to have left the other undone. You blind guides, who strain out a gnat, and swallow a camel!*

Fifth, He portrays them as greedy and evil.

Matthew 23:25-26
Woe to you, scribes and Pharisees, hypocrites! For you clean the outside of the cup and of the platter, but within they are full of extortion and unrighteousness. You blind Pharisee, first clean the inside of the cup and…platter…its outside may become clean also.

Sixth, the Lord Jesus displays the spiritual deadness that was deep inside.

Matthew 23:27-28
Woe to you, scribes and Pharisees, hypocrites! For you are like whitened tombs, which outwardly appear beautiful, but inwardly are full of dead men's bones, and of all uncleanness. Even so you also outwardly appear righteous to men, but inwardly you are full of hypocrisy and iniquity.

Lastly, Christ asserts that are murderers in their hearts as they oppress those who disagree.

Matthew 23:29-31
Woe to you, scribes and Pharisees, hypocrites! For you build the tombs of the prophets, and decorate the tombs of the righteous, and say, "If we had lived in the days of our fathers, we wouldn't have been partakers with them in the blood of the prophets." Therefore you testify to yourselves that you are children of those who killed the prophets.

Paul continues by stating that these people of the last days "have denied its power." They do not realize the real power of a devoted life to God and instead rely on their own devious ways. Here, he implies that they understand it and refuse to accept it. They choose their own wisdom and wiles.

So, some of these individuals will present themselves as religious people participating in devout appearing activities but will descend deeper into the darkness of their extremely proud, power-hungry, blind, foolish, hypocritical, greedy, evil, spiritually dead, and dark hearts. These kinds of people will persecute Christ's followers just as their fathers did the Old Testament prophets.

Matthew 23:33-35
Fill up, then, the measure of your fathers. You serpents, you offspring of vipers, how will you escape the judgment of Gehenna? Therefore behold, I send to you prophets, wise men, and scribes. Some of them you will kill and crucify; and some of them you will scourge in your synagogues, and persecute from city to city; that on you may come all the righteous blood shed on the Earth, from the blood of righteous Abel to the blood of Zachariah son of Barachiah, whom you killed between the sanctuary and the altar.

Paul finishes the thought with, "turn away from these, also." The word "turn away" refers to the idea of "shunning" these people. We cannot allow ourselves to be carried away by the qualities that we admire in them which are outward and ultimately fake. They will appear to be better followers than we are, but they are feigning their godliness. Then, they will use this fake godliness to persecute Christians as if they were the true spokesman for God, though they are not.

Their Self-Centered Love

In four of the characteristics Paul discusses in this lengthy passage, he uses a common term so we will take these four together. The term is "lovers or friends of."

The first characteristic of these last days people is their love of themselves. As one loves another person with great focus and intensity, this last day's person loves himself.

2 Timothy 3:2
For men [and women] will be lovers of self [self-centered], lovers of money, boastful, arrogant, blasphemers, disobedient to parents, unthankful, unholy.

This common Greek term refers to a "friendship love." There are several words for our English "love" in the Bible and the word used here describes a "love between friends." It is a relational term that speaks of a close and abiding friendship. One that is characterized by love.

In the ancient world, friendship was seen as incredibly important. As a result, it was characterized by much respect, loyalty, and endurance. In the Scriptures, we can clearly see numerous characteristics of friends mentioned.

First, friends come to the aid of other friends. Luke, the inspired writer, utilizes this word "friend" when he describes the people closest to a Centurion. The leader's servant was very sick, and they traveled a long distance to find Jesus and ask if he would come and heal him. Not just anyone was sent to speak to Jesus in his behalf.

Luke 7:6
Jesus went with them. When he was now not far from the house, the centurion sent friends to him, saying to him, "Lord, don't trouble yourself...I am not worthy for you to come under my roof."

Second, friends will meet the needs of other friends even if it is inconvenient to do so. Jesus tells the story of a man with a friend who is traveling on a journey and stops at his home late for sustenance.

Luke 11:5-6
He said to them, "Which of you, if you go to a friend at midnight, and tell him, 'Friend, lend me three loaves of bread.' For a friend of mine has come to me...and I have nothing to set before him.

Third, friends are companions along life's difficult road. Not only did Jesus call His followers "disciples," but He also called them "friends."

Luke 12:4
I tell you, my friends, don't be afraid of those who kill the body, and after that have no more that they can do.

Fourth, friends celebrate the many great things that occur in their lives. This story of Jesus involves a man who found his lost sheep.

Luke 15:6
When he comes home, he calls together his friends and his neighbors, saying to them, "Rejoice with me, for I have found my sheep which was lost!"

Fifth, friends are concerned about all of the different aspects of their friends' lives especially spiritual ones. Here Cornelius calls his friends to his home because he knows Peter will preach what God wants him to hear and he wants them to hear it also.

Acts 10:24
On the next day they entered into Caesarea. Cornelius was waiting for them, having called together his relatives and his near friends.

Sixth, friends care for and also bring refreshment to other friends. Paul, the apostle, was under arrest and then brought to Rome for trial to sort out the accusations against him by the Jews.

THE PERSECUTION OF THE SAINTS AND HOW TO OVERCOME IT

Acts 27:3
The next day, we touched at Sidon. Julius [his guard] treated Paul kindly, and gave him permission to go to his friends and refresh himself.

Seventh, friends treat friends with tender affection and honor. Paul encourages this showing of love among saints.

Romans 12:10
In love of the brothers [Christians] be tenderly affectionate to one another; in honor preferring one another.

So, Paul uses a derivative of this powerful word to speak of the growing increase of people who will have a close and abiding relationship with themselves. They come to their own aid first, then others. They will continually meet their own needs no matter how inconvenient it is to anyone else. These people will be their own best companions caring and refreshing themselves along life's difficult road. When good things happen, they will celebrate and exalt themselves. These people have a constant and continual love affair with themselves! When they appear as if they need people, it is only because it satisfies something they want or desire.

We see this with Judas, the betrayer who only thought of himself. He pilfered money out of the collection box for the poor and pretended to love the Lord and follow Him. Judas ate a final meal with Jesus though he knew that he would betray him by leading a mob to his secret location in order to kill Him. Judas took the small amount of thirty pieces of silver and walked up to his supposed friend and kissed Him on the cheek to identify Jesus for His arrest.

Here is a man who is self-centered and completely in love with himself. Though He heard the words, he failed to heed them. He was committed to his own satisfaction alone. He desires to bring himself joy.

John 6:64
"But there are some of you who don't believe." For Jesus knew from the beginning who they were who didn't believe, and who it was who would betray him.

John 12:6
Now he said this, not because he cared for the poor, but because he was a thief, and having the money box, used to steal what was put into it.

John 13:2
During supper, the devil having already put into the heart of Judas Iscariot, Simon's son, to betray him.

John 18:2
Now Judas, who betrayed him, also knew the place, for Jesus often met there with his disciples.

Matthew 26:15
And said, "What are you willing to give me, that I should deliver him to you?" They weighed out for him thirty pieces of silver.

John 18:3
Judas then, having taken a detachment of soldiers [Roman] and officers [Jewish temple guards] from the chief priests and the Pharisees, came there with lanterns, torches, and weapons.

Luke 22:47
While he was still speaking, behold, a multitude, and he who was called Judas, one of the twelve, was leading them. He came near to Jesus to kiss him.

The first evil that will increase is the last days is the love people have for themselves. These are people unconcerned with the beliefs, values, feelings, or needs of others because the only thing on their minds is them. They believe that what they think is right and they will seek whatever they need or want as they love themselves. They will want all the delights that their flesh desires and the world offers. We, as Christians, through our shining lights, will expose their sin and selfishness. Then persecution will come.

Their Greedy Desires

Another characteristic of these last days is that people will grow in their love for money. Greed will fill their hearts and Christians will be in the way.

2 Timothy 3:2
For men will be lovers of self, lovers of money, boastful, arrogant, blasphemers, disobedient to parents, unthankful, unholy.

The word translated "lovers of money" is one word in the Greek and comes from a root that means deep friendship with money. It is their close friend. They are in love with money. They have a relationship with it. It matters greatly to them. Money will be their own best companion caring and refreshing them along life's extremely difficult road. When more money comes, they will celebrate and exalt it. These people have a continual love affair with money!

After Jesus Christ explained that no man could serve two masters, both God and wealth, the Pharisees did nothing but scoff at Him and mock this "nonsense." Then, Luke provides the reason.

Luke 16:14
The Pharisees, who were lovers of money, also heard all these things, and they scoffed at him.

They laughed at Him because they were not going to give up their wealth. This was absolutely ludicrous to them.

During one journey of the Lord's a rich young man came to Him asking how he might find eternal life. The Lord told him to keep the commandments. The man declared that he had kept them all. So, Jesus gave Him a simple task to point out the real issue keeping him from eternal life.

Mark 10:21-23
Jesus looking at him loved him, and said to him, "One thing you lack. Go, sell whatever you have, and give to the poor, and you will have treasure in heaven; and come, follow me, taking up the cross." But his face fell at that saying, and he went away sorrowful, for he was one who had great possessions. Jesus looked around, and said to his disciples, "How difficult it is for those who have riches to enter into God's Kingdom!"

The response that this man gave to Jesus was absurd. No one can keep the whole law. The purpose of God's law was to expose man's inability to live righteously. It was to show men that they were unable to stop sinning. They were to live under constant conviction, which would drive them to God.

Romans 3:23
For all have sinned, and fall short of the glory of God.

Instead, the man should have confessed his sins before Jesus and repented. To expose the wickedness in his heart, Jesus gave him a command which would expose the struggle with greed in his heart. The sin of greed was holding him back.

It will be the greed that brings opposition to us. As the societies of the world are swayed by the demands of the marketplace to buy their goods to feel happy, there will be more and more pressure put upon the saints to pursue these same things. When we, as believers, refuse to make money and the possessions that they can acquire the subject of our worship, persecution will come.

Their Pleasure Seeking

Since these people of the last days will be in a relationship with themselves and also with money, the next logical step is to fall into love with pleasure. In 2 Timothy 3, Paul adds another quality, they are "lovers of pleasure." Do you see the contrast? The light loves God and His righteousness, but the darkness loves pleasure and its sin.

2 Timothy 3:4
Traitors, headstrong, conceited, lovers of pleasure rather than lovers of God.

Though their deep relationship should be with God, rather it was with pleasure. Pleasing themselves is their pursuit and not the Lord. They have an abiding love relationship with pleasure. They pursue after it the way Christians pursue after God. Their idol is their lusts. When Christians stand in the way of their evil sensual pursuits, persecution will come.

In his second letter to the Thessalonians, Paul speaks of the coming lawless one and the judgment that will ensue. To contrast those who will be judged and believers who will not he characterizes them as to what they take pleasure in.

2 Thessalonians 2:12
That they all might be judged who didn't believe the truth, but had pleasure in unrighteousness.

In their self-centeredness, they sought sin and wickedness for fun and pleasure rather than God.

STANDING YOUR GROUND

To Titus, Paul describes their former lives without Christ.

Titus 3:3
For we were also once foolish, disobedient, deceived, serving [as a slave] various lusts and pleasures, living in malice and envy, hateful, and hating one another.

Notice, they did not simply take pleasure in unrighteousness but served it. The word speaks of slavery. Their various lusts and pleasures became their masters. This is always the end of self-centeredness.

A good example of self-love, and the love of money and pleasure is Zacchaeus, the tax-collector. The law allowed these officials to charge the people of Israel what Rome had designated; their fee could be whatever they desired. As a result, these men gouged the Jewish people and became rich. If someone did not pay, the tax collectors would try and intimidate him into paying through threats or physical force. Since Zacchaeus was one of the "chief" tax collectors, he received a percentage of the amount of taxes collected by every tax collector that was under him. They were despised by the fellow Jews because they were working for Romans.

As long as these Roman foreigners received what they were due, the tax-collectors could charge any amount for their fees whatsoever. As a result, they often would require large amounts of money from the Jewish people, which was essentially extorted from them.

The Hebrews referred to them as "sinners" which meant that they were the lowest class of people in their country. They were unclean, defiled, and outcasts. The Jewish law stated that these evil people were to be avoided and not allowed to enter the home of a Jew or the synagogue. This was Zacchaeus.

Luke 19:2
There was a man named Zacchaeus....a chief tax collector, and he was rich.

We know that he had taken much from the people due to his deep love of his closest companions (himself, money, and pleasure) because when he came to Christ, he was willing to pay a great restitution.

Luke 19:8
Zacchaeus stood and said to the Lord, "Behold, Lord, half of my goods I give to...poor. If I have wrongfully exacted anything of anyone, I restore four times as much."

Fortunately, this man came to Christ, but many others are on the broad road and reject the Lord. They do not have a love relationship with God. So, when these people encounter the lights of Christians who are Christ-centered and serving the Lord Jesus, they cannot stand it. These people will see Christians as standing in the way of the satisfaction of the love and companionship they have of themselves, money, and the pleasures that can be found in all that the world has to offer people in the satisfaction of their desires. This will create in them a deep displeasure in them toward us which will pour forth in hostility.

Their "Good" Hating

The last description of these people using the root word for "friend" is its opposite. These people who do not love God, do not love "good" either.

2 Timothy 3:3
Without natural affection, unforgiving, slanderers, without self-control, fierce, not lovers of good.

This phrase "not lovers of good" means no relationship with good. These perpetrators of evil have no love or friendship with "good" of any kind. Their thoughts, words, and actions are directed toward hating "good." They do not appreciate any good that is shown to them and will not show any good to others. Our light of "goodness" causes them to hate us.

John describes these "lusts of the flesh" in his first letter by putting these strong desires, passions, and feelings into three simple categories.

1 John 2:15-17
Don't love the world or the things that are in the world. If anyone loves the world, the Father's love isn't in him. For all that is in the world, the lust of the flesh, the lust of the eyes, and the pride of life, isn't the Father's, but is the world's. The world is passing away with its lusts, but he who does God's will remains forever.

The "lusts of the flesh" refers to the appetites of the body. The body desires the excesses of food, drink, and sex. This is anything that is "not good" but evil, sinful, and wicked. The "lusts of the eyes" refers to anything the eyes will crave that sparkles, titillates them, and is beautiful. It may be physical appearance, clothes, and jewelry. The "pride of life" refers to the boastful and arrogant pride in living. However, people live which can be "boasted about" comes under this category. This may be expensive cars and luxurious homes. It could be extravagant vacations and high-end technology of all kinds. If neutral, these things will not be enjoyed within the bounds of good, but outside them.

In Romans 1, he presents one of the results of wicked and evil behavior.

Romans 1:32
Who, knowing the ordinance of God, that those who practice such

things are worthy of death, not only do the same, but also approve of those who practice them.

As they participated in every kind of sin wickedness, they also recruited others to be even more sinful. The more who sin, the more who will persecute the lights exposing that sin.

Their Prideful Words

The world will increase in its wickedness and therefore in its opposition as it grows in its pride and the desire to boast about the positions, status, and possessions it has. The more it boasts, the more it wants to boast.

2 Timothy 3:2
For men [and women] will be lovers of self...of money, boastful, arrogant, blasphemers, disobedient to parents, unthankful, unholy.

"Boastful" in Greek means "empty pretender." These people boast about how great they are, but it is fake. It is a facade put forth for their selfish ends. Everything they say and do is a make-believe role. They know how to get what they want.

They pretend that their positions, status, and possessions have such great value in life when they don't. They dress up, give each other numerous awards, participate in parades, have fabulous parties, and speak endlessly about themselves but really have no significance or real importance.

This pretense goes all the way back to the Garden where the Serpent pretended that he was interested in the good of Adam and Eve and only wanted the best for them. Even his own appearance as a serpent was fake and a pretense. Then he feigned an interest in Eve and her wellbeing which was farthest from his mind.

Genesis 3:1-5
Now the serpent was more subtle than any animal of the field which Yahweh God had made. He said to the woman, "Has God really said, 'You shall not eat of any tree of the garden?'" The woman said to the serpent, "We may eat fruit from the trees of the garden, but not the fruit of the tree which is in the middle of the garden. God has said, 'You shall not eat of it. You shall not touch it, lest you die.'" The serpent said to the woman, "You won't surely die, for God knows that in the day you eat it, your eyes will be opened, and you will be like God, knowing good and evil."

John the Baptist lost his own head because of the boastful words of Herod Antipas, the ruler of the Jews. The king and his brother's wife Herodias divorced both their spouses and married each other which violated God's law. John spoke out against their sin. As a result, John was imprisoned by Herod. He was in chains at the time of this banquet. On this occasion, Herod made a great boast.

Matthew 14:6-7
But when Herod's birthday came, the daughter of Herodias danced...and pleased Herod. Whereupon he promised with an oath to give her whatever she should ask.

Then, the daughter of Herodias danced before Herod the Tetrarch at a huge banquet. In a drunken daze Herod before all his guests (with prideful words) offered her up to half of his entire kingdom. When the daughter inquired of her mother, she told her to ask for John the Baptist's head on a platter.

The king could not refuse her. Though his boastful words were foolish, he was prideful and would not embarrass himself by admitting this and letting John live. It was more important to him to protect and guard his high status among all of those attending.

Matthew 14:8-10
She, being put forward by her mother, said, "Give me...on a platter the head of John the Baptizer." The king was grieved, but for the sake of his oaths, and of those who sat at the table with him, he commanded it to be given, and he sent and beheaded John in the prison.

John the Baptist was killed because he stood up for true righteousness among God's people. This angered Herodias because she did not like his righteous light exposing her sin. The empty pretense and boastful words of Herod forced him to commit an act that he didn't want to do. He was a prideful pretender. These people are constantly imposing their sinful values upon righteous Christians.

Their Prideful Hearts

Paul continues his discussion by describing what is in the hearts of these people. It all comes down to one wicked and sinful attitude: pride.

2 Timothy 3:2
For men will be lovers of self...of money, boastful, arrogant, blasphemers, disobedient to parents, unthankful, unholy.

"Arrogant" refers to people who believe in their inner hearts that they are superior to everyone else and display that attitude for all to see. In their own minds, they are superior and think, speak, and act in a way that is far superior to everyone else. To them, the regular population of people are uncouth, lazy, stupid, foolish, messy, and of no account.

This prideful display is condemned by James when he contrasts the pride of those without Christ to the humility of those in Christ.

James 4:6
But he gives more grace. Therefore it says, "God resists the proud, but gives grace to the humble."

There is no place for pride in the Christian life. So, when we display our humility as we let our lights shine, this will be labeled by the proud as weakness and they will attempt to take advantage of us.

An example of this is Herod Agrippa. He was the nephew of Herodias. In Acts 12, he put James, the apostle, to death with the sword. When it pleased the people, he imprisoned Peter also. After God rescued Peter with the help of an angel. The Lord decided it was time to demonstrate His power to this king.

Acts 12:21-23
On an appointed day, Herod [Agrippa] dressed himself in royal clothing, sat on the throne, and gave a speech to them. The people shouted, "The voice of a god, and not of a man!" Immediately an angel of the Lord struck him, because he didn't give God the glory, and he was eaten by worms and died. His pride displeased God.

This is what eventually happens eternally to the prideful. Until judgment day arrives, the number of these people who are full of pride and putting it on display in their arrogance will increase and their pride will grow and grow. They will see believers as naive, unenlightened, and desperately in need of the psychological crutch that religion provides. The saints are viewed as even more inferior than the population they mock and scorn.

To them, we are laborers and workers, not professionals and scientists. They think Christians have not evolved into the superior values and beliefs that they have. Followers of Christ must be tolerated but eventually they will feel we will need to be isolated or eliminated. They will accuse the saints of intolerance as they are being intolerant of them. When they come after us, we must be willing and able to stand our ground against them.

Their Scornful Mocking

Now, Paul continues in his list of wickedness increasing in the last days with "blasphemers." Those in the last days will grow in their blasphemy.

2 Timothy 3:2
For men [and women] will be lovers of self, lovers of money, boastful, arrogant, blasphemers, disobedient to [their] parents, unthankful, unholy.

The Greek word translated "blasphemous" means "to speak evil, slanderous, reproachful, railing, and abusive things." Of the three times the word is used in the New Testament, it is in reference to God not simply slandering in general.

Paul uses it to describe his words and behavior toward Christ and his followers before his salvation.

1 Timothy 1:13
Although I [Paul] used to be [as the unsaved Saul] a blasphemer, a persecutor, and insolent. However, I obtained mercy, because I did it ignorantly in unbelief.

In several places in the book of Acts, the apostle presents more details as to what happened. Luke describes how Paul actually came to believe in Jesus as Savior and Lord.

Acts 9:1-2
But Saul [Paul], still breathing threats and slaughter against the

disciples of the Lord, went to the high priest, and asked for letters from him to the synagogues of Damascus, that if he found any who were of the Way...he might bring them bound to Jerusalem.

Much later, Paul attempted to keep a vow in order to show support to the Jews when they turned on him and accused him of taking a Gentile into the temple. The Romans intervened in order to protect Paul and he asks permission to give his testimony to the Jews of his former blaspheming.

Acts 22:4-5
I persecuted this Way to the death, binding and delivering into prisons both men and women. As also the high priest and all the council of the elders testify, from whom also I received letters to the brothers...traveled to Damascus to bring them also who were there to Jerusalem in bonds to be punished.

Later, Paul defends himself to King Herod Agrippa. He had been taken to the Roman governor for protection years earlier from the Jews who desired to murder kill him. Since this governor was unsure of what to do, he King Agrippa to hear his case.

Acts 26:9-11
I myself most certainly thought that I ought to do many things contrary to the name of Jesus of Nazareth. This I also did in Jerusalem [where church began]. I both shut up many of the saints in prisons, having received authority from the chief priests, and when they were put to death, I gave my vote against them. Punishing [persecuting] them often in all the synagogues, I tried to make them blaspheme [rail against the Lord]. Being exceedingly enraged against them, I persecuted them even to foreign cities.

Notice, Paul hunted the innocent Christians wherever they went. Why? He wanted to wipe out the very name of Jesus Christ from the land. This was his blasphemy!

The word is used of false witnesses who stood up against Stephen. This man, who was full of faith and power, was going about performing great wonders and signs among the people when a group of Jews opposed him.

Acts 6:10-14
They weren't able to withstand the wisdom and the Spirit by which he spoke. Then they secretly induced men to say, "We have heard him speak blasphemous words against Moses and God." They stirred up the people, the elders, and the scribes, and came against him and seized him, and brought him...to the council, and set up false witnesses who said, "This man never stops speaking blasphemous words against this holy place and the law. For we have heard him say that this Jesus...will destroy this place, and will change the customs which Moses delivered to us."

This group could not compete against his wisdom from the Spirit of God, so they accused him of blasphemy. They were trying to stir up the leaders by asserting that Stephen was speaking slanderous and reproachful words which were against the temple and the law. His railing was abusive to the holiness and majesty of God. And they were lies.

These are the people who criticize the Lord and then His believers. They will accuse us of being intolerant of others' behavior and then are intolerant against us. These are the scoffers, mockers, and scorners who do everything in their power to silence Christians. They will accuse believers of being divisive, inhuman, and intolerant. These people will present us as standing in the way of man's progress.

Their Rebellious Attitude

In verse two, Paul adds another characteristic to his list. They are disobedient to their parents. Though this may seem to be a childhood issue, it is not. This disobedience can flow from childhood to adolescence and into adulthood and affect their responses to those in authority.

2 Timothy 3:2
For men [and women] will be lovers of self, lovers of money, boastful, arrogant, blasphemers, disobedient to [their] parents, unthankful, unholy.

The Greek word which is translated "disobedient" is the negative or direct opposite of another word. The root is the word "persuasion" which carries a unique idea. First, one is persuaded, then believes in the person and what they ask them to do. As a result, they comply and submit to their instruction or commands. The obedience grows out of being persuaded in their own minds to the point of compliance. People presented their case and others complied because it seemed reasonable. This persuasion to being obedient can be either for actions concerning good or evil. It is important to note this aspect of the word to understand its negative.

Matthew 27:20
Now the chief priests and the elders [all the Jewish leaders] persuaded the multitudes to ask for Barabbas, and destroy Jesus.

Acts 14:19
But some Jews from Antioch and Iconium came there, and having persuaded the multitudes, they stoned Paul, and dragged him out of the city, supposing that he was dead.

Acts 27:11
But the centurion gave more heed to the master and to the owner of the ship than to those things which were spoken by Paul.

It is used in the deeply spiritual sense of being persuaded to believe in Christ.

THE PERSECUTION OF THE SAINTS AND HOW TO OVERCOME IT

Acts 17:4
Some of them were persuaded, and joined Paul and Silas, of the devout Greeks a great multitude, and not a few of the chief women.

Acts 18:4
He [Paul] reasoned in the synagogue every Sabbath, and persuaded Jews and Greeks.

Acts 19:8
He [Paul] entered into the synagogue, and spoke boldly for a period of three months, reasoning and persuading about the things concerning God's Kingdom.

This word does not have a connotation of trickery or selling; but instead, it indicates a true persuasion. Once convinced, it leads to real trust. This trust then produces the desire to be obedient. In this case, it is a persuaded obedience to parents.

In our context, it is the opposite of this. These people are disobedient to their parents because they are not persuaded by any means to yield their wills enough to obey. It is not that their own parents have not convinced them that they are worthy of their obedience and so they disobey. Instead, these people cannot be persuaded by that which is natural, normal, and cultural to obey as other children do. They cannot be persuaded to give up their own will to yield it to the authority of parents. These kinds of people submit to no one.

This was seen as especially heinous in the ancient world where disobedience of parents was seen as terribly shameful and sinful. It is nothing like it is today in the modern world where "rebellion against parents" is seen as the norm and is mostly tolerated.

Deuteronomy 21:18-21
If a man has a stubborn and rebellious son, who will not obey the

voice of his father or the voice of his mother, and though they chasten him, will not listen to them; then his father and his mother shall take hold of him and bring him out to the elders of his city, and to the gate of his place. They shall tell the elders [the leaders] of his city, "This our son is stubborn and rebellious. He will not obey our voice. He is a glutton and a drunkard." All the men of his city shall stone him to death with stones. So you shall remove the evil from among you. All Israel shall hear, and fear.

As is mentioned in this passage, it is not just disobedience that is condemned, but the licentious living it results in.

In Proverbs 30, wise Solomon speaks of this rebellion and outright disobedience of these people.

Proverbs 30:17
The eye that mocks at his father, and scorns obedience to his mother: the ravens of the valley shall pick it out, the young eagles shall eat it.

Since they have rejected the training and discipline of their parents, they are rebellious, undisciplined, and do not follow rules. They did not trust their parents and will not trust any other authority. If they become intolerant of Christians, they will attack their Christian parents first then others. The law will not persuade to restrain themselves.

Their Willful Ingratitude

The people in the last days will be an ungrateful lot who will attribute all blessings to themselves and thank no one.

2 Timothy 3:2
For men [and women] will be lovers of self...of money, boastful, arrogant, blasphemers, disobedient to parents, unthankful, unholy.

Similar to the last word discussed, this is the negative of a Greek word that refers to "demonstrating thankfulness and gratitude for an unmerited favor and blessing." The root word of this Greek term is translated in the New Testament as "grace."

Ephesians 2:5-9
Even when we were dead through our trespasses, made us alive together with Christ (by grace you have been saved), and raised us up with him, and made us to sit with him in the heavenly places in Christ Jesus, that in the ages to come he might show the exceeding riches of his grace in kindness toward us in Christ Jesus; for by grace you have been saved through faith, and that not of yourselves; it is the gift of God, not of works, that no one would boast.

We see this grace pouring out into our salvation. Its verb form carries the idea of showing grace and unmerited favor to someone.

Luke 7:21
In that hour he cured many of diseases and plagues and evil spirits; and to many who were blind he gave sight.

Romans 8:32
He who didn't spare his own Son, but delivered him up for us all, how would he not also with him freely give us all things?

1 Corinthians 2:12
But we received, not the spirit of the world, but the Spirit which is from God, that we might know the things that were freely given to us by God.

2 Corinthians 2:10
Now I also forgive whomever you forgive anything. For if indeed I have forgiven anything, I have forgiven that one for your sakes....

Ephesians 4:32
And be kind to one another, tender hearted, forgiving each other, just as God also in Christ forgave you.

Colossians 2:13
You [Christians] were dead through your trespasses and the uncircumcision of your flesh. He made you alive together with him, having forgiven us all our trespasses.

Therefore, the opposite means to be ungrateful, thankless, and lacking a sense of blessing when one is given something or forgiven by someone.

One clear example is seen in an encounter Jesus had with ten lepers in Luke 17.

Luke 17:11-19
As he was on his way to Jerusalem, he was passing along the borders of Samaria and Galilee. As he entered into a certain village, ten men who were lepers met him, who stood at a distance. They lifted up their voices, saying, "Jesus, Master, have mercy on us!" When he saw them, he said to them, "Go and show yourselves to the priests." As they went, they were cleansed. One of them, when he saw that he was healed, turned back, glorifying God with a loud voice. He fell on his face at Jesus' feet, giving him thanks...he was a Samaritan. Jesus answered, "Weren't the ten cleansed? But where are the nine? Were there none found who returned to give glory to God, except this stranger?" Then he said to him, "Get up, and go your way. Your faith has healed you."

The nine lepers were cured by a gracious act of God but only one came back thankful. This demonstrated that he was the true believer in God. The ungodly do not give thanks. They are not grateful to God for anything.

These entitled people believe that the world owes them.

They simply deserve what they get. They will not care about all that was done for them in the past but instead act as if they themselves had either obtained it or they deserve it. How will they see our graciousness and forgiveness? It may appear as just another sign of our "pathetic weakness" and then they may try and take advantage of us or harass us.

Their Unholy Hearts

At the end of 2 Timothy 3:2, Paul asserts that people in the last days will be unholy.

2 Timothy 3:2
For men will be lovers of self, lovers of money, boastful, arrogant, blasphemers, disobedient to parents, unthankful, unholy.

Here, Paul continues with another negative of a word that means, "sacred, devoted to God, or undefiled by sin." This word is distinguished by the word "devout" which we have looked at already. One's religious activity is not focused on the pure, clean devotion of the person. These undefiled ones have little filthiness and uncleanness of sin, wickedness, or evil in their lives. The word has the idea of being above and separate from anything that would, could, or should defile them.

The word is used of the "purity and sacredness" of Christ.

Acts 2:27
Because you will not leave my soul in Hades, neither will you allow your Holy One to see decay.

Hebrews 7:26
For such a high priest was fitting for us: holy, guiltless, undefiled, separated from sinners, and made higher than the heavens.

Revelation 15:4
Who wouldn't fear you, Lord, and glorify your name? For you only are holy. For all the nations will come and worship before you. For your righteous acts have been revealed.

Revelation 16:5
I heard the angel of the waters saying, "You are righteous, who are and who were, O Holy One, because you have judged these things.

Christ is the "Holy One." The Lord Jesus is absolutely pure, clean and cannot be conceived as undergoing any filthiness of decay in His body. This is the reason why the Lord's body was transformed in the grave. Also, notice, the word is used as a title for him. Not only did He act holy, but Christ was completely holy in every aspect of His thoughts, words, and deeds. No one questioned this and no one would. He was beyond reproach.

The word is used to speak of the hands of prayer. As they are lifted to God, the hands represent a sacred, pure, clean, undefiled act of devotion. They are symbolic of the devoted act itself.

1 Timothy 2:8
Therefore I want the men in every place to pray, lifting up holy hands, without wrath and dissension.

Paul draws on this word to describe a quality of elders who are in charge. People understand that they seek purity and an undefiled life. The elders will be viewed as sacred, devoted to the Lord, and not involved in the filthiness of dark, wicked sins.

Titus 1:8
But hospitable, loving what is good, sensible, just, devout [acting in a sacred way], self-controlled.

The opposite would obviously be unclean, defiled, and filthy in their sinfulness, perversions, and wicked pleasures. This is the idea that Paul wants to present. These people of the last days are unclean in their many thoughts, words, and deeds.

It is used only one other place in the New Testament and that is in Paul's letter to Timothy. In this passage, the apostle was explaining to his child in the faith that the law was given to expose sin. It was meant to present God's character and His utter and absolute holiness and righteousness. As man comes face to face with the law, he sees how corrupt and filthy he really is from his wickedness. This drives him to Christ because he desperately needs the forgiveness of the Savior. Paul connects many synonyms to this word.

1 Timothy 1:9
As knowing this, that law is not made for a righteous man, but for the lawless and insubordinate, for the ungodly and sinners, for the unholy and profane, for murderers of fathers and murderers of mothers, for man slayers.

So, we can see that "unholy" would be the kinds of thoughts, words, and actions which are the very opposite of sacred, devout, and pure. This is God's standard.

So, these hordes of people in the last days will love and practice wickedness. They will mock and scorn piety and devotion to Christ. They will chide believers for not being hip and current. They will criticize the church for its boring and irrelevant practices. The world has become enlightened, and the church will need to become more entertaining. They will seek and pursue every kind of evil the world offers. They will attempt to entice believers into their filthiness or force them to socially or legally tolerate it whether they like it or not. Christians will feel their pressure over and over to accept their unholy dealings. When Christians fall into their sin, they will rejoice. They will desire us to be as dirty as they are. If we won't, their tolerance will wane. If we resist, we will feel their wrath and persecution will come.

Their Lack of Natural Affection

As Paul continues his description of the characteristics of people living in the last days, the apostle moves on to their utter lack of natural affection. These people have something missing in their humanity.

2 Timothy 3:3
Without natural affection, unforgiving, slanderers, without self-control, fierce, not lovers of good.

This phrase in the Greek carries the idea of being unsociable, lacking human affection, or the natural and proper love one might have for family or friends. They will disregard the blueprint of love and affections God put within them.

The word appears to be derived from the opposite of "family love." The Greeks distinguished between different kinds of love and familial love is the one referred to here. This would be the opposite of it. So, they are lacking natural familial love. They do not care about family or marriage relationships. To them, it may be done out of necessity, business reasons, or for other purposes but it is not valued. They do not treat family differently than strangers.

One illustration of this lack of natural affection was Laban in the Old Testament. He took advantage of his nephew Jacob who needed a place to hide. After his deception of his brother Esau, Jacob fled to his Uncle Laban's household. On the way, he met Laban's youngest daughter Rachel and fell madly in love with her. To marry her, Jacob pledged to work seven years for free. After the seven years, Laban switched his daughters on their wedding night and Jacob married Leah instead. Jacob was also allowed to marry Rachel but only if he committed to another seven years. After fourteen years, Jacob, Leah, and Rachel wanted to head back to his father's household.

Laban persuaded his nephew to stay and gave him his own flock. This way he could build his own wealth. Then, whenever Jacob's flock prospered Laban would change the agreement to take Jacob's sheep. This drove him to leave.

Genesis 31:41-42
These twenty years I have been in your house. I served you fourteen years for your two daughters, and six years for your flock, and you have changed my wages ten times. Unless the God of my father, the God of Abraham, and the fear of Isaac, had been with me, surely now you would have sent me away empty. God has seen my affliction...the labor of my hands, and rebuked you last night.

After he departed, rather than apologize for taking such advantage of him, he encouraged Jacob to make a treaty with him. He was only concerned with assuring there would no retaliation on Jacob's part.

Genesis 31: 52
May this heap [of stones] be a witness, and the pillar be a witness, that I will not pass over this heap to you, and that you will not pass over this heap and this pillar to me, for harm.

Here again, there was no real affection for his nephew Jacob, and he used and abused him.

The unbelievers of the last days will have little natural familial affection and will desire to take advantage of their family relationships. If any of their family members will not respond, they will be persecuted.

Their Argumentative Demeanor

In verse 3, Paul lists the next characteristic. These people would not be willing to reconcile. They would rather remain alienated from those who crossed them.

2 Timothy 3:3
Without natural affection, unforgiving, slanderers, without self-control, fierce, not lovers of good.

This word "unforgiving" in the Greek is another negative from a word which refers to the pouring out of a libation to God. It is a sacrificial term used of offering a drink rather than food as a sacrifice and pouring out onto the altar.

Paul uses it to speak of His service to the Lord God as he ministered to the Philippians.

Philippians 2:17-18
Yes, and if I am poured out on the sacrifice and service of your faith, I rejoice, and rejoice with you all. 18 In the same way, you also rejoice, and rejoice with me.

He also uses the word to describe how his constant and continual offering of himself in service finally brought his demise.

2 Timothy 4:6
For I am already being offered...the time of my departure has come.

When you refer to the opposite of this root word, it carries the concept of "an unwillingness to offer oneself in service to others in regard to making peace or a truce." These people will not bend to anyone else's will or desire. They absolutely refuse to forgive, reconcile, or even come to mutually agreed upon terms.

The Pharisees are an example of the argumentative kinds of people that we have been discussing. This quarreling group essentially hounded the Lord Jesus wherever He went and pounded Him with questions and arguments in order to trick Him into saying something which will provide them an excuse to arrest him.

Matthew 16:1
The Pharisees and Sadducees came, and testing him, asked him to show them a sign from heaven.

Matthew 19:3
Pharisees came to him, testing him, and saying, "Is it lawful for a man to divorce his wife for any reason?"

Matthew 22:35
One of them, a lawyer, asked him a question, testing him.

Luke 11:16
Others, testing him, sought from him a sign from heaven.

They did not want a real discussion with the Lord Jesus but only desired to deceive him into slipping up. Then, they could accuse Him of breaking the law. They had their Jewish tradition, and they would not depart from it. When Jesus would not bend, they killed Him.

They want what they want when they want it. Whenever their desires come in conflict with Christian values, they will not tolerate anything but their way. These are the people who "shout down" others. They never let up on their attempt to shut people down through their many picket lines, at the conferences and presentations, in the office lunchrooms, and standing at the podium in most of the college classrooms. They will never stop, nor will they ever give in. As with the Pharisees, these difficult ones will become less and less patient with Christians until finally they have had enough. Their minds are closed and if believers won't change then they must be silenced or eliminated.

Their Constant Gossip

In verse 3, Paul adds another wicked quality which deals primarily with personal attacks on our person rather than our gospel. They get personal and it doesn't matter if they're lying or not.

2 Timothy 3:3
Without natural affection, unforgiving, slanderers, without self-control, fierce, not lovers of good.

This word "slanderers" in the Greek language comes from the root word meaning "to throw across" or "send over." It was a common word for throwing something. It was utilized by Jesus to speak of throwing tasteless salt away or an eye that caused one to stumble.

Matthew 5:13
You are the salt of the Earth; but if the salt has become tasteless, how can it be made salty again? It is no longer good for anything, except to be thrown out and trampled under foot by men.

Matthew 5:29
If your right eye makes you stumble, tear it out and throw it from you; for it is better for you to lose one of the parts of your body, than for your whole body to be thrown into hell.

Numerous times, it was used for "casting" a fishing net into the sea.

Matthew 4:18
Now as Jesus was walking by the Sea of Galilee, He saw two brothers, Simon who was called Peter, and Andrew his brother, casting a net into the sea; for they were fishermen.

The word eventually came to be used to indicate throwing accusations toward others. So, in this context it refers to those in the last days who are accusers, slanderers, and malicious gossips. It is also the word translated "Devil."

This word is translated as the "Devil" thirty-four times in the New Testament. In Revelation 12:10, Satan is an accuser who slanders the saints day and night before their God.

Revelation 12:10
I heard a loud voice in heaven, saying, "Now the salvation, the power, and the Kingdom of our God, and the authority of his Christ has come; for the accuser of our brothers has been thrown down, who accuses them before our God day and night."

A powerful illustration is the Devil's accusations of Job. He was a righteous man and Satan could not wait to accuse him of loving God only when things were going well.

Job 1:8-11
Yahweh said to Satan, "Have you considered my servant, Job? For there is no one like him in the Earth, a blameless and an upright man, one who fears God, and turns away from evil." Then Satan answered Yahweh, and said, "Does Job fear God for nothing? Haven't you made a hedge around him, and around his house, and around all that he has, on every side? You have blessed the work of his hands...his substance is increased in the land. But stretch out your hand ...touch all...he has...he will renounce you to your face."

So, Satan moved the Sabeans to attack and then kill his servants and destroy his livestock. He caused fire from the sky to consume his sheep and servants watching them. The accuser instigated the Chaldeans to murder the camels and the servants who kept watch. Finally, he brought a great wind which caused the roof of the house to fall upon his children and all died. Job did not sin. Then, he returned to God and accused him again. Then, Satan struck Job with horrible sores over his entire body which brought incessant pain.

Job 2:4-6
Satan answered Yahweh, and said, "Skin for skin. Yes, all that a man has he will give for his life. But stretch out your hand now, and touch his bone and his flesh, and he will renounce you to your face." Yahweh said to Satan, "Behold, he is in your hand. Only spare his life."

Like Satan these people do the same. Jesus called Satan the father of unbelievers. Why? They are simply acting as their father does. Jesus declared that his accusers were of their father the Devil.

John 8:44
You are of your father, the devil...you want to do the desires of your father. He was a murderer from the beginning, and doesn't stand in the truth, because there is no truth in him. When he speaks a lie, he speaks on his own; for he is a liar, and its father.

The apostle John calls unbelievers the children of the Devil. They are the offspring of Satan.

1 John 3:10
In this the children of God are revealed, and the children of the devil. Whoever doesn't do righteousness is not of God, neither is he who doesn't love his brother.

So, there will be people whose focus will be on slandering and accusing Christians of every form of evil. They will be pointing out the misdeeds of Christians constantly or even accusing them of bad intentions when good is done. They may attack those who believe in Christ behind their backs.

Their Uncontrollable Impulses

In verse 3, Paul comments on their inability to control any of their impulses.

2 Timothy 3:3
Without natural affection, unforgiving, slanderers, without self-control, fierce, not lovers of good.

Again, this word is another negative of a Greek root word which focuses on the power and might to bring dominion.

It is utilized several times to refer to God's strength and power.

Ephesians 1:19
And what is the surpassing greatness of His power toward us who believe. These are in accordance with the working of the strength of His might.

Colossians 1:11
Strengthened with...power, according to His glorious might, for the attaining of all steadfastness and patience; joyously.

This power then gives Him dominion or control over all things.

1 Peter 5:11
To Him be dominion [control over] forever and ever. Amen.

Jude 1:25
To the only God our Savior, through Jesus Christ our Lord, be glory, majesty, dominion and authority, before all time and now and forever. Amen.

So, we see that the word refers to one's strength, might, and power which gives one dominion over something. In this case, it would be referring to dominion over oneself. If the person does not have control or dominion over himself or herself, then this term in 2 Timothy 3:3 would be used.

In the negative, it would indicate that one has no power or strength to have dominion over his impulses. He has no self-control. When they get angry, they lash out. They have no patience with people. If they desire something, they take it. They must follow every impulse and whim.

The synagogue members of Nazareth during the ministry of Jesus are a good illustration of this.

Luke 4:16-17
He [Jesus] came to Nazareth, where he had been brought up. He entered, as was his custom, into the synagogue on the Sabbath day, and stood up to read. The book of the prophet Isaiah was handed to him. He opened the book, and found the place where it was written.

The custom at this time was for visiting Rabbis to stand up and give some insight into the Scriptures. So, Jesus stood up to read a passage from Isaiah about the coming Messiah.

Luke 4:18-19
The Spirit of the Lord is on me, because he has anointed me to preach good news to the poor. He [God] has sent me [the Messiah] to heal the broken hearted, to proclaim release to the captives, recovering of sight to the blind, to deliver those who are crushed, and to proclaim the acceptable year of the Lord.

Then, the Jesus declared that it was He who was spoken of in that passage clearly proclaiming that Isaiah was talking about Him. He was the Messiah.

Luke 4:20-21
He [Jesus] closed the book, gave it back to the attendant, and sat down. The eyes of all in the synagogue were fastened on him. He began to tell them, "Today, this Scripture has been fulfilled in your hearing."

At first, they wondered about what he was actually saying, since He was just a carpenter's son. Then Jesus indicted the people by proclaiming no miracle had happened in their city because of their hardened hearts.

He does this by telling the story of Elijah feeding only the starving widow and Elisha the leper Naaman. He excluded Israel because of their hard hearts. Suddenly, these people became angry and could not control the impulsive rage that they felt for this "self-proclaimed Messiah."

Luke 4:28-30
They were all filled with wrath in the synagogue, as they heard these things. They rose up, threw him out of the city, and led him to the brow of the hill that their city was built on, that they might throw him off the cliff. But he, passing through the middle of them, went his way.

In the last days, the people who have no self-control will see Christians as standing in their way of what they want. They will not be able to control their impulses, thoughts, words, and actions pouring out of their desires. They will have no toleration for those who are standing in the way of their satisfaction. When their evil turns toward Christians, there is no telling what they might do. Out of their wicked hearts can come every kind of persecution.

Their Extreme Brutality

Paul continues his portrayal of these wicked people by speaking of their brutality.

2 Timothy 3:3
Without natural affection, unforgiving, slanderers, without self-control, fierce, not lovers of good.

This Greek word translated "fierce" means "savage, fierce, and brutal." This speaks of violence and the worst of human savagery and barbarity. These kinds of people will not think twice about performing horrific acts upon believers who disagree with them.

In Hebrews 11, the author describes this savage brutality that was directed toward God's people.

Hebrews 11:37-38
They [God's people] were stoned. They were sawn apart. They were tempted. They were slain with the sword. They went around in sheep skins...in goat skins; being destitute, afflicted, ill-treated (of whom the world was not worthy), wandering in deserts, mountains, caves, and the holes of the Earth.

In his prophecy of the suffering servant, Isaiah describes these horrific atrocities that would be directed toward the Lord Jesus many years earlier.

Isaiah 53:4-7
Surely he has borne our sickness, and carried our suffering; yet we considered him plagued, struck by God [the Father], and afflicted. But he was pierced for our transgressions. He was crushed for our iniquities. The punishment that brought our peace was on him; and by his wounds we are healed.... Yahweh has laid on him the iniquity of us all. He was oppressed, yet when he was afflicted he

didn't open his mouth. As a lamb...led to the slaughter, and as a sheep that before its shearers is silent, so he didn't open his mouth.

Even a cursory reading of a book of martyrs or the history of Christianity will reveal the unlimited unleashing of pure human brutality to punish Christians. As we know, Paul says that more is coming.

Their Merciless Betrayals

The apostle continues with his next characteristic of those who live in the last days. They will betray others. This is the reason he calls them "traitors."

2 Timothy 3:4
Traitors, headstrong, conceited, lovers of pleasure rather than lovers of God.

This word translated "traitors" comes from two root words in the Greek: "before" and "to give." Therefore, it means "to give information before it is necessary." It came to refer to those who betray others because they provide the necessary information before it should be known. These are betrayers.

This was the word used of Judas concerning his betrayal of Jesus in Luke 6.

Luke 6:16
Judas the son of James; and Judas Iscariot, who also became a traitor.

First, he had pretended to be a follower of Jesus.

Matthew 10:1-4
He called to himself his twelve disciples, and gave them authority

over unclean spirits, to cast them out, and to heal every disease and every sickness. Now the names of the twelve apostles are these. The first, Simon, who is called Peter; Andrew, his brother; James the son of Zebedee; John, his brother; Philip; Bartholomew; Thomas; Matthew the tax collector; James the son of Alphaeus; Lebbaeus, who was also called Thaddaeus; Simon the Canaanite; and Judas Iscariot, who also betrayed him.

As the pressure mounted to arrest Jesus, He had to go into hiding until the time designated by the Father.

John 7:30-31
They sought therefore to take him; but no one laid a hand on him, because his hour [time] had not yet come. But of the multitude, many believed in him. They said, "When the Christ comes, he won't do more signs than those which this man has done, will he?"

Judas offered to tell the Jewish leaders where Jesus was so they could arrest Him but only if they would pay him.

Matthew 26:14-16
Then one of the twelve, who was called Judas Iscariot, went to the chief priests, and said, "What are you willing to give me, that I should deliver him to you?" They weighed out for him [Judas] thirty pieces of silver. From that time he sought opportunity to betray him.

Even though Jesus had indicated at the last supper that He knew what Judas was about to do, Judas continued with his plan anyway. Jesus clearly identified His betrayer and traitor to be Judas.

John 13:26
Jesus therefore answered, "It is he to whom I will give this piece of bread when I have dipped it." So when he had dipped the piece of bread, he gave it to Judas, the son of Simon Iscariot.

When the time had come, he led the crowd to Jesus and kissed Him on the cheek to point Him out so there would be no mistakes.

John 18:2-5
Now Judas, who betrayed him, also knew the place, for Jesus often met there with his disciples. Judas then, having taken a detachment of soldiers and officers from the chief priests and the Pharisees, came there with lanterns, torches, and weapons. Jesus therefore, knowing all the things that were happening to him, went out, and said to them, "Who are you looking for?" They answered him, "Jesus of Nazareth." Jesus said to them, "I am he."

Luke 22:47-48
While he was still speaking, behold, a multitude, and he who was called Judas, one of the twelve, was leading them. He came near to Jesus to kiss him. But Jesus said to him, "Judas, do you betray the Son of Man with a kiss?"

Just like Judas, they will betray anybody who is in their way. Since these people will turn on each other, they cannot trust anyone. They will act as if they are loyal to Christians and turn their back on them if persecution comes.

Their Wicked Recklessness

In verse 4, Paul continues his portrayal of these evil men and describes them as headstrong.

2 Timothy 3:4
Traitors, headstrong, conceited, lovers of pleasure rather than lovers of God.

The word in the Greek translated "headstrong" comes from a root word that means "to fall." The term was used literally for people falling down for variety of reasons with a wide range of results. It also came to refer metaphorically to falling into evil and wickedness.

Here are several examples when the word referred to the falling down in worship and respect.

First, it is used to describe the Magi who came from the East. They fell down in worship of the baby Jesus.

Matthew 2:11
They came into the house and saw the young child with Mary, his mother, and they fell down and worshiped him. Opening their treasures, they offered to him gifts: gold, frankincense, and myrrh.

Second, Mark utilizes this term to portray Jairus' falling down at Christ's feet begging Him to heal his daughter.

Mark 5:22-23
Behold, one of the rulers of the synagogue, Jairus by name, came; and seeing him...fell at his feet, and begged him much, saying, "My little daughter is at the point of death. Please come and lay your hands on her, that she may be made healthy, and live."

Third, when Luke recorded the incident involving a leper entreating Jesus to cure him of leprosy, he said the leper fell on his face before Him.

Luke 5:12
While he was in one of the cities, behold, there was a man full of leprosy. When he saw Jesus, he fell on his face, and begged him, saying, "Lord, if you want to, you can make me clean."

Here are some examples of the word used literally for something evil or dangerous. First, Jesus compares the false leaders of the Jews who taught their people lies as the blind leading the blind. Then, he says what will happen to them in the end.

Matthew 15:14
Leave them alone. They are blind guides of the blind. If the blind guide the blind, both will fall into a pit.

Second, Matthew presents the true story of the demon-possessed boy who continually fell into the fire.

Matthew 17:15
Lord, have mercy on my son, for he is epileptic [lunatic], and suffers grievously; for he often falls into the fire, and often into the water.

Third, the term referred to falling. When Jesus was about to heal on the Sabbath, He asked the people if they would pull a fallen animal or son out of a well on this day.

Luke 14:5
He answered them, "Which of you, if your son or an ox fell into a well, wouldn't immediately pull him out on a Sabbath day?"

This root word was also utilized metaphorically to speak of falling into sin. Paul uses it to warn believers not to fall into evil.

1 Corinthians 10:12
Therefore let him who thinks he stands be careful that he doesn't fall.

When John wrote the letters to the churches in the book of Revelation, Jesus tells the church at Ephesus to repent from where they have fallen away. Though the Ephesians were a powerful church of ministry, they had forgotten why they were doing it. They had lost their first love.

Revelation 2:5
Remember therefore from where you have fallen, and repent and do the first works; or else I am coming to you swiftly, and will move your lamp stand out of its place, unless you repent.

Therefore, the negative idea came to denote our word in this text. So, the word came to mean "falling into something without thinking with negative consequences attached." It can be readily translated "reckless." The actual word is used only one other place in the New Testament which provides a beautiful example of "reckless" behavior.

In Acts 19, Paul traveled to Ephesus to preach the gospel and had such a powerful impact that huge crowds of people were turning from their idolatrous, evil ways to Christ. This began to hurt the silver merchants who made their living off the purchasing of silver idols of Artemis. The city was filled with them.

A man named Demetrius met with all the craftsmen in the city and explained that not only were their livelihoods on the line but the very worship of their goddess. Since this may affect all of Asia, they had to do something. Then, Luke described what happened as the crowd became convinced that their fortunes were about to be destroyed by Paul and his own "magic arts."

Acts 19:28-31
When they heard this they were filled with anger, and cried out, saying, "Great is Artemis of the Ephesians!" The whole city was filled with confusion, and they rushed with one accord into the theater, having seized Gaius and Aristarchus, men of Macedonia, Paul's companions in travel. When Paul wanted to enter in to the people, the disciples didn't allow him. Certain also of the Asiarchs, being his friends, sent to him and begged him not to venture into the theater.

There was chaos in the assembly. It had turned into was a huge disturbance. This went on for over two hours before someone finally addressed the commotion to put an end to the chaos before someone was killed.

Acts 19:32-34
Some therefore cried one thing, and some another, for the assembly was in confusion. Most of them didn't know why they had come together. They brought Alexander [substitute for Paul] out of the multitude, the Jews putting him forward. Alexander beckoned with his hand, and would have made a defense to the people. But when they perceived that he was a Jew, all with one voice for a time of about two hours cried out, "Great is Artemis of the Ephesians!"

Then the town clerk stood up amid the frenzied crowd and intervened warning them of the "rash" (the same word) actions they were about to take.

Acts 19:35-41
When the town clerk had quieted the multitude, he said, "You men of Ephesus, what man is there who doesn't know that the city of the Ephesians is temple keeper of the great goddess Artemis, and of the image which fell down from Zeus? Seeing then that these things can't be denied, you ought to be quiet, and to do nothing rash. For you have brought these men here, who are neither robbers of temples nor blasphemers of your goddess. If therefore Demetrius and the craftsmen who are with him have a matter against anyone, the courts are open, and there are proconsuls. Let them press charges against one another. But if you seek anything about other matters, it will be settled in the regular assembly. For indeed we are in danger of being accused concerning today's riot, there being no cause. Concerning it, we wouldn't be able to give an account of this commotion." When he had...spoken, he dismissed...assembly.

These people of the last days are rash and reckless in their words and deeds. They foolishly think nothing of what they do by impulse. Consequences do not matter to them because nothing they do is thought through or carefully considered. Christians who fall into their hands will bear the brunt of anything their evil impulses desire. They will take whatever risk to punish and persecute Christians who do not agree.

Their Foolish Conceit

As the apostle continues in verse 4 with his long list of attributes, he says that they will be conceited.

2 Timothy 3:4
Traitors, headstrong, *conceited*, lovers of pleasure rather than lovers of God.

This Greek word comes from a root word meaning "to cause or emit smoke, raise smoke, to smoke." The root is only used once in the New Testament when Isaiah is quoted by Jesus.

Matthew 12:20-21
He won't break a bruised reed. He won't quench a smoking flax, until he leads justice to victory. In his name, the nations will hope.

Here, He is referring to Himself as the true Messiah who is coming to save the broken, suffering people. He compared these afflicted ones to "bruised reeds" and "smoking flax." The first analogy speaks of reeds that become bruised. In Ancient times, reeds had many uses by the common people. One involved them being cut and made into a flute so music could fill the void in their difficult lives. When they became bruised or bent, they were broken and thrown away. When the music was gone, they would return to their desperation and despair. Rather than crush them as the oppressors did, the Messiah would come and deliver them, and they would be surrounded with joy again as they had with music.

In the second analogy, the poor would set flax on fire to provide light and warm themselves. Eventually, it would smolder until the fire had gone out and there was no light or warmth. These people would again return to their despair. Rather than quenching the fire as the oppressors would do, the Messiah would come to bring salvation. True justice in both situations would be meted out.

The smoke of the burning flax would physically surround the people warming themselves and fill the area. As a result, it began to be used metaphorically to speak of the conceited who attempt to surround people with their presence, words, and actions whether they like it or not. This is what is in Paul's mind when he uses this descriptive word. They do not bring the warmth and light of the burning flax; but instead, it was the choking smoke of a smoldering fire just about to go out.

Paul uses the word in two other places. The first was in his letter to young Pastor Timothy. In his correspondence, the apostle lists the characteristics of leaders (elders) in the church.

1 Timothy 3:6-7
Not a new convert, lest being puffed up he fall into the same condemnation as the devil. Moreover he must have good testimony from those who are outside, to avoid falling into reproach and the snare of the devil.

Here, the apostle is concerned that new believers should not become elders because they could become "puffed up" or "extremely conceited." In our analogy, they will envelope everyone in the smoke of their powerful new leadership and fall into the same condemnation as the Devil who fell from pride. They will want it all and do whatever has to be done to achieve it.

Second, he repeats the term later on in the letter to speak of the people that Timothy had encountered who wanted to spend their time among the brethren in foolish discussions of no consequence leading to arguing and disputes. In their conceit, they were obsessed with this. Timothy was not to get involved with these men in their verbal battles.

1 Timothy 6:4-5
He is conceited, knowing nothing, but obsessed [as if sick with a disease] with arguments, disputes, and word battles, from which come envy, strife, insulting, evil suspicions, constant friction of people of corrupt minds and destitute of the truth, who suppose that godliness is a means of gain [from disputing]. Withdraw yourself from such.

This is an unrelenting prideful obsession with their thoughts and opinions resulting in arguing, fighting, suspicion, and friction between themselves and others. This is "pride to the extreme." They believe that not only are they always right but will pursue their "rightness" to the end. These people have a big presence and will seek to intimidate all those around them including Christians. They will argue with us but never come to Jesus Christ. As their numbers increase so will their intensity toward foolish conceit which will pour forth into persecution.

Their Predatory Nature

As the apostle continues in verse 6, he describes the last days as filled with people who are predators.

2 Timothy 3:6
For some of these are people who creep into houses, and take captive gullible women loaded down with sins, led away by various lusts.

First, these people "creep" into houses. The root of this Greek word "creep" refers literally to the "setting" of the sun. It's used by two authors to describe the same event. Jesus was in Capernaum, and he was healing people at sunset. So, it has the idea of a sun appearing to "sink" into the horizon.

Mark 1:32
At evening, when the sun had set, they brought to him all who were sick, and those who were possessed by demons.

Luke 4:40
When the sun was setting, all those who had any sick with various diseases brought them to him; and he laid his hands on every one of them, and healed them.

From this root, the word Paul uses came to refer to one who sinks or inserts himself into a situation. It is as subtle and smooth as the setting of the sin. It was literally used of the putting on of a garment (nice and easy). It is translated "creep" due to the context. So, these kinds of people slink into the houses of easily influenced (gullible) women who are "loaded down with sins, led away by various lusts."

The word "loaded" carries the concept of "overwhelmed, heaped up with, or overloaded" by sins. The root word refers to an "urn or receptacle that carries the bones of the dead." These women are carrying on their own bodies the dead bones of sin.

This occurs simply because they are "lead away, directed or guided by, even attached to" their own lusts, passions, and forbidden desires. These cravings are "manifold, have many aspects, or are of various colors." This makes these women very easy targets to capture them either physically, emotionally, or even financially and use them for whatever they want or need.

The Samaritan woman in John 4 is one example. On his way to Galilee, Jesus and His disciples stopped at a village in Samaria called Sychar. Wearied from His journey, Jesus sat down at a well and asked His disciples to go into town about one half of a mile away and retrieve some food. Around six in the evening, a Samaritan woman came to fetch water from the well. Though current Jewish custom did not allow men or rabbis to speak to any women in public, Jesus decided to speak to the woman.

He knew that she was a woman of lusts, passions, and forbidden desires and satisfied it through many husbands. He wanted to gently confront her and offer the living water He could provide to wash it away. So, the Lord Jesus began a conversation about the water she was physically seeking and the spiritual water He could provide. So, He asked her for a drink.

John 4:7
A woman of Samaria came to draw water. Jesus said to her, "Give me a drink."

The Samaritan woman was stunned and inquired as to why a Jewish man would even speak to her let alone ask her for something. He replied that if she knew the gift of God that was sitting before her, she would request of Him living water (He was the well providing the water of eternal life). After a brief discussion about this water, he indicts her with a command.

John 4:16-18
Jesus said to her, "Go, call your husband, and come here." The woman answered, "I have no husband." Jesus said to her, "You said well, 'I have no husband,' for you have had five husbands; and he whom you now have is not your husband. This you have said truly."

By referring to her husband, He desired to bring to her consciousness the dead bones of sin in her life. It is fair to assume that in an ancient patriarchal society, she had also been the victim of these five husbands; the man the woman was living with now did not seem to mind her history. A woman in that society would have to have been shielded by the men in her life who desired to take advantage of her.

We know that she was an outcast because she alone and getting water at an unusual hour of the day. She could not get water with the other women and had to fetch it alone and unprotected. Rather than taking advantage of her, Jesus offered her salvation. Rather than repent and receive Him as Savior and Lord, the woman left her water pot and ran into the city. Eventually, many arrived and heard Jesus.

These people of the last days will be vicious predators of the gullible, lustful, and burdened. They may be preachers, who are wolves in sheep's clothing. However, they arrive, they promise relief but only ransack the lives of the weak. Regarding Christians, they will search for those among us who are immature, weak, and struggling with sin. These will be led away by them and down a path of wickedness and unrighteousness. Their persecution will be to prey on them, drag them into further sin and enjoy their fall from grace.

Their Feigned Desire to Learn

In 2 Timothy 3:7, Paul turns to another important aspect of these people. Some will appear to be truly searching for the truth, but it is a pretense.

2 Timothy 3:7
Always learning, and never able to come to the knowledge of the truth.

These are the "religious people" we see who appear to be completely dedicated to seeking the truth. They will usually be in the higher levels of leadership and responsibility in the different religions of the world and even under the auspices of Christianity. Paul says that they are at "all times, always learning." The word "learning" has the idea of "increasing in knowledge and being informed" concerning truth.

The Greek word translated "truth" nearly always refers to God's truth revealed in the Scriptures.

John 17:17
Sanctify them in your truth. Your word is truth.

John 3:21
But he who does the truth comes to the light, that his works may be revealed, that they have been done in God.

Galatians 5:7
You were running well! Who interfered with you that you should not obey the truth?

Ephesians 1:13
In whom you also, having heard the word of the truth, the Good News of your salvation [this plus all the Scriptures] — in whom, having also believed, you were sealed with the promised...Spirit.
So, these individuals actually read, study, and discuss the truth revealed in the Bible about God. They may even be so-called experts in the Scriptures. Yet, these are not able to discern the real truth within it. They cannot comprehend the true knowledge it is revealing.

The word "able" comes from a word whereby we get the English word "dynamite." It refers to real explosive power. No matter how much knowledge they attain, they have no spiritual, explosive power to fully understand it. They are never able to come to the truth no matter how much time and effort they put in.

This exact same word is used by Paul when he speaks of an unbeliever who attempts to understand the Scriptures.

1 Corinthians 2:14
Now the natural man doesn't receive the things of God's Spirit, for they are foolishness to him, and he can't [is not able to] know them, because they are spiritually discerned.

You see, they have no Spirit of God inside them to illuminate the truth or enlighten them as to what it means. They cannot understand it though they may think they are experts. Their desire cannot bring about the knowledge of the truth.

John explains to his readers, who were Christians, that they have the Holy Spirit who can guide them into all truth. He calls it "the anointing."

1 John 2:27
As for you, the anointing [Holy Spirit] which you received from him remains in you, and you don't need for anyone to teach you. But as his anointing teaches you concerning all things, and is true, and is no lie, and even as it taught you, you will remain in him.

This does not mean we should not study the Scriptures to understand them; but simply, we have the Spirit to guide us into the truth as we study.

The Lord Jesus promised that when He left the Earth, He would send the "Spirit of Truth" to His disciples when he left so they would remember what He had said.

John 14:17
The Spirit of Truth.... You know him, for he lives with you....

John 16:13
However when...the Spirit of Truth, has come, he will guide you into all truth, for he will not speak from himself; but whatever he hears, he will speak. He will declare to you things that are coming.

Unfortunately, these religious people have no Spirit, so they learn and learn but are not able to find the truth even though it is right in front of them. Why? They misinterpret it or add and subtract from it until it is something else altogether.

This beautifully describes the Pharisees and other Jewish leaders. These people hounded Jesus asking question after question appearing to be searching for the truth. They knew the Scriptures quite well but had added and subtracted so much from them that they could not see the true intent of the law and could not understand the Spirit's work in Christ.

In the first incident, they attribute Christ's healing of the multitudes to the Devil's power rather than to God's. These leaders who are "learning and never able to see the truth" actually accuse Him of being possessed.

Matthew 9:32-34
As they went out, behold, a mute man who was demon possessed was brought to him. When the demon was cast out, the mute man spoke. The multitudes marveled, saying, "Nothing like this has ever been seen in Israel!" But the Pharisees said, "By the prince of the demons [the Devil], he casts out demons."

Later, this happened again because they had not "learned" from the first incident.

Matthew 12:22-24
Then one possessed by a demon, blind and mute, was brought to him and he healed him, so that the blind and mute man both spoke and saw. All the multitudes were amazed, and said, "Can this be

the son of David?" But when the Pharisees heard it, they said, "This man does not cast out demons, except by Beelzebul, the prince of the demons."

Since they attempt to learn but "never really understand," Christ indicts them for their foolish and illogical reasoning. They were viewing these incidences which verified that He was from God but were not able to come to that real truth behind what He did. This was nothing less the power of God, but they could not see it.

Matthew 12:25-29
Knowing their thoughts, Jesus said to them, "Every kingdom divided against itself is brought to desolation, and every city or house divided against itself will not stand. If Satan casts out Satan, he is divided against himself. How then will his kingdom stand? If I by Beelzebul cast out demons, by whom do your children cast them out? Therefore they will be your judges. But if I by the Spirit...cast out demons, then God's Kingdom has come upon you. Or how can one enter into the house of the strong man, and plunder his goods, unless he first bind the strong man? Then he will plunder his house.

These people of the last days claim to be the truth seekers among the religious leaders, professors, intellectuals, and scientists. They are continually learning about the truth; yet they are in an endless cycle of spiritual ignorance. No matter how much effort is expended, they will never comprehend the truth because deep inside them they have no desire for the things of God.

These unconvinced people will browbeat many Christians into thinking that Christianity is based on fairy tales, myths, and the musings of foolish dreamers. In reality, it will their false beliefs that will indict them on the day in which they are judged for their false tales.

Their Religious Opposition

Now the apostle continues the list of characteristics of "these" people he had just been describing by revealing one of the reasons why they were not able to come to the truth. They continually resisted or opposed the very truth that they were reading and studying.

2 Timothy 3:8
Even as Jannes and Jambres opposed Moses, so do these [refers to the people of verses 1-7] also oppose the truth; men corrupted in mind, who concerning the faith, are rejected.

The Greek word translated "oppose" means "to set oneself against, to withstand, to resist." It comes from two words: one is a preposition meaning "against" and the other word is a verb meaning "to stand." Therefore, it refers to "taking a stand against" someone or something.

The root of this word is the verb "to stand." It could refer to simply a person standing in the upright position in the normal course of life.

Matthew 12:46
While he was yet speaking to the multitudes, behold, his mother and his brothers stood outside, seeking...him.

Matthew 13:2
Great multitudes gathered to him, so that he entered into a boat, and sat, and all the multitude stood on the beach.

Matthew 20:3
He went out about the third hour, and saw others standing idle in the marketplace.

Since people will stand for issues, it came to mean "a stand for something or someone."

Therefore, the Greek word is used in Acts for the physical standing up for a cause.

On the day of Pentecost, Peter stood before the huge crowd and preached the gospel.

Acts 2:14
But Peter, standing up with the eleven, lifted up his voice, and spoke out to them, "You men of Judea, and all you who dwell at Jerusalem, let this be known to you, and listen to my words."

The angel who released the apostles from prison gave this powerful command from the creator Himself. They were to continue preaching the Word.

Acts 5:20
Go *stand* and speak in the temple to the people all the words of this life.

In Athens, the apostle Paul stood up before the idolatrous people whose city was full of idols and preached a message about the "unknown God" that they were worshipping in ignorance.

Acts 17:22
Paul stood in the middle of the Areopagus, and said, "You men of Athens, I perceive that you are very religious in all things.

In the letters of Paul, rather than for literal standing, the apostle used the word metaphorically for "taking a stand for someone or something. This became an important word that the apostle utilized.

Romans 11:20
True; by their unbelief they were broken off, and you stand by your faith. Don't be conceited, but fear.

2 Corinthians 1:24
Not that we control your faith, but are fellow workers with you for your joy. For you stand firm in faith.

Ephesians 6:11
Put on the whole armor of God, that you may be able to stand against the wiles of the devil.

It these passages, we are to stand for the truth. Here, Paul uses the opposite. Rather than standing for the truth, these people of the last days stand against the truth. This word is used many times but in particular of two people who stood against Paul.

Here, Paul warns Timothy about a resister of the truth who did Paul much harm.

2 Timothy 4:14-15
Alexander, the coppersmith, did much evil to me. The Lord will repay him according to his deeds, of whom you also must beware; for he greatly opposed our words.

Whatever Alexander did, it was evil enough for this harsh indictment.

Luke used the word for another one who opposed Paul.

Acts 13:6-8
When they [Paul and others] had gone through the island to Paphos, they found a certain sorcerer, a false prophet, a Jew, whose name was Bar Jesus, who was with the proconsul, Sergius Paulus, a man of understanding. This man [Sergius] summoned Barnabas and Saul, and sought to hear the word of God [the truth]. But Elymas the sorcerer (for so is his name by interpretation) withstood them [the truth], seeking to turn aside the proconsul from the faith.

Here, this magician did everything he could to keep Sergius from hearing the truth of God, but this made Paul only more determined which led to a terrible rebuke.

Acts 13:9-12
But Saul, who is also called Paul, filled with the Holy Spirit, fastened his eyes on him, and said, "Full of all deceit and all cunning, you son of the devil [the real source], you enemy of all righteousness, will you not cease to [never stops] pervert the right ways of the Lord? Now, behold, the hand of the Lord is on you, and you will be blind, not seeing the sun for a season!" Immediately a mist and darkness fell on him. He went around seeking someone to lead him by the hand. Then the proconsul, when he saw what was done, believed, being astonished at the teaching of the Lord.

Just as Alexander and Elymas opposed the truth of God, Paul mentions another two who did the same but years and years earlier. This was Jannes and Jambres who had resisted Moses. Though they are not mentioned in the Scripture, their names were passed down through Jewish history. These were among the magicians who were at Pharaoh's side when Moses came a second time to speak to the ruler of Egypt.

You may remember that Moses and Aaron presented to Pharaoh God's demand to release His people. The ruler's response was to remove the straw the Hebrews were given but to continue the quota of bricks they were to make. This only angered the Hebrews, and they criticized Moses. After complaining to God, He issued Moses a second command to go to Pharaoh again and this time His servant Moses was to demonstrate God's power by turning his rod into a snake.

Exodus 7:10-13
Moses and Aaron went into Pharaoh, and they did so, as Yahweh had commanded: and Aaron [the spokesman] cast down his rod before Pharaoh and before his servants, and it became a serpent.

Then Pharaoh also called for the wise men and the sorcerers. They also, the magicians of Egypt, did the same thing with their enchantments. For they [Jannes and Jambres] each cast down their rods, and they [the rods] became serpents: but Aaron's rod swallowed up their rods. Pharaoh's heart was hardened, and he didn't listen to them; as Yahweh had spoken.

Notice, this opposition was serious and supernatural. It involved real demonic power against Moses. Of course, God's power is so much greater than the devil's power, but the implication is pretty clear. Their opposition may involve something not of this world.

So, these religious people may come from the ranks of the world's religions including Christianity or even the world of shamans, witches, and sorcerers. They will be passionate about their teachings especially when it involves the Holy Bible but, in their learning, will resist the truth. They will vehemently oppose our interpretations. They are unwilling to consider another's. Everyone else is wrong. Period.

When focused on Christians, they will be much like the false magicians (Jannes and Jambres) who opposed Moses in the court of Pharaoh. They will stand against them in the courts of law, in the forums of public opinion, and in the personal interactions of families and friends. They speak with great authority and against those who name Christ as Savior and Lord. If necessary, they will call upon the Devil and use their magical arts to curse Christians.

Their Corrupted Minds

Another characteristic of these people of the last times is that they are utterly corrupt in their minds. This corruption refers to the truth of God's revelation.

THE PERSECUTION OF THE SAINTS AND HOW TO OVERCOME IT

2 Timothy 3:8
Even as Jannes and Jambres opposed Moses, so do these also oppose the truth; men corrupted in mind, who concerning the faith, are rejected.

The Greek word translated "corrupted" comes from two root words: a preposition meaning "through" and a root word meaning "to destroy, corrupt, and be depraved." So, it means to "be destroyed, corrupted, and depraved through and through." In this case, it is throughout the mind.

Paul uses the root word (corrupted) to describe a person's former manner of depraved living without God.

Ephesians 4:22
That you put away, as concerning your former way of life, the old man, that grows corrupt after the lusts of deceit.

He uses the word to describe the people of God (a temple) and speaks of false teachers corrupting them with lies.

1 Corinthians 3:17
If anyone destroys God's temple, God will destroy him; for God's temple is holy, which you are.

It is used by the apostle to show how relationships with evil people can destroy the good morals of believers. Some think it is the reverse, but it is not. The corrupters influence the Christian toward evil.

1 Corinthians 15:33
Don't be deceived! Evil companionships corrupt good morals.

As one can see, this word refers to the corruption of both sin and error. We have seen that the corrupted mind is full of dark thoughts producing dark words and actions.

In the 2 Timothy 3 passage, Paul uses the word derived from this root word to describe the minds of these people of the last days. Their minds are "destroyed, depraved, and corrupted" through and through. The darkness of sin and error has fully penetrated their minds. There is no moral or doctrinal light in them.

How Paul uses the root word to speak of the mind of Eve being corrupted by the wiles of Satan disguised as a serpent is a perfect example of this.

2 Corinthians 11:3
But I am afraid that somehow, as the serpent deceived Eve in his craftiness, so your minds might be corrupted from the simplicity that is in Christ.

Eve's mind was persuaded to think differently about God and His motives (the darkness of error).

Genesis 3:4-5
The serpent said to the woman, "You won't surely die, for God knows that in the day you eat it, your eyes will be opened, and you will be like God, knowing good and evil."

He told Eve that God had lied, and she would not die. He desired to shed doubt on the Lord's motives and purposes by implying that God knew something that she also should know. He knew what evil was and she needed to know this also. This would change everything for her.

The serpent claimed she would be God-like if she ate.

Genesis 3:6-7
When the woman saw that the tree was good for food, and that it was a delight to the eyes, and that the tree was to be desired to make one wise, she took some of its fruit, and ate; and she gave

some to her husband with her, and he ate it, too. Their eyes were opened [here's the corruption], and they both knew that they were naked [lust came]. They sewed fig leaves...and made coverings for themselves.

When Eve took a good long look at the fruit in her hand, her lusts took over. The fruit was suddenly beautiful as she gazed at it and would be delicious to eat. So, she and Adam ate. This is the second aspect of corruption and darkness: lusts bringing forth sin. Now, their thoughts were corrupted because their eyes were opened to sin's many possibilities. One of them was now sexual sin. As a result, they quickly covered themselves. Fortunately, the corruption had not filled their entire minds. In the apostle's description in his letter, he explains it has filled the minds of the people of the last days. In these men of the last days, the corruption had fully destroyed their thinking and their minds were filled with depravity. In the contrast of Jannes and Jambres with Moses, Paul is most likely referring to the depraved minds of those in the religious hierarchy which were the corrupted clergy, ministers, or other religious leaders.

Jesus knew that though the Pharisees and other religious leaders appeared holy and righteous, they had minds that were totally corrupt. When Jesus preached His Beatitudes, he contrasted their ancient interpretation of God's laws with His interpretation. Their "righteousness" was only outward, but God's had to do with the inner heart and mind.

Matthew 5:27-28
You have heard that it was said, "You shall not commit adultery;" but I tell you that everyone who gazes at a woman to lust after her has committed adultery with her already in his heart.

Here, Jesus moves literally to the heart of the issue. These leaders had determined that they could lust all they wanted in their "corrupt minds" but as long as they did not actually commit the lewd act, they were sinless. Jesus says that this was not true. The act in the mind was just as much a sin.

So, the apostle Paul is speaking of people in the last days with dark minds filled with falsehoods and wickedness. They may look religious or "good" on the outside, but their minds are filled with lies, lusts, and evil. True Christians represent the exact opposite of who they truly are. The clean, pure minds and actions of believers will drive them insane and make them capable of every kind of persecution.

Their "Disqualified" Faith

Another characteristic of these people of the last times is that they are "rejected" regarding the faith. They have failed the test when it comes to their faith. They have not proved themselves to be Christians.

2 Timothy 3:8
Even as Jannes and Jambres opposed Moses, so do these also oppose the truth; men corrupted in mind, who concerning the faith, are rejected.

The Greek word translated "rejected" refers to the "failing of a test." It carries the idea that beliefs, words, and actions do not demonstrate authenticity. In this context, it refers to their opposition of truth (wrong beliefs) and their depraved minds (producing wrong actions) disqualify them from salvation. Since beliefs and fruit display salvation, they have the wrong ones and are rejected by God.

Below, Paul contrasts his humble faith to the prideful ones of the Corinthian faction who opposed him. He asked them to examine their own selves to see if they are believers.

2 Corinthians 13:5
Examine your own selves, whether you are in the faith. Test your own selves. Or don't you know as to your own selves, that Jesus Christ is in you [through His Holy Spirit]? – unless indeed you are disqualified.

If they thoroughly look at their beliefs, words, and actions will it demonstrate the Christ that is in them or not?

Then, Paul defends himself and his companions with a powerful declaration that they are qualified because they do demonstrate the characteristics that display their true faith.

2 Corinthians 13:6-7
But I hope that you will know that we aren't disqualified.

In Titus 1, Paul takes a tough stand against false teachers plaguing Titus and his ministry who by their wicked deeds showed themselves to be disqualified.

Titus 1:16
They profess that they know God, but by their deeds they deny him, being abominable, disobedient, and unfit for any good work.

In Hebrews, the author compares those who refused to believe in the Lord Jesus Christ to thorns and thistles among branches which must be rejected and burned.

Hebrews 6:8
But if it bears thorns and thistles, it is rejected and near being cursed, whose end is to be burned.

So, these people of the last days, mostly religious leaders, will be disqualified as to having authentic faith. Because they are missing the truth and holiness that is in a believer's heart, they will come after us.

Their Evident Foolishness

In these last days religious leaders will get to the point where they are foolish in every way. Their imbecilic minds and decisions will become utterly obvious for all to see. People will begin to see them for who they really are. Why? Their foolish acts from their corruption and opposition to the truth will make it evident to all.

2 Timothy 3:9
But they will proceed [advance] no further. For their folly will be evident to all men, as theirs also came to be.

The Greek word for "folly" is the negative of the word for "mind." Therefore, Paul is speaking of "no mind" meaning "lack of reason" about something. It refers to thinking in a way that completely lacks any kind of reasoning faculties. They demonstrate sheer stupidity in their words and actions which displays what is in their hearts.

This word is used only one other time in the entire New Testament. Here, Luke described an event where the Lord Jesus appeared to break the Sabbath law. This day was to be a day of rest. Of course, the Pharisees went far beyond God's intentions for that day with a long list of rules. Jesus desired to point this out. This incident involved healing of a man with a severely withered arm which was considered work and a violation of the Sabbath law.

Luke 6:6
It also happened on another Sabbath that he entered into the synagogue and taught. There was a man there, and his right hand was withered. The scribes and the Pharisees watched him, to see whether he would heal on the Sabbath, that they might find an accusation against him. But he knew their thoughts; and he said to the man who had the withered hand, "Rise up, and stand in the

middle." He arose and stood. Then Jesus said to them, "I will ask you something: Is it lawful on the Sabbath to do good, or to do harm? To save a life, or to kill?" He looked around at them all, and said to the man, "Stretch out your hand." He did, and his hand was restored as sound as the other.

When Jesus challenged the Jewish laws and authority, Luke used the word to describe their incredibly impulsive reaction.

Luke 6:11
But they were filled with rage and talked with one another about what they might do to Jesus.

Though this word is translated "rage", that is an assumption on the part of the translators. The King James Translation gives the very best sense of it when they translate the word "madness."

Luke 6:11
And they were filled with madness; and communed one with another what they might do to Jesus.
The leaders "went crazy, became completely unreasonable, and went out of their minds" when they saw this violation of their laws. Their religious authority was being undermined. This "Jesus" had to go.

These religious people of the last days will become more and more unthinking when it comes to the sins conjured up in their corrupted, depraved minds and opposition of God's truth. They will say and do things that upon reflection by any reasonable person will be considered absolutely insane and stupid. We see this in the numerous cover ups of sexual immorality in many religious organizations. These groups cover up the immoral sin rather than expose and punish it. This encourages its continued existence.

Sometimes, the immorality will be so rationalized that it will look normal and acceptable. Upon scrutiny, it is easily seen and exposed. Because, their foolishness will be repeated by them over and over, it will eventually appear normal. These people will not be patient with the saints because their light will always be exposing this.

Their Blocked Advancement

Paul describes the constant blocking of their advancement in their corruption and opposition. They will go forward and be exposed. Then, they will regroup and try again.

2 Timothy 3:9
But they will proceed [advance] no further. For their folly will be evident to all men, as theirs also came to be.

The word translated "proceed" is the same word we dealt with in 2 Timothy 3 describing the increase in evil.

2 Timothy 3:13
But evil men...impostors will grow worse and worse, deceiving and being deceived.

It referred to the hard work of a special group of soldiers who would be sent ahead of the Roman army when there was no road to advance. These soldiers would cut a broad way through the brush and build a road for the army to march through. They would make a pioneer advance with great effort.

Paul is explaining that these corrupted individuals will work hard to metaphorically cut through the intertwined branches of righteousness and goodness to commit their evil, corrupt, and godless acts. They will exert much effort!

He utilizes the term in the same way earlier in his letter to describe the progress of ungodliness in general.

2 Timothy 2:16
But shun empty chatter, for it will go further in ungodliness.

Though the ungodly and unrighteous may progress and also advance, these specific Jannes and Jambres types of religious people will be blocked over and over.

He says that they will advance "no further." The word for "further" refers to an increase in quantity and quality.

2 Timothy 3:9
But they will proceed [advance] no further. For their folly will be evident to all men, as theirs also came to be.

No matter how these corrupt people try to increase in their sin both in quantity and quality, it will get halted every time. Why is that? Their sin is exposed. Then they will try again. If they cannot recover, then others will come. This will be an ongoing process throughout this long period of last days. We will never be rid of them.

Their Continual Exposure

In the last part of the verse, Paul asserts that folly will be evident like the unreasoning actions of Jannes and Jambres.

2 Timothy 3:9
But they will proceed [advance] no further. For their folly will be evident to all men, as theirs also came to be.

The Greek word "evident" comes from two words. The first is a preposition meaning "out of" and a root word meaning "clear, certain, evident." This root is used in several places in the New Testament.

First, it is used of Peter's accent which made it clear he was from Galilee.

Matthew 26:73
After a little while those who stood by [at his arrest] came and said to Peter, "Surely you are also one of them, for your speech makes you known."

Second, it refers to the reasoning process that makes one idea clear from another.

1 Corinthians 15:27
For, "He put all things in subjection under his feet." But when he says, "All things are put in subjection", it is evident that he is excepted who subjected all things to him.

Third, in Galatians 3, Paul argues that justification does not come from the law because no one can live by it. This truth was "evident" to them. They could see the facts about the law and easily discern that no one could be justified by it because no one could fully align their lives to it in perfect obedience.

Galatians 3:11-12
Now that no man is justified by the law before God is evident, for, "The righteous will live by faith." The law is not of faith, rage and "The man who does them will live by them."

The word Paul uses in 2 Timothy 3 is similar except it has an added preposition meaning "out of". This indicates that the clarity grows "out of" the inner evil insanity of these corrupt people. Their foolhardy thinking is made obvious by their foolhardy words and behavior. No one will have any reservations as to whether these people are wickedly "mad," because it will be clear to all. A viewing of their behavior and a little reasoning removes doubt. In fact, "all" can see it.

Then, Paul compares them to what happened to Jannes and Jambres. In the confrontation with those two corrupt, depraved men, God exposed their madness, and their folly was stopped. Their opposition to the truth led to their "insanity" in thinking that they could outperform a servant of the Lord God Almighty. This became utterly manifest when "God's snake" easily gobbled up theirs.

These religious zealots and others will be clearly seen. As these predators arise, they will commit their dark, corrupted deeds from their opposition to the truth. Eventually, their thoughtless, foolish, unreasoning actions will expose them, and they will be rejected only for another to arise. With them will come untold persecution of true Christians who through their holy testimony and righteous deeds will expose the darkness they have inside these madmen with the light of Christ.

The Jewish Pharisees are a powerful example of people who were similar to Jannes and Jambres. They hounded Jesus relentlessly and He continually exposed them for who they really were. They were always attempting to trap Jesus in a supposed violation of God's laws. Often, Jesus would challenge them due to the misinterpretation of God's Word.

On one occasion, they asked Jesus to explain who a man's wife in heaven would be if he took a series of wives due to their multiple deaths. Jesus' response was immediate.

Matthew 22:29
But Jesus answered them, "You are mistaken, not knowing the Scriptures, nor the power of God.

At this question, the Lord rebukes them for not knowing the answer from the Scriptures that they so quickly defended. Also, they did not understand the power God had.

Matthew 22:30
For in the resurrection they [the saints] neither marry, nor are given in marriage, but are like God's angels in heaven.

How could they not comprehend this? We know from this passage in 2 Timothy 3 that they were reading the Scriptures but were constantly opposing the truth and using it for their own financial gain. These people will use the Scriptures to persecute Christians by claiming that the true believers are not following the teachings of Word.

Their Evil Nature

In verse 13, the apostle comes to the crux of the issue when he described these people of the last days who will bring persecution upon God's saints: they are evil people.

2 Timothy 3:13
But evil men and impostors will grow worse and worse, deceiving and being deceived.

What is evil? The answer is whatever God says it is. God defines evil and good which is falling short of God's glory which is the standard.

Romans 3:23
For all have sinned, and fall short of the glory of God.

To fall short of God's glory is to fall short of all that He is. It is thinking, saying, or doing something less than what He would do. It is having qualities unlike His perfect ones.

THE PERSECUTION OF THE SAINTS AND HOW TO OVERCOME IT

In the garden, evil was the eating of a tree that God told Adam and Eve not to eat.

Genesis 2:17
But you shall not eat of the tree of the knowledge of good and evil; for in the day that you eat of it, you will surely die.

Man and woman ate of that tree and sinned. This continued until God decided to destroy the earth and start over.

Genesis 6:5
Yahweh saw that the wickedness of man was great in the Earth, and that every imagination of the thoughts of man's heart was continually only evil.

To receive a better understanding of evil. it is important to dig deeper into the many New Testament passages which discuss this concept.

Matthew 5:45
That you may be children of your Father who is in heaven. For he makes his sun to rise on the evil and the good, and sends rain on the just and the unjust.

Matthew 7:17-18
Even so, every good tree produces good fruit; but the corrupt tree produces evil fruit. A good tree can't produce evil fruit, neither can a corrupt tree produce good fruit.

Matthew 12:34
You offspring of vipers, how can you, being evil, speak good things? For out of the abundance of the heart, the mouth speaks.

Matthew 12:35
The good man out of his good treasure brings out good things, and the evil man out of his evil treasure brings out evil things.

Matthew 13:49
So will it be in the end of the world. The angels will come and separate the wicked from among the righteous.

Second, evil involves the inner heart which produces evil words and actions. It is these that really defile the man not something on the outside.

Matthew 15:19-20
For out of the heart come evil thoughts, murders, adulteries, sexual sins, thefts, false testimony, and blasphemies. These are the things which defile [make unclean] the man; but to eat with unwashed hands doesn't defile the man."

Third, evil is compared to darkness.

Luke 11:34
The lamp of the body is the eye. Therefore when your eye is good, your whole body is also full of light; but when it is evil, your body also is full of darkness.

Fourth, the word "evil" is used to describe the demons and not the "good angels."

Acts 19:15
The evil spirit answered, "Jesus I know, and Paul I know, but who are you?"

Acts 19:16
The man in whom the evil spirit was leaped on them, and overpowered them, and prevailed against them, so that they fled out of that house naked and wounded.

Fifth, they tried to accuse the apostle Paul of numerous violations against the Jews and Romans, but they were not able to substantiate any evil he did.

THE PERSECUTION OF THE SAINTS AND HOW TO OVERCOME IT

Acts 25:18
Concerning whom, when the accusers stood up, they brought no charge of such things as I supposed.

Sixth, evil is compared to good, and we are to "abhor" evil while we cling to "good." These are seen as opposites of each other in every way.

Romans 12:9
Let love be without hypocrisy. Abhor that which is evil. Cling to that which is good.

Seventh, evil is used of the Devil when he is called the "Evil One." The Devil fell short of His glory at his rebellion against God and will continue to do so until he is finally stopped at the end of all things. The Devil caused a myriad of angels to fall also. Now as always, He desires to condemn as many people as he can in order to take them to his own realm of punishment.

Matthew 5:37
But let your "Yes" be "Yes" and your "No" be "No." Whatever is more than these is of the evil one.

Matthew 6:13
Bring us not into temptation, but deliver us from the evil one. For yours is the Kingdom, the power, and the glory forever. Amen.

Matthew 13:19
When anyone hears the word of the Kingdom, and doesn't understand it, the evil one comes, and snatches away that which has been sown in his heart. This is what was sown by the roadside.

Matthew 13:38
The field is the world; and the good seed, these are the children of the Kingdom; and the darnel weeds are the children of the evil one.

Luke 11:4
Forgive us our sins, for we ourselves also forgive everyone who is indebted to us. Bring us not into temptation...deliver us from the evil one.

John 17:15
I pray not that you would take them from the world, but that you would keep them from the evil one.

Ephesians 6:16
Above all, taking up the shield of faith, with which you will be able to quench all the fiery darts of the evil one.

1 Thessalonians 5:15
See that no one returns evil for evil to anyone, but always follow after that which is good, for one another, and for all.

2 Thessalonians 3:3
But the Lord is faithful, who will establish you, and guard you from the evil one.

1 John 3:12
Unlike Cain, who was of the evil one, and killed his brother. Why did he kill him? Because his deeds were evil, and his brother's righteous.

So, Paul describes the unbelieving people of the last days as evil, wicked, unrighteous, and lacking good. When they encounter Christians who are good, holy and righteous due to Christ's death on the cross and their faith in Him, they react. They have not become whole and healthy in Christ; instead, their deep spiritual sicknesses and raw spiritual wounds will drive them to persecute Christians. They will hate their light as they did Christ's light. They will never tolerate the light shining on their evil, sin, and wickedness. This will continue to increase until the end.

Their False Fabrication

In 2 Timothy 3:13, Paul adds an additional description when he calls them "impostors." These people are deceivers and fakers. They tell lies as a matter of course, especially lies about the Bible. In fact, they are "faker fakes" than others.

2 Timothy 3:13
But evil men and impostors will grow worse and worse, deceiving and being deceived.

The Greek word translated "imposters" is used only here in the New Testament. It is used in secular Greek literature for "wailers and howlers." It also referred to street jugglers and enchanters because they uttered a kind of howl.

It came to carry the meaning of fake and false imposters of religion. The word deals with the lowest, most debased level of fakery. They are imposters but are not very good at it. These people are like bad magicians who are still able to fool many because they are always hustling their religious wares.

The term is used in one passage in the Septuagint (LXX) (the Greek translation of the Old Testament) which provides some insight into its meaning.

Proverbs 26:22
The words of a whisperer are as dainty morsels, they go down into the innermost parts.

To understand this Greek word, we can see what Hebrew word it translates in the LXX. The Hebrew word means "murmurer, whisperer, backbiter, slanderer, or tale-bearer." In this context, it is best understood as a "religious tale-bearer." They pretend to know God and His ways. Yet, these are fabrications to further their own personal agendas and evil goals.

This same Hebrew word is used in other passages. First, it is utilized to speak of the liar who lies and separates friends. He whispers into the ear of another the lie that his friend has done something evil.

Proverbs 16:28
A perverse man stirs up strife. A whisperer separates close friends.

Second, in Proverbs 26, it describes gossips who tell lies and leave. When this occurs, the lies are forgotten and the argument over them ceases. He repeats this in chapter 18.

Proverbs 26:20
For lack of wood a fire goes out. Without gossip, a quarrel dies down.

Proverbs 18:8
The words of a whisperer are as dainty morsels, they go down into the innermost parts.

So, whisperers are liars. They speak falsehoods and every kind of error.

The next phrase describes the true impact of the lies on the hearer.

Proverbs 26:22
The words of a whisperer are as dainty morsels, they go down into the innermost parts.

The word translated "dainty morsels" literally carries the idea of something "swallowed quickly and greedily." They taste delicious but "wound" you in the inner most part of your belly. Their words taste sweet but when digested, they wound the hearer rather than the one being slandered. This is evil.

The final phrase in the verse describes the impact of these lies.

Proverbs 26:22
The words of a whisperer are as dainty morsels, they go down into the innermost parts.

In the Hebrew, these two words are only one term. It means "innermost or inward part of a chamber, room, or parlor." Here, it is used of the inner person or deepest part of the heart. Their lies run very deep and wound the person in the deepest part of their hearts.

First, the word was utilized physically to speak of inner rooms. In the first example, Joseph sees his brothers after they arrive to purchase food to survive the famine. They do not know that this high official is their brother, but Joseph does.

Genesis 43:30
Joseph hurried, for his heart yearned over his brother; and he sought a place to weep. He entered into his room, and wept there.

Second, Moses warns Pharaoh that if he does not let God's people go, a plague of frogs will come and penetrate even the deepest parts of their homes.

Exodus 8:3
And the river shall swarm with frogs, which shall go up and come into your house, and into your bedroom, and on your bed, and into the house of your servants, and on your people, and into your ovens, and... kneading troughs.

Third, Elisha is predicting the movements of this king, and they cannot understand how he could get information that is only spoken in his home's inner chamber.

2 Kings 6:12
One of his servants said, "No, my lord, O king; but Elisha, the prophet who is in Israel, tells the king of Israel the words that you speak in your bedroom."

Therefore, it came to mean the inner rooms or chambers of the heart which is deep inside a person.

Fourth, Solomon also uses the word to speak of the inner dimensions of the heart of every single person. This would be where the emotions, deep urges, and desires reside. It our inner most being.

Proverbs 20:30
Wounding blows cleanse away evil, and beatings purge the innermost parts.

So, these people of the last days are characterized as those who are whispering false doctrines into the ears of their listeners that sound so sweet but are bitter wounds that will dig deep into their inner hearts and hurt them spiritually and eternally. This will damn their unbelieving souls to hell for all eternity.

Among the Christians, they are cheap fakes. They may come in the guise of Christian experts, theologians, fantastic speakers, professors, and scientists and bear false tales about God and the Bible. They claim that they are making it more relevant, or much more hip, or even fit better with scientific knowledge. People will accept their lies because they sound so good and are easier to believe than the faith-based claims of the Bible.

In Acts 20, Paul warns the elders in Ephesus that when he left wolves in sheep's clothing would come to deceive them. Prophets wore the wool of sheep as coats.

Acts 20:29-30
For I know 1hat after my departure, vicious wolves will enter in among you, not sparing the flock. Men will arise from among your own selves, speaking perverse things, to draw away the disciples after them. Therefore watch, remembering that for a period of three years I did not cease to admonish everyone night and day....

The prophets identified themselves by wearing a cloak made out of sheep skins. Paul explains that these wolves will be wearing the same cloaks and will pawn themselves off as true teachers of God but will be spiritual wolves.

Some examples might be the preaching and teaching of the jugglers and enchanters on television and on the pulpits of megachurches promising the blessings of a "god" who is only loving, gracious, and merciful and not righteous, holy, and just. They will be experts in entertaining the people with their practical, relevant, humorous, sermons, but have little if any truth in them. They are seducers who persecute those who love the Lord by leading them astray and making those who are unsaved think they are saved.

Their Deceiving Actions

Paul wraps up his list in verse 13, by saying that they are "deceiving and being deceived."

2 Timothy 3:13
But evil men and impostors will grow worse and worse, deceiving and being deceived.

Previously, we have learned that the word "grow" means to "promote, further, advance, proceed, or make progress."

The English word translated "deceive" means "to cause to stray, to lead astray, lead aside from the right way, to go astray, and to wander and roam about." This is wandering away from the light into the darkness and being led astray from truth and holiness to error and evil.

The words "deceived" and "being deceived" are the same words in the Greek; One is active, and one is passive.

The word connotes the physical wandering of people and animals.

Hebrews 11:38
(Of whom the world was not worthy), wandering in deserts, mountains, caves, and the holes of the Earth.

Matthew 18:13
If he finds it, most certainly I tell you, he rejoices over it more than over the ninety-nine which have not gone astray.

When used spiritually, it is the wandering away from truth and right morals to lies and evil living.

Here are examples of deceptions with doctrinal error.

Galatians 6:7
Don't be deceived. God is not mocked, for whatever a man sows, that he will also reap.

Hebrews 3:10
Therefore I was displeased with that generation, and said, "They always err in their heart...they didn't know my ways."

James 5:19
Brothers, if any among you wanders from the truth...someone turns him back.

1 John 1:8
If we say that we have no sin, we deceive ourselves, and the truth is not in us.

1 John 3:7
Little children [Christians], let no one lead you astray. He who does righteousness is righteous, even as he is righteous.

This doctrinal error then leads to moral sin. It is how this flows into wickedness. What is believed turns into action.

Jesus discussed the kinds of moral sin into which these deceivers lead people.

1 Corinthians 6:9
Or don't you know that the unrighteous will not inherit God's Kingdom? Don't be deceived. Neither...sexually immoral, nor idolaters, nor adulterers...male prostitutes, nor homosexuals.

1 Corinthians 15:33
Don't be deceived! "Evil companionships corrupt [or destroy] good morals."

Titus 3:3
For we were also once foolish, disobedient, deceived, serving various lusts and pleasures, living in malice and envy, hateful, and hating one another.

Both words are in the present tense denoting continuous action. The main verb translated "grow" is in the future tense and indicates that this deception will be getting worse.

First, they continually deceive people. Jesus spoke of the rise of these deceivers who will lead the people astray into doctrinal error and moral evil.

Matthew 24:4
Jesus answered them, "Be careful that no one [the evil and seducers] leads you astray."

Luke 21:8
He said, "Watch out that you don't get led astray, for many will come in my name, saying, 'I am he,' and, 'The time is at hand.' Therefore don't follow them."

1 John 2:26
These things I have written to you concerning those who would lead you astray.

Jesus accused these evil leaders of deliberately seeking to deceive the masses.

Matthew 24:5
For many will come in my name, saying, "I am the Christ," and will lead many astray.

Matthew 24:11
Many false prophets will arise, and will lead many astray.

Matthew 24:24
For there will arise false christs, and false prophets, and they will show great signs and wonders, so as to lead astray, if possible, even the chosen ones.

Second these false teachers deceive because they are being deceived. The Lord Jesus accused these leaders of being deceived and Peter taught this also. Both Jesus and Peter testified to this important truth.

THE PERSECUTION OF THE SAINTS AND HOW TO OVERCOME IT

Matthew 22:29
But Jesus answered them, "You are mistaken, not knowing the Scriptures, nor the power of God.

2 Peter 2:15
Forsaking the right way, they went astray, having followed the way of Balaam the son of Beor, who loved the wages [money earned] of wrongdoing.

The one who is ultimately deceiving the deceivers is the great deceiver himself: Satan.

Revelation 12:9
The great dragon was thrown down, the old serpent, he who is called the devil and Satan, the deceiver of the whole world. He was thrown down to the Earth...his angels were thrown down with him.

These people are lying to everyone. Yet, they themselves are being lied to by others. In the passage, Paul stated that they would grow worse and worse. How? The more they are deceived, the more they will deceive. Like numerous door to door salesmen, they try to sell you something that won't work. They are like the merchants of old selling elixirs and potions promising healing when they could not heal. They promise financial prosperity, physical healing, and a special mystical relationship with the Lord for all. Yet, they cannot produce these things because they are false teachings. Here is the irony of it all. They themselves are being deceived by others. Someone sold them the elixir and potions and so they too are being lied to.

Those "mentors" are feeding them lies in their books, leadership groups, conferences, and messages. Then they proclaim and propagate the same falsehoods to others. They will persecute true Christians verbally by mocking them and calling them cold, legalistic, and divisive when the real believers stand for the doctrinal and moral purity. They will speak confidently, but their wisdom is the lies of liars.

Their Final End

In 2 Timothy 3, Paul doesn't discuss what finally happens to these people of the last days, but the Jesus and John do.

First, Jesus stated that the church cannot be persecuted out of its existence. In Matthew 16, after Peter's declaration concerning Jesus as the Christ and Son of the living God, the Lord makes His own proclamation.

Matthew 16:17-18
Jesus answered him, "Blessed are you, Simon Bar Jonah, for flesh and blood has not revealed this to you, but my Father who is in heaven. I also tell you that you are Peter, and on this rock [the truth of who Christ is that Peter just declared] I will build my assembly, and the gates of Hades will not prevail against it.

Second, John reveals the brutal end of the deceiver when it will all be over for him.

Revelation 20:10
The devil who deceived them was thrown into the lake of fire and sulfur, where the beast and... false prophet are also. They will be tormented day and night forever and ever.

In Revelation 20, John describes the final judgment of those who were deceived and deceiving others.

Revelation 20:11-12
I saw a great white throne, and him who sat on it, from whose face the earth and the heaven fled away. There was found no place for

them. I saw the dead, the great and the small, standing before the throne, and they opened books. Another book was opened, which is the book of life. The dead were judged out of the things which were written in the books, according to their works.

Yet, in the meantime the world's opposition will grow until it encompasses the earth.

Now, we can understand the evil characteristics that are spawned from the darkness of the human condition. When our light exposes their sins and resultant judgment, those who desire to continue in their sins will do anything to turn our bright lights off. Therefore, we must be prepared to stand our ground against the evil people Paul describes.

STANDING YOUR GROUND

Chapter 3

Expect a Contentious Opposition

As we have just seen, we are living in the last days, we do not know how long the era will last but we do know that the world (of non-believers) is becoming increasingly wicked which will result in an escalation of persecution. Since this book deals with every aspect of persecution, this chapter will describe the numerous forms in which this opposition may come.

Why is this important? The entire New Testament is filled incidences of people's resistance to the gospel. If the inspired writers described these events, then they must be critical in our understanding of what can occur if we share the gospel.

Secondly, Jesus promised that this would happen to His followers. He described how His disciples would experience persecution as He had.

John 15:20
Remember the word that I said to you: "A servant is not greater than his lord." If they persecuted me, they will also persecute you. If they kept my word, they will keep yours also.

In the Beatitudes, the Lord Jesus explains that the righteous will find intolerance and hostility in the world.

Matthew 5:10-11
Blessed are those [believers living holy lives] who have been persecuted for righteousness' sake, for theirs is the Kingdom of Heaven. Blessed are you when people reproach you, persecute you, and say all kinds of evil against you falsely, for my sake.

Thirdly, we must open our eyes and face this possibility realistically and know how we are to behave. We must know what we will face and how to stand our ground.

Matthew 10:16
Behold, I send you out as sheep among wolves. Therefore be wise as serpents, and harmless as doves.

When we read the book of Acts, often, we are struck by how many received Christ in those early years, but we fail to notice the larger group that did not. Whether we like it or not, we must always remember that most will not come to Christ; therefore, most will react negatively in some way. Jesus warned us that the road to destruction was broad and to life narrow.

Matthew 7:13-14
Enter in by the narrow gate; for wide is the gate and broad is the way that leads to destruction, and many are those who enter in by it. How narrow is the gate, and restricted is the way that leads to life! Few are those who find it.

In Acts chapters 2 and 4, after Peter's two great sermons, Luke records that thousands came to Christ.

Acts 2:41
Then those who gladly received his word were baptized. There were added that day about three thousand souls.

Acts 4:4
But many of those who heard the word believed, and the number of the men came to be about five thousand.

Yet, there were many thousands who would have been in Jerusalem at the time who did not respond to the gospel. As the apostles, Paul, and others spread throughout the Earth preaching the gospel, they were met with a wide variety of reactions from mild intolerance to violent murder. We can study the different kinds of negative responses to prepare ourselves. This is one reason that accounts were written.

A Physical Retribution

When Christians proclaim a gospel of sin and judgment coupled with a Savior who is the only way to heaven, there will be negative reactions. Most will not accept this gospel. Some will desire to respond physically and violently to the message.

In Acts chapter 5, Christ's apostles were arrested for their preaching of the good news. They were brought before the Jewish Sanhedrin and ordered not to preach. In verses 29-32, Peter declared to these leaders that they must obey God, not men. Peter then preached the gospel to them. They became angry and wanted to see them dead.

Acts 5:29-32
But Peter and the apostles answered, "We must obey God rather than men. The God of our fathers raised up Jesus, whom you killed, hanging him on a tree. God exalted him with his right hand to be a Prince and a Savior, to give repentance to Israel, and remission of sins. We are His witnesses of these things; and so also is the Holy Spirit, whom God has given to those who obey him."

In Acts chapter 7, when Stephen preached to this exact council, his indictment for sin cut deep into their hearts. They became so enraged that they stoned Stephen to death. The words of the gospel can enrage people because it condemns them to eternal fire. They are unwilling to accept it and repent, so they must kill the messenger. Why? They love their sin and refuse to believe it will be judged forever.

The words of the gospel are not only salvation for those who believe but condemnation for those who don't.

Acts 7:54-58
Now when they heard these things, they were cut to the heart, and they gnashed at him with their teeth. But he, being full of the Holy Spirit, looked up...into heaven, and saw the glory of God, and Jesus standing on the right hand of God, and said, "Behold, I see the heavens opened, and the Son of Man standing on the right hand of God!" But they cried out with a loud voice, and stopped their ears, and rushed at him with one accord. They threw him out of the city, and stoned him. The witnesses placed their garments at the feet of a young man named Saul.

Violence came to others also. In Acts 12, Luke records that Herod Agrippa decided to persecute some of the Christians, so he put James to death. This was the first apostle who was martyred for the faith.

Acts 12:2-3
Now about that time, King Herod stretched out his hands to oppress some of the assembly. He killed James, the brother of John, with the sword. When he saw that it pleased the Jews, he proceeded to seize Peter also. This was during the days of unleavened bread.

In his second letter to the Corinthians, Paul described the numerous persecutions he experienced at the hands of those in the darkness who rejected the light.

2 Corinthians 6:4-8
But in everything commending ourselves [the apostle and his companions], as servants of God, in great endurance, in affliction...hardships...distresses...beatings...imprisonments...riots...labors...watchings [sleeplessness due to dangers], in fastings [for his current and future converts]; in pureness, in knowledge, in patience, in kindness, in the Holy Spirit, in sincere love, in the

word of truth, in the power of God; by the armor of righteousness on the right hand and on the left, by glory and dishonor, by evil report and good report; as deceivers, and yet true.

Later in the letter, the apostle continues his description of the intense harm done to him for the sake of the gospel.

2 Corinthians 11:24-27
Five times from the Jews I received forty stripes minus one. Three times I was beaten with rods. Once I was stoned. Three times I suffered shipwreck. I have been a night and a day in the deep. I have been in travels often, perils of rivers, perils of robbers, perils from my countrymen, perils from the Gentiles, perils in the city, perils in the wilderness, perils in the sea, perils among false brothers; in labor and travail, in watchings often, in hunger and thirst, in fastings often, and in cold and nakedness.

In 2 Corinthians 11, Paul summarizes all of his suffering for the name of Christ.

2 Corinthians 4:11
For we who live are always delivered to death for Jesus' sake, that the life also of Jesus may be revealed in our mortal flesh.

He was being handed over to death daily as they attempted to murder him for Christ's sake. We must be willing to look death in the face for Christ.

A Personal Accusation

Often, Christians will not be persecuted in a physical way as they share the gospel, live righteously, and assemble; instead, they might be personally attacked. This may involve slander, libel, personal lies, and the insulting of Christians by calling them a host of derogatory names.

In Acts chapter 6, Stephen was accused by the Sanhedrin of speaking "blasphemies" against Moses and God. This was the worst possible accusation one could make to a Jew. The Hebrew people believed in one God alone.

Acts 6:11-14
Then they secretly induced men who said, "We have heard him speak blasphemous words against Moses and God." They stirred up the people, the elders, and the scribes, and came on him and seized him, and brought him into the council, and set up false witnesses who said, "This man never stops speaking blasphemous words against this holy place and the law. For we have heard him say that this Jesus of Nazareth will [physically] destroy this place, and will change the customs which Moses delivered to us."

In Acts 16, Paul cast out the demon in a fortune telling slave girl. Since she could no longer use demonic magic to tell fortunes, her masters lost much of their income. They brought Paul before the magistrates and charged him with stirring up strife in the city and presenting to the people anti-Roman customs to observe. All were lies.

Acts 16:20-21
When they had brought them to the magistrates, they said, "These men, being Jews, are agitating our city, and set forth customs which it is not lawful for us to accept or to observe, being Romans."

In Acts 17, Paul was dismissed by the secular scholars as nothing more than a "babbler."

Acts 17:18
Some of the Epicurean and Stoic philosophers also encountered him. Some said, "What does this babbler want to say?" Others said, "He seems to be advocating foreign demons," because he preached Jesus and the resurrection.

The Greek word "babbler" means "seed picker." It referred to sparrows who flew around picking up numerous scraps of seed and food from the ground. They were accusing Paul of simply picking up bits and pieces of other people's ideas and were pawning them off as his own.

When Paul preached the gospel to Festus, in Acts 26, the ruler called him crazy and told him that all of his learning was finally driving him insane. He saw Paul's great mind, but his words didn't match. To Festus the good news was the words of a mad man. What an insult!

Acts 26:24
As he thus made his defense, Festus said with a loud voice, "Paul, you are crazy [mad]! Your great learning is driving you insane!"

In Galatians 1:10, Paul describes a group of false prophets who had crept into the church. They believed that a Gentile must become a circumcised Jew to become a Christian. To belittle Paul and his "Gentile gospel without circumcision," they accused him of being a man-pleaser.

Galatians 1:10
For am I now seeking the favor of men, or of God? Or am I striving to please men? For if I were still pleasing men, I wouldn't be a servant of Christ.

To them, it was a gospel without circumcision and the various demands of the Jewish rules and codes which made it too easy because there were no works.

In 1 Corinthians 9, still others of their kind who had infiltrated the church in their city indicted him for preaching only for the money he could receive. They claimed Paul was greedy and an opportunist.

STANDING YOUR GROUND

1 Corinthians 9:3-7
My defense to those who examine me is this: Have we no right to eat and to drink? Have we no right to take along a wife who is a believer, even as the rest of the apostles, and the brothers of the Lord, and Cephas? Or have only Barnabas and I no right to not work? What soldier ever serves at his own expense? Who plants a vineyard, and doesn't eat of its fruit? Or who feeds a flock, and doesn't drink from the flock's milk?

They portrayed Paul as a greedy man who cared only about money the Corinthian church could contribute to ministry.

Some people attacked him personally calling him strong in his letters but weak in his speaking skills and personal appearance.

2 Corinthians 10:10
For, "His letters," they say, "are weighty and strong, but his bodily presence is weak, and his speech is despised."

This was not that unusual because Jesus Christ was also charged with being mad, crazy, and insane.

Mark 3:20-21
The multitude came together again, so that they could not so much as eat bread. When his friends heard it, they went out to lay hold on him: for they said, "He is insane."

In John 7, the brothers of Jesus had not yet believed in Him and questioned His motives. So, they insisted that the Lord leave them and go into the region of Judea.

John 7:2-5
Now the feast of the Jews, the Feast of Booths, was at hand. His brothers therefore said to him, "Depart from here, and go into Judea, that your disciples also may see your works which you

do....no one does anything in secret, and himself seeks to be known openly. If you do these things, reveal yourself to the world." For even his brothers didn't believe in him.

The brothers of Jesus sarcastically chided him for wanting to be known so openly. The Jew's Feast of Booths was about to occur, so they challenged Jesus to perform His works there. This way everyone would know who He was.

Often, the Lord Jesus ate among the unsaved to share the gospel with them. That is, He was invited to be a dinner guest and then to speak. This was a cultural practice. As a result, some accused the Lord Jesus of being a drunkard and a glutton.

Luke 7:34
The Son of Man [Jesus] has come eating and drinking, and you say, "Behold, a gluttonous man, and a drunkard; a friend of tax collectors and sinners!"

In verse 35, the Lord Jesus responded. Luke records Jesus' explanation of the accusations against Him, "The Son of Man [a title Jesus used of Himself] has come eating and drinking, and you say, 'Behold, a gluttonous man, and a drunkard; a friend of tax collectors and sinners."

Jesus implied that once salvation was brought to the people with whom he ate and drank, He would be vindicated.

Nathanael's initial reaction to his brother concerning Jesus was to question Christ's birth town and its reputation which in his estimation was meager and inconsequential.

John 1:46
Nathanael said to him [Philip], "Can any good thing come out of Nazareth?" Philip said to him, "Come and see."

He inquired as to whether anything good could come out of Nazareth. This town was not considered a town with a great reputation. It was as if the town that the Lord Jesus came from disqualified His claims to be deity.

The people of Nazareth accused the Lord Jesus of being just a simple carpenter.

Mark 6:3
Isn't this the carpenter, the son of Mary, and brother of James, Joses, Judah, and Simon? Aren't his sisters here with us?" So, they were offended at him.

Believers who share, assemble, and live the gospel must be prepared for personal accusations.

As we can now see, some of those people who don't know Christ, may react to our gospel by attacking us personally.

An Outright Rejection

Some unbelievers might not react negatively to Christians physically, nor accuse them personally, but might simply reject their gospel.

When Paul preached the gospel in Athens, Luke records one particular group's negative reaction. This response was not pleasant by any means.

Acts 17:32
Now when they heard of the resurrection of the dead, some mocked; but others said, "We want to hear you yet again...."

He wrote that the people were just sneering at and mocking everything he said. This essentially is outright rejection.

When Paul arrived in Corinth, he entered the synagogue to proclaim the good news as was his custom. Many did not react in a positive way, but instead with outright rejection.

Acts 19:9
But when some were hardened and disobedient, speaking evil of the Way [name for Christians] before the multitude, he departed from them, and separated the [true] disciples, reasoning daily in the school of Tyrannus.

As soon as Paul entered Rome as a prisoner, he called together the Jewish leaders to explain his chains.

Acts 27:21-24
They said to him, "We neither received letters from Judea concerning you, nor did any of the brothers come here and report or speak any evil of you. But we desire to hear of you what you think. For, as concerning this sect [thought they were a sect of Judaism], it is known to us that everywhere it is spoken against." When they had appointed him a day, they came to him into his lodging in great number. He explained to them, testifying about the kingdom of God, and persuading them concerning Jesus, both from the law...and from the prophets...morning until evening. Some believed the things which were spoken, and some disbelieved.

Notice, Luke records that some citizens believed and some simply did not. We will be faced with those people who may embrace our light (message, love, and lifestyle) and those people who do not. Those who do not may completely reject everything we say concerning Christ.

A Total Indifference

Some unbelievers may hear the good news, see our love, and observe our holy living and just won't care. It is not that they reject the gospel outright, but instead have absolutely no interest in Jesus or His Father. In fact, in many religiously tolerant countries, this may be the main reaction. They are indifferent to the gospel. They are not for or against Jesus. They are not interested in who He is or what He did.

When Paul and Barnabas traveled to the city of Antioch of Pisidia, Paul preached a powerful sermon in the synagogue. Many asked him to come back and preach again on the next Sabbath.

Acts 13:44
The next Sabbath [the next Saturday] almost the whole city was gathered together to hear the word of God.

Notice, Luke records that "almost" the whole town came out to hear him. He indicates that some did not. Obviously, this is due to indifference. So, some were saved, and some were indifferent. Oftentimes, Christians focus on the ones who respond or the ones who reject, yet others may have a reaction of indifference.

In Acts 18, Paul preached the gospel and was dragged before the proconsul of Achaia and accused of instigating people to worship God contrary to the law.

Acts 18:14-16
But when Paul was about to open his mouth, Gallio said to the Jews, "If indeed it were a matter of wrong or of wicked crime, Jews, it would be reasonable that I should bear with you; but if they are questions about words and names and your own law, look to it yourselves. For I don't want to be a judge of these matters." He drove them from the judgment seat.

Notice, Gallio responds with indifference. He was not at all interested in listening and judging things as trivial as the religious vocabulary, customs, and laws. He was apathetic. Those evil people responded to the proconsul's indifference by beating the leader of the Jewish synagogue, Sosthenes, in the presence of this important man. Still, this Roman leader was unaffected. We must understand that some might be completely indifferent to Jesus and His gospel. No matter how much we try, they are not interested.

A Blind Confusion

Some people, no matter how simply a Christian explains the gospel to them, no matter how much time is taken, will not be able to understand it. They will not comprehend our love for one another and ministry together or why we desire to live righteously. No amount of explanation will aid in their comprehension. Christians may assume that perhaps some additional information is all that is necessary to bring them to Christ when they are actually blinded by their own hardened hearts and not ignorant understanding. We must be aware of this difference as we share the gospel.

This is one of the reactions referred to by Jesus Christ in His parable concerning the various seeds that were sowed. In Matthew 13, the Lord described a farmer who had thrown seeds by the side of the road, and it was devoured by birds. In verse 19, Jesus explained that some hear the Word and do not understand it.

Matthew 13:19
When anyone hears the word of the Kingdom, and doesn't understand it, the evil one comes, and snatches away that which has been sown in his heart. This is what was sown by the roadside.

Notice, immediately, the Devil intercedes and snatches the seed away from them.

How does this happen? In Ephesians 4, Paul identifies the unbeliever as one who is futile in his mind, darkened in his understanding, and alienated from the life of God because of the ignorance in him. Why? It is due to the person's hardness of heart and the giving of himself over to sensuality and impurity among other evils. The hardness of heart causes the ignorance and lack of understanding. They create their own confusion.

Ephesians 4:17-18
This I say therefore, and testify [to you] in the Lord, that you no longer walk as the rest of the Gentiles also walk, in the futility of their mind, being darkened in their understanding, alienated from the life of God, because of the ignorance that is in them, because of the hardening of their hearts.

In his second letter to the Corinthians, Paul writes that the god of this world has blinded the mind of the unbelieving so they cannot see the light. Once man has rejected this creation knowledge, Satan blinds them further. This is their state.

2 Corinthians 4:4
In whom the god of this world has blinded the minds of the unbelieving, that the light of the gospel of the glory of Christ, who is the image of God, should not dawn on them.

In his earlier letter, Paul asserts that a natural man does not accept the supernatural things of God due to his inability to understand them. Our message, fellowship, and lifestyle are utterly foolish to them because their hearts are so utterly hardened.

1 Corinthians 2:14
Now the natural man doesn't receive the things of the God's Spirit, for they are foolishness to him, and he can't know them, because they are spiritually discerned.

So, when we share the gospel, some will react negatively out of blind ambition.

A Vain and Prideful Investigation

There are those who take great delight in philosophical, metaphysical, and theological discussions. There are those, who will listen to the gospel, discuss the concepts, and even investigate Christianity but only as an intellectual exercise. They endeavor in their pride to have an intellectual debate concerning Christianity and the Bible.

They usually want to begin with the origin of dinosaurs, or whether Cain had to incestuously marry his sister. These people want to find the controversy or supposed errors in the Bible and then go head-to-head with a believer. It is wasteful and useless because the discussion goes nowhere. These people are not truly seeking wisdom but only to hear themselves talk.

In 1 Corinthians 1, the apostle contrasts the wisdom of the world with the foolishness of God. The world in their great wisdom could not find God but He can only be found in the folly of what Christians preach. To the unsaved who are perishing it is foolishness but to those being saved it is the power of God. These vain and prideful wise men investigate and research, discuss and pontificate but will never find God. God can only be found in the humble good news by a person with a seeking heart. The Spirit will only enlighten the understanding of those who have been called and have softened their hearts toward God.

1 Corinthians 1:18
For the word of the cross is foolishness to those who are dying, but to us who are saved it is the power of God.

1 Corinthians 1:22-25
For Jews ask for signs, Greeks seek after wisdom, but we preach Christ crucified; a stumbling block to Jews, and foolishness to Greeks, but to those who are called, both Jews and Greeks, Christ is the power of God and the wisdom of God. Because the foolishness of God is wiser than men, and the weakness of God is stronger than men.

An example of such a group is found in Acts 17. Luke records that Paul entered Athens and was provoked in his spirit by all the idols that he observed. Athens was one of the ancient philosophical, intellectual, and cultural centers of the world. They desired to represent virtually every god that could possibly exist in the universe. In case they missed one, they had an idol whose inscription read, "To the unknown God."

In verses 18-20, Paul encountered several of the Epicurean and Stoic philosophers who resided in the city. When the apostle began to proclaim the gospel, they became interested in what Paul had to say. Their vain and prideful intellectual pursuits had once again begun. This is what they did daily. This is who they really were. They totally thrived on ranting, raving, speculating, formulating, discussing, and coming to all kinds of conclusions that they thought were brilliant but in reality, were lies.

Acts 17:18-21
Some [not all] of the Epicurean and Stoic philosophers also encountered him. Some said, "What does this babbler want to say?" Others said, "He seems to be advocating foreign demons," because he preached Jesus and the resurrection. They took hold of him, and brought him to the Areopagus, saying, "May we know what this new teaching is, which is spoken by you? For you bring certain strange things to our ears. We want to know therefore what these things mean."

In verse 18, some criticized him, and others thought Paul was proclaiming some kind of a strange deity, but they all wanted to understand this new teaching. They needed to know more about his gospel. So, they brought Paul to the Areopagus, which was a sort of philosophical, theological court to discern whether new teachings were from the gods. One might be fooled into thinking that they were completely open and interested in understanding the Jewish rabbi's new teachings. In fact, they were not.

In the next verse, Luke adds that these Athenians were very well known for spending much of their time in nothing else but hearing and discussing new ideas. They loved this!

Acts 17:21
Now all the Athenians and the strangers living there spent their time in nothing else, but either to tell or to hear some new thing.

The truth was not the important issue. It was the discussion, all the ideas that were new and different, and the intellectual exercise involved that was important.

Timothy had to deal with these pseudo-intellectuals. Paul describes men like these in his first letter to Timothy as ones who have turned aside to fruitless discussion. These people wanted to be teachers of the law, but they made confident assertions about matters they knew nothing about.

1 Timothy 1:3-7
As I urged you when I was going into Macedonia, stay at Ephesus that you might command...men not to teach a different doctrine, and not to pay attention to myths and endless genealogies, which cause disputes...from which things some, having missed the mark, have turned away to vain talking, desiring to be teachers of the law, though they understand neither what they say, nor about what they strongly affirm.

In chapter 6, Paul, the apostle, describes them as teaching a different doctrine. They did not consent to sound words but were conceited and really knew nothing.

1 Timothy 6:3-5
If anyone teaches a different doctrine, and doesn't consent to sound words, the words of our Lord, Jesus Christ, and to the doctrine which is according to godliness; he is conceited, knowing nothing, but obsessed with arguments, disputes, and word battles, from which come envy, strife, reviling, evil suspicions, constant friction of men of corrupt minds and destitute of the truth, who suppose that godliness is a means of gain. Withdraw yourself from such.

They were utterly obsessed with disputes, word battles, and arguments. They assumed their nonsense would ultimately result in greater godliness.

These people appeared as seriously committed Christians with intellectual integrity. They also presented themselves as people who were seeking real answers concerning the truth, but it was all a facade. These false believers simply enjoyed discussions of philosophical, metaphysical, and theological issues. They wanted to know about Christ, discuss spiritual concepts, and talk and talk about Christianity. They pursued after this vain and prideful intellectual pleasure, but not for knowledge. This consumed so much of Timothy's time.

The apostle then warned his son in the faith in to avoid all of this worldly, empty chatter and opposing arguments of false knowledge. Timothy was to guard and protect the truth of God that had been entrusted to him. This guarding did not involve endless arguments.

1 Timothy 6:20-21
Timothy, guard [keep an eye] that which is committed to you, turning away from the empty chatter and oppositions of what is

falsely called knowledge [false], which some profess, and thus have wandered from the faith.

A Christian may attempt to discuss the gospel with these vain and prideful investigators, but the conversation will go around and around. This will culminate in the Christian's endless frustration but in their immense delight. These "free thinkers" investigate Christianity like they investigate every philosophical, metaphysical, or theological system. They do it to feel superior about themselves. Pride is the motivating factor.

A Feigned Interest

There might be some people who will feign interest in the presentation of the gospel, our assembling together in love or our righteous lifestyle because they want something from believers. They may be seeking a handout, support in their political campaign, or even a romantic date. They will play the part of someone pursuing the truth but have ulterior motives driving them.

Two infamous people in Scripture illustrate this particular negative reaction. The first is found in Luke 23 when the Lord was in the midst of His trial and imprisonment. Christ appeared before the judgment seats of Annas, Caiaphas, and the Sanhedrin. Unfortunately for them, none had the power to condemn someone to death.

This had to be done by Pilate, the Roman governor. Pilate examined Him and found no guilt worthy of death or even imprisonment. Then Pilate discovered that Jesus was from Galilee. Since Herod Antipas was in Jerusalem at the time, Pilate sent the Lord to face him. Herod had jurisdiction over Galileans.

The ruler of the Jews was ecstatic. He had always desired to see one of the miracles of Jesus.

Luke 23:8
Now when Herod saw Jesus, he was exceedingly glad, for he had wanted to see him for a long time, because he had heard many things about him. He hoped to see some miracle done by him.

The chief priests and scribes stood by vehemently accusing the Lord, but Jesus said nothing. The Messiah did not speak, nor did He offer a sign or miracle to Herod.

So, Herod put his pretense aside.

Luke 23:10-12
The chief priests and the scribes stood, vehemently accusing him. Herod with his soldiers humiliated him and mocked him. Dressing him in luxurious clothing, they sent him back to Pilate. Herod and Pilate became friends with each other that very day, for before that they were enemies with each other.

He allowed his soldiers to mock, mistreat, and dress Jesus up in the regal robe of a king and then return Him to Pilate.

Another example occurred when Paul stood before Felix, the Roman Procurator of Judea, in similar circumstances. In Acts 24, Paul preached the gospel to Felix. When Paul spoke of the judgment to come, Felix became frightened and sent Paul away. He was hoping to be bribed by Paul, so he often called for Paul to discuss his case with him. Felix feigned interest hoping to be bribed but it didn't work.

Acts 24:26
Meanwhile, he also hoped that money would be given to him by Paul, that he might release him. Therefore also he sent for him more often, and talked with him.

An unbeliever might simulate interest in the gospel, church, or our lives due to something they might desire from us, such as approval, advice, praise, or perhaps a friendship or possibly romantic relationship. Since Christians cannot look into the heart to discern motives, they must rely upon God to expose the other's ulterior motives.

God exposed the deeper motives of Simon the magician in Acts 8:13-24, when he tried to buy the power of the Holy Spirit from Peter and John after he had been baptized by Philip.

Acts 8:18-19
Now when Simon [the Magician] saw that the Holy Spirit was given through the laying on of the apostles' hands, he offered them money, saying, "Give me also this power, that whoever I lay my hands on may receive the Holy Spirit."

Peter's response was quick and harsh.

Acts 8:20-23
But Peter said to him, "May your silver perish with you, because you thought you could obtain the gift of God with money! You have neither part nor lot in this matter, for your heart isn't right before God. Repent therefore of this, your wickedness, and ask God if perhaps the thought of your heart may be forgiven you. For I see that you are in the gall of bitterness...in the bondage of iniquity."

As one can see, interest in the gospel may be faked for a motive that is not admirable and we should be on the alert.

A Personal Admiration

As Christians proclaim the good news, invite people to church, live their lives before the world, there might be some who pay attention to them out of admiration. They are not really listening to the message but are wrapped up in the speaking ability and skills of the messenger. They enjoy the way or manner in which the speaker talks, acts, or lives. They may be attracted to the community atmosphere of the church. They may admire their righteousness.

Herod the Tetrarch is the perfect example of this personal admiration. Mark records the horrific event of the reluctant beheading of John the Baptist by Herod in his gospel.

Mark 6:20-28
For Herod feared John, knowing that he was a righteous and holy man, and kept him safe. When he heard him, he did many things, and he heard him gladly.

Here, Herod considered John to be a righteous and holy man and feared him but also used to hear him gladly and with joy. This indicates Herod really enjoyed listening to John. There is no indication that John's words actually had any real impact on Herod's unrighteous living.

Herod did not release John, nor repent or be baptized by John, but just enjoyed his rhetorical skills. He enjoyed John's many presentations. Then, Herod made an impulsive oath. He promised to give the dancing daughter of Herodias up to half the kingdom but instead she asked for John's head on a platter. Herod executed John to preserve his reputation.

Mark 6:21-28
When a...day had come, that Herod on his birthday made a supper for his lords, and the high captains, and the chief men of Galilee; and when the daughter of Herodias herself came in and danced, she pleased Herod and those reclining with him. The king said to the young lady, "Ask me whatever you want, and I will give it to you." He swore to her, "Whatever you shall ask of me, I will give

you, up to half of my kingdom." She went out, and said to her mother, "What shall I ask?" She said, "The head of John the Baptizer." She came in immediately with haste to the king, and asked, "I want you to give me right now the head of John the Baptizer on a platter." The king was exceedingly sorry, but for the sake of his oaths, and of his dinner guests, he didn't wish to refuse her. Immediately the king sent forth a soldier of his guard, and commanded to bring John's head, and he went and beheaded him in the prison, and brought his head on a platter, and gave it to the young lady; and the young lady gave it to her mother.

In Acts 4, when Peter and John gave a defense before the Sanhedrin, Luke indicated that these leaders marveled at the confidence of these two men since they were uneducated and untrained. The Jewish leaders admired their boldness and rhetorical skills but not their message. It offended them terribly, but their courage and eloquence did inspire them. They two apostles had great presentations. The people loved to hear them, but their gospel was rejected. The eloquence they could handle but the frightful judgment for sin and condemnation to eternal punishment was too much to bear.

Acts 4:13
Now when they saw the boldness of Peter and John, and had perceived that they were unlearned and ignorant men, they marveled. They recognized that they had been with Jesus.

This occurred frequently with many of the prophets of the Old Testament. The people admired the messenger but not the message.

In Ezekiel 33, the Lord God spoke to the prophet Ezekiel and described how the people treated him. He compared Ezekiel to a woman singing a sensual song. They liked his voice and how his message was delivered. They "liked him as a person," but never listened and obeyed his message.

Ezekiel 33:30-33
As for you, son of man, the children of your people talk of you by the walls and in the doors of the houses, and speak one to another, everyone to his brother, saying, Please come and hear what is the word that comes forth from Yahweh. They come to you as the people comes, and they sit before you as my people, and they hear your words, but don't do them; for with their mouth they show much love, but their heart goes after their gain. Behold, you are to them as a very lovely song of one who has a pleasant voice, and can play well on an instrument; for they hear your words, but they don't do them. When this comes to pass, (behold, it comes,) then shall they know that a prophet has been among them.

People may admire the Christian and listen over and over to the gospel message but never accept it as the truth. A pastor or evangelistic speaker who is actually speaking the truth of the Scriptures may be drawing quite a crowd but not all of them will receive Christ because they are just enjoying listening to him speak but do not want to deal with their sin.

A Religious Acceptance

Some people may respond to the gospel with a religious acceptance. They may see Christians as religiously similar in some way to them even though they will never believe their message. They will accept them as religiously related. They are willing to listen but will never believe. They will interact with them but will never believe their gospel of Christ. They are willing to associate with the saints but will not accept their gospel message. They have no problem with agreeing to disagree because they are all religiously connected. They all share a common religious bond.

First, this can be observed in one reaction of the many philosophers in Athens to Paul.

Acts 17:18
Some of the Epicurean and Stoic [prideful] philosophers also encountered him. Some said, "What does this babbler want to say?" Others said, "He seems to be advocating foreign demons," because he preached Jesus and the resurrection.

Here, some thought Paul was proclaiming strange deities. The word "foreign" connotes "strange or unusual." He was proclaiming the gods and deities of which they were not familiar. The statue of the unknown god in town allowed for the possibility of many additional divine beings that had not been honored. Perhaps, his God was among the unknown.

Acts 17:23
For as I passed along, and observed the objects of your worship [idols], I found also an altar with this inscription: "TO AN UNKNOWN GOD." What therefore you worship in ignorance, this I announce to you.

Second, numerous Jews and Romans saw Christianity as nothing more than a sect of Judaism.

Acts 18:12-14
But when Gallio was proconsul of Achaia, the Jews with one accord rose up against Paul and brought him before the judgment seat, saying, "This man persuades men to worship God contrary to the law." But when Paul was about to open his mouth, Gallio said to the Jews, "If indeed it were a matter of wrong or of [some] wicked crime, you Jews, it would be reasonable that I should bear with you."

They thought that among the Hebrews that there were the Pharisees who were strict adherents to the law of God. The sect called the Sadducees were much more liberal in their understanding. They did not believe in the resurrection or angels. The Zealots had believed that politics and the law went hand in hand. So now, there arose another Jewish group who were followers of Jesus. In these early days, the Christians gathered in the synagogue and the Jewish temple without opposition. This added to the misconception.

Acts 3:1
Peter and John were going up into the temple at the hour of prayer, the ninth hour.

James 2:2
For if a man with a gold ring, in fine clothing, comes into your assembly, and there come in also a poor man in filthy clothing.

Public officials, such as, Pilate and Gallio had viewed Jesus Christ and His followers as part of the Jewish religion.

Luke 23:4
Pilate said to the chief priests and the multitudes, "I find no basis for a charge against this man.

Acts 18:14-15
But when Paul was about to open his mouth, Gallio said to the Jews, "If indeed it were a matter of wrong or of wicked crime, Jews, it would be reasonable that I should bear with you; but if they are questions about words and names and your own law, look to it yourselves. For I don't want to be a judge of these matters."

These officials put them in the same religious group. If they had decided to associate with one group, then they would with the other also.

There might be people in the lives of Christians who may view themselves as a part of Christianity. They may accept some of the Christian truths but not every one of them. This has happened with some of the cults who desperately desire to be seen under the "cloak" of Christianity. Yet, they have a different Jesus and a false gospel. Some denominations may also find themselves wearing this banner which can be seen in the over-arching bubble of Christianity.

Sometimes, people will make the claim to be spiritual, but not religious and are able to coexist with Christians without much furor. Perhaps, unbelievers enter the church but are never confronted about their lack of belief. All the believers assume they are saved. They become a part because the church makes them feel good or "centers" them. The people are so friendly, so they want to stay.

A Sympathetic Support

There might be those who will identify with a Christian's serious commitment, sympathize with his plight, and even support his cause but not become true Christians. There are humanitarian people who will join hands with true believers in their good works toward man but not come to Christ as Savior and Lord.

In Acts 27, Luke describes a man such as this. His name is Julius. Paul was on his way to Rome to stand trial. Julius was the centurion in charge. In verses 1-3, he treats Paul with great consideration by allowing him to visit his friends and receive their care. Julius was a kind humanitarian who was concerned about the needs of Paul.

Acts 27:1-3
When it was determined that we should sail for Italy, they delivered Paul [the apostle] and certain other prisoners to a centurion named Julius, of the Augustan band. Embarking in a ship of Adramyttium, which was about to sail to places on the coast of Asia, we put to sea [for Rome], Aristarchus, a Macedonian of Thessalonica, being with us. The next day, we touched at Sidon.

Julius treated Paul kindly, and gave him permission to go to his friends and refresh himself.

Later, when their ship encountered a terrible storm and rammed into a barrier reef near an island, Julius took action. Since it meant death for the soldiers if any prisoner escaped, the crew decided to kill all the prisoners on board the ship. How could this be since it had been predicted that he would travel to Rome? In the Lord's providence, God intervened through an unlikely unbeliever. Luke records this event.

Acts 27:42-43
The soldiers' counsel was to kill the prisoners, so that none of them would swim out and escape. But the centurion, desiring to save Paul, stopped them from their purpose, and commanded that those who could swim should throw themselves overboard first to go to the land.

This Roman soldier who was in command stopped them from bringing harm to Paul though Julius wasn't a Christian. He did not accept Paul's gospel of Christ but simply lent Paul sympathetic support.

As with Julius, Pilate had sympathetic support for Jesus. In the gospel accounts, He tried to release Him by sending him to Herod. He tried to exonerate Christ by beating Him. Perhaps, this would satisfy their jealousy. The governor even gave the Jewish leaders the option of providing clemency for Jesus, rather than Barabbas. Unlike Jesus, this evil man was a criminal who had committed heinous crimes against Jews. Nothing worked. Unfortunately, the governor could not take the political pressure and succumbed.

Matthew 27:24
So, when Pilate saw that nothing was gained, but rather that a disturbance was starting, he took water, and washed his hands

before the multitude, saying, "I am innocent of the blood of this righteous person. You see to it."

There might be those who listen to the presentation of the gospel and desire to provide sympathetic support. They may empathize with their humanitarian goals, agree with their holy lifestyle, adhere to some of their values, even admire their courage to speak but do not believe in their gospel. Their association is strictly philanthropic. They might have corresponding goals, comparable charitable activities, and similar altruistic aspirations but only on a human level. They had no spiritual connection in Christ.

A Fearful Resistance

There might be some who will become so fearful of what Christians say that they will rebuff these saints. If believers proclaim the true gospel which involves condemnation and judgment for sin, these people may become utterly terrified and want nothing to do with them. In Romans 2, the apostle Paul describes God's law within the heart of every man that continually accuses him of sin and judgment.

Romans 2:15
In that they show the work of the law written in their hearts, their conscience testifying with them, and their thoughts among themselves accusing or else excusing them.

In Romans 1, Paul explained that this is suppressed, and the gospel loosens sin's grip. Then fear of judgment may come.

Romans 1:18
For the wrath of God [bringing judgment] is revealed from heaven against all ungodliness and unrighteousness of men, who hinder the truth in unrighteousness.

This occurred with Felix when Paul presented the gospel to Him. He experienced this very dread!

Acts 24:25
As he reasoned about righteousness, self-control, and the judgment to come, Felix was terrified, and answered, "Go your way for this time, and when it is convenient for me, I will call you to me."

Often, Christians are afraid to alienate the unsaved, so they leave sin and judgment out of their gospel presentation. When this occurs, how can unbelievers repent in order to be saved? It does not allow for this critical response. No one enters into the kingdom of God without repentance.

The saints should allow people to become afraid because this will drive them to repentance. Though the unsaved may reject this at first, they might repent later. This is the Lord's way.

1 Corinthians 14:24
But if all prophesy, and someone unbelieving or unlearned comes in, he is reproved by all, and he is judged by all.

In fear, they will seek to find the only deliverance from their horrifying future at the cross of the crucified Christ and their redemption through His resurrection. This is the powerful work of the Spirit.

An Impassioned Rage

When Christians present the true gospel, invite people to their churches, live their lives righteously in front of some, these people might react by passionately raging in response. This rage may be expressed in a wide variety of ways from verbal to physical persecution. The anger may be very deep-seated, intense, and arousing a fury. This impassioned rage will pour forth into persecution.

In Luke 4, the Lord Jesus Christ spoke in the synagogue of Nazareth among his own family and friends, neighbors, and fellow citizens.

Luke 4:29
And they rose up, and threw him out of the city, and led him to the brow of the hill that their city was built on, that they might throw him off the cliff.

When He was finished, they were so enraged, they attempted to cease Him and throw Him off the edge of the cliff right outside the city.

In Acts 7, the leaders of Israel were cut to the quick by Stephen's words, so they covered their ears, gnashed their teeth, shouted with one voice, and seized him.

Acts 7:54
Now when they heard these things, they were cut to the heart, and they gnashed at him with their teeth.

Acts 7:57
But they cried out with a loud voice, and stopped their ears, and rushed at him with one accord. They threw him out of the city, and stoned him [until dead]. The witnesses placed their garments at the feet of a young man named Saul.

They were in such frenzy that these distinguished religious officials of Israel stoned and murdered him in cold blood.

In Acts 14, the Jews of Antioch and Iconium journeyed to Lystra in order to stir up the people of Lystra against Paul and his companions.

Acts 14:19
But some Jews from Antioch and Iconium came there, and having persuaded the multitudes, they stoned Paul, and dragged him out of the city, supposing that he was dead.

Because their feelings of anger and rage had such intensity, they stoned him, dragged his body out of the city, and left it to rot.

All that happened was predicted by Jesus when He sent His disciples out into the world to preach His gospel. He warned them to be aware that all men will loathe them because of His name. They would have to endure until the end. This hatred can burst into raging fury.

Matthew 10:22
You will be hated by all men for my name's sake, but he who endures to the end, the same will be saved.

Again, Jesus refers to these various types of incidences. The Lord repeatedly announced to His disciples that people would hate them on account of Him. The Lord Jesus warned His followers that hating Him would mean hating them. This is a bitter pill to swallow; No one wants people to hate them, but it comes with Jesus.

Luke 6:22
Blessed are you when men shall hate you, and when they shall separate you from them and reproach you, and throw out your name as evil, for the Son of Man's sake.

In John 15, Jesus explains the real reason that the world despises them. Unbelievers will hate them because they hate the Lord Jesus Christ! They want control of their lives and are unwilling to relinquish it. The saved will be viewed as one's who foolishly gave up their liberty for a lie.

John 15:18-19
If the world hates you, you know that it has hated me before it hated you. If you were of the world, the world would love its own. But because you are not of the world, since I chose you out of the world, therefore the world hates you.

Christians will be seen as part of the world. This system will not love and embrace them but hate and rage against them. If Christians want to be embraced by the pop culture, they will be disappointed. They will be compelled to remove any discussion of sin and judgment. Christ and His true gospel, not the one dressed up in a pretty package without sin, will be hated by the world system; therefore, His followers will also be despised. Saints might experience an angry fury from unbelievers when the gospel is shared.

A Relentless Pursuit

Another negative reaction by unbelievers could be the relentless pursuit of the messengers. They become incensed by the message, love, or lifestyle and follow those who are active in their faith everywhere they go. These pursuers then agitate the other listeners until they are stirred into frenzy. They continue until finally they lash out at those who are living their faith.

When Paul preached in Pisidian Antioch and many came out to hear him, the Jews became jealous, and they stirred up some of the leading men and prominent women of the city against Paul. This animosity toward Paul and those with him led the persecutors to throw them out of the region.

Acts 13:44-45
The next Sabbath [Saturday] almost the whole city was gathered together to hear the word...But when the Jews saw the multitudes,

they were filled with jealousy, and contradicted the things which were spoken by Paul, and blasphemed.

Acts 13:48-50
As the Gentiles heard this, they were glad, and glorified the word of God. As many as were appointed to eternal life believed. The Lord's word was spread abroad throughout all the region. But the Jews urged on the devout women of honorable estate, and the chief men of the city, and stirred up a persecution against Paul and Barnabas, and threw them out of their borders.

In Acts 14, the apostle Paul traveled to Iconium in Galatia and preached the gospel powerfully in the synagogue to the Jews. After his presentation there were two reactions. Some believed, but others did not.

Acts 14:1-7
It happened in Iconium that they entered together into the synagogue of the Jews, and so spoke that a great multitude both of Jews and of Greeks believed. But the disobedient Jews stirred up and embittered the souls of the Gentiles against the brothers. Therefore they stayed there a long time, speaking boldly in the Lord, who testified to the word of his grace, granting signs and wonders [miracles] to be done by their hands. But the multitude of the city was divided. Part sided with the Jews, and part with the apostles. When some of both the Gentiles and the Jews, with their rulers, made a violent attempt to insult them and to stone them [to death], they became aware of it, and fled to the cities of Lycaonia, Lystra, Derbe, and the surrounding region. There they [Paul and Barnabas] preached the gospel.

These others stirred up the Gentiles against the apostle Paul in the city. The entire town was divided between these two groups. The antagonistic mob pursued Paul so they might stone him to death and be rid of him once and for all. So, the apostle and his companions fled.

In verses 8-19, Paul arrived in Lystra and healed a man. The people thought he and Barnabas were gods, but Paul denied it and preached a strong gospel. As a result, the Jews from Antioch and Lystra relentlessly pursued Paul to this city and incited the citizens against him. The crowd stoned Paul dragged him out of the city and left him for dead.

Acts 14:9
But some Jews from Antioch and Iconium came there, and having persuaded the multitudes, they stoned Paul, and dragged him out of the city, supposing that he was dead.

In Acts 17, Luke records that Paul preached in the city of Thessalonica, angered the Jews, a mob formed, and he fled.

Acts 17:5
But the unpersuaded Jews took along some wicked men from the marketplace, and gathering a crowd, set the city in an uproar. Assaulting the house of Jason, they sought to bring them out to the people.

Acts 17:9-10
When they had taken security from Jason and the rest, they let them go. The brothers immediately sent Paul and Silas away by night to Berea. When they arrived, they went into the Jewish synagogue.

In the next passage, Paul shared the good news with the Bereans. As they were searching the Scriptures for answers, the Jews who lived in Thessalonica had heard that Paul had now entered the city. Immediately, they pursued after him, stirred up the crowds, and Paul ran for his life.

Acts 17:13-15
But when the Jews of Thessalonica had knowledge that the word of God was proclaimed by Paul at Berea also, they came there likewise

agitating the multitudes. Then the brothers immediately sent out Paul to go as far as to the sea, and Silas and Timothy still stayed there. But those who escorted Paul brought him as far as Athens. Receiving a commandment to Silas and Timothy that they should come to him very quickly, they departed.

By Acts 23, the intensity of some Jews had grown to such a level, a plot was hatched to ambush and assassinate him. Paul finished preaching to the Jewish council in Jerusalem and they responded with antagonism and outrage.

Acts 23:12-14
When it was day, some of the Jews banded together, and bound themselves under a curse, saying that they [the Jews] would neither eat nor drink until they had killed Paul. There were more than forty people who had made this conspiracy. They came to the chief priests and the elders, and said, "We have bound ourselves under a great curse, to taste nothing until we have killed Paul.

The Romans perceived that things were quickly getting out of hand, so they seized Paul. While in their custody, these assassins approached the council requesting that they send for Paul. On his way, they planned to murder him.

When the nephew of Paul discovered this, he informed the centurion in charge. This centurion believed Paul was in terrible danger, so the officer sent Paul to Caesarea at night. He was accompanied by two hundred soldiers and seventy horsemen with two hundred spearmen. The assassins may be in a relentless pursuit to assassinate Paul, but the apostle would be heavily guarded.

Some Christians might not experience the terror of this kind of hostile pursuit but must be aware of its possibility. All the saints should remember that Peter compared Satan to a hungry, roaring lion, who is prowling around because he is seeking someone (a Christian) to devour. He is a powerful angel who desires to destroy our witness and will use all of his demons to accomplish this.

1 Peter 5:8
Be sober and self-controlled. Be watchful. Your adversary the devil, walks about like a roaring lion, seeking whom he may devour.

An Associative Persecution

When Christians proclaim the gospel, assemble in love, and live holy lives, sometimes people will persecute family, friends, acquaintances, or anyone in some way associated with them. Perhaps, for some reason, they cannot persecute the actual Christian, so they oppress those who have been associating with them. This might be difficult for the believer to handle since it involves others.

In Acts 17, Paul's preaching again incensed some of the Jews in Thessalonica. The Jews then recruited some wicked men from the marketplace to assist them. This angry mob went to the house of Jason, where they perceived Paul was staying, to seize him. When the mob discovered Paul had left, they grabbed Jason and other Christians and dragged them before the city's governing authority.

Acts 17:6
When they didn't find them, they dragged Jason and certain brothers before the rulers of the city, crying, "These who have turned the world upside down have come here also.

Since they could not persecute Paul himself, they decided to persecute the ones that they thought were harboring and supporting him in his "proselytizing" of his particular faith in Jesus Christ who rose from the dead.

In Acts 19, Paul's many conversions in Ephesus angered the businessmen who were earning much from the worship of their goddess, Artemis. These evil entrepreneurs began losing vast amounts of income. So, the angry businessmen, artisans, and idolaters, began to enrage the Ephesians over the defaming of Artemis. The crowds were thrown into such an agitation and confusion that they grabbed the traveling companions of Paul, Gaius, and Aristarchus, and rushed with them into the theater for a confrontation.

It seems that Gaius and Aristarchus would be a great way to attract Paul if he was hiding. Perhaps, these two big supporters of Paul could become the crowd's objects of wrath if he did not appear. Regardless, Paul's companions were persecuted due to their association with the apostle.

Though sharing the good news of Jesus Christ, enjoying fellowship in the church, and living for the Lord of our lives is a rewarding experience, it might also be a dangerous one for the family, acquaintances, and associates of Christians who are having an impact on the world. If the world hates us, they may take note of those to whom we associate. They may view our family and friends in a more hostile way.

In John 15:20, Jesus warned His disciples that a student is not above his teacher in persecution.

John 15:20
Remember the word that I said to you: "A servant is not greater than his lord." If they persecuted me, they will also persecute you. If they kept my word, they will keep yours also.

If they persecuted Him, they would persecute them. As has been previously seen, they may also persecute other people associated with them. We must be aware that those involved with us may receive the persecution intended for us.

A Political Opportunism

Some will respond negatively to the church, even to the point of persecution, as a political opportunity to advance themselves or their agenda in some way. These unbelievers might not be particularly angry or hateful of Christians but could see the personal and political advantage of rejecting them. The torment or mistreatment of the saved may win them some kind of political victory or allow some important political influence over others.

The Herod dynasty was not only blood-thirsty but was also looking for opportunities to advance politically. In Acts 12, Herod Agrippa martyred James, the apostle and brother of John. When it pleased the Jews, he imprisoned Peter also.

Acts 12:1-4
Now about that time, Herod the king put forth his hands to oppress some of the assembly. He killed James, the brother of John, with the sword. When he saw that it pleased the Jews, he proceeded to seize Peter also. This was during the days of unleavened bread. When he had captured him, he put him in prison, and delivered him to four squads of four soldiers each to guard him, intending to bring him out to the people after the Passover.

In Acts 24, Paul stood on trial before Felix, the Roman governor. Felix left Paul in prison in Caesarea for two years and then turned him over to his successor Festus because he wanted to gain favor with the Jews.

Acts 24:27
But...two years were fulfilled, Felix was succeeded by...Festus, and desiring to gain favor with the Jews, Felix left Paul in bonds.

If he had released Paul, the Jews would have been angered. Felix did not want to lose any political support.

Festus saw the same kind of opportunity. In Acts 25, the Jews begged him to put Paul on trial. Festus met with both parties and heard the Jew's accusations and Paul's defense.

Acts 25:6-8
When he [Festus] had stayed among them more than ten days, he went down to Caesarea, and on the next day he sat on the judgment seat, and commanded Paul to be brought. When he [Paul] had come, the Jews who had come down from Jerusalem stood around him, bringing against him many and grievous charges which they could not prove, while he said in his defense, "Neither against the law of the Jews, nor against the temple, nor against Caesar, have I sinned at all." But Festus, desiring to gain favor with the Jews, answered Paul and said, "Will you go up to Jerusalem, and there be judged of these things before me?"

Like His predecessor, He wanted to gain favor with the Jews and asked Paul if he would return to Jerusalem. Paul realized Festus was attempting to appease these Jews, so he exercised his Roman right and appealed to Caesar. As can be seen, persecution was for sometimes for political ends. Some are motivated by the gain of political advantage. When they meet evangelizing believers, they may hurt them to attain a political victory. Political influence can powerfully motivate.

A Merchant Reprisal

Some people might not react directly to the gospel itself but respond to what the gospel has done in someone's life. In this case, someone's financial gain has been curtailed. When certain unbelievers come to Christ, they may have incurred some sinful and wicked financial debts or obligations they can no longer meet. They might be involved in an industry that falls short of God's standard for righteousness and must quit. Therefore, businesspeople or merchants, with whom they work, may retaliate against the persons who instigated these changes in their lives.

One example may be a drug dealer who comes to Christ. The suppliers of the drug dealer might become enraged that their partner is no longer available to deal. Their businesses will be affected, and their income will decline. Or perhaps, a gang member turns his life over to the Lord and quits the gang. This person may hold an important position in their financial endeavors or have critical information concerning their illegal dealings. This may result in targeting not only the dealer but the person who turned him to the light.

A prostitute might find the Lord and turn away from her handler. He might find this situation utterly unacceptable in his dark world of perversion. He may search out the one who impacted her to obtain revenge for his financial losses. Similarly, others may have a network who are financially invested in their mutual sins. When they turn to Christ, the network might retaliate. These perpetrators of sinful and illegal gain could desire to exact retribution upon those who share the gospel. There may be the reprisal of the merchants involved. Christians must be aware of this possibility.

This principle springs directly from the experience of the apostle Paul mentioned before in other contexts. In Acts 16, Paul arrived in Philippi and preached the gospel. A demon possessed slave girl followed them proclaiming that they were servants of the Most High God.

Acts 16:16-18
It happened, as we were going to prayer, that a certain girl having a spirit of divination (fortune telling) met us, who brought her masters much gain by fortune telling. The same, following after Paul and us, cried out, "These men are servants of the Most High God, who proclaim...salvation!" This she did for many days. But

Paul, becoming distressed, turned and said to the spirit, "I charge you in the name of Jesus Christ to come out of her!" It came out that very hour.

After many days, Paul became annoyed and cast the spirit of divination out of her body. Most likely, Paul did not want her fortune telling to be associated with his ministry. Once the demon was exorcized, her magical skills ceased. They no longer had her as an asset. This upset her masters, and they reacted violently toward him because of what he had done.

Acts 16:19
But when her masters saw that the hope of their gain was gone, they laid hold on Paul and Silas...dragged them into the marketplace before the rulers.

So, they dragged Paul before the city magistrates. The city officials proceeded to beat him and throw him into prison. These evil merchants wanted revenge upon Paul because their income from their wicked gain was gone. Money can motivate men to commit some evil deeds.

A similar persecution occurred in Ephesus. The apostle Paul preached the gospel there and many came to Christ. They forsook their worship of Artemis to such an extent that the silver merchants who made idols were losing business and so were others.

Acts 19:23-30
About that time there arose no small stir [disturbance] concerning the Way....Demetrius, a silversmith, who made silver shrines of Artemis, brought no little business to the craftsmen, whom he gathered together, with the workmen of like occupation, and said, "Sirs, you know that by this business we have our wealth...Paul has persuaded and turned away many people, saying that they are no gods, that are made with hands....the temple of the great goddess

Artemis will be counted as nothing, and her majesty destroyed..." When they heard this they were filled with anger, and cried out, saying, "Great is Artemis of the Ephesians!" The whole city was filled with confusion, and they rushed with one accord into the theater, having seized Gaius and Aristarchus, men of Macedonia, Paul's companions in travel. When Paul wanted to enter into the people, the disciples didn't allow him.

These business owners from many trades banded together to exact retribution upon the apostle. After stirring their fellow idolaters up into a hysterical frenzy, Paul could have been killed. The Christians would not allow Paul even to enter the theater so he could make a defense. Finally, a key city official convinced the angry crowd to disperse from their gathering.

Christians should understand that some unbelievers may have evil financial relationships. When they come to Christ, these evil connections might not appreciate the loss of their financial income as these new believers turn their lives fully over to Christ. Merchant's reprisals upon the messenger may result from this new life.

A Religious Animosity

When one begins to share the gospel, those who hear may not be coming to Christ out of a religious vacuum. They may have important religious connections that will be disrupted or severed. As the saints draw people from the ranks of false religions, other members may retaliate. The religious fervor they may feel for their beliefs could suddenly be directed in anger and retribution toward the messengers of the gospel. They will not want their devout adherents turning away from their sacred religion. Consider the different persecutors of Jesus in the New Testament. Many were religious people who were very zealous.

Who was it that really persecuted the Lord? The religious council, the Sanhedrin, persecuted Him because Christ was drawing many people away from their influence. It was the religious leaders of the Jews that hounded him and accused him of breaking Mosaic Law every opportunity they could. It was these religious zealots, who plotted His death and badgered the Romans into crucifying Him. In history, it was religious people who did the most damage to Christians.

In Luke 6, when the Lord Jesus entered the synagogue on the Sabbath, He encountered a man with a withered hand. The scribes and Pharisees watched Him intently. Would He heal him on the Sabbath and defy their religious beliefs and customs? When He did, their rage flared to a frenzy. Then, they began plotting against Him.

Luke 6:6-11
It also happened on another Sabbath that he entered into the synagogue and taught. There was a man there, and his right hand was withered. The scribes and the Pharisees watched him, to see whether he would heal on the Sabbath, that they might find an accusation against him. But he knew their thoughts; and he said to the man who had the withered hand, "Rise up, and stand in the middle." He arose and stood. Then Jesus said to them, "I will ask you something: Is it lawful on the Sabbath to do good, or to do harm? To save a life, or to kill?" He looked around at them all, and said to him, "Stretch out your hand." He did, and his hand was restored as sound as the other. But they were filled with rage, and talked with one another about what they might do to Jesus.

These same officials led the mob that came to arrest Jesus. In Mark 14, the Lord was betrayed and arrested by the chief priests, scribes, and elders.

Mark 14:43
Immediately, while he was still speaking, Judas, one of the twelve,

THE PERSECUTION OF THE SAINTS AND HOW TO OVERCOME IT

came -- and with him a multitude with swords and clubs, from the chief priests, the scribes, and the elders.

These religious examples of holy living were accompanied by many temple guards and Roman soldiers with a group of common people and many unsavory characters. Yet, these Jews were in charge! They were the driving force behind the religious fervor of Christ's persecution and ultimate murder.

Before Annas, a Jewish religious official, the Lord Jesus was struck in the face.

John 18:19-23
The high priest therefore asked Jesus about his disciples and about his teaching. Jesus answered him, "I spoke openly to the world. I always taught in synagogues, and in the temple, where the Jews always meet. I said nothing in secret. Why do you ask me? Ask those who have heard me what I said to them. Behold, they know the things which I said." When he had said this, one of the officers standing by slapped Jesus with his hand, saying, "Do you answer the high priest like that?" Jesus answered him, "If I have spoken evil, testify of the evil; but if well, why do you beat me?"

Before the high priest Caiaphas, they blind-folded Jesus and beat him with their fists.

Matthew 26:62-67
The high priest stood up and said to him, "Have you no answer? What is this that these testify against you?" But Jesus stayed silent. The high priest answered him, "I adjure you by the living God that you tell us whether you are the Christ, the Son of God." Jesus said to him, "You have said so. Nevertheless, I tell you, after this you will see the Son of Man sitting at the right hand of Power, and coming on the clouds of the sky." Then the high priest tore his clothing, saying, "He has spoken blasphemy! Why do we need any more witnesses? Behold, now you have heard his blasphemy. What

do you think?" They answered, "He is worthy of death!" Then they spat in his face and beat him with their fists, and some slapped him, 68 saying, "Prophesy to us, you Christ! Who hit you?"

Here, the soldiers didn't believe that He was even a prophet, but they demanded that He prophecy and kept slapping and hitting Him.

In Matthew 27, it was the Sanhedrin who condemned the Lord Jesus to death and led him to Pilate.

Matthew 27:4-7
Saying, "I have sinned in that I betrayed innocent blood." But they said, "What is that to us? You see to it." He threw down the pieces of silver in the sanctuary, and departed. He went away and hanged himself. The chief priests took the pieces of silver, and said, "It is not lawful to put them into the treasury, since it is the price of blood." They took counsel, and bought with them the potter's field, to bury strangers in.

They did not have the power to execute anyone according to Roman law or His life would have ended there. This group of religious leaders, who were to be the example of piety, righteousness, and love, then badgered and taunted Pilate into crucifying the innocent Jesus Christ. Instead, they chose to release an insurrectionist and murderer into society to continue his malicious actions upon innocent citizens. They chose to condemn someone who was the epitome of love, compassion, and righteousness.

As has been seen over and over, the apostles and disciples received exactly the same treatment. Christians must know that sharing the gospel might upset the strongly religious in their families, among their friends, and neighbors. It might instigate retaliation from members of their religious group, church, or institution.

Christians may face retribution from religious employees or managers among their work force or fellow colleagues within their profession. They may not tolerate the Christian values or righteous words and actions. As has been noted, usually the persecution is even more intense because the persecutors think they are truly serving their god(s) when they criticize or harm Christians.

A False Brethren Interference

As Christians become active in their faith, Satan might send some false brethren to interfere with their ministry efforts. Often, Christians do not consider the possibility that so-called Christians from their own church or organization could obstruct their evangelistic efforts. Yet, this could easily happen from tares, he could sow among the wheat, within their own Christian group. No one imagines opposition from their own local church members, but it can especially if they are false brethren among the true.

Matthew 13:25
But while people slept, his enemy came and sowed darnel also among the wheat, and went away.

In Galatians 2, the apostle describes some false teachers who followed him into the area of Galatia.

Galatians 2:4
This was because of the false brothers secretly brought in, who stole in to spy out our liberty which we have in Christ Jesus, that they might bring us into bondage.

There, they attempted to bring the brethren, who had been freed by the gospel, back into the bondage of their Jewish customs. Their efforts disrupted Paul's evangelism ministry.

These disrupters were even able to persuade Peter and Barnabas to stop eating with the Gentiles. As a result, Paul had to curtail his activities for the gospel and confront Peter.

Galatians 2:11-14
But when Peter came to Antioch, I resisted him to his face, because he stood condemned. For before some people came from James, he ate with the Gentiles. But when they came, he drew back and separated himself, fearing those who were of the circumcision. And the rest of the Jews joined him in his hypocrisy; so that even Barnabas was carried away with their hypocrisy. But when I saw...they didn't walk uprightly according to the truth of the Good News, I said to Peter before them all, "If you, being a Jew, live as the Gentiles do, and not as the Jews do, why do you compel the Gentiles to live as the Jews do?

Again, in 2 Corinthians 11, the Devil sent several false brethren into the Corinthian church to continually disrupt Paul's ministry. The attack of these fake and false brethren might occur on numerous fronts.

These tares among the wheat might question the internal motives of the evangelist. These false Christians will not like the actions of true witnesses.

1 Thessalonians 2:3-5
For our exhortation is not of error, nor of uncleanness, nor in deception. But even as we have been approved by God to be entrusted with the gospel, so we speak; not as pleasing men, but God, who tests our hearts. For neither were we at any time found using words of flattery, as you know, nor a cloak of covetousness (God is witness).

Colossians 1:10
That you may walk worthily of the Lord, to please him...bearing fruit in every good work, and increasing in the knowledge of God.

They might criticize our evangelistic methods as they did Paul's.

2 Corinthians 11:7
Or did I commit a sin in humbling myself that you might be exalted, because I preached to you God's gospel for nothing?

Often, they will criticize our personal call.

2 Corinthians 11:5
For I reckon that I am not at all behind [lack anything] the very best apostles.

2 Corinthians 11:23
Are they servants of Christ? (I speak as one beside himself) I am more so; in labors more abundantly, in prisons more abundantly, in stripes above measure, in deaths often.

They may challenge our doctrinal beliefs.

Galatians 1:6-11
I marvel that you are so quickly deserting him who called you in the grace of Christ to a different gospel; and there isn't another gospel. Only there are some who trouble you, and want to pervert the gospel of Christ. But even though we, or an angel from heaven, should preach to you any gospel other than that which we preached to you, let him be cursed. As we have said before, so I now say again: if any man preaches to you any gospel other than that which you received, let him be cursed.... But I [Paul] make known to you, brothers, concerning the gospel which was preached by me, that it is not according to man.

This can cause havoc to the ministry and testimony of many Christians. It can even ruin their reputation and example in the church and community. In the end, this will hinder the service they are rendering to God.

In Acts 20, Paul cautioned the Ephesian elders to beware of savage wolves that would arise from among them and would draw the flock away. Notice, these wolves will be leaders among them.

Acts 20:28-30
Take heed, therefore, to yourselves, and to all the flock, in which the Holy Spirit has made you overseers, to shepherd the assembly of the Lord and God which he purchased with his own blood. For I know that after my departure, vicious wolves will enter in among you, not sparing the flock. Men will arise from among your own selves, speaking perverse things, to draw away the disciples after them.

They may be full-time false ministers thwarting the efforts of the true ones in order to discredit them. Often, they might discredit them by simply declaring that the true minister's preaching or evangelistic methods are outdated, his gospel not hip enough, or his presentation not geared to the right audience. The Bible must be the only source of the veracity of such claims.

A Christian Misunderstanding

As believers live their Christian lives before the people, they may receive many negative reactions from those, who do not understand their ministry, inside their own church. Not only could these real saints be opposed by false brethren among them, but true believers who may be ignorant of biblical truth. Understanding the vast knowledge contained within the Scripture is a daunting task. Often, Christians choose to rely upon others for truth, rather than dig for it themselves in the Bible. This creates in them a susceptibility to error. These saints may read a book, listen to a sermon, or contemplate the subject themselves, and think they know all about a biblical topic. When others depart from this limited knowledge, they shun them.

This is exactly what happened in the early church. In Acts 10, Peter had just brought Cornelius and the members of his household to Christ in Caesarea. This display of God's great mercy upon a Gentile provided fuel for a challenge to Peter's methods. In Acts 11, Peter arrived in Jerusalem and some in the church immediately began to question him concerning his regular eating with the Gentiles which was a forbidden Jewish custom. Gentiles were not even allowed into a Jewish home under any circumstances.

Acts 11:2-3
When Peter had come up to Jerusalem, those who were of the circumcision contended with him, saying, "You went into uncircumcised men, and ate with them!"

Then in the rest of the chapter, Peter defended himself by explaining that the gospel was to be given to the Gentiles also. Then He summed it up in verses 17-18.

Acts 11:17-18
If then God gave to them the same gift as us, when we believed in the Lord Jesus Christ, who was I, that I could withstand God?" When they heard these things, they held their peace, and glorified God, saying, "Then God has...granted to the Gentiles repentance to life!"

When Paul completed his first missionary journey and arrived in the church at Antioch, Paul and Barnabas shared the great things God had done through them (Acts 14:26-27). This included winning numerous Gentiles to the faith and planting many churches. In Acts 15:1-3, some men traveled from Judea claiming that the Gentiles had to be circumcised to be saved. This caused such a problem that it provoked a calling of the Jerusalem council. The apostles as well as the whole church would have to become involved. Some of the Christians did not fully understand what the Lord God was now doing and opposed their many methods. They did not necessarily understand that this was hindering ministry.

As was seen previously, Paul spent a large amount of his time defending his ministry to the saints. In Galatia, it was so hostile that Paul had to ask them who had bewitched them. This occurs because Satan comes as an angel of light through his emissaries and will attempt to lead the brethren astray.

2 Corinthians 11:13-15
For such men are false apostles, deceitful workers, masquerading as Christ's apostles. And no wonder, for even Satan masquerades as an angel of light. It is no great thing therefore if his ministers also masquerade as servants of righteousness, whose end will be according to their works.

It also comes from the spiritual immaturity of Christians. On numerous occasions, the apostle had to admonish, teach, exhort, and encourage the church at Corinth on so many issues because they were still spiritual babies.

1 Corinthians 3:1-3
Brothers, I couldn't speak to you as to spiritual, but as to fleshly, as to babes in Christ. I fed you with milk, not with meat; for you weren't yet ready. Indeed, not even now are you ready, for you are still fleshly. For insofar as there is jealousy, strife, and factions among you, aren't you fleshly, and don't you walk in the ways of men?

He complained that they still needed spiritual milk when they should be eating meat. These babies gave him the most trouble during his ministry on earth.

Unfortunately, Christians should understand that within their own churches or ministries, they may find opposition. There may be those who attempt to thwart their sharing of the gospel in some way due to ignorance of the Scriptures. It is important to note that everything Christians do, including the sharing of the gospel, must be judged by the Scriptures. Paul exhorts the church to examine everything carefully. All doctrine is included in this powerful mandate.

1 Thessalonians 5:21-22
Test all things, and hold firmly that which is good. Abstain from every form of evil.

John demands that believers test the spirits (Holy Spirit or demons) behind the teaching of others.

1 John 4:4
You are of God, little children, and have overcome them; because greater is he [Spirit] who is in you than he [Satan] who is in the world.

The Scriptures alone validate all ministries.

A Satanic Opposition

Why would the devil bother harassing Christians who are making an impact for Christ? When people begin to have an impact on the world, they may experience great opposition from this serpent of old. While Job was living righteously, this deceiver took notice and questioned his real motivation and desires.

Job 1:9
Then Satan answered Yahweh, and said, "Does Job fear God for nothing?

Christians should expect Satan to take notice of them when they begin to share the gospel. The Devil's attention will turn toward those who are rescuing his captive unbelievers from the domain of darkness and continually transferring them to God's kingdom of light.

Colossians 1:13
Who delivered us [believers] out of the power of darkness, and translated us into the kingdom of the Son of his love.

This opposition is found from the very outset of Christ's ministry. Jesus told those who opposed Him that they were of their father, the Devil.

John 8:44
You are of your Father, the devil, and you want to do the desires of your father. He was a murderer from the beginning, and doesn't stand in the truth, because there is no truth in him. When he speaks a lie, he speaks on his own; for he is a liar, and...father of it.

When Peter attempted to stop Christ from his journey to the cross, the Lord replied with a rebuke to Satan.

Matthew 16:22
Peter took him aside, and began to rebuke him, saying, "Far be it from you, Lord! This will never be done to you."

Later, the Lord Jesus revealed something astonishing to this disciple. Satan had demanded permission to sift him like wheat and implied it had been granted by God. When he had turned back to the Lord (from the denial), Peter was to strengthen his brothers.

Luke 22:31
The Lord said, "Simon, Simon, behold, Satan asked to have you, that he might sift you as wheat."

Peter must have been reminded of this prophecy while he was weeping in deep grief over his denial of the Lord.

In 1 Thessalonians 2:18, Paul described the opposition he was experiencing from the Devil in his evangelistic ministry.

1 Thessalonians 2:18
Because we wanted to come to you -- indeed, I, Paul, once and again -- but Satan hindered us.

This crafty, cunning fallen angel was attacking him. The Greek word translated "hindered" in the Greek means "to cut into, to impede one's course by cutting off his way." This old serpent was cutting off Paul's way so he could not share the gospel. He was thwarting Paul's efforts. Christians should realize that Satan may become active in their lives, as they become active in faith. Christians can take solace in the fact that God is always in control. Those who will be saved will be saved in spite of Satan's attacks.

A Complete Annihilation

Some may not only desire to persecute the followers of Jesus but to literally stamp it out of a city, region, country, or the whole world. This is accomplished through the murder of Christians, the forcing of believers out of an area legally and through threats, or even confiscating or destroying all sacred or non-sacred documents pertaining to the truths of Christianity.

We have seen this throughout history under the various persecutions of the Roman emperors and even into modern times as various rulers of countries kill Christians in large numbers, force them to flee to other nations, and forbid missionaries or Bibles to enter the country.

When a new Pharaoh came into power who did not know Joseph, he was fearful of the growing number and influence of Hebrews in his land. So, he ordered the Jewish midwives to kill every male Hebrew.

Exodus 1:15-17
The king of Egypt spoke to the Hebrew midwives, of whom the name of the one was Shiphrah, and the name of the other Puah, and he said, "When you perform the duty of a midwife to the Hebrew women, and see them on the birth stool, if it is a son, then you shall kill him; but if it is a daughter, then she shall live." But the midwives feared God and didn't do what the king of Egypt commanded them, but saved the baby boys alive.

In the New testament, we see the beginnings of this kind of reaction as the Jews attempted to destroy the witness of Christianity in the early days of the church. Their goal was not to stop Christianity but eliminate it. In Galatians 1, Paul discusses his own desire to annihilate Christianity when the apostle describes his motivation prior to coming to Christ.

Galatians 1:23
But they only heard: "He who once persecuted us now preaches the faith that he once tried to destroy."

You see, Paul wanted to destroy Christianity.

In Acts 9, Luke uses the same Greek word to describe the apostle Paul's intent and actions. He struck fear into the people because they knew he wanted to annihilate them all.

Acts 9:21
All who heard him were amazed, and said, "Isn't this he who in Jerusalem made havoc [destruction] of those who called on this name? And he had come here intending to bring them bound before the chief priests!"

In Galatians 1:13, he describes his method.

Galatians 1:13
For you have heard of my way of living in time past in the Jews' religion, how that beyond measure I persecuted the assembly of God, and ravaged it.

Paul used numerous methods of persecution that could not be measured. He literally did everything humanly possible to wipe this new blasphemy off the face of the Earth. Some might want to completely destroy us.

A Blasphemy Attempt

Another way in which some might persecute Christians is to require them to verbally reject their God in front of others. It is not enough to simply punish them for their beliefs, but they want the satisfaction of these renouncing their God. This is what Saul's actions attempted to achieve.

In Acts 26, Paul explained to King Agrippa the amazing change Christ had made in his life and describes what he had done to believers before becoming a Christian.

Acts 26:11
Punishing them often in all the synagogues, I tried to make them blaspheme. Being exceedingly enraged against them, I persecuted them even to foreign cities.

He was working hard at finding these saints and forcing them to "blaspheme" against the Lord who saved them.

This Greek word translated "blaspheme" refers to "railing at, reviling, speaking reproachfully, or cursing." He wanted them to curse their God in front of him. This is the place he desired to put the Christians. He wanted them to have no other choice than to curse and rail against their Savior and Lord God. Christians must be prepared to face this kind of persecution.

A Verbal Mockery

Many will persecute Christians simply with their scornful and mocking words. This is what they did to Jesus. In Mark 10, Jesus predicted this mockery, His suffering and death. This was to prepare His disciples for the horror of what was to come. It was necessary for this to occur to redeem man and prove His deity.

Mark 10:34
They will mock him, spit on him, scourge him, and kill him. On the third day he will rise again.

In Matthew 26, the Roman soldiers dressed Jesus in a robe of purple and mocked Him. It was a mockery that was harsh and vicious.

Matthew 27:29
They braided a crown of thorns and put it on his head, and a reed in his right hand; and they kneeled down before him, and mocked him, saying, "Hail, King of the Jews!"

While the Lord Jesus was on the cross, the people walking by mocked and scoffed at Him. They sneered, laughed at, and chided Him in their unbelief.

Mark 15:29-30
Those who passed by blasphemed him, wagging their heads, and saying, "Ha! You who destroy the temple, and build it in three days, save yourself, and come down from the cross!"

Matthew 27:39-40
Those who passed by blasphemed him, wagging their heads, and saying, "You who destroy the temple, and build it in three days, save yourself! If you are the Son of God [Messiah], come down from the cross!"

In Luke 6:22, Jesus warned His disciples that they would be mocked also.

Luke 6:22
Blessed are you when men shall hate you, and when they shall separate you from them and reproach you, and throw out your name as evil, for the Son of Man's sake.

They will scoff at believers as they scoffed Jesus with every kind of cursing, coarse joking, and critical humor. We might become the topic of their vulgar jesting as they humiliate us.

An Indecent Disrespect

There may be some who will show their disrespect using gestures that offend and dishonor Christians. They will desire to be as offensive as they can because they hate our purity. In Matthew 27 and Mark 15, the two writers recorded that the Roman soldiers kneeled before our Savior, spit on Him, and beat Him with a reed.

Matthew 27:30
They spat on him, and took the reed and struck him on the head.

Mark 15:15
Pilate, wishing to please the multitude, released Barabbas to them, and delivered Jesus, when he had flogged him, to be crucified.

These are all signs of great disrespect for the King of Kings.

When the Lord was being examined by Annas, the high priest, a soldier did not like the way Jesus was speaking to him, so he disrespectfully slapped the Lord Jesus.

John 18:20-23
Jesus answered him, "I spoke openly to the world. I always taught in synagogues, and in the temple, where the Jews always meet. I said nothing in secret. Why do you ask me? Ask those who have heard me what I said to them. Behold, these know the things which I said." When he had said this, one of the officers standing by slapped Jesus with his hand, saying, "Do you answer the high priest like that?" Jesus answered him, "If I have spoken evil, testify of the evil; but if well, why do you beat me?"

In Acts 23, the apostle Paul was being examined by the Jewish Council and Luke records how they demonstrated their disrespect to him.

Acts 23:1-2
Paul, looking steadfastly at the council, said, "Brothers, I have lived before God in all good conscience until this day." The high priest, Ananias, commanded those who stood by him to strike him on the mouth.

While Paul was making his defense to the leaders, the high priest had him struck on the mouth. What a powerful sign of dishonor!

Christians must be prepared to be dishonored as their Savior and His apostles were dishonored.

An Infamous Reputation

Others may persecute the saints by attempting to destroy their reputations. This is what the Jews did to Paul.

THE PERSECUTION OF THE SAINTS AND HOW TO OVERCOME IT

In Acts 21, the apostle was trying to make a gesture of reconciliation to the Jewish people by keeping a vow and they immediately turned the crowd at the temple against him with evil presumptions.

Acts 21:27-30
When the seven days were almost completed, the Jews from Asia, when they saw him [Paul] in the temple, stirred up all the multitude and laid hands on him, crying out, "Men of Israel, help! This is the man who teaches all men everywhere against the people, and the law, and this place. Moreover, he also brought Greeks into the temple, and has defiled this holy place!" For they had seen Trophimus, the Ephesian, with him [Paul] in the city, and they supposed that Paul had brought him into the temple. All the city was moved, and the people ran together. They seized Paul and dragged him out of the temple. Immediately the doors were shut."

There slanderous accusations were always the same: Paul blasphemed their Jewish God and spoke against the customs of the Romans.

Acts 16:20-21
When they had brought them to the magistrates, they said, "These men [Paul and Silas], being Jews, are agitating our city, and set forth customs which it is not lawful for us to accept or to observe, being Romans."

In Acts 13:50, the Jewish leaders stirred up the devout and prominent women and the chief men of the city with their many slanders and lies and caused them to be thrown out of the city.

Acts 13:50
But the Jews urged on the devout women of honorable estate, and the chief men [leaders] of the city, and stirred up a persecution against Paul and Barnabas, and threw them out of their borders.

In Acts 14, they stirred up the people in Iconium and Paul and his companions had to flee.

Acts 14:5
When some of both the Gentiles and the Jews, with their rulers, made a violent attempt to mistreat and stone them, 6 they became aware of it, and fled to the cities of Lycaonia, Lystra, Derbe, and the surrounding region.

They followed him to Lystra and agitated the people with their lies which resulted in Paul's stoning to the very edge of death.

Acts 14:19
But some Jews from Antioch and Iconium came there, and having persuaded the multitudes, they stoned Paul, and dragged him out of the city, supposing that he was dead.

Christians should be prepared for slanderous lies to be told about them for Christ's sake.

A Mob Association

One of the techniques that persecutors will use against Christians is to enlist the aid of unsavory characters who have nothing better to do than to stir up strife. It was the Jewish leaders accompanied by a mob that arrested Jesus.

Matthew 26:47
While he was still speaking, behold, Judas, one of the twelve, came, and with him a great multitude with swords and clubs, from the chief priest and elders of the people.

Paul experienced this same thing in Thessalonica where an unsavory mob were recruited to come after him.

Acts 17:5
But the unpersuaded Jews took along some wicked men from the marketplace, and gathering a crowd, set the city in an uproar."

Wicked men are stirred up for a fight [incited] not because of what we preach or how we live but simply because they enjoy a good scuffle. The people who persecute Christians may take along a mob willing to maim for any reason.

A Continual Imprisonment

Some governments will persecute Christians by throwing them into prison and incarcerating them for a length of time. Not every Christian may experience this, but many have. The apostles were imprisoned on several occasions.

In Acts 4, Peter healed a lame man and then preached a powerful sermon bringing many into the kingdom of God.

Acts 4:4
But many of those who heard the word believed, and the number of the men came to be about five thousand.

As a result, the apostles were arrested.

Acts 5:18
And laid hands [arrested] on the apostles, and put them in public custody.

Since the murder of James pleased the people, King Herod arrested Peter to put him to death.

Acts 12:3
When he saw that it pleased the Jews, he proceeded to seize Peter also. This was during the days of unleavened bread.

Peter's ministry was initiated with constant imprisonment.

As Saul (before becoming Paul) persecuted the church, he bound Christians in chains and dragged them off to prison.

Acts 8:3
But Saul ravaged the assembly, entering into every house, and dragged both men and women off to prison.

When Paul became a Christian and began preaching the gospel, the Jews were constantly trying to have him arrested and often succeeding. One of those times occurred in the city of Philippi. The merchants were deeply angered when Paul cast a demon out of a fortune telling slave girl they owned. So, they brought him before the leaders of the city.

Acts 16:22-24
The multitude rose up together against them, and the magistrates tore their clothes off of them, and commanded them to be beaten with rods. When they...laid many stripes on them, they threw them into prison, charging the jailer to keep them safely, who, having received such a charge, threw them into the...prison, and secured their feet in the stocks.

He was mobbed by the Jews and unfairly imprisoned by the Romans because they were unsure what to do with him.

Acts 24:26-27
He hoped that way that money would be given to him by Paul, that he might release him. Therefore also he sent for him more often, and talked with him. But when two years were fulfilled, Felix was succeeded by Porcius Festus, and desiring to gain favor with the Jews, Felix left Paul in bonds.

Paul was in custody for over two years. Once Felix became governor, he wanted to return Paul to the Jewish Council.

This forced Paul to appeal to Caesar which led to a much longer time since he had to be transferred to Rome and await a trial. So, Christians must be prepared to face even prison time for the sake of their glorious Lord.

A Planned Assassination

Some may even plot the assassinations of certain leaders who are Christian. We know that for some time, the Jewish leaders planned to kill Jesus. This happened early on in the Lord's three-year ministry.

John 7:1
After these things, Jesus walked in Galilee, for he would not walk in Judea, because the Jews sought to kill him.

This continued until it led to Christ's death on the cross. In Mark 14, Mark describes this very assassination plot.

Mark 14:1
It was now two days before the feast of the Passover and the unleavened bread, and the chief priests and the scribes sought how they might seize him [Jesus] by deception, and kill him.

The same assassination plots happened to Paul from the very beginning. A short time after Paul received Christ the Jews were after him. They did not just want to imprison him but to kill him.

Acts 9:23
When...days were fulfilled, the Jews conspired together to kill him.

Wherever he went, they would try to stop his ministry until finally they had had quite enough of his preaching and bound themselves together in a secret pact to kill him. Once this pact had been pact made, they informed the Sanhedrin in order to illicit their help.

Acts 23:12-15
When it was day, some...Jews banded together, and bound themselves under a curse, saying that they would neither eat nor drink until they had killed Paul. There were more than forty people who had made this conspiracy. They came to the chief priests and the elders, and said, "We have bound ourselves under a great curse, to taste nothing until we have killed Paul Now therefore, you with the council inform the commanding officer that he should bring him down to you tomorrow, as though you were going to judge his case more exactly. We are ready to kill him...."

What was the result of all of this? The Centurion in charge of Paul whisked him away to the governor for protection. Christians must understand that the enemies of the gospel can be very serious in their attempts to destroy Christ and His followers.

An Outright Murder

Some will desire our deaths and not hide in secret but kill us for all to see. In Matthew 24, Jesus warned His disciples of the murders of His followers.

Matthew 24:9
Then they will deliver you up to oppression, and will kill you. You [ultimately Christians] will be hated by all of the nations for my name's sake.

This is eventually what happened.

In Matthew 14, John the Baptist's head was served up on a platter for the world to see.

THE PERSECUTION OF THE SAINTS AND HOW TO OVERCOME IT

Matthew 14:11
His head was brought on a platter, and given to the young lady: and she brought it to her mother.

In John 19, they crucified Jesus Christ on a cross in front of the Jewish and Roman world.

John 19:33
But when they came to Jesus, and saw that he was already dead, they didn't break his legs.

In Acts 7, the leaders rushed Stephen and murdered him through stoning. This was a painful, horrifying way to die.

Acts 7:58
They threw him out of the city [Jerusalem], and stoned him. The witnesses placed their garments at the feet of a young man named Saul.

In Acts 12, the apostle James, who was the brother of John and one of the Lord Jesus' closest companions, was killed by putting him to death with a sword which was ordered by Herod. All of this was done in a public forum for all to see.

Acts 12:2
He killed James, the brother of John, with the sword.

In Acts 8, Saul's terrifying persecution of the saints led to more boldness. Many will not be afraid to kill Christians in full view of all, especially when they have the governor and people's approval.

Acts 8:1-4
Saul was consenting to his death. A great persecution arose against the assembly which was in Jerusalem in that day. They were all scattered abroad throughout the regions of Judea and

Samaria, except for the apostles. Devout men buried Stephen, and lamented greatly over him. But Saul ravaged the assembly, entering into every single house, and dragged both men and women off to prison. Therefore those who were scattered...went around preaching the word.*

For the next two thousand years, Christians were killed for their faith in almost every nation in the world. The light of Jesus in us that exposes their sin becomes too much for some to bear and they must seek our deaths to stop us. This has only emboldened believers to share the gospel and live holy lives even more.

A Territorial Banishment

Sometimes, rather than kill Christians, they will simply be banished. They will be kicked out of a region or territory. Often, they would never be allowed to return to their homes. In Acts 13, Luke records what happened to Paul in Antioch of Pisidia.

Acts 13:50
But the Jews urged [spurred on] on the devout women of honorable estate, and the chief men of the city, and stirred up a persecution against Paul and Barnabas, and threw them out of their borders.

We know for certain that the apostle John was banished to the remote island of Patmos where he had his final vision of the end.

Revelation 1:9
I John, your brother and partaker with you in oppression and kingdom and perseverance which are in Jesus, was on the isle that is called Patmos because of God's Word and the testimony of Jesus Christ.

This might happen in neighborhoods, towns, cities, regions, and even countries.

A Sustained Effort

Christians must realize that persecution may continue for years in an area or region. The New Testament demonstrates the sustained effort the Jews made in persecuting Christ.

In John 5, Jesus healed a lame man on the Sabbath, and it wasn't long before they were after Him.

John 5:15-16
The man went away, and told the Jews that it was Jesus who had made him well. For this cause the Jews persecuted Jesus, and sought to kill him, because he did these things on the Sabbath.

Their effort began early on in His ministry and continued throughout his years of ministry until it ended in His death.

John 7:44-46
Some of them would have arrested him, but no one laid hands on him. The officers therefore came to the chief priests and Pharisees, and they said to them, "Why didn't you bring him?" The officers answered, "No man ever spoke like this man!"

While Jesus was in Perea, Herod discovered that the Lord Jesus was there and sought to kill Him.

Luke 13:31
On that same day, some Pharisees came, saying to him, "Get out of here, and go away, for Herod wants to kill you."

After Jesus was requested by Martha and Mary to return to save their brother, the disciples took issue with Him.

John 11:8
The disciples told him, "Rabbi, the Jews were just trying to stone you, and are you going there again?"

He went anyway and raised Lazarus from the dead which only increased their efforts to seize Him.

John 11:47-48
The chief priests therefore and the Pharisees gathered a council, and said, "What are we doing? For this man [Jesus] does many signs. If we leave him [the Lord] alone like this, everyone will believe in him, and the Romans will come and take away both our place and our nation."

Finally, they decided to murder Him. His death became paramount in their minds.

John 11:53
So, from that day forward they took counsel that they might put him to death.

We know that in the same way, they went after the apostles on numerous occasions.

Acts 4:1-3
As they spoke to the people, the priests and the captain of the temple and the Sadducees came to them, being upset because they taught the people and proclaimed in Jesus the resurrection from the dead. They laid hands on them, and put them in custody until the next day, for it was now evening.

Acts 5:16-18
The multitude...bringing sick people...those who were tormented by unclean spirits: and they were all healed. But the high priest rose up...and they were filled with jealousy and laid hands on the apostles, then put them in public custody.

And as we have already seen, the apostle Paul also had a constant barrage of persecution toward him. We must be ready for this.

As one can see, persecution comes in a wide variety of forms. Whenever believers are sharing the good news of sin, judgment, and salvation through Christ alone, assembling together in love, and living righteously for Him, their lights will shine into the darkness of the world. As our lights expose their sins and the coming judgment, many will do anything to turn our bright lights off. We must continue to shine them so some may be saved.

A Friendship Destruction

Before Christians become believers, they may be involved in many immoral, unethical, illegal, or other sinful activities with their unsaved friends. After they repent, they will begin their process toward holiness and righteousness as they now live for Christ. This is called sanctification. In his first letter to the Thessalonians, Paul speaks about this new process.

1 Thessalonians 4:3-8
For this is the will of God: your sanctification [holiness], that you abstain from sexual immorality, that each one of you know how to control his own body in sanctification and honor, not in the passion of lust, even as the Gentiles who don't know God, that no one should take advantage of and wrong a brother or sister in this matter; because the Lord is an avenger in all these things, as also we forewarned you and testified. For God called us not for uncleanness, but in sanctification. Therefore, he who rejects this doesn't reject man, but God...has given his Holy Spirit to you.

The Greek word translated "sanctification" comes from a root word meaning "set apart, separate, or wholly different."

As we pursue Christ, we will more and more desire to live His holy (wholly different) way which will set us more and more apart from the unrighteous things of the world. This must include the activities we may be involved in with our many friends. We will not give up on them, but we will have to discontinue our engagement in these activities.

In his first letter, Peter addresses this very issue.

1 Peter 4:2-3
That you no longer should live the rest of your time in the flesh for the lusts of men, but for the will of God. For we have spent enough of our past time doing the desire of the Gentiles, and having walked in lewdness, lusts, drunken binges, orgies, carousings, and abominable idolatries.

Here is a brief description of the numerous evil activities, we might be engaged in with our companions.

Then, Peter indicates that there may be repercussions. Our friends may think it is "strange" that we have stopped doing the things we enjoyed together before our conversion. Yet, this is what Christians must do.

1 Peter 4:4
They think it is strange that you don't run with them into the same excess of riot, blaspheming.

The Greek word translated "strange" is not "weird" or "odd," but refers to "a foreigner, alien, or stranger in a land." They may begin to view you as a stranger among them. This could result in a wide variety of negative behaviors toward us. We could be ostracized from the group completely or placed on the periphery and not invited to even their neutral or even pure activities. Or they could respond in any of the many ways we have already discussed.

One example of how friends can respond to our desire to no longer participate in the dark deeds of unbelief is found in the final words of the apostle Paul in his second letter to Timothy. Here Paul describes a companion that abandoned him.

2 Timothy 4:10
For Demas having loved this present world has deserted me and gone to Thessalonica.

Demas was mentioned as Paul's ministry companion in two letters.

Colossians 4:14
Luke the beloved physician and Demas greet you.

Philemon 24
As do Mark [the gospel's author] Aristarchus, Demas, and Luke, my fellow workers.

The word translated "deserted" means more than leaving someone, it carries the idea of "complete abandonment at a critical time." Demas completely abandoned Paul when he needed him most. He was in his final Roman imprisonment awaiting his trial before Caesar Nero. Then, Paul gives the reason that he left: he loved the present world. We would expect Paul to use the Greek word for relationships which is translated "brotherly love," but he doesn't. He describes his love with the word Paul used for "loving" God. The root of the word is "to value or prize." When used of the God's love for us, it describes a love that values and then pours forth into sacrifice.

Romans 5:8
But God commends his own love toward us, in that while we were yet sinners, Christ died for us.

The term is used to describe our love for one another as the saints of God.

Romans 13:8
Owe no one anything, except to love one another; for he who loves his neighbor has fulfilled the law.

So, Demas "valued" this present world much more than he "prized" his relationship to Paul. In fact, he loved it so much he sacrificed his relationship to Paul for it and deserted him. The phrase "this present world" refers to "the current period of time." Demas loved living in the culture, clothes, and lifestyles of the world. He loved the "lewdness, lusts, drunkenness, orgies, carousings and the abominable idolatries" that the world could offer a person at the time in which he lived.

This could mean that our friends might suddenly see us as "strangers" among them. Because they value and prize the living of their lives with its sinful pleasures and evil delights, we can no longer participate with them which may bring retaliation. This could take the form of shunning, backbiting, slandering, mocking, or scoffing. We should respond by loving them but not their deeds.

A Familial Hostility

When someone comes to Christ, they do not receive Him in a vacuum; instead, they welcome Jesus Christ into a life filled with family, friends, neighbors, and others. This may lead some of them to become hostile to the new believer and respond negatively in the of the ways discussed. We know that the brothers and sisters of the Lord Jesus did not believe that He was the Messiah at first and then mocked Him for attempting to become well known.

THE PERSECUTION OF THE SAINTS AND HOW TO OVERCOME IT

John 7:1-10
After these things, Jesus was walking in Galilee, for he wouldn't walk in Judea, because the Jews sought to kill him. Now the feast of the Jews, the Feast of Booths, was at hand. His brothers therefore said to him, "Depart...and go into Judea, that your disciples also may see your works which you do. For no one does anything in secret while he seeks to be known openly. If you do these things, reveal yourself to the world."

Here, the family is traveling to Jerusalem to celebrate the feast and His brothers mock Him by telling Him to go into Judea and show everyone what He can do. Since he seeks to be known publicly, He needs to be seen.

Then, John provides the explanation for why they would say such a thing to Jesus.

John 7:5-6
For even his brothers didn't believe in him. Jesus therefore said to them, "My time has not yet come, but your time is always ready.

Jesus responds not by condemning them but by offering all of them salvation.

Jesus grew up in Nazareth. Since these were His people, His message should be well received, but it was not.

Luke 4:28-30
They were all filled with wrath in the synagogue, as they heard these things. They rose up, threw him out of the city, and led him to the brow of the hill that their city was built on, that they might throw him off the cliff. But he, passing through the middle of them, went his way.

After declaring that He was the Messiah and Servant of Isaiah 61, they responded with great hostility. Why?

Mark 6:5-6
He could do no mighty work there...laid his hands on a few sick people, and healed them. He marveled because of their unbelief.

Once again, those who know us will not necessarily embrace us when they discover we have Jesus, the Savior and Lord, in our lives.

Christians should expect this kind of reaction because the Lord Jesus gave us this warning.

Matthew 10:34
Don't think that I came to send peace on the Earth. I didn't come to send peace, but a sword. For I came to set a man at odds against his father, and a daughter against her mother, and a daughter-in-law against her mother-in-law. A man's foes will be those of his own household.

The sword will be Jesus Christ. He will divide households, friends, teammates, and others. Why? It is not because we are hostile to them; it is because they are hostile to Him and then to us.

They might make us choose between Jesus or them, we must choose Jesus.

Matthew 10:37
He who loves father or mother more than me is not worthy of me; and he who loves son or daughter more than me isn't worthy....

This is part of bearing crosses and giving up lives for Him.

Matthew 10:38-39
He who doesn't take his cross and follow after me isn't worthy of me. He who seeks his life will lose it; and he who loses his life for my sake will find it.

As we can see, we might experience real hostility from our spouses, siblings, families, or relatives.

A Demonic Accusation

One of the accusations that the Lord Jesus received over and over was His message and power was from the Devil. One incident occurred after healing a demon-possessed man.

Matthew 12:22-24
Then one [man] possessed by a demon, blind and mute, was brought to him; and he healed him, so that the blind and mute man both spoke and saw. All the multitudes were amazed, and said, "Can this be the son of David?" But when the Pharisees heard it, they said, "This man does not cast out demons except by Beelzebul, the prince of the demons."

This was the exact opposite of everything Jesus was. It was a foolish response to a divine act. They did not want people to believe in Him.

Before this incident, the Lord warned them of accusations that they would encounter because of Him.

Matthew 10:24
A disciple is not above his teacher, nor a servant above his lord. It is enough for the disciple that he be like his teacher... the servant like his lord. If they have called the master of the house Beelzebul, how much more those of his household!

So, we should not be surprised if people, especially religious ones, accuse us of being false teachers from the Devil.

Thus far, we have learned that persecution will come if we know Christ and are willing to shine our lights. Since we are living in the last days, we know that evil will increase. Therefore, persecution will also grow. We discovered the many ways that man's hostility toward us may arise due to our salvation. When we know this, we can be prepared.

Chapter 4

Keep the Divine Perspective

In order to "stand our ground" in persecution no matter how terrifying, it is crucial to understand the divine purpose of this. Why does God allow persecution in the first place? The answer to this question always brings to mind the larger question of trials in general. Why does God allow so many trials?

What is revealed in the Scriptures can be divided into two parts. One is the general trials of life, and the other is the specific trials of persecution. In this book, persecution will be discussed and the larger question of trials in general will be left to another book.

In John 15, the Lord Jesus was preparing His disciples for His departure from this Earth and gave them a warning.

John 15:18
If the world hates you, you know that it has hated me before it hated you.

John 15:20
Remember the word that I said to you: "A servant is not greater than his lord." If they persecuted me, they will also persecute you. If they kept my word, they will keep yours also.

So, we know that believers will be treated in the same way as their Lord. They cannot live like Him and not be treated in the same way as He was treated. This will definitely include every kind of persecution whether it is displayed in a word, action, or even a thought or attitude.

God's Sovereign Will

Before we begin our study, something must be made very clear. The Lord is in control of all persecution of His people. Every attitude, thought, word, and deed against us has been allowed by Him. Though Lucifer rebelled in the heavenlies, and mankind rebelled on the Earth, God has never for one moment lost control of His universe. The Lord never gave up total sovereignty over everything that occurs including our harm. Everything happens according to His will. Men may make their many plans, but the Lord almighty decides whether it will happen.

Solomon wrote of this truth.

Proverbs 16:9
A man's [good or evil] heart plans his course, but Yahweh directs his steps.

Proverbs 16:33
The lot [a dice-like rock] is cast into the lap, but its every decision is from Yahweh.

Proverbs 19:21
There are many plans in a man's heart, but Yahweh's counsel will prevail.

In Daniel chapter 4, the ruler of the Babylonian kingdom, Nebuchadnezzar, was struck with the mind of a wild animal because of his arrogance and pride. After eating grass and living as an animal for seven years, God restored his mind according to the prophecy of Daniel.

Then this mighty king came to know the sovereignty and power of the one true God. In humility and adoration this most powerful ruler on Earth made this declaration.

Daniel 4:35
All the inhabitants of the Earth are reputed as nothing; and he does according to his will in the army of heaven, and among the inhabitants of the Earth; and none can stay his hand, or tell him, What do you?

God controls all things, even our persecution. In fact, the Lord claims full responsibility for both the good and evil things that occur in the entire universe including the Earth and heavenly places. God makes this very announcement in the words of Isaiah.

Isaiah 45:7
I form the light, and create darkness; I make peace, and create evil. I am Yahweh, who does all these things.

God Himself says that He creates both peace and calamity like He created the light and darkness.

This proclamation is a "Hebrew parallelism" which entails the use of two different statements that have similar and parallel thoughts. We observe physical light or darkness and are sure it is from God. In the same way, when we see peace or calamity (no matter what it seems), we are sure it is from God. We can be as certain that our calamity (persecution) is from God's hand as we are about all the light and darkness coming from Him.

This includes the physical maladies of birth or afterward. When God called Moses at the burning bush to speak to Pharaoh on His behalf and lead His people out of bondage in Egypt, this humble shepherd complained. He felt that he didn't possess the rhetorical skills needed to accomplish this powerful feat. The Lord's response gives us great insight into His sovereignty over all that is in the universe. Moses recorded God's response.

Exodus 4:11
Yahweh said to him, "Who made man's mouth? Or who makes one mute...deaf...seeing, or blind? Isn't it I, Yahweh?"

All imperfections including deafness, blindness, and others are as much from the Lord God as are physical perfections. God decides these things and He is never surprised. This does not necessarily mean that He did not allow the natural processes to work, the sin of a mother to take its toll, the unredeemed and cursed creation to affect someone, or even the harm of persecution, it simply means He takes absolute responsibility for it as His own decision. Either He allowed it to happen or did it directly.

In the same way, the Lord claims to be sovereign over the movement of armies and nations which also persecute His people. In Amos 3, the prophet warns sinful, unrepentant Israel of a mighty army that will be coming against them for their sin. Then, in verse 6, he presents a general principle in the form of a rhetorical question answered in the affirmative.

Amos 3:6
Does the trumpet alarm sound in a city, Without the people being afraid? Does evil befall a city, And Yahweh hasn't done it?

Here again, these two statements are parallel. When the trumpet sounds to warn of an approaching enemy, people become afraid. This is a true and authentic principle of life. In the same way, when evil occurs in a city (usually by an enemy army), God has done this. It is the hand of God. We can be assured that the Lord God is right there controlling and limiting all things.

As Jeremiah grieved over the destruction of Jerusalem by the Babylonians, the prophet asks a rhetorical question that provides a powerful truth about God.

Lamentations 3:37-38
Who is he who says, and it comes to pass, when the Lord doesn't command it? Doesn't evil and good come out of the mouth of the Most High?

Jerusalem and all who will read his writing better know that this destruction by the Babylonian army was from God.

In Lamentations 2, Jeremiah provides God's perspective on the coming Babylonian army which will conquer Judah.

Lamentations 2:17
Yahweh has done that which he purposed; he has fulfilled his word that he commanded in the days of old; He has thrown down, and has not pitied: He has caused the enemy to rejoice over you; he [God] has exalted the horn of your adversaries.

Of course, though Babylon is used as an instrument of God's fury, it would also be judged for its acts of unrelenting treachery against nations. This is absolute control.

Isaiah 43:14-15
Thus says Yahweh, your Redeemer, the Holy One of Israel: For your sake I have sent to Babylon, and I will bring down all of them as fugitives, even the Chaldeans, in the ships of their rejoicing.

What about the Devil? Doesn't he run rampant? You can rely on the Scriptures' depiction of Satan's divine imposed limitations toward God's people. This serpent of old must receive permission from the Lord. This is either directly (by asking) or indirectly (by God allowing it) to make sure he is operating according to God's plan. This includes persecuting God's people.

In Job 1-2, we see Satan receiving permission to persecute Job to test his faith on two different occasions.

Job 1:12
Yahweh said to Satan, "Behold, all that he has is in your power. Only on himself don't stretch out your hand." So Satan went out from the presence of Yahweh.

Job 2:6
Yahweh said to Satan, "Behold, he is in your hand. Only spare his life."

In Luke 22, Jesus told Peter and the other disciples that the Devil had asked permission to sift them like wheat and the Father (implied) had given permission. Jesus then told Peter that He had prayed that his faith would not fail during this difficult trial.

Luke 22:31-34
The Lord said, "Simon, Simon, behold, Satan asked to have you, that he might sift you as wheat...I prayed for you, that your faith wouldn't fail. You, when once you have turned again, establish your brothers." He said to him, "Lord, I am ready to go with you both to prison and to death!" He said, "I tell you, Peter, the rooster will by no means crow today, before you deny that you know me three times."

In 1 Peter 5, Peter compares the Devil to a desperate and hungry lion on the prowl for food. These creatures prowl for prey to eat.

1 Peter 5:8
Be sober and self-controlled. Be watchful. Your adversary, the devil, walks around [prowls about] like a roaring lion [hungry and on the move], seeking whom [Christians] he may devour.

Lucifer cannot prowl or devour anyone without permission. He knows God can and will stop him any time he strays outside of the will of our all-powerful Father.

THE PERSECUTION OF THE SAINTS AND HOW TO OVERCOME IT

We must understand that God may have much larger purposes in His divine mind than just our immediate well-being. Joseph was sold into slavery by his ten brothers. He was purchased by Potiphar and ran his household. When Joseph refused the sexual advances of his wife, she accused him of attempted rape, and her husband threw Joseph into prison.

There Joseph interpreted the dreams of two of Pharaoh's servants which came to pass. The one who was restored to his position then related to Pharaoh the story of Joseph. When the emperor had his own dreams, Joseph interpreted them as referring to seven years of plenty and then seven years of famine in the world.

As a result, Joseph was given authority over the entire land of Egypt and their collection and distribution of food. After the famine came, his father sent his brothers to Egypt to obtain this sustenance. When Joseph discovered this, he brought his entire family to Egypt in order to protect them during this difficult time in which the world would face famine. The father, Jacob, showed favoritism to Joseph, his youngest at the time.

This made his brothers jealous and angry. Joseph intensified their feelings by wearing a special coat around and bragging of dreams that indicated he would eventually rule over them. His brothers responded by selling him into slavery out of spite for him. Potiphar's wife wanted to satisfy her lust and took revenge on Joseph for refusing her. So, she accused him of attempting to rape her and he was thrown into prison.

In Genesis 50, Joseph told his brothers that though they had purposed evil in what they did to him, God had His own reasons for allowing all of this.

Genesis 50:20
As for you, you meant evil against me, but God meant it for good, to bring to pass, as it is this day, to save many people alive.

The "good" that the Lord God intended was to preserve the future nation of Israel represented in the twelve sons of Jacob who would have died in the famine. Therefore, though Jacob and his favored son contributed to these events, Joseph attributed them to God's hand.

Since Christ had to be born of the Jews in the line of King David, this preserved the Messianic line. Joseph saved many others in the world through his management of Egypt's vast resources. Also, the Lord God set into place the necessary elements for the greatest event in the history of Israel: the deliverance of his people out of Egypt by Moses. As a result, He also created the most powerful sign of His Son's work on the cross: the Passover. All of these events occurred due to the evil motives of men and the righteous motives of God.

Amid all these purposes, God desires is to administer "good." The good of His people, as Paul explains in Romans 8, is uppermost in His mind.

Romans 8:28
We know that all things work together for good for those who love God [believers], to those who are called according to his purpose.

Here, he uses the term "all" which means "all." This indicates God has His hand in everything (all things) that happens in His vast universe including the heavenly places. The apostle does not say, "we know that all things Christians do."

This working (whether good or evil) occurs for our good and the good of others. As we will see, those others may not only be believers but even potential believers who may be saved through the persecution and torment that is inflicted upon us.

So, when we find ourselves in a situation of persecution where it seems God is absent and everything appears out of control, He is there, and He is in control. We may think that the Lord did not choose the situation of persecution we find ourselves in, but this is not true.

God claims responsibility for everything that goes on in His universe. He is not fooled or surprised by what happens. He does not come along and comfort us by saying that He is sorry and did not have anything to do with what happened. He did and for good reason. Though Christians may not see the reasons clearly, this does not mean they do not exist. Not only do they exist but they are extremely important in the plan of God. If not, they would not be a part of our lives.

God's Sovereign Purposes

As was previously mentioned, being persecuted because of Christ is almost inevitable for those who are saved. As evil increases so will persecution. One way to be mentally prepared is to understand God's purposes for persecution. Why does He not deliver us instead?

In Matthew 24, as the Lord sits on the Mount of Olives, He predicts the persecution of His disciples and all others who follow Him.

Matthew 24:8-9
But all these things are the beginning of birth pains. Then they will deliver you up to oppression, and will kill you. You will be hated by all of the nations for my name's sake.

Here is a brief list of some of the most important reasons for God's allowance of persecution. This is not an exhaustive list. We should use these to embrace our suffering for Christ, trust in His sovereignty over it, and stand our ground which will glorify His Only Son Jesus in the process.

His Continued Suffering

When we are persecuted, we can know that it is actually intended for our Savior and Lord. His suffering continues through our lives. In Colossians 1, Paul describes his intense, unimaginable sufferings for Christ.

Colossians 1:24
Now I rejoice in my sufferings for your sake, and fill up on my part that which is lacking of the afflictions of Christ in my flesh for his body's sake, which is the assembly.

The apostle Paul saw himself as suffering for their sakes because it was him who brought the gospel to them. Yet, more importantly, He saw himself as a vessel to persecute because Christ is no longer in the flesh and they cannot harm Him. Paul is, so they can take their animosity out on Him.

We suffer because the world has not filled up the cup of their animosity toward the Lord Jesus. They want to make Him suffer but He has risen, so we are the next best thing to harm. Paul saw this as a great privilege. This is the reason that the apostle rejoiced in his suffering and the reason we should also.

According to Revelation 19, John, the apostle, reveals that the world will attempt to persecute Christ physically one more time. This will be at his Second Coming of our Lord and Savior Jesus Christ, His angels, and saints.

Revelation 19:19-21
I saw the beast, and the kings of the Earth, and...armies, gathered together to make war against him who sat on the horse, and against his army. The beast was taken, and with him the false prophet who worked the signs in his sight, with which he deceived those who had received the mark of the beast and those who worshiped his image. They two were thrown alive into the lake of fire that burns with sulfur. The rest were killed with the sword of him who sat on the horse, the sword which came forth out of his mouth. All the birds were filled with their flesh.

Even when the Lord returns in all His glory, they will refuse to repent, refuse to recognize His deity, and in futility attempt to blow Him and His armies (angels and Christians) out of the sky. Then, all those persecuted His Son and His people, including the false prophet and man of lawlessness, will be finished. Persecution is an honor and privilege. Why? We have the opportunity to be a "stand in" as it were for Christ as the world hates and pours their wrath upon Him. Since He is no longer on Earth, they hurt and harm us instead. What a privilege!

Our Divine Manifestation

When we are persecuted and stand up for Jesus Christ, we manifest His life in us. We demonstrate to people that He is alive and in our midst. The world can see Christ living in us as we endure persecution. This is what God desires for us. As the apostle Paul experienced persecution even to the point of death, he knew this was a demonstration that Jesus was still alive in him. The apostle spoke of this wonderful and powerful manifestation.

2 Corinthians 4:10-11
Always carrying in the body the putting to death of the Lord Jesus,

that the life of Jesus may also be revealed in our body. For we who live are always delivered to death for Jesus' sake, that the life also of Jesus may be revealed in our...flesh.

Jesus was active in the world and still proclaiming that His kingdom had come through Paul's proclamation and his suffering for the Lord's sake.

These enemies of the Lord attempted to crucify Christ in Paul's body and the bodies of his companions again and again. They hated Christ and could never get away from His presence in His disciples. We reveal God as we suffer for Him. They will know through us that He lives! So, when we share the gospel, assemble in love, or live righteously and the world persecutes us, we manifest that Christ is still alive!

Our Divine Identification

As we are beaten and tortured for our faith, those wounds that we bear are like the brands of an owner on his cattle. In Galatians 6, Paul presents a powerful analogy: the stripes bruises, and scars from his floggings and beatings were the branding of Christ. He was owned by the Lord and everyone could see it. They could literally observe it on his body. Those horrible mutilations stated, "I am His!"

Galatians 6:17
From now on, let no one cause me any trouble, for I bear the marks of the Lord Jesus branded on my body.

In the Hebrew world, a slave could receive his freedom in the seventh year of service. If the bondservant desired to remain because he loved his master, he could request the master to brand him and he would permanently be owned by him. This was God's holy law. Moses explained this.

Deuteronomy 15:16-17
It shall be, if he tell you, I will not go out from you; because he loves you and your house, because he is well with you; then you shall take an awl, and thrust it through his ear to the door, and he shall be your servant forever. Also to your maid-servant you shall do likewise.

In the same way, physical marks from persecution should be viewed as if they were brands that were burned into our flesh to identify our owner Jesus Christ. It demonstrates our loyalty and devotion to Him.

Our Divine Fellowship

When we partner with Jesus as we minister for Him, we will suffer as He suffered. Paul called this true fellowship. The Philippians were disturbed when they heard Paul was under arrest in Rome awaiting his trial before Caesar. They had lost much of their joy because they loved Paul. In the letter, the apostle describes how he now viewed his past life as a prominent Jew to his current life as a servant of God. His past life was metaphorically "garbage" compared to all He had possessed in Christ.

Philippians 3:7-11
However, what things were gain to me, these have I counted loss for Christ. Yes most assuredly, and I count all things to be loss for the excellency of the knowledge of Christ Jesus, my Lord, for whom I suffered the loss of all things, and count them nothing but refuse, that I may gain [Jesus] Christ and be found in him, not having a righteousness of my own, that which is of the law, but that which is through faith in Christ, the righteousness which is from God by faith; that I may know him, and the power of his resurrection, and the fellowship of his sufferings, becoming conformed to his death; if by any means I may attain to the resurrection from the dead.

It did not matter where he was or what had happened to him. Why? All of his former possessions, prominence, and material and worldly comfort were considered nothing but refuse and rubbish when compared to the surpassing value of knowing Christ. The word translated "refuse" did not refer to simply garbage, but the dirty filthy grime left at the bottom. You see, when the apostle came to Christ, he lost everything that pertained to his "own righteousness" and gained "Christ's righteousness" by faith. Now, he had new purposes which were to know Christ intimately (through his Word, of course), to partner Himself with Christ in suffering, and to eventually conform himself to His Lord's death.

Paul wanted to "fellowship" with Christ in His sufferings. The word translated "fellowship" means "partnership." To fellowship is to partner in something. He partnered with Christ in ministry by proclaiming the kingdom of God (the gospel) and now he desired to accept and partner with Him in the resultant suffering of persecution. He explained this to the Philippians because they were so discouraged over his persecution. He declared that they no longer needed to be disturbed because this is exactly what he desired in his sharing of the gospel. He did not care any longer about the comforts of life. So, there was no need for their concern. He counted them as garbage. This persecution was his deep fellowship with Christ, and he knew Christ would provide so much more in heaven for him. God provide the same for us. If this fellowship comes, we must embrace it.

A Continued History

The persecution of God's people extends back to the very beginning of the human race. It begins with the trickery the Devil uses in the form of a serpent to cause Eve to stumble into sin.

THE PERSECUTION OF THE SAINTS AND HOW TO OVERCOME IT

Genesis 3:4-6
The serpent said to the woman, "You won't surely die, for God knows that in the day you eat it, your eyes will be opened, and you will be like God, knowing good and evil." When the woman saw that the tree was good for food, and that it was a delight to the eyes, and that the tree was to be desired to make one wise, she took of the fruit of it, and ate; and she gave some to her husband...and he ate.

Through his temptation Adam rebelled. Paul described this when he discussed the place of man in God's plan.

1 Timothy 2:13-14
For Adam was first formed, then Eve [order of creation]. Adam wasn't deceived, but the woman, being deceived, has fallen into disobedience [deception vs. rebellion].

We know it was him, the Devil, because John confirmed it.

Revelation 12:9
The great dragon was thrown down, the old serpent, he who is called the Devil and Satan, the deceiver of the whole world. He was thrown down to the Earth, and his angels were thrown down with him.

It extends through time to the eminent rise of the Man of Lawlessness who will be possessed by the Devil himself and will torment the saints for days and days. Then this evil one will attempt to kill all of God's people during the tribulation chasing them throughout the earth.

Revelation 13:6-7
He [beast] opened his mouth for blasphemy against God, to blaspheme his name, and his dwelling, those who dwell in heaven. It was given to him to make war with the saints, and to overcome them. Authority over every tribe, people, language, and nation was given to him.

Finally, Satan gathers a massive army to persecute Christ at the end of the thousand-year reign.

Revelation 20:7-10
And after...thousand years, Satan will be released from his prison, and he will come out to deceive the nations which are in the four corners of the Earth, Gog and Magog, to gather them together to the war; the number of whom is as the sand of the sea. They went up over the width of the Earth, and surrounded the camp of the saints, and the beloved city. Fire came down out of heaven from God, and devoured them. The devil who deceived them was thrown into the lake of fire and sulfur, where the beast and the false prophet are also. They will be tormented day and night forever and ever.

As we peer into the Old Testament, the author of Hebrews calls those who were persecuted "cloud of witnesses" in Hebrews 12.

Hebrews 12:1
Therefore let us also, seeing we are surrounded by so great a cloud of witnesses, lay aside every weight and the sin which so easily entangles us, and let us run with patience the race that is set before us.

Here, he describes the Christian life and its many obstacles as a race which must be run without the entanglements of sin and self-imposed burdens or weights. He has in view a long journey with many obstacles of persecution because he uses the word patience indicating a patient endurance in the midst of obstacles.

Secondly, the author imagines a stadium of onlookers which are saints who have suffered in the Old Testament. They are "cheering believers on" as they run the race of the Christian life throughout the church age. They were the first who had gone through the persecution we may experience, and they are still speaking today through their lives of faith.

Hebrews 11:4
By faith, Abel offered to God a more excellent sacrifice than Cain, through...he had testimony given to him that he was righteous, God bearing witness with respect to his gifts; and through it he, being dead, still speaks.

He continues with a list of these people of great faith and all their heroic acts and the suffering that they faced. Then, it ends with these words.

Hebrews 11:32-34
What will I more say? For the time will fail me if I tell of Gideon, Barak, Samson, Jephthah, David, Samuel, and the prophets; who, through faith, subdued kingdoms, worked out righteousness, obtained promises, stopped the mouths of lions, quenched the power of fire, escaped the edge of the sword, from weakness were made strong, grew mighty in war, and turned to flight armies....

This "cloud of witnesses" was an indication that we are in a long line of persecuted saints which extends all the way back to Adam and then Abel who was slain by Cain for his righteousness.

As we suffer, we, as Christians, are now a part of a long history of true believers who have stood their ground as an example to us. They have "obtained a testimony." They have endured their persecution by faith and now can testify that it is worth all the suffering. They are at the present enjoying their blessed rewards in heaven.

By faith, we can know that they are on the other side of suffering rejoicing in their privilege of suffering for His name. If they ran the race standing their ground against the ravages of hate for Jesus Christ, so can we. We are all a part of the persecution of God's people for thousands of years. There will be many more trials and tribulations to come as the Lord God prepares His church for His Beloved Son's triumphant return. This return will be a glorious display of the faith of myriad of believers glorifying God.

A Pioneer Advance

As we shine our lights in the midst of a dark and perverse world, they will persecute us. At times, God will use this persecution to advance his gospel to people that we would not otherwise be able to reach. This is seen so clearly in the ministry of the apostle Paul.

Romans 15:23-25
But now, no longer having any place in these regions, and having these many years a longing to come to you, whenever I journey to Spain, I will come to you. For I hope to see you on my journey, and to be helped on my way there by you, if first I may enjoy your company for a while. But now, I say, I am going to Jerusalem, serving the saints.

Yet, he was never able to travel there because of his other pressing concerns. In Acts 19, Luke records Paul's words of determination.

Acts 19:21
Now after these things had ended, Paul determined in the spirit, when he had passed through Macedonia and Achaia, to go to Jerusalem, saying, "After I have been there, I must also see Rome."

Please notice again, his great desire to visit was to no avail. Later, the apostle was arrested in Jerusalem because he had supposedly taken a Gentile into the temple. When Paul had testified before the Jewish leaders, he was able to divide the council into two groups theologically and they were unable to find unity as to what they should do to him. This left Paul in the hands of the Romans.

That night, God appeared to Paul and encouraged him by telling him that the apostle would be going to Rome as he had wished and would stand before the emperor.

Acts 23:11
The following night, the Lord [Christ] stood by him [Paul], and said, "Cheer up, Paul, for as you have testified about me at Jerusalem, so you must testify also at Rome."

Paul was placed under strict house arrest with the Roman governor Festus and remained there for two years. Festus hoped Paul would bribe him, but he did not. So, for two years, he knew that he was going to Rome but not how.

Then Felix replaced Festus and he listened to the apostle's plea and decided to return him to the Jewish authorities. At this point, Paul exercised an important Roman right to appeal to Caesar as a last resort.

Acts 25:11
For if I have done wrong, and have committed anything worthy of death, I don't refuse to die; but if none of those things is true that these accuse me of, no one can give me up to them. I appeal to Caesar!

Apparently, as Paul saw Felix's desire to send Paul back to Jerusalem, he realized God had given him the opportunity he needed to travel to Rome (though it would be in chains).

During his arrest in Rome, the Philippian church had sent emissaries to assist Paul both financially and in ministry.

They were concerned for Paul's welfare. They loved him and struggled with the reason God would allow such a thing to happen. When Paul writes his letter to the beloved church, he explains God's great purpose.

Philippians 1:12-14
Now I desire to have you know, brothers, that the things which happened...have turned out rather to the progress of the gospel; so that my bonds became revealed in Christ throughout the whole praetorian guard, and to all the rest; and that most of the brothers [and sisters] in the Lord, being confident through my bonds, are more abundantly bold to speak the word of God without fear.

Though Paul's imprisonment appeared a random incident of persecution, it was actually a well-planned strategy by God to take the good news to groups of people who never would have heard it otherwise heard.

The Greek word "progress" was used of Romans soldiers building roads where there were none for their armies to advance. Often, there would be thick brush that had to be cleared away for the armies to proceed. The soldiers would have to cut their way through it and build a road to advance the army. Paul is explaining that his imprisonment cut a way through the obstacles to provide a path for the good news.

He was able to make a pioneer advance of the gospel in the city because he saw himself as an ambassador in chains to all who surrounded him.

Ephesians 6:20
For which I am an ambassador in chains; that in it I may speak boldly, as I ought to speak.

When Paul arrived in Rome, He was not jailed but had to rent a place and was guarded the emperor's own soldiers.

THE PERSECUTION OF THE SAINTS AND HOW TO OVERCOME IT

Acts 28:16
When we entered into Rome, the centurion delivered the prisoners to the captain of the guard, but Paul was allowed to stay by himself with the soldier who guarded him.

First, Paul shared the gospel with the Praetorian guards to whom he was chained.

Philippians 1:13
So that it became evident to the whole palace guard, and to all the rest, that my bonds are in Christ.

The guards would have to listen to the gospel day after day.

Second, the good news infiltrated into the very palace of the emperor himself (his home and his offices).

Philippians 4:22
All the saints [Christians] greet you, especially those who are of Caesar's household.

Notice, Paul mentions the new believers in the household of Caesar. How would they have heard unless Paul told them.

Third, Paul was able to wake up a sleeping church. The church in Rome had been silenced due to social pressure.

Philippians 1:14
And that most of the brothers in the Lord, being confident through my bonds, are more abundantly bold to speak the word of God without fear.

Because of Paul's boldness, the saints were also emboldened to once again share their faith. Many Romans now heard the word because of Paul's example. This was a pioneer advance of the gospel into their lives.

Fourth, we know through Pauls' letter to Philemon, that Paul encountered a runaway slave named Onesimus. We do not know the exact circumstances that led to Paul sharing the gospel with him, but we do know he did and Onesimus came to Christ Jesus.

Philemon 1:10
I beg you for my child, whom I have become the father of in my chains, Onesimus.

This newborn Christian ministered alongside Paul for quite some time and the apostle desired to keep him. Finally, Paul had to return him to his master, Philemon. Since Paul also brought him to Christ, Philemon might be willing to forego the usual punishment of branding or death if Paul pleaded for the converted slave.

In his letter, the apostle describes the pioneer advance of the gospel in the slave's life.

Philemon 1:15-16
For perhaps he was therefore separated from you for a while, that you would have him forever, no longer as a slave, but more than a slave, a beloved brother, specially to me, but how much rather to you...in the flesh...in the Lord.

Fifth, since he could have visitors, Paul met with many Jews during that time. Some came to a saving faith in Jesus Christ through his presentation of the gospel.

Acts 28:23-24
When they had appointed him a day, they came to him into his lodging in great number. He [Paul] explained to them, testifying about the kingdom of God, and persuading them concerning Jesus, both from the law of Moses and from the prophets, from morning until evening. Some believed...and some disbelieved.

Acts 28:30-31
Paul stayed two whole years in his own rented house, and received all who went in...preaching the kingdom of God, and teaching the things concerning the Lord...with all boldness, without hindrance.

While imprisoned, Paul was able to meet with numerous people and had won many of them to Christ.

Without this pioneer advance of the gospel in their lives through Paul's persecution, how would they have heard? Here again, God's sovereignty takes full control and works out all the circumstances so these Jews could come to Christ.

So, if persecution comes, we must ask ourselves if God has placed us in a situation to share the gospel with some who would never have heard the gospel otherwise.

A Ministry Consequence

When believers decide to become active in their faith by sharing the gospel and building Christians up, persecution will be the natural result. Many times, Jesus warned His disciples of this persecution to come. If we shine our lights, the darkness will retaliate.

Matthew 10:16-17
Behold, I send you forth as sheep in the midst of wolves. Therefore be wise as serpents, and harmless as doves. But beware of men: for they will deliver you up to councils, and in their synagogues they will scourge you.

He uses the analogy of wolves preying on sheep to devour them. These spiritual wolves will attack them as viciously as real wolves attack unsuspecting innocent sheep. He did not want them to be unaware of their attacks but prepared. They were to handle these wolves as snakes would with great caution, shrewdness, and wisdom. Essentially, they were aware of the danger and wise about dealing with it. Yet, no matter how much they desired to retaliate against them, they were never to respond with evil.

Jesus goes on to explain that this will occur while they are in ministry not when they are sitting in their houses doing absolutely nothing for God.

Matthew 10:21-23
Brother will deliver up brother to death, and the father his child. Children will rise up against parents, and cause them to be put to death. You will be hated by all men for my name's sake, but he who endures…the same will be saved. But when they persecute you in this city, flee into the next, for most assuredly I tell you, you will not have gone through the cities of Israel, until the Son of Man has come.

Paul, Peter, and the others were constantly experiencing persecution because they were active in ministry. In order to stand our ground, Christians must understand that all of this is in the plan of God and God is in control. We are required to obey God amid chaos and find comfort in the Scriptures.

A Willingness to Suffer

From the moment we became Christians, the possibility of persecution became a reality. In fact, in the parable of the seeds, Jesus describes the seed of the gospel being scorched by the heat of persecution and finally dying.

In His parable, the Lord Jesus Christ describes a farmer that throws seeds he desires to see grow among the rocks and then describes what happens to them.

THE PERSECUTION OF THE SAINTS AND HOW TO OVERCOME IT

Matthew 23:5-6
Others fell on rocky ground, where they didn't have much soil, and immediately they sprang up, because they had no depth of Earth. When the sun had risen, they were scorched. Because they had no root, they withered away.

Here, Jesus explains the true meaning of this important and powerful parable to His disciples. The men needed to fully understand what it took to be a kingdom member.

Matthew 23:20-21
What was sown on the rocky places, this is he who hears the word and immediately with joy receives it; yet he has no root in himself, but endures for a while. When oppression or persecution arises because of the word, immediately he stumbles.

The person whose faith is not deep enough to save, stumbles and falls away when persecution comes. Why? They were unwilling to suffer for the Lord.

We know this because only the last seed which produced fruit represented the truly saved. Jesus describes the seed in the good soil.

Matthew 23:8
Others fell on good soil and yielded fruit: some one hundred times as much, some sixty, and some thirty.

The Lord Jesus explains this seed and soil to His disciples so they could understand the important truths concerning the fruits all God's children produce.

Matthew 23:23
What was sown on the good ground, this is he who hears the word and understands it, who most certainly bears fruit and produces, some one hundred times as much, some sixty, and some thirty."

So, true believers have good soil where the seed is deep and when persecution comes, they are willing to suffer for the Lord and stand against the onslaught. Sometime after Peter's great declaration that Jesus was the Christ, the Son of the Living God, the Lord Jesus began to predict His future suffering and death.

Matthew 16:21
From that time, Jesus began to show his disciples that he must go to Jerusalem...suffer many things from the elders, chief priests, and scribes, and be killed, and the third day be raised up.

Immediately Peter rebuked the Lord for even the thought of this.

Matthew 16:22
Peter took him aside and began to rebuke him, saying, "Far be it from you, Lord! This will never be done to you."

The Lord responded firmly with His own rebuke.

Matthew 16:23
But he turned and said to Peter, "Get behind me, Satan! You are a stumbling block to me, for you are not setting your mind on the things of God, but on the things of men."

Then the Lord Jesus instructed the disciples concerning their attitudes toward suffering.

Matthew 16:24-27
Then Jesus said to his disciples, "If anyone desires to come after me, let him deny himself, take up his cross, and follow me. For whoever desires to save his life will lose it, and whoever will lose his life for my sake will find it. For what will it profit a man if he gains the whole world and forfeits his life? Or what will a man give in exchange for his life? For the Son of Man will come in the

glory of his Father with his angels, and then he will render to everyone according to his deeds."

In essence, Jesus is stating that the true believer will have to be willing to deny himself, take up the cross of persecution and suffering that He had, and follow Him. Christians have to be willing to lose their Earthly lives in persecution and even death. Then, they will gain new lives in heaven with Christ. What's the point of gaining all that the world has to offer and then losing their eternity in hell?

In this chapter, we have discovered that God is sovereign over all that goes on in our lives including persecution. In fact, He has sacred purposes for our suffering on behalf of His Son. We learned that it is the divine manifestation that Christ is alive and in our hearts. Also, it identifies us as His and His alone. It is the display of our divine fellowship as we partner with Christ for the advance of the gospel. We saw that we are part of a long history of suffering for Him and it keeps Christians on the move to advance the gospel in new places. Then, we studied the concept that persecution is the natural consequence of sharing the gospel. Finally, we have come to understand that believers must be willing to suffer for Christ which is a part of the fruits of the true seed of salvation planted in their hearts.

STANDING YOUR GROUND

Chapter 5

Beware of Satan's Schemes

Our persecution originates with Satan and his demons. In Revelation, John refers to Lucifer and "his angels." These are the fallen angels that chose to follow Lucifer in his rebellion. They became "his" angels and now rank under him.

Revelation 12:9
The great dragon was thrown down, the old serpent, he who is called the Devil and Satan, the deceiver of the whole world. He was thrown down to the Earth, and his angels were thrown down with him.

He and they have great power as angels, but they are no match for God. We see in Job 1-2, that this evil serpent was able to control the winds, send fire from the skies, influence powerful armies, strike humans with illness, and kill any creature except other angels. Therefore, they are formidable, powerful beings.

Job 1:14-19
That there came a messenger to Job, and said, "The oxen were plowing, and the donkeys feeding beside them, and the Sabeans attacked, and took them away. Yes, they have killed the servants with the edge of the sword, and I alone have escaped to tell you." While he was still speaking, there also came another, and said, "The fire of God has fallen from the sky, and has burned up the sheep and the servants, and consumed them, and I alone have escaped to tell you." While he was still speaking, there came also another, and said, "The Chaldeans made three bands, and swept down on the camels, and have taken them away, yes, and killed the servants with the edge of the sword; and I alone have escaped to tell

you." While he was still speaking, there came also another, and said, "Your sons and your daughters [Job's] were eating and drinking wine in their oldest brother's house...behold, there came a great wind from the wilderness, and struck the four corners of the house, and it fell on the young men, and they are dead...."

Job 2:7-8
So Satan went out from the presence of Yahweh, and struck Job with painful sores from the sole of his foot to his head. He took for himself a potsherd to scrape himself with, and he sat among the ashes.

In Ephesians 6, Paul makes it clear that these powerful, fallen angels are our real enemies. They are a well-organized group of beings with levels of rank and responsibility. Every Christian must understand that Lucifer will not allow the unsaved to leave his evil domain without a fight. The Devil's strategy is to oppose all that God is doing in and through us (especially those living seriously for the Lord).

Ephesians 6:11-12
Put on the whole armor of God, that you [believers] may be able to stand against the wiles of the devil. For our wrestling is not against flesh and blood but against the principalities, against the [angelic] powers, against the world's rulers of the darkness of this age [the last days], and against the spiritual hosts of wickedness in the heavenly places.

Notice, Paul says the Devil has "wiles." These are "cunning arts, trickery, and deceit." Also, Lucifer and his dark minions throw fiery projectiles at us. In battle, the enemy would light these objects on fire before throwing them.

Ephesians 6:16
Above all, taking up the shield of faith, with which you will be able to quench all the fiery darts [also arrow, javelin] of the evil one.

Paul wrote to the Thessalonians that he had a great desire to see them, but Satan intervened. In his second letter to the Corinthians, he spoke of Satan's wicked schemes.

1 Thessalonians 2:17-18
But we, brothers, being bereaved of you for a short season, in presence, not in heart, tried even harder to see your face with great desire, because we wanted to come to you -- indeed, I, Paul, once and again -- but Satan hindered us.

2 Corinthians 2:11
That no advantage may be gained over us by Satan; for we are not ignorant of his schemes.

Paul knew the many schemes and flaming missiles of the Devil that were aimed toward those who know Jesus Christ.

As only an evil serpent can do, he will spit out his venom until he is finally vanquished into the lake of fire for all eternity.

Revelation 20:10
The devil who deceived them was thrown into the lake of fire and sulfur, where are also the beast and the false prophet. They will be tormented day and night forever and ever.

The following are some of the schemes Satan has developed in his wicked opposition to God's kingdom from the very beginning as he persecutes God's people to prevent them from bringing others into the kingdom of the Son.

The Attempt to Destroy the Messiah

Satan attempted to destroy the Messiah who would fulfill the plan of redemption. It began with Herod. After speaking to the wise men, he determined that the Messiah must have been born within two years of their arrival. Herod ordered all the Hebrew children who were under two years of age to be slaughtered.

Matthew 2:16
Then Herod, when he saw that he was mocked by the wise men, was exceedingly angry, and sent forth, and killed all the male children who were in Bethlehem, and in all the surrounding countryside, from two years old and under, according to the exact time which he had learned from the wise men.

Was the Devil behind all of this? Of course, he was. The next recorded incident occurred at the temptation.

In Matthew 4, the Devil appeared to the Lord Jesus in the wilderness and tempted Him in His humanity. He wanted to give Jesus Christ an easy way out from the pain and torment of the wretched cross. This would destroy God's eternal plan of redemption.

Matthew 4:1-3
Then Jesus was led up by the Spirit into the wilderness to be tempted by the devil. When he had fasted forty days and forty nights, he was hungry afterward. The tempter came and said to him, "If you are the Son of God, command that these stones become bread."

During His ministry, the Lord was constantly hounded by Jewish leaders attempting to destroy His witness. They were constantly accusing the Lord of teaching precepts contrary to Moses.

Matthew 19:3
Pharisees came to him, testing him, and saying, "Is it lawful for a man to divorce his wife for any reason?"

They viewed the Lord's actions as breaking the law.

Matthew 12:1-7
At that time, Jesus went on the Sabbath day through the grain fields. His disciples were hungry and began to pluck heads of grain and to eat. But the Pharisees, when they saw it, said to him, "Behold, your disciples do what is not lawful to do on the Sabbath." But he said to them, "Haven't you read what David did, when he was hungry, and those who were with him; how he entered into the house of God, and ate the show bread, which was not lawful for him to eat, neither for those who were with him, but only for the priests? Or have you not read in the law, that on the Sabbath day, the priests in the temple profane the Sabbath, and are guiltless? But I tell you that one greater than the temple is here. But if you had known what this means, 'I [God] desire mercy...not sacrifice,' you would not have condemned the guiltless."

He was accused of doing the works of demons using the power of their leader the Devil.

Matthew 12:24
But when the Pharisees heard it, they said, "This man does not cast out demons, except by Beelzebul, the prince of the demons."

These men pursued Jesus to find something against Him.

In John 8, the Lord's response spoke right to the issue. The Lord pronounced that they were of their father the Devil and they were being used by Satan to destroy Christ's work.

John 8:44
You are of your father [like a father], the Devil, and you want to do the desires of your father. He was a murderer from the beginning, and doesn't stand in the truth, because there is no truth in him. When he speaks a lie, he speaks on his own; for he is a liar, and its father.

Unfortunately, the serpent had fooled them into thinking they were serving God.

The Attempt to Influence the Disciples

The Serpent sought to influence the disciples of the Lord. In Matthew 16, Jesus declared that He would suffer, be killed, and be raised up on the third day. Peter disagreed.

Matthew 16:22-23
Peter took him aside, and began to rebuke him, saying, "Far be it from you, Lord! This will never be done to you." But he turned, and said to Peter, "Get behind me, Satan! You are a stumblingblock to me, for you are not setting your mind on the things of God, but the things of men."

He declared that this would never happen. Christ's reply was to rebuke the Devil who was behind Peter's remark.

In Luke 22, Jesus Christ told Peter that Satan had asked God, the Father, permission to sift him like wheat. The Devil desired to put Peter and the disciples to the test.

Luke 22:31-32
The Lord said, "Simon, Simon, behold, Satan asked to have you, that he might sift you as wheat, but I prayed for you, that your faith wouldn't fail...when once you have turned again, establish your brothers."

Then Jesus comforted Peter with the knowledge that He had prayed for him. After he turned back to the Lord, Peter was to strengthen his brothers. This "sifting" was presented to Peter in the form of questions relating to whether he knew Jesus or not. Being fearful, Peter denied that he knew Jesus three times fulfilling the prophecy.

Luke 22:34
He said, "I tell you, Peter, the rooster will by no means crow today, before you deny that you know me three times."

Satan's ultimate attempt was his possession of Judas, one of the twelve, who betrayed the Lord Jesus.

John 13:27
After the morsel, then Satan entered into him. Jesus therefore said to him, "What you do, do quickly."

Judas was used to aid the Jews in killing the Lord.

Psalm 22:11-13
Don't be far from me, for trouble is near. For there is none to help. Many bulls have surrounded me. Strong bulls...have encircled me. They [demons] open their mouths wide against me, Lions tearing prey and roaring.

This only led to victory when Christ resurrected. Satan had bruised the Messiah on the heel, and Christ had crushed him on the head, as was predicted.

Genesis 3:15
I will put enmity between you and the woman, and between your offspring and her offspring. He will bruise your head, and you will bruise his heel.

The saints may face similar attacks of the Devil. We all must be prepared to stand firm against them.

The Preparation of an Opposing Plan

Satan created his own false messiahs from the dispersion at Babylon throughout history.

Luke 21:8
He said, "Watch out that you don't get led astray, for many will come in my name, saying, 'I AM,' and, 'The time is at hand.'" Therefore don't follow them.

Lucifer and his demons created their own fake religions.

2 Corinthians 11:4-5
For if he who comes preaches another Jesus, whom we did not preach, or if you receive a different spirit, which you did not receive, or a different gospel, which you did not accept, you put up with that well enough. For I reckon that I am not at all behind the very best apostles.

He also sent his own false prophets to proclaim his lies and deceive God's people.

Matthew 24:11
Many false prophets will arise, and will lead many astray.

His counterattack against Jesus Christ, His gospel, and His apostles are his own counterfeits. He creates prophets and teachers that sound like believers.

In 2 Corinthians 11, the apostle Paul asserts that Satan disguises himself to look exactly like an angel of light.

2 Corinthians 11:14-15
And no wonder, for even Satan masquerades [disguises] as an angel of light...his ministers...masquerade as [God's] servants of righteousness, whose end will be according to their works.

So, the devil dresses himself up to appear just a minister of truth and dresses his servants up the same way. His strategy is simple. While the true light is shining, he will put up false lights all around the true one.

These are the ones involved in false religions today. They have their own beliefs, history, traditions, and practices and mock the true church. If given the chance some of them would destroy every Christian on the face of the Earth. Some in the name of their god look forward to a day when all Christians are subservient to them.

In 1 John 4, John declares that the demon spirits behind all of these false religions are from the world.

1 John 4:5
They are of the world. Therefore they speak of the world, and the world hears them.

They speak as from this system and the world listens to them. Those who do not know the Lord are truly listening to them. When authentic Christians inevitably encounter the unbeliever, Satan will be trying to draw them away with his own false prophets and then Christians will be persecuted.

The Perversion of the True Gospel

Not only does the Devil propagate his own gospel outside the church but attempts to pervert the true gospel inside the church.

In Galatia, false teachers had entered the church claiming that the Gentile Christians had to become circumcised and keep certain tenets of the law to be saved.

Galatians 1:6-7
I marvel that you are so quickly deserting him who called you in the grace of Christ to a different gospel; and there isn't another gospel. Only there are some who trouble you, and want to pervert the gospel of Christ.

Here, Paul asserts this was not a different gospel, but an alteration or perversion of the real gospel. This was not a different gospel, but a heresy of the true one.

In 2 Peter 2, Peter spoke of these false prophets who had come and had secretly introduced destructive heresies.

2 Peter 2:1
But there also arose false prophets among the people, as among you also there will be false teachers, who will secretly bring in destructive heresies, denying...the Master who bought them, bringing on themselves swift destruction.

In Acts 20, Paul warned the elders at Ephesus that men would rise from among them and speak an alternate gospel.

Acts 20:30
Men will arise from among your...selves, speaking perverse things, to draw away the disciples after them.

In Jude 4, Jude, the half-brother of Jesus, describes some ungodly men who had secretly crept into the church. They turned God's grace into indecency and denied the Savior. These were perversions of the gospel.

Jude 1:4
For there are certain men who crept in secretly, even those who were long ago written about for this condemnation: ungodly men, turning the grace of our God into indecency, and denying our only Master, God, and Lord, Jesus Christ.

In Paul's second letter to Timothy, he describes the empty chatter and ungodliness of Hymenaeus and Philetus. Paul did not often name names unless the words and deeds were public and so outrageous that they deserved to face a public rebuke which these two men did.

2 Timothy 2:17-18
And their word [of false teachers] will consume like gangrene, of whom is Hymenaeus and Philetus; men who have erred concerning the truth, saying that the resurrection [from the dead] is already past, and overthrowing the faith of some.

They claimed the resurrection from the dead had already occurred, which had affected the faith of some Christians. He was worried that their error (perversion of the gospel) would spread much like gangrene. There will be those who present themselves as true Christian evangelists and will set about perverting the truth of God.

The Disruption of Evangelistic Efforts

Satan disrupts the saint's evangelistic efforts. This serpent accomplishes this evil activity in numerous ways. Paul was sent a difficult thorn in the flesh, which was most likely something physical like his eyesight. It seems reasonable because something other than a physical malady would not have been life long. His thorn was life long. He called this "thorn" a messenger of Satan.

2 Corinthians 12:7
By reason of the exceeding greatness of the revelations, that I should not be exalted excessively, there was given to me a thorn in the flesh, a messenger of Satan to buffet me, that I should not be exalted excessively.

Satan might send someone to counteract what Christians say, such as Elymas, the court magician. This worker of evil interrupted Paul's gospel testimony to Sergius Paulus. In Acts 13, the apostle was traveling throughout the island and preaching the gospel. The court magician could not let them near Sergius and lose his own status and opposed him.

Acts 13:8
But Elymas the sorcerer (for so is his name by interpretation) withstood them, seeking to turn aside the proconsul from the faith.

The evil one can send one of his emissaries to wrongly associate with believers, such as the demon-possessed slave girl in Philippi. She followed Paul and his other companions everywhere they went making declarations about them. She would shout that they were the servants of God proclaiming the way to salvation.

This was a true statement, but the Devil was attempting to associate their ministry with her wicked fortune telling. This would confuse people and dim the light of the gospel. People would think Paul and his companions were just like her and reject the gospel based on her poor reputation. Paul became so annoyed that He decided to cast the demon out of her once and for all.

Acts 16:16-18
It happened, as we were going to prayer, that a certain girl having a spirit [demon] of divination met us, who brought her masters much [financial] gain by fortune telling. The same, following after Paul and us, cried out, "These men are servants of the Most High God, who proclaim to us the way of salvation!" This she [slave] did for many days. But Paul, becoming distressed, turned and said to the spirit, "I charge you in the name of Jesus Christ to come out of her!" It came out that very hour.

In 2 Thessalonians 2, this fake god and constant accuser of the brethren, will send false believers into our paths.

2 Thessalonians 2:1-2
Now we beg you, brothers, concerning the coming of our Lord Jesus Christ, and our gathering together to him, to the end that you won't be quickly shaken in your mind, nor yet be troubled,

either by spirit, or by word, or by letter as from us, saying that the day of Christ had come.

This is exactly what happened in Thessalonica, and they led many astray. These false believers had a false gospel which deceived them.

He will slander these Christians and shed doubt on much of their credibility. They will mistreat and harass them.

Galatians 1:10
For am I now seeking the favor of men, or of God? Or am I striving to please men? For if I were still pleasing men, I wouldn't be a servant of Christ.

2 Corinthians 11:5
For I [Paul] reckon that I am not at all behind the very best apostles.

Philippians 1:28-30
And in nothing frightened by the adversaries, which is for them a proof of destruction, but to you of salvation, and that from God. Because it has been granted to you on behalf of Christ, not only to believe in him, but also to suffer on his behalf, having the same conflict which you saw in me, and now hear is in me.

The evil one controls a myriad of demons to carry out these disruptions. The church must test these spirits.

1 John 4:1
Beloved, don't believe every spirit, but test the spirits, whether they are of God, because many false prophets have gone out into the world.

Paul declares that some Christians will fall away and follow the teachings of deceitful spirits and demons.

1 Timothy 4:1
But the Spirit says expressly that in later times some will fall away from the faith, paying attention to seducing spirits and doctrines of demons.

Believers should be careful in their many associations with others as they share the gospel. Some might have been sent from the Devil as one of his many schemes to interrupt their presentations of the truth. This is a more subtle form of persecution. They cannot afford to allow this evil deceiver to outwit them. Believers can never underestimate the schemes of Satan as he works in the lives of his unbelievers. We, as saints, must constantly realize that this demonic serpent is not omnipotent, omnipresent, or omniscient as their God is. Yet, he is still an extremely powerful angel. They cannot afford to overestimate his power, or underestimate God's sovereignty.

Christians must take this knowledge about the Devil to heart. They should not be foolish enough to think that Satan is going to allow them to walk into his domain and pull his subjects out of his domain without opposition. There will be a battle for the souls of those who hear the gospel. We will be of good courage because the victory is ours. Therefore, we will stand our ground against opposition.

Chapter 6

Counter with a Holy Action

Now, we come to the first of our numerous reactions to persecution. These are responses that should be made when our persecutors are not intending physical harm to ourselves or others. These acts to counter persecution are to be taken when our abuse for Christ is somewhat minor and cannot be avoided. If Christians are taken captive or restricted in their activities, these are the attitudes and actions they may take. These acts of love come from the teachings of Jesus on how to treat our enemies. The reactions we must have toward persecutors are the same as the ones we are to have toward our enemies. They comprise the same group. Our enemies will persecute us and those who persecute us will be our enemies. The Lord taught that His people are to love, bless, do good to, pray for, not resist, and forgive their enemies. We do not behave out of hate, anger, or revenge.

One of the purposes of the instruction of the Lord was to present God's true intent behind the divine law to Israel. God's offspring completely misunderstood His intent in the law because they had over time reinterpreted and added so many additional mandates to His righteous commandments. Then, they attempted daily to meticulously obey these man-made decrees or ordinances. This produced in them a false sense of righteousness. Their intent and motives could be evil as long as their outward actions appeared devout. He intended to correct this false notion by properly interpreting the law from God's point of view which had been lost. This required preaching God's true commandments and then to properly interpret them. The original intent behind the Lord God's ordinances had to be restored.

STANDING YOUR GROUND

In Matthew 5:38-45 and Luke 6:27-36, Jesus challenges two of the decrees. One decree was "Take an eye for and eye, and a tooth for a tooth." Another of the decrees was "Love your neighbor and hate your enemies." All of the first precept and the first part of the second precept came directly from the Old Testament. The second part of the second maxim was added essentially through human logic. In the first saying, the Jews misinterpreted God's law and His intent behind the law. In the second, the Jews added a part He did not intend.

Matthew 5:38-45
You have heard that it was said, "An eye for an eye, and a tooth for a tooth." But I tell you, don't resist him who is evil; but whoever strikes you on your right cheek, turn to him the other also. If any man would go to law with you and take away your coat, let him have your cloak also. Whoever compels you to go one mile, go with him two. Give to him who asks you, and don't turn away him who desires to borrow from you. You have heard that it was said, "You shall love your neighbor, and hate your enemy." But I tell you, love your enemies, bless those who curse you, do good to those who hate you, and pray for those who spitefully use you and persecute you, that you may be sons of your Father who is in heaven. For he makes his sun to rise on the evil and the good, and sends rain on the just and the unjust.

Luke 6:27-36
But I tell you who hear, love your enemies, do good to those who hate you, bless those who curse you, and pray for those who insult you. To him who strikes you on the cheek, offer also the other; and from him who takes away your cloak, don't withhold your coat also. Give to everyone who asks you, and don't ask him who takes away your goods to give them back again. As you desire that men should do to you, likewise do to them also. If you love those who love you, what credit is that to you? For even sinners love those who love them. If you do good to those who do good to you, what

credit is that to you? For even sinners do the same. If you lend to those from whom you hope to receive, what credit is that to you? Even sinners lend to sinners, to receive back as much. But love your enemies, and do good, and lend, expecting nothing back; and your reward will be great, and you will be sons of the Most High; for he is kind toward the unthankful and evil. Therefore, be merciful, even as your Father is also merciful.

Once properly interpreted by Jesus, God's people were given the appropriate reactions they should take when any minor persecution comes their way. In them, Jesus describes the relationship that believers should maintain amid their persecutors, enemies, and unbelievers even if they must take the more drastic action discussed in future chapters.

The concept of "an eye for an eye" comes from three Old Testament passages.

Exodus 21:23
But if any harm follows, then you must take life for life.

Leviticus 24:19-20
If a man cause a blemish in his neighbor; as he has done, so shall it be done to him: breach for breach, eye for eye, tooth for tooth; as he has caused a blemish in a man, so shall it be rendered to him.

Deuteronomy 19:21
Your eyes shall not pity; life [shall go] for life, eye for eye, tooth for tooth, hand for hand, foot for foot.

These were judicial laws set up for the nation of Israel to govern its people. They were not to be moral precepts for individuals to follow in their relationships and dealings with others. The context of each of these passages simply involves dispensing justice by society. The moral precepts involved dispensing love by individuals.

The concept of "love your neighbor" is also found in the Old Testament, but without the second part.

Leviticus 19:18
You shall not take vengeance, nor bear any grudge against the children of your people; but you shall love your neighbor as yourself: I am Yahweh.

That second part was added later by the Jewish leaders.

God commands that the individual not take vengeance, but instead, should love his neighbor. They disregarded the first portion and added instead "hate your enemies" as the logical conclusion. This allowed them to hate anyone who was against them and more importantly authorized them to hate in God's name.

To love, bless, do good to, pray for, meet the needs of, and forgive someone's enemies are difficult tasks, something opposite to how the world would respond. Just before Jesus uttered these commandments Matthew 5, the Lord made a powerful statement to the Jewish people.

Matthew 5:19-20
Whoever, therefore, shall break [disobey] one of these least commandments, and teach others to do so, shall be called least in the Kingdom of Heaven; but whoever shall do and teach them shall be called great in the Kingdom of Heaven. For I tell you, that unless your righteousness exceeds that of the scribes and Pharisees, there is no way you shall enter into the Kingdom of Heaven.

Jesus declared that unless their righteousness exceeded the Scribes and the Pharisees, they could not possibly inherit the kingdom of heaven. God's standards are far higher than any of man's, in fact higher than the highest of his man-made standards.

Jesus explained in Matthew 5:45 and Luke 6:31-35, the five reasons why Christians need to take the much higher path of righteousness, even towards enemies. We must remember that these are supernatural acts instigated by the Spirit in us.

The Display of God's Character

First, Jesus explained to believers that loving their enemies constantly demonstrates that they are children of God. In Matthew 5:45, He asserts believers do these things that they may be children of their heavenly Father. Children act like their parent.

Matthew 5:45
That you may be children of your Father who is in heaven. For he makes his sun to rise on the evil and the good, and sends rain on the just and the unjust.

Second, loving enemies is a quality or characteristic of God Himself. Jesus goes on to present in the same verse that God makes the sun rise and rain fall to bless all people both the just and unjust.

Matthew 5:45
That you may be children of your Father who is in heaven. For he makes his sun to rise on the evil and the good, and sends rain on the just and the unjust.

Third, saints should be holier than unbelievers. In verses 46-47, the Lord Jesus explains that even the tax-gatherers (a hated, heathen group) love people who love them and greet their friends.

In the parallel passage in Luke 6, Jesus extends this doing good even to lending.

Luke 6:34
If you lend to those from whom you hope to receive, what credit is that to you? Even sinners lend to sinners, to receive back as much.

Jesus pointed out that even sinners lend to those who they know will return what was borrowed. The love of Christians for enemies requires love at a supernatural level.

Fourth, a believer's reward for loving his enemies will be great. Jesus implies in Matthew 5:46, that there is not much reward in Christians loving those who love them. In Luke 6:35, He says that if the saints love their enemies, do good to them, and lend to them expecting nothing in return, then their reward will be great.

Matthew 5:46
For if you love those who love you, what reward do you have? Don't even the tax collectors do the same?

Luke 6:35
But love your enemies, and do good, and lend, expecting nothing back; and your reward will be great, and you will be sons of the Most High; for he is kind toward the unthankful and evil.

Fifth, the children of God are to imitate their Father. In these two passages the Lord says that they are to be perfect and merciful as their Father God is perfect and merciful.

Matthew 5:48
Therefore you shall be perfect, just as your Father...is perfect.

Luke 6:36
Therefore be merciful, even as your Father is also merciful.

Sixth, this is a part of a believer's testimony to the world. Even before these words, Jesus teaches us that we should be salt and shining lights to all. As people witness our behavior toward them, they will see God's character displayed.

Matthew 5:13-16
You are the salt of the Earth, but if the salt has lost its flavor, what will it be salted with? It is then good for nothing, but to be cast out and trodden under the feet of men. You are the light of the world. A city set on a hill can't be hid. Neither do you light a lamp, and put it under a bushel basket, but on a stand; and it shines to all who are in the house. Even so, let your light shine before men; that they may see your good works, and glorify your Father who is in heaven.

Our shining lights and savory salt always manifest God's person, purpose, and power to the world. Christians exhibit His person in that these are His characteristics, not man's. They portray His purpose since men can so clearly see He exists and loves all men. They display His power because these actions require supernatural power to exhibit. Since unsaved people will see His person, purpose, and power in their Christian lives, they will know these believers are from the one true God. This prepares their hearts to fully hear His saving message.

These lights must continually shine even in the face of persecution and enemy attack. This salt must continually remain tasty even in the midst of mistreatment and enemy opposition. When Christians are tormented, harassed, and cursed for Christ's sake, they do not respond with revenge and retaliation, which is a human approach. Instead, they are to react in love, blessing, good works, prayer, meeting needs (not resisting), and forgiveness. In this, God is manifested, the good news can be presented, and God's power to save lives will be unleashed. Unbelievers will be able to identify Christians as the ones who have the true God in their lives.

We see these principles in other passages of the Bible as well. To love, bless, do good to, pray for, not resist, and forgive one's enemies were declared by God Himself to Moses. In Exodus 34, the Lord shows the backside of His glory to His servant and declares His holy characteristics.

Exodus 34:6-7
Yahweh passed by before him, and proclaimed, "Yahweh! Yahweh, a merciful and gracious God, slow to anger, and abundant [bountiful, overflowing] in lovingkindness and truth, keeping lovingkindness for thousands [innumerable], forgiving iniquity and disobedience and sin; and that will by no means clear the guilty, visiting the iniquity of the fathers on the children, and on the children's children, on the third and on the fourth generation.

These attributes comprise His character. Even though men are in total rebellion against Him, God's character does not change. Whether men are enemies or children of God, they will experience His attributes (though not always in the same way). This does not mean that we are to be doormats and allow unbelievers to behave in any way they like toward us. God does not allow this and nor should we.

In Romans 1:19-20, Paul declared that God's deity, power, and attributes are clearly seen through his creation.

Romans 1:19-20
Because that which is known by God is revealed in them, for God revealed it to them. 20 For the invisible things of him since the creation of the world are clearly seen, being perceived through the things that are made, even his everlasting power and divinity; that they may be without excuse.

In Acts 14, the apostle Paul proclaims that God's creation also displays to the world His grace and mercy through the rain he provides.

Acts 14:17
Yet he didn't leave himself without witness, in that he did good and gave you rains from the sky and fruitful seasons, filling our hearts with food and gladness.

This rain produces fruitful seasons which will satisfy their hearts with food and with gladness. His blessing upon them in creation will prepare them for the gospel.

Christians are growing more and more into the image of Christ, they will find themselves more and more loving, blessing, doing good to, praying for, not resisting, and forgiving their enemies. This is due to the transformation of their thinking, speaking, feeling, and behaving into more and more Christlikeness. Paul discloses to the Corinthians that believers are beholding the glory of the Lord in a mirror and being transformed into the same image of Christ from glory to glory.

2 Corinthians 3:18
But we all, with unveiled face beholding as in a mirror the glory of the Lord, are transformed into the same image from glory to glory, even as from the Lord, the Spirit.

As we are being transformed, we are loving our enemies as Christ did. We are constantly growing in this critical area of the Christian life.

John has a similar thought regarding believers. In 1 John 2, John tells his readers that if Christians abide in Him, they ought to walk as He walked. Of course, this would involve His behavior toward His persecutors.

1 John 2:6
He who says he remains in him ought himself also to walk just like he walked.

In its simplest understanding, Christ loved His enemies and as we walk like Him, we will too.

In John 14, the apostle Paul indicates that true believers will obey this command. Why? The Lord Jesus explains that those who love Him will obey His many commands. They will display this love through their obedience.

John 14:15
If you love me, keep my commandments.

John 14:23
Jesus answered him, "If a man loves me, he will keep my word. My Father will love him, and we will come to him, and make our home with him."

They will walk as their Savior and Lord walked. They will demonstrate God's holy character and person and behave like Him toward their persecutors.

When His children come to share the good news, then unbelievers will know they are from God. Christians will behave like the God they know from His own creation and blessing. Even if they persecute them, the character of God's grace, mercy, love, and blessing will manifest itself through the words and actions of His children. Again, they will know that those who proclaim the gospel are truly from God and God alone.

In Matthew 5:44 and Luke 6:27, Jesus declares that the saints are to love their enemies.

Matthew 5:44
But I tell you, love your enemies, bless those who curse you, do good to those who hate you, and pray for those who spitefully use you and persecute you.

THE PERSECUTION OF THE SAINTS AND HOW TO OVERCOME IT

Luke 6:27
But I tell you who hear, love your enemies, do good to those who hate you.

In Romans 13, Paul explains that it is the responsibility of governing authorities to be avengers of God. They constitute God's own powers avengers of His wrath.

Romans 13:1-4
Let every soul be in subjection to the higher authorities, for there is no authority except from God, and those who be are ordained by God. Therefore...who resists...authority, withstands the ordinance of God; and those who withstand will receive to themselves judgment. For rulers are not a terror to the good work, but to the evil. Do you desire to have no fear of the authority? Do that which is good, and you will have praise from the same, for he is a servant of God to you for good. But if you do that which is evil, be afraid, for he doesn't bear the sword in vain; for he is a minister of God, an avenger for wrath to him who does evil.

Christians are to show love toward their enemies, and the government is to prosecute them for any harm or violation of the law done to believers. One is personal and the other is judicial. The personal precepts involve love. The judicial precepts involve justice. Saints do not avenge, nor bear any grudge, but love their neighbors as themselves.

This is first seen in the Old Testament in Leviticus 19 when God sets forth His laws that the people of Israel must follow. This was a fundamental principle of living which was to be obeyed.

Leviticus 19:18
You shall not take vengeance, nor bear any grudge against the children of your people...you shall love your neighbor as yourself: I am Yahweh.

In Romans 12, Paul quotes Moses in Deuteronomy 32 and fully reiterates the importance of not taking vengeance upon others, but letting God do His judicial work.

Romans 12:19
Don't seek revenge yourselves, beloved, but give place to God's wrath. For it is written, "Vengeance belongs to me; I will repay, says the Lord."

Deuteronomy 32:35
Vengeance is mine, and recompense, At the time when their foot shall slide: For the day of their calamity is at hand, The things that are to come on them shall make haste.

Here, the apostle clearly explains that vengeance belongs to God. It is His divine responsibility.

In 2 Thessalonians 1, Paul praises the Thessalonians for their patient endurance of the suffering of persecution which is a sign of the righteous judgment of God. He will repay their affliction.

2 Thessalonians 1:4-10
So that we ourselves boast about you in the assemblies of God for your patience and faith in all your persecutions and in the afflictions which you endure. This is an obvious sign of the righteous judgment of God, to the end that you may be counted worthy of the kingdom of God, for which you also suffer. Since it is a righteous thing with God to repay affliction to those who afflict you, and to give relief to you that are afflicted with us, when the Lord Jesus is revealed from heaven with his mighty angels in flaming fire, giving vengeance to those who don't know God, and to those who don't obey the gospel of our Lord Jesus, who will pay the penalty: eternal destruction from the face of the Lord and from the glory of his might, when he comes to be glorified in his saints, and to be admired among all...who have believed....that day.

When persecution comes and is somewhat minor and also unavoidable, then Christians should be concerned with the spiritual matters of their enemies first. How the saints treat unbelievers in the ways that have been discussed is critical. Christians may seek justice from their government and pray for justice also which will be dealt with later in this book.

Psalm 94:1-7
Yahweh, you God to whom vengeance belongs, You God to whom vengeance belongs, shine forth. Rise up, you judge of the Earth. Pay back the proud what they deserve. Yahweh, how long will the wicked, How long will the wicked triumph? They pour out arrogant words. All the evil-doers boast. They break your people in pieces, Yahweh, And afflict your heritage. They [evil-doers] kill the widow and the alien, And murder the fatherless. They say, "Yah will not see, Neither will Jacob's God consider."

Revelation 6:9-11
When he opened the fifth seal, I saw underneath the altar the souls of those who had been killed for the word of God, and for the testimony which they held. They cried with a loud voice, saying, "How long, Master, the holy and true, do you not judge and avenge our blood on those who dwell on the Earth?" There was given to each one of them a white robe. It was said to them that they should rest yet for a little time, until their fellow servants and their brothers, who would also be killed even as they were....

This does not imply that believers cannot defend themselves as the law allows. Though we answer to men, we answer to a higher authority who is God.

The Showing of Love

In Matthew 5:44 and Luke 6:27, Jesus explains Christians are to love their enemies, the ones who persecute them.

Matthew 5:44
But I tell you, love your enemies, bless those who curse you, do good to those who hate you, and pray for those who spitefully use you and persecute you.

Luke 6:27
But I tell you who hear, love your enemies, do good to those who hate you.

The word "love" in this simple passage is not the concept of romantic love, but something much deeper. The Greek word essentially means to value or prize someone or something. This word was utilized by Jesus and His disciples to speak of valuing to the point of sacrifice.

The classic use of the word is found in John 3:16, where Jesus asserts that God so loved the world that He gave His Son. God so valued the world that He gave, even though it was hostile to Him.

John 3:16
For God so loved the world, that he gave his one and only Son, that whoever believes in him should not perish, but have eternal life.

Christians are to so love the world that they also will give, even though it is hostile to them. Sacrificial giving is crucial in demonstrating this love to the world and distinguishing the true people of God from the false people of God. This also distinguishes the true gospel from the false gospel.

This coincides with the great commandments that Jesus acknowledged in Luke 10.

Luke 10:27
He [lawyer] answered, "You shall love the Lord your God...and your neighbor as yourself."

Men are to love God and love their neighbors as themselves. When a lawyer asked Him who truly was this neighbor, he referred to, Jesus told the story of the Good Samaritan in verses 30-36. This poignant story indicated that his neighbor went beyond all races, genders, and creeds to anyone in need. Even enemies of Christ's saints may be in need and would obviously be their neighbor. In the story, this Jewish man, who was robbed and beaten, was aided by a Samaritan man. The Samaritans and Jews hated each other and were enemies. However, as God's people love themselves, they are to love their enemies.

Luke 10:30-36
Jesus answered, "A... man was going down from Jerusalem to Jericho, and he fell among robbers, who both stripped him and beat him, and departed, leaving him half dead. By chance a certain priest was going down that way. When he saw him, he passed by on the other side. In the same way a Levite also, when he came to the place, and saw him, passed by on the other side. But a certain Samaritan, as he journeyed, came where he was. When he saw him, he was moved with compassion, came to him, and bound up his wounds, pouring on oil and wine. He set him on his own animal, and brought him to an inn, and took care of him. On the next day, when he departed, he took out two denarii, and gave them to the host, and said to him, 'Take care of him. Whatever you spend beyond that, I will repay you when I return.' Now which of these three [who passed by] do you think seemed to be a neighbor to him who fell among the robbers?"

This is also found in the Old Testament. In Proverbs 11, Solomon declares that despising one's neighbor displays a lack of wisdom. Later in Proverbs 14, he calls it sin.

Proverbs 11:12
One who despises his neighbor is void of wisdom, but a man of understanding holds his peace.

Proverbs 14:21
He who despises his neighbor sins, But blessed is he who has pity on the poor.

In Romans 13, Paul writes again that Christians are to owe nothing to anyone except to love one another.

Romans 13:8
Owe no one anything, except to love one another; for he who loves his neighbor has fulfilled the law.

Believers are to have only one debt toward their neighbors. This debt is to love them. This love fulfilled the law. If one summed up all God's commandments toward others, it would be to love one's neighbor, whether they are enemies or not.

No matter what kind of negative reactions Christians may receive from the world, unbelievers are to be loved by those saints, especially ones who become their enemies. The Lord desires all unbelievers to be valued, prized, and loved which issues forth in sacrifice as He did for us. Of course, there are many facets to this love.

The Giving of Blessings

Not only are Christians to love their enemies but are also to give a blessing to them. In the passages of Matthew 5:44 and Luke 6:28, believers are commanded to bless everyone who curses them. Providing a blessing was a very familiar concept in the Old Testament. It had a specific meaning that is important to note.

Luke 6:28
Bless those who curse you, and pray for those who insult you.

A typical kind of blessing is found in Ruth 2 when Boaz went out into his fields. When Boaz found his reapers, he greeted them with a particular expression.

Ruth 2:3-5
She went, and came and gleaned in the field after the reapers: and she happened to come to the portion of the field belonging to Boaz, who was of the family of Elimelech. Behold, Boaz came from Bethlehem, and said to the reapers, "Yahweh be with you." They answered him, "Yahweh bless you." Then said Boaz to his servant who was set over the reapers, "Whose young lady is this?"

This exchange of greetings was meaningful. This expressed the genuine and heartfelt desire that the other person would find safety and protection in God.

In Numbers 6, the Lord God told Moses to have Aaron bless the people of Israel with the words the Lord gave him to speak.

Numbers 6:22-27
Yahweh spoke to Moses, saying, "Speak to Aaron and to his sons, saying, 'This is how you shall bless the children of Israel.' You shall tell them, 'Yahweh bless you, and keep you. Yahweh make his face to shine on you, And be gracious to you. Yahweh lift up his face toward you, And give you peace.' So they shall put my name on the children of Israel; and I will bless them."

This was a general blessing which asked God to pour out His grace upon them. This would be common grace. This is the grace that He provides for believers and unbelievers. This does not refer to the exclusive blessings that are given to His children in Christ.

In Romans 12, Paul commands the church to bless those who persecute them and not curse them.

Romans 12:14
Bless those who persecute you; bless, and don't curse.

The apostle encourages Christians to give their persecutors and enemies a blessing like that of Boaz. The city of Rome was the seat of the Caesars. These despots were responsible for the persecution of saints using many horrific methods of terror. Martyrdom became a common way of life in many periods of this city's history. Yet, these saints were to bless their persecutors.

Paul endured many of these kinds of persecutions at the hand of the Jews and Gentiles. In 1 Corinthians 4, the apostle describes his response to those who cursed him. He would give a blessing in return.

1 Corinthians 4:12
We toil, working with our own hands. Being reviled, we bless. Being persecuted, we endure.

He would wish God's grace upon those who railed against him. Though his words could have been unkind; instead, he blessed them. Believers who are persecuted should provide a blessing upon their persecutors or enemies, both in their hearts and from their mouths.

It is important to note that this blessing for unbelievers will always be in light of the knowledge that God desires to forgive them as He forgave us if they repent. If they do not repent, then justice will eventually come to them, and we will be avenged. In light of these two scenarios, we can bless them because God is in control and will do what needs to be done. Perhaps, as we greet them, silently we would beg God in our hearts to work in their lives and bring them to His Son and if not, to avenge us. The saints who have been killed during the tribulation cry out for vengeance.

Revelation 6:9-11
When he opened the fifth seal, I saw underneath the altar the souls of those who had been killed for the Word of God, and for the testimony of the Lamb which they had. 10 They cried with a loud voice, saying, "How long, Master, the holy and true, until you judge and avenge our blood on those who dwell on the Earth?" A long white robe was given to each of them. They were told that they should rest yet for a while, until their fellow servants and their brothers, who would also be killed even as they were, should complete their course.

Here, we have the implication that God would avenge them when His plan had finally been accomplished. This will be discussed at length in another chapter.

The Doing of Good

Not only are all Christians to love and bless their enemies, but they are to do good to them. In Matthew 5:44 and Luke 6:27, all believers are commanded by the Lord Jesus to do good to those who hate them.

Matthew 5:44
But I tell you, love your enemies, bless those who curse you, do good to those who hate you, and pray for those who spitefully use you and persecute you.

Luke 6:27
But I tell you who hear, love your enemies, do good to those who hate you.

When His followers are seeking to do good works for God's glory, they should consider their enemies or persecutors as the recipients of their righteous deeds and aspirations. They can choose to do good to them as well as others.

In Acts 14, both Paul and Barnabas entered Lystra and healed a man who had been lame from birth. Thinking they were gods (Hermes and Zeus), the people responded by worshiping and making sacrifices to them.

Aghast by this inappropriate response, Paul and Barnabas tore their robes and declared to the crowd that they were mere men. Instead, they had come to proclaim the true God. It was time for the citizens of Lystra to turn toward the Lord who had been testifying to these people throughout history.

Acts 14:14-17
But when the apostles, Barnabas and Paul, heard of it, they tore their clothes, and sprang into the multitude, crying out, "Men, why are you doing these things? We also are men of like passions with you, and bring you good news, that you should turn from these vain things to the living God, who made the sky and the Earth and the sea, and all that is in them; who in the generations gone by allowed all the nations to walk in their own ways. Yet he didn't leave himself without witness, in that he did good and gave you[b] rains from the sky and fruitful seasons, filling our hearts with food and gladness."

Paul explains that the true deity, whom they represented, had been sending rain from heaven and producing fruitful seasons to satisfy their hearts with food and gladness.

In essence, the Lord's person, purpose, and power had been on display all along through His goodness. The point is that doing good to enemies is an important characteristic of the Lord God and believers are to behave in the same way with their persecutors. Once again, God pours His grace out on His enemies and so should we.

In John 5:29, Jesus pronounced that those who did good deeds would proceed to a resurrection of life.

THE PERSECUTION OF THE SAINTS AND HOW TO OVERCOME IT

John 5:29
And will come forth; those who have done good, to the resurrection of life; and those who have done evil, to the resurrection of judgment.

Paul teaches the same concept in Romans 2, when he wrote about glory, honor, and peace.

Romans 2:10
But glory and honor and peace to every man who works good, to the Jew first, and also to the Greek.

In Matthew 5, Jesus indicated that His people should let their light shine before men, so that all will see His goodness in them and glorify God.

Matthew 5:16
Even so, let your light shine before men; that they may see your good works, and glorify your Father who is in heaven.

Here, the term "men" would include his enemies.

In Ephesians 2, Paul views God's church as His divine workmanship, created in Christ Jesus for good works.

Ephesians 2:10
For we are his workmanship, created in Christ Jesus for good works [deeds], which God prepared before that we would walk in them.

Then he encourages his readers to walk in them. These good works must extend to persecutors, enemies, and unbelievers in general. We must do good to all men regardless of evil.

In 2 Peter 2, Peter commands Christian slaves with unruly and mean masters to be submissive with all respect.

2 Peter 2:18-20
For, uttering great swelling words of emptiness, they entice in the lusts of the flesh, by licentiousness, those who are indeed escaping from those who live in error; promising them liberty, while they themselves are bondservants of corruption; for by whom a man is overcome, by the same is he also brought into bondage. For if, after they have escaped the defilement of the world through the knowledge of the Lord and Savior...they are...entangled therein and overcome, the last state has become worse with them than the first.

The apostle argues that when these slaves, who believe in Jesus, suffer unjustly, yet submit and respect their masters, this finds favor with God. Would that not be a good work toward a persecutor or an enemy?

In Romans 15, the apostle exhorts all believers to bear the weaknesses of those who are weak and not just seek their own pleasure.

Romans 15:1-3
Now we who are strong ought to bear the weaknesses of the weak, and not to please ourselves. Let each one of us please his neighbor for that which is good, to be building him up. For Christ also didn't please himself. But, as it is written, "The reproaches of those who reproached you fell on me."

Then Paul provides a general principle. The saved are to please their neighbors (including enemies) for good and for their edification or building up. So, pleasing neighbors for their good is good works.

In chapter twelve, Paul asserts that the saints of God should overcome evil with good. This includes their enemies and persecutors. Why? Enemies and persecutors desire to bring evil upon believers; this should be overcome with much good works.

THE PERSECUTION OF THE SAINTS AND HOW TO OVERCOME IT

Romans 12:21
Don't be overcome by evil, but overcome evil with good.

In 1 Corinthians 10:24, he reiterates this command to the church in Corinth. Again, he writes that they are to seek the good of their neighbors (anyone in need). The implication is clear.

1 Corinthians 10:24
Let no one seek his own, but each one his neighbor's good.

So, a characteristic of true believers are good works, but not just to believers, but also persecutors, enemies, and anyone else.

In Galatians 6, Paul exhorted the Galatians to do good to all men, while they had the opportunity, especially ones of the household of the faith. The first priority of doing good is to other Christians and then to everyone.

Galatians 6:10
So then, as we have opportunity, let us work that which is good toward all men, and especially toward those who are of the household of the faith.

What do good deeds entail? John explains that loving the brethren involves these four essential parts: word, tongue, deed, and truth.

1 John 2:15
Don't love the world, neither the things that are in the world. If anyone loves the world, the Father's love isn't in him.

Doing good deeds towards a neighbor involve both good words and actions. Though this might be difficult in the humanity of Christians to conceive of speaking and acting good toward enemies, it has always been God's way. If He had not done good (sending His Son) to the saints though they were His enemies through unbelief, they would still be dead in their sins. So, believers do good to those who oppose them because God did the same for them.

The Offering of Prayer

Not only are all Christians to bless their enemies but pray for them. In Matthew 5:44 and Luke 6:28, Christians are told to pray for those who mistreat them and persecute them. This may not be easy but is what God desires.

Matthew 5:44
But I tell you, love your enemies, bless those who curse you, do good to those who hate you, and pray for those who spitefully use you and persecute you.

Luke 6:28
Bless those who curse you, and pray for those who insult you.

What should our prayer requests be for these enemies of ours? The first answer is their salvation.

In his first letter to Timothy, Paul tells his son in the faith to pray for all men. Why must Christians do this? Why is this so important?

1 Timothy 2:3-4
For this is good and acceptable in the sight of God our Savior; who desires all people to be saved and come to full knowledge of the truth.

God desires for men to be saved. Would this also include unbelievers? Of course, it would.

Before Christians believed in the Lord Jesus Christ, they were unbelievers, who may have reacted negatively to the gospel. The Bible has numerous accounts of formerly hostile unbelievers who eventually received the Lord. These became illustrations of God's person, purpose, and power. Since He sometimes calls unsaved persecutors to His Son, Christians need to pray for their salvation. The saints need to see them as lost and beg God to move their hearts to repent.

Nicodemus, the teacher of the Jews, began in John 3 with negative reactions to Jesus and His gospel. He is not spoken of again until John 19 when he brought the spices to anoint the dead body of the Lord Jesus.

John 19:39-42
Nicodemus also came, he who at first came to Jesus by night, bringing a mixture of myrrh and aloes, about a hundred Roman pounds. So they took Jesus' body, and bound it in linen cloths with the spices, as the custom of the Jews is to bury. Now in the place where he was crucified there was a garden. In the garden a new tomb in which no man had ever yet been laid. Then because of the Jews' Preparation (for the tomb was near at hand) they laid Jesus there.

Sometime between these two events, Nicodemus became a believer in Jesus. Before this, Nicodemus was an important member of the Sanhedrin. He must have participated in the variety of ways this Jewish council hounded, mocked, and discredited Jesus, which ultimately led to the murder of the Lord Jesus. This teacher of Israel reacted negatively at first, later he believed. Perhaps, the Lord prayed for Nicodemus when He went off to pray, though he was an enemy. He knew He would come to Him.

As has been noted, Paul was a vicious persecutor of the church. His negative reactions to the good news went to the furthest extremes against believers: tracking the newborn Christians, storming into their private homes, hauling off these innocent people, throwing these virtuous saints into prison, and eventually martyring them.

Acts 8:1-3
Saul was consenting to his death. A great persecution arose against the assembly which was in Jerusalem in that day. They were all scattered abroad throughout the regions of Judea and Samaria, except for the apostles. Devout men buried Stephen, and lamented greatly over him. But Saul ravaged the assembly, entering into every house, and dragged both men and women off to prison.

Acts 9:1-2
But Saul, still breathing threats and slaughter against the disciples of the Lord, went to the high priest, and asked for letters from him to the synagogues of Damascus, that if he found any who were of the Way, whether men or women, he might bring them bound to Jerusalem.

He began with negative reactions, lavishing in being both an enemy and persecutor of the church. Eventually, he came to Christ.

Acts 9:5
He said, "Who are you, Lord?" The Lord said, "I am Jesus, whom you are persecuting.

Perhaps, those believers who were fleeing from Saul prayed for his salvation.

Paul and the other apostles witnessed many enemies and persecutors of Christians transformed into supporters and proclaimers of the gospel. In Acts 16, Paul was thrown into prison in Philippi. It can be reasonably assumed the jailer did not give him a warm reception, since he was ordered to put Paul and Silas into the stocks to secure them from escape. In verses 35-41, Paul did a good work in the jailer's life by saving him from killing himself.

Acts 16:35-41
But when it was day, the magistrates sent the sergeants, saying, "Let those men go." The jailer reported these words to Paul, saying, "The magistrates have sent to let you go; now therefore come out, and go in peace." But Paul said to them, "They have beaten us publicly, without a trial, men who are Romans, and have cast us into prison! Do they now release us secretly? No, most assuredly, but let them come themselves and bring us out!" The sergeants reported these words to the magistrates, and they were afraid when they heard that they were Romans, and they came and begged them. When they had brought them out, they asked them to depart from the city. They went out...the prison, and entered into Lydia's house. When they had seen the brothers, they comforted them, and departed.

This gave Paul the opportunity to share the good news and he and his whole household came to the Savior. The jailer went from negative reactions to the gospel and being an enemy and persecutor to one of the original members of the newly founded church at Philippi. Perhaps, Paul and Silas were praying for the jailer even while their limbs were stretched out in the stocks.

In Acts 18, the apostle was resisted, mocked, criticized, and eventually thrown out of the Jewish synagogue in the city of Corinth. Of course, the leader of the synagogue was involved. How could he not have been?

Acts 18:4-7
He [Paul] reasoned in the synagogue every Sabbath, and persuaded Jews and Greeks. But when Silas and Timothy came down from

Macedonia, Paul was compelled by the Spirit, testifying to the Jews that Jesus was the Christ. When they opposed him and blasphemed, he shook out his clothing and said to them, "Your blood be on your own heads! I am clean. From now on, I will go to the Gentiles!" He departed there, and went into the house of a certain man named Justus, one who worshiped God, whose house was next door to the synagogue.

When Paul was instructing in the house next door, owned by Titius Justus, Crispus, the leader of the Jewish synagogue, received Christ with his household. He was transformed into a staunch advocate and proclaimer of Jesus Christ.

Acts 18:8
Crispus...ruler of the synagogue, believed in the Lord with all his house [family and servants included]. Many of the Corinthians, hearing, believed and were baptized.

In previous discussions of Paul's missionary journeys, it has been continually demonstrated that the hostile Jews and Gentiles, though they were enemies of Christians, ultimately became believers. Could Paul have been praying for Crispus and these others? Yes.

When Paul was imprisoned, the Philippian church was concerned about his well-being. They loved Paul, supported him financially and with providing fellow ministers as the apostle proclaimed the gospel.

Acts 28:30-31
Paul stayed two whole years in his own rented house, and received all who went into him, preaching...teaching the things concerning the Lord Jesus Christ with all boldness without hindrance.

In Philippians 1, Paul explained that there was a greater progress of the gospel in Rome.

THE PERSECUTION OF THE SAINTS AND HOW TO OVERCOME IT

Philippians 1:12-13
Now I desire...you know, brothers, that the things which happened to me have turned out rather to the progress of the gospel; so that my bonds became revealed in Christ throughout the whole praetorian guard, and to all the rest.

God was advancing the gospel into Rome. How was God accomplishing this? In verse 13, the apostle reasoned that the slumbering church in Rome had awakened because of his boldness. The saints in the capital city of the Roman Empire were now out boldly preaching Christ. The whole Praetorian Guard had heard the gospel among many others who were coming to him.

In Philippians 4, the letter closes with his final example of the gospel's advancement, when he sent a greeting from those who now believed from Caesar's own household. This would most likely be the servants who waited on Paul and perhaps a relative.

Philippians 4:22
All the saints greet you, especially those who are of Caesar's household.

All of this was taking place right in the emperor's own city while Caesar Nero was a horrific persecutor of the church. Perhaps, Paul was praying for these guards and household members while imprisoned.

Why are all these examples important? God can and does bring the persecutors and enemies of the gospel to Christ. No man or woman is beyond the reach of the all-powerful, almighty, sovereign God. Consequently, salvation should be the first thing on the lips of believers, as they are praying for their enemies and persecutors. What else is more important than their salvation? Is it a good life?

Christians should regularly bring the unsaved to God in prayer, especially those who respond negatively to the good news. They are to pray for the salvation of their persecutors.

The Unwillingness to Resist

In Matthew 5:39-41 and Luke 6:29-30, Jesus declared that His followers should not "resist their enemies."

Matthew 5:39-42
But I tell you, don't resist him who is evil...whoever strikes you on your right cheek, turn to him the other also. 40 If any man would go to law with you and take away your coat, let him have your cloak also. Whoever compels you to go one mile, go with him two. Give to him who asks you, and don't turn away him who desires to borrow from you.

Luke 6:29-30
To him who strikes you on the cheek, offer also the other; and from him who takes away your cloak, don't withhold your coat also. Give to everyone who asks you, and don't ask him who takes away your goods to give them back again.

The Greek word translated "resist" means to oppose or to stand against. A careful reading of the context demonstrates that it has to do with enemies in need.

In Matthew 5:42, after providing three examples of not resisting enemies, the Lord Jesus presents a general guiding principle. His followers are to give to every person who asks or wants to borrow.

They should not oppose them because they are enemies. When people need something the saints have, they should generously provide it for them, even if they are persecutors.

He is contrasting this to their concept of "take an eye for an eye and a tooth for a tooth." This would dictate that when enemies ask, Christians should resist them or deprive them of what they need, because they don't deserve it. This is not what God does. He provides for the needs of all mankind.

Therefore, the three examples the Lord provides has to do with someone who is in need. The first illustration involves the shaming and humiliating of believers who have offended their enemies. In Matthew 5:39 and Luke 6:29, this enemy of the believer slaps him on the right cheek.

Matthew 5:39
But I tell you, don't resist him who is evil; but whoever strikes you on your right cheek, turn to him the other also.

Luke 6:29
To him who strikes you on the cheek, offer also the other; and from him who takes away your cloak, don't withhold your coat also.

Being hit on the right cheek would indicate the believer was hit backhanded with the enemy's right hand. A straight slap would hit the left cheek. In ancient times, this slap was a challenge; it was a sign of humiliation to the offender by an offended person.

In the context, an unbeliever becomes offended, while he is in need. The Christian has no obligation to give him what he desires, even though he may think he deserves it. When the Christian refuses, he slaps him. The believer should let the enemy humiliate him. This is the reason Jesus said that His followers should just turn the other cheek. Let him humiliate the believer even more. Real Christians do not retaliate when humiliated. Yet, it would be better if he had just provided it for him. Self-defense is not an issue here. This was not an act of violence, but a challenge to a believer.

The man was not punching him in the face but demanding a response. It was not a slap that injured the face but the pride.

The second illustration involves an enemy who thinks a Christian possesses what he needs, so he sues the believer in court. In this example, the enemy needs the coat of the saint and believes that he legally should possess it. As a result, he sues the saint for it. Someone does not sue another unless he needs something that the other possesses and believes the law will support him. He needs this Christian's tunic. In some way, he believes it is his, so he decides to sue. Jesus says that he should just give him the undergarment.

The third illustration involved soldiers who were in need of help. These military men did not need objects from others, but physical help. By law, soldiers could ask regular citizens to carry their pack for them for a distance. As an example, Simon the Cyrene was required to carry the cross of Jesus as the Lord struggled with it.

Matthew 27:32
As they came out, they found a man of Cyrene, Simon by name, and they compelled him to go with them, that he might carry his cross.

The Roman soldiers were hated by the Jewish people and were considered enemies and persecutors. The implication was powerful. This hated Roman soldier asks a Jew to walk a mile with his pack. He is to take it two miles. So, when an enemy is in need of physical help, a believer should give him twice as much as he needs.

Paul discusses this same principle in the book of Romans. In Romans 12, the apostle Paul clearly states that Christians are to never repay evil for evil, but to seek peace with men, if it is possible.

THE PERSECUTION OF THE SAINTS AND HOW TO OVERCOME IT

Romans 12:17-20
Repay no one evil for evil. Respect what is honorable in the sight of all men. If it is possible, as much as it is up to you, be at peace with all men. 19 Don't seek revenge yourselves, beloved, but give place to God's wrath. For it is written, "Vengeance belongs to me; I will repay, says the Lord." Therefore "If your enemy is hungry, feed him. If he is thirsty, give him a drink. For in doing so, you will heap coals of fire on his head."

Here believers are given another aspect to Christ's mandate to never seek vengeance.

It is easy to withhold something that an enemy needs out of vengeance. Christians must understand that God will avenge, believers must feed their enemies. If they are cold, then give them coats to wear and warm themselves. One of the results of these good deeds done in kindness is that they heap hot coals upon their heads (a reference to humiliating them with good). Christians are to overcome evil with good. When we do this, everyone will see the difference in our approaches and theirs (which is retaliation rather than doing good). Then, we can share the reason for these good works which is the gospel. This is a wonderful opportunity.

The point of the Lord is extremely clear. His followers are nothing like their unbelieving counterparts. They will go out of their way and beyond their comfort to meet the needs of people. Does someone need something a believer has and tries to humiliate him to get it? There is no need to challenge him because he can have it. Does someone sue a believer because he needs something the believer might be wearing? He should not bother, because he will give him two articles of clothing. Does someone need a believer to help him carry something some distance? There is no problem because he will carry it twice as far. Believers are not like other people even their enemies will be helped.

The Willingness to Forgive

Christians should forgive their persecutors and enemies. Though this concept is not seen in these Matthew and Luke passages which were mentioned earlier, nevertheless, it is an important consideration. There are several passages in the Bible that attest to the importance of this principle. In any discussion of how Christians should treat their enemies.

In Luke 23:34, the Lord is hanging on the cross, dripping with blood from the crown of thorns and the nails in his hands and feet.

Luke 23:34
Jesus said, "Father, forgive them, for they don't know what they are doing." Dividing his garments among them, they cast lots.

In His excruciating pain from the horrifying tortures and beatings, agonizing in the slow process of dying, humiliated from the mocking of the people, He cried to the Father to forgive these ignorant persecutors.

The Romans, who were doing all the dirty work the Jews could not do, did not realize that they were really crucifying the ultimate King of Kings and Lord of Lords. The common Jews, who were standing around the cross, shouting insults at the Lord, could not fully understand that their longed-for Messiah, was hanging from that cursed tree. The frightened disciples who were hiding from the leaders and the mob could not comprehend, that their great moment of victory in salvation had not been lost in that dying man. Instead, it was about to be completed when the price was paid, and Christ had risen from the dead. Even, many of the rulers, who were caught up in their self-righteous pride, could not perceive that the veil of the temple was about to be split into two. The lamb would be sacrificed, and the new eternal high priest would enter the Holy of Holies to forever represent them. Their sacred redeemer had come, and they could not see this.

In the midst of his deep pain, Christ knowing all of this, looked down with great compassion, and cried out for the Father's forgiveness. Christians know through their study of the Scriptures, that the prayer could only be fulfilled if all of these ignorant, hardhearted persecutors and enemies of the cross, received the soon to be risen Son of God as Savior and Lord. Yet, implied in the merciful cry to His Father, is a God who became truly man, and as man forgave His persecutors.

In Acts 7, Stephen preached before the Sanhedrin and indicted them for their sin. They responded by rushing him, dragging him out of the city, and stoning him to death.

Acts 7:54-59
Now when they heard these things, they were cut to the heart, and they gnashed at him with their teeth. But he, being full of the Holy Spirit, looked up steadfastly into heaven, and saw the glory of God, and Jesus standing on the right hand of God, and said, "Behold, I see the heavens opened, and the Son of Man standing on the right hand of God!" But they cried out with a loud voice, and stopped their ears, and rushed at him with one accord. They threw him out of the city, and stoned him. The witnesses placed their garments at the feet of a young man named Saul. They stoned Stephen as he called out, saying, "Lord Jesus, receive my Spirit!"

In his final words in Acts 7, Stephen took up Jesus Christ's compassionate mantle and begged God to forgive them even though he was about to die at their hands.

Acts 7:60
He kneeled down, and cried with a loud voice, "Lord, don't hold this sin against them!" When he had said this, he fell asleep.

I am sure he forgave them for the same reasons. Once again, forgiveness from God must be obtained through and only through His Son. Once again, implicit in his compassionate words is his own forgiveness of these murderers.

The question then arises, "Does the Bible explicitly teach that Christians are to forgive their unbelieving enemies and persecutors?" Most Christians acknowledge that they must forgive their fellow saints.

Ephesians 4:32
And be kind to one another, tenderhearted, forgiving each other, just as God also in Christ forgave you.

Colossians 3:13
Bearing with one another, and forgiving each other, if any man has a complaint against any; even as Christ forgave you, so you also do.

Yet, most Christians are not so sure of the specific teaching concerning the forgiveness of those who have not turned to Christ. Are believers to forgive? The answer is yes.

All Christians are compelled by their Lord and Savior to forgive anyone and everyone, believer or unbeliever, friend or foe, brother or acquaintance, and persecutor or supporter for any and all transgressions! This is a tall order. This is not human, but a real supernatural phenomenon. In the gospels and epistles, it clearly states that saints are to forgive both other believers and unbelievers. Why? Saints are forgiven by God. Because they have experienced forgiveness, they must show forgiveness.

In Matthew 6, during the Sermon on the Mount, the Lord Jesus declared that prayers should end with some powerful words of forgiveness of others.

THE PERSECUTION OF THE SAINTS AND HOW TO OVERCOME IT

Matthew 6:12
Forgive us our debts, as we also forgive our debtors.

Also, in Mark 11, on His way to Jerusalem, Jesus explained to His disciples that whenever they stood praying, they should forgive, if they had anything against anyone.

Mark 11:25
Whenever you stand praying, forgive, if you have anything against anyone; so that your Father, who is in heaven, may also forgive you your transgressions.

Then, when Jesus was asked how to pray by His disciples, He delivered the Lord's Prayer a second time.

Luke 11:4
Forgive us our sins, For we ourselves also forgive everyone who is indebted to us. Bring us not into temptation, But deliver us from the evil one.

There is no distinction between believers and unbelievers. Jesus utilizes the words "debtors," "anyone," and "everyone." So, forgiveness is extended to all. He makes no distinction in the kinds of transgressions that ought to be forgiven. They must all be forgiven. Therefore, Christians must forgive their enemies and persecutors for what they do against them, no matter how bad the persecution.

One might ask the question, "What about justice?" It is for the Lord to determine when He will administer His justice in this life as these two examples show. He can directly judge and condemn which he does on a regular basis. We not always know when and how He does, it but He does.

Luke 13:1-4
Now there were some present at the same time who told him about

the Galilaeans, whose blood Pilate had mixed with their sacrifices. Jesus answered them, "Do you think that these Galilaeans were worse sinners than all the other Galilaeans, because they suffered such things? I tell you, no, but, unless you repent, you will all perish in the same way. Or those eighteen, on whom the tower in Siloam fell, and killed them; do you think that they were worse offenders than all the men who dwell in Jerusalem?

Acts 12:23
Immediately an angel...struck him, because he didn't give God the glory, and he was eaten by worms, and he died.

Christians know that His justice will be administered at the great white throne of Christ. This is where every single transgression anyone has committed against believers will be judged. Their names and specific sins against them will be presented to the unsaved to be judged and punished.

Revelation 20:11-15
I saw a great white throne, and him who sat on it, from whose face the Earth and the heaven fled away. There was found no place for them. I saw the dead, the great and the small, standing before the throne. Books were opened. Another book was opened, which is the book of life. The dead were judged out of the things which were written in the books, according to their works. The sea gave up the dead who were in it. Death and Hades gave up the dead who were in them. They were judged, each one according to his works. Death and Hades were thrown into the lake of fire. This is the second death, the lake of fire. If anyone was not found written in the book of life, he was cast into the lake of fire.

Christians must understand, if any of their enemies or persecutors receives Jesus Christ, they too will be forgiven of all their sins, including the persecution. These enemies of the cross, if they repent and believe in Jesus as Savior and Lord, they will be forgiven, as those they persecuted were forgiven of all their sins. There is no better illustration of this than the apostle Paul. He saw himself as the worst of sinners who found forgiveness.

1 Timothy 1:15-17
The saying is faithful, and worthy of all acceptance, that Christ Jesus came into the world to save sinners; of whom I am chief. However, for this cause I obtained mercy, that in me as chief, Jesus Christ might display all his patience, for an example of those who were going to believe in him to eternal life. Now to the King eternal, immortal, invisible, to God who alone is wise, be honor and glory forever and ever. Amen.

Forgiveness can extend to all as God extended forgiveness to us.

It is important to understand that the majority of people will react negatively to the gospel. If the road is narrow that proceeds to life, most people will not follow it. Instead, they will respond with one or more of the negative reactions that were previously mentioned. For every person who comes to Christ, many others will not. Jesus explained this in just a few words.

Matthew 22:14
For many are called, but few chosen.

Most will never come to Christ and will react in some kind of negative way.

We have discussed the holy acts we are to take to stand our ground in the midst of persecution that is minor and unavoidable. We should utilize these first if possible.

STANDING YOUR GROUND

Chapter 7

Submit in Human Affairs

As we consider the reactions to persecution, we will see four different kinds of responses. The first is a legal response which involves submission, restraint, adjudication, or even defiance of governing authorities. The second response to persecution entails avoiding it all together either verbally or behaviorally. The third one involves facing the persecution directly with a strong verbal presentation. The last response deals with the physical defense of ourselves and others. It is critical that we understand these four kinds of responses. Otherwise, the many words and actions God's people took when facing harm or death will be confusing and leave us in a state of immobility when persecution comes. This chapter and the next three discuss our legal response and should be read as one unit.

Our first response, as Christians, to all authorities of the government and its laws is to humbly submit in all human affairs including persecution when it does not involve the non-negotiables (direct and clear commands of God) of the Christian faith. These non-negotiables will be discussed in detail in the chapter on defiance of the law to obey a divine command. Our fundamental response is humble submission. The Holy Scriptures provide guidelines on what we are to think, say, and do regarding governmental authorities. The Bible provides several critical passages which discuss these biblical principles. They are Romans 13:1-8, 1 Peter 2:13-17, 1 Timothy 2:1-4, Titus 3:1, and Titus 3:8. Since these passages are filled with so much powerful truth, we will look at some portions briefly, some more extensively, and others will by necessity be left out.

Our normal pattern of behavior toward any governing authority is simple: we are to submit. If we must defy them according to Scriptural principles, it comes from a pattern of obedience. As Christians, we must understand exactly who these authorities are. There are three Greek terms used by the apostles which make their identities clear. Of course, we must know exactly who should be obeyed.

First, believers must obey "higher authorities." These are referred to as simply "authorities" (with or without "higher" as an adjective).

Titus 3:1
Remind them to be in subjection to rulers and to authorities, to be obedient [to authorities - verb form], to be ready for every good work.

Romans 13:1-3
Let every soul be in subjection to the higher authorities, for there is no authority except from God, and those who exist are ordained by God. Therefore he who resists the authority, withstands the ordinance of God; and those who withstand will receive to themselves judgment. For rulers are not a terror to the good work, but to the evil. Do you desire to have no fear of the authority? Do that which is good, and you will have praise from the same.

The word translated "authority" in these passages in the Greek is a general term that refers to "those who have the power of choice or the liberty of doing as one pleases." It is used of different types of authorities who are either divine, angelic, or human. Since we are interested in the human realm, we will focus on these.

It is used of various kinds of authorities of different ranks in the military and society. It referred to a Roman Centurion who was a commander of one hundred soldiers.

THE PERSECUTION OF THE SAINTS AND HOW TO OVERCOME IT

Matthew 8:8-9
The centurion answered, "Lord, I'm not worthy for you to come under my roof. Just say the word, and my servant will be healed. For I am also a man under authority, having under myself soldiers. I tell this one, 'Go,' and he goes; and tell another, 'Come,' and he comes; and tell my servant, 'Do this,' and he does it."

It speaks of the authority of a Roman governor over a province or region.

Luke 20:20
They watched him, and sent out spies, who pretended to be righteous, that they might trap him in something he said, so as to deliver him [Jesus] up to the power and authority of the governor.

Also, it referred to Herod's rank and authority as the ruler of the Jewish nation.

Luke 23:7
When he found out that he was in Herod's jurisdiction, he sent him to Herod, who was also in Jerusalem during those days.

It described the authority of Pilate, the Roman governor.

John 19:10
Pilate therefore said to him, "Aren't you speaking to me? Don't you know that I have power [authority] to release you, and have power [authority] to crucify you?"

It also spoke of religious authorities of Jesus' day, such as the Sanhedrin (the Jewish council).

Acts 26:10
This I also did in Jerusalem. I both shut up many of the saints in prisons, having received authority from the chief priests, and when they were put to death I gave my vote against them.

When Paul describes these authorities, he added "higher." This Greek word translated "higher" means "to stand out, rise above, to be superior in rank, authority, or quality." Here, he is referring to anyone who is above the average citizen in rank or authority.

Second, these authorities were regional leaders, and the Greek words were usually translated "governors."

1 Peter 2:14
Or to governors, as sent by him for vengeance on evildoers and for praise to those who do well.

It referred to Pilate, the governor over the region of Judea, who gave the order to crucify Jesus.

Matthew 27:2
And they bound him, and led him away, and delivered him up to Pontius Pilate, the governor.

It was used of Felix who succeeded Pilate as governor. Then, Festus succeeded Felix. Both these men held Paul for over two years each in custody.

Acts 23:26
Claudius Lysias [the commanding officer in charge of Paul] to the most excellent governor Felix: Greetings.

Acts 26:30
The king rose up with the governor, and Bernice, and those who sat with them.

Third, these "authorities" would be rulers in general. The next Greek term is a general term for various types and ranks of rulers. These would refer to authorities at the lower end of government.

Romans 13:3
For rulers are not a terror to the good work, but to the evil. Do you desire to have no fear of the authority? Do that which is good, and you will have praise from the same.

Titus 3:1
Remind them to be in subjection to rulers and to authorities, to be obedient, to be ready for every good work.

Also, the term was used to refer to religious officials.

Luke 8:41
Behold, there came a man named Jairus, and he was a ruler of the synagogue. He fell down at Jesus' feet, and begged him to come into his house.

John 3:1-2
Now there was a man of the Pharisees named Nicodemus, a ruler of the Jews. The same came to him by night, and said to him, "Rabbi, we know that you are a teacher...from God, for no one can do these signs...unless God is with him."

It was used of local town officials.

Luke 12:58
For when you are going with your adversary before the magistrate, try diligently on the way to be released from him, lest perhaps he drag you to the judge, and the judge deliver you to the officer, and the officer throw you into prison.

Also, at times, this Greek term was used to refer to rulers of the nations in general.

Matthew 20:25
But Jesus summoned them, and said, "You know that the rulers of the nations lord it over them, and...exercise authority over them.

Acts 4:26
The kings of the Earth take a stand, and the rulers take council together, against the Lord, and against his Christ.

As can be seen, these words are synonyms referring to superior authorities of any rank. So, we must submit to any official who ranks above us.

We are also to obey kings and the head of nations. The term translated "king" refers to the supreme ruler or highest authority in the land. This would include presidents, prime ministers, and other rulers.

1 Peter 2:13
Therefore subject yourselves to every ordinance of man for the Lord's sake: whether to the king, as supreme.

1 Peter 2:17
Honor all men. Love the brotherhood. Fear God. Honor the king.

1 Timothy 2:1-2
I exhort [beseech, entreat] therefore, first of all, that petitions, prayers, intercessions, and givings of thanks, be made for all men: for kings and all who are in high places; that we may lead a tranquil and quiet life in all godliness and reverence.

Though he had a different title, this Greek word would include emperors like Caesar in Rome.

Matthew 1:6
Jesse became the father of King David. David became the father of Solomon by her who had been Uriah's wife.

Matthew 18:23
Therefore the Kingdom of Heaven is like a...king, who wanted to reconcile accounts with his servants.

THE PERSECUTION OF THE SAINTS AND HOW TO OVERCOME IT

Mark 6:22
When the daughter of Herodias herself came in and danced, she pleased Herod and those sitting with him. The king said to the young lady, "Ask me whatever you want, and I will give it to you."

Acts 12:1
Now about that time, King Herod stretched out his hands to oppress some of the assembly.

Of course, in modern times, the word refers to presidents, prime ministers, and even dictators who are acting within their legal authority. Therefore, we should submit to them.

Fourth, we are to submit to human ordinances.

1 Peter 2:13-14
Therefore subject yourselves to every ordinance of man for the Lord's sake: whether to the king, as supreme; or to governors, as sent by him for vengeance on evildoers and for praise to those who do well.

The word translated "ordinance" literally means "creation" and is translated this way due to the context.

Mark 10:5-6
But Jesus said to them, "For your hardness of heart, he wrote you this commandment...from the beginning of the *creation*, God made them male and female.

Though it is used for creation almost everywhere else, in this context, it refers to the created laws, policies, or procedures created by kings and governors. Therefore, these refer to the numerous laws these authorities create. This would include the statutes and ordinances of towns, cities, states, regions, provinces, and nations.

In Romans 13:1, we are given the standard by which we judge the "divine legitimacy" of these superior authorities. They must be "established." The rulers that are to be obeyed must have been established in the past and continually set in place. We are not talking at all about authorities who are in the process of being "established" either by election or force. This is an important distinction. Once a superior authority is established and continually in place, then we must believe by faith that this is God's doing.

Romans 13:1
Let every soul be in subjection to the higher authorities, for there is no authority except from God, and those who exist are ordained [established] by God.

The verb translated "exist" is in the present tense which indicates a continual "existence" in present time. This portion of the biblical passage can best be translated, "those who are continually existing in the present are established by God." Authorities that are to be obeyed are the ones currently in existence. We cannot wait until some other candidate comes into office or some other government comes into existence to submit. We are to submit to those in power now. Whatever the future may hold does not determine our obedience now.

This other critical word in this passage is translated by the English word "ordained." The Greek word speaks of "putting something in order, stationing, arranging, or assigning a place to something, and appointing someone to a position of responsibility." It is used to designate the mountain the Lord Jesus Christ had specifically picked out to meet His disciples after the resurrection.

Matthew 28:16
But the eleven disciples went into Galilee, to the mountain where Jesus had sent them.

Also, it is used of God appointing believers to eternal life.

Acts 13:48
As the Gentiles heard this, they were glad, and glorified the word of God. As many [unsaved people] as were appointed to eternal life believed.

Luke used it to describe the selection, appointment, and establishment process of Paul and Barnabas to represent the church at the Jerusalem Council in Antioch.

Acts 15:1-3
Some men came down from Judea and taught the brothers, "Unless you are circumcised after the custom of Moses, you can't be saved." Therefore when Paul and Barnabas had no small discord and discussion...they appointed Paul and Barnabas...some others of them, to go up to Jerusalem to the apostles and elders about this question. They...passed through...Phoenicia and Samaria, declaring the conversion of the Gentiles. They caused great joy to all the brothers.

The risen Jesus speaks of the numerous responsibilities He had determined Paul would have in His service to Him using this word. Jesus ordered, appointed, established, and ordained specific things He wanted Paul to do for Him.

Acts 22:10
I said, 'What shall I do, Lord?' The Lord said to me, 'Arise, and go into Damascus. There you will be told about all things which are appointed for you to do.'

The word is in the perfect tense which denotes authorities who were selected, appointed, and established in the past with continuing results (their current existence) are the ones established by God. The verb is in the passive voice which means the ordaining happened to them by an outside force.

Of course, this force was God. Though they think they were active in their establishment, actually they were passive. God is the one who established them. How can we possibly know? They still exist. This ordination by our God does not legitimize wicked or despotic behavior which was used in past history by kings to force the people to accept their evil.

Now that we understand who the legitimate authorities are, how are we to respond? The terms "submit" and "obey" have been used as a general word for the many terms used to speak of our proper behavior toward authorities that have been established by God. In this next section, we will discuss the specific terms used to describe our Christian behavior toward these God-ordained authorities.

Our Willing Subjection

Paul and Peter clearly command us to subject ourselves to higher authorities and their laws, policies, and ordinances. We find this in three passages where Paul and Peter use the same Greek term to speak of this submission and what it exactly entails regarding obedience.

Romans 13:1
Let every soul be in subjection to the higher authorities, for there is no authority except from God, and those who exist are ordained by God.

Romans 13:5
Therefore you need to be in subjection, not only because of the wrath, but also for conscience' sake.

1 Peter 2:13
Therefore subject yourselves to every ordinance of man for the Lord's sake: whether to the king, as supreme.

This verb means "to arrange under, to subordinate, to subject, to obey, to submit to another's control, or to yield to another's admonition." This term was also a military term meaning "to arrange [troop divisions] in a military fashion under the command of a leader."

It was used of Jesus submitting to His parents when He was a young boy.

Luke 2:51
And he went down with them, and came to Nazareth. He was subject to them, and his mother kept all these sayings in her heart.

The seventy used the term to describe how the demons were subject to them as they cast the demons out. These evil angels had to submit to the seventy.

Luke 10:17
The seventy returned with joy, saying, "Lord, even the demons are subject to us in your name!"

Jesus repeats the term in His admonition to them. They were to rejoice in a greater truth.

Luke 10:20
Nevertheless, don't rejoice in this, that the spirits are subject to you, but rejoice that your names are written in heaven."
It is used to speak of the flesh's unwillingness to submit.

It is used to portray the flesh as not being willing to put itself under the law of God.

Romans 8:7
Because the mind of the flesh is hostile towards God; for it is not subject to God's law, neither indeed can it be. Here it describes the Jews unwillingness to submit to God.

Romans 10:3-4
For being ignorant of God's righteousness, and seeking to establish their own righteousness, they [the Jews] did not subject themselves to the righteousness of God. For Christ is the fulfillment of the law for righteousness to everyone who believes.

The word is used to describe our relationship to our Lord Jesus as we submit to Him.

Ephesians 5:24
But as the assembly is subject to Christ, so let the wives also be to their own husbands in everything.

The Greek word was utilized to speak of the subjection of slaves to their masters.

Titus 2:9
Exhort servants to be in subjection to their own masters, and to be well-pleasing in all things; not contradicting.

1 Peter 2:18
Servants, be in subjection to your masters with all fear; not only to the good and gentle, but also to the wicked.

Also, it was used to refer to all things coming in subjection to Christ.

Hebrews 2:8
You...put all things in subjection under his feet." For in that he subjected all things to him...left nothing that is not subject to him. But now we don't see all things subjected to him, yet.

As we see clearly, this term refers to Christians arranging, subordinating, and subjecting their wills under the law. In Romans 13:1, the verb translated "be in subjection" is a command which is in the present tense. This indicates that the action is already going on and must continue. It could be translated, "Let us keep on being subjected to the higher authorities." Apparently, the Roman Christians were being submissive to those in authority, and Paul commands them to keep on submitting.

In Romans 13:5, Paul discusses the same truth again and adds a new aspect. The same verb in this passage is in the middle voice. This refers to a people doing something for themselves. Therefore, Christians are to be subjecting themselves to the authorities and should not have been forced. In Peter's passage, the verb translated "subject" is in the aorist tense indicating that the readers of the letters of Peter were not subjecting themselves and needed to start. Here, we see the lack of consensus of obedience in the Body of Christ. Some of the saints were submitting, others had stopped and needed to begin again, and still others had to start for the first time.

Our Constant Reminder

In another passage where Paul uses the same term of subjection, he commands Titus to be continually reminding the believers to obey the laws. This constant reminder is a critical aspect of our behavior toward the law. In the same way, we should be reminding each other and ourselves that God desires subjection to the authorities.

Titus 3:1
Remind them to be in subjection to rulers and to authorities, to be obedient, to be ready for every good work.

The verb that is translated "remind" is in the present tense indicating a regular and constant bringing to remembrance of these truths. In our case, we may have to journey back to these principles time and time again. We are told often in the New Testament to remember important truths.

2 Timothy 2:14
Remind them of these things, charging them in the sight of the Lord, that they don't argue about words, to no profit, to the subverting of those who hear.

2 Peter 1:12
Therefore I will not be negligent to remind you...though you know them, and are established in the present truth.

One of the reasons that we must be reminded is that we know we are no longer tied to this Earth. In fact, Paul tells us to keep our minds on the spiritual things.

Romans 8:5
For those who live according to the flesh set their minds on the things of the flesh, but those who live according to the Spirit, the things of the Spirit.

We also know that we are no longer of the Earth. We have a new citizenship which is in heaven.

Philippians 3:20
For our citizenship is in heaven, from where we also wait for a Savior, the Lord Jesus Christ.

Due to this heavenly citizenship, we are now foreigners on the Earth.

1 Peter 2:10-11
 In the past, you were not a people, but now are God's people, who had not obtained mercy, but now have obtained mercy. Beloved, I beg you as foreigners and pilgrims, to abstain from fleshly lusts, which war against the soul.

So, it may become easy for us to think that we are no longer bound to the laws of the land. This simply is not true. We are still bound but for a different reason. The unsaved choose to obey or not to obey for various secular reasons, and we obey to please the Lord.

Our Unwillingness to Resist

As we continue, we will look at the subtle, more indirect actions we must take to subject ourselves to all authorities. Though these truths could be considered under "reasons for submitting ourselves," I prefer to see them as actions that we must take. In Romans 13:2, the apostle Paul our submission by describing what happens if Christians refuse.

He calls this "resisting." To submit to authorities is to be unwilling to resist God's ordinance. Why? When we resist authorities, we are really resisting God. Therefore, we must be unwilling to resist something God established. This action has its focus in the right place: God!

Romans 13:2
Therefore he [anyone] who resists the authority, withstands the ordinance of God; and those who withstand will receive to themselves judgment.

This Greek word translated "resist" is the opposite of the word "ordained" that was found in Romans 13:1. Here Paul is indulging in some wordplay to get his meaning across. If "ordained" refers to put in order, station, arrange, or assign a place for something, or to appoint someone," then resisting would be the opposite. We would be disrupting the divine "order, placement, station, or arrangement of His governing authorities. Not only this, but believers would definitely be resisting the divine appointment to their responsibilities.

So, we must be willing not to resist them. This Greek word translated "resist" is used to refer to Jews disrupting God's order of salvation found in the gospel by Paul.

Acts 18:6
When they opposed him and blasphemed, he shook out his clothing and said to them, "Your blood be on your own heads! I am clean. From now on, I will go to the Gentiles!"

The word is utilized by both James and Peter to speak of God's disruption of the order of the "proud" in society. This means He will not allow them to get a hold on people to oppress them.

James 4:6
But he gives more grace. Therefore it says, "God resists the proud, but gives grace to the humble."

1 Peter 5:5
Likewise, you younger ones, be subject to the elder. Yes, all of you clothe yourselves with humility, to subject yourselves to one another; for "God resists the proud...gives grace to the humble."

Also, James uses the word to describe how the poor are not able to disrupt the placement of the rich in society. They cannot resist them.

James 5:6
You have condemned, you have murdered the righteous one. He doesn't resist you.

This word is strong and speaks of disruption and upheaval. Therefore, for Christians to subject themselves to the laws, they must be willing to say to themselves, "I am never going to resist authorities established by God. This is God's order, and it is what He desires for me."

Our Unwillingness to Withstand

In the same way, another indirect principle is also found in Romans 13:2.

Romans 13:2
Therefore he [believers] who resists the authority, withstands the ordinance of God; and those who withstand will receive to themselves judgment.

The verb translated "withstands" comes from two words: "to stand" and the preposition "against." Therefore, it means "to stand against someone or something."

Luke utilizes the word as he describes the withstanding of Elymas against Paul. When the apostle was attempting to share the good news with Sergius Paulus, this false prophet kept interfering.

Acts 13:6-7
When they had gone through the island to Paphos, they [Paul and his entourage] found a certain sorcerer, a false prophet, a Jew, whose name was Bar Jesus [Elymas], who was with the proconsul [a ruler], Sergius Paulus, a man of understanding. This man [Sergius] summoned Barnabas and Saul, and sought to hear the word of God.

When Paul was summoned, the sorcerer stepped in to stop him. He didn't want to lose his high status in the court.

Acts 13:8
But Elymas the sorcerer (for so is his name by interpretation) withstood them, seeking to turn aside the proconsul from the faith.

The "withstanding" was so strong that the apostle rebuked him and struck him blind.

Acts 13:9-11
But Saul, who is also called Paul, filled with the Holy Spirit, fastened his eyes on him, and said, "Full of all deceit and all cunning, you son of the devil [the one behind his hostility], you enemy of all righteousness, will you not cease to pervert the right ways of the Lord? Now, behold, the hand of the Lord is on you, and you will be blind, not seeing the sun for a season!" Immediately a mist and darkness fell on him. He went around seeking someone to lead him by the hand.

In his letter to the church in Galatia, Paul portrays his stand against Peter with this word. Peter had stopped eating with the Gentiles as he adhered to the lies of the Judaizers. They taught that the Gentiles had to become circumcised and obey the Jewish ceremonial laws to be saved. He would not take a stand against them, so Paul stood against Peter.

Galatians 2:11
But when Peter came to Antioch, I resisted [withstood] him to his face, because he stood condemned.

In Romans 9, Paul declares that God is so powerful that no one can "withstand" His will.

Romans 9:19
You will say then to me, "Why does he still find fault? For who withstands his will?"

In his letter to Timothy, Paul uses this term to describe the magicians in Pharaoh's court who stood against Moses. These were the ones who threw their staffs down and turned them into snakes, but the snake from the staff of Moses ate the other two.

2 Timothy 3:8
Even as Jannes and Jambres opposed Moses, so do these also oppose

the truth; men corrupted in mind, who concerning the faith, are rejected.

So, Paul is explaining that any unwillingness to submit to the governing authorities is essentially standing against an ordinance of our God. When we stand against authority, we stand against God's order. So, as Christians, we must be unwilling to stand against anything that God has ordained and established which as we have seen is a government that is currently existing. This main verb is in the perfect tense which indicates that the withstanding of authorities brings continuing consequences. These are the consequences of defying God's command from Paul and God's ordinance for the order of society.

The Unwillingness to Practice Evil

Another indirect way we should submit ourselves to those authorities who govern us to be unwilling to "do evil." If we commit ourselves to not doing evil, then we will submit to the governing authorities.

Romans 13:3
For rulers are not a terror to the good work, but to the evil. Do you desire to have no fear of the authority? Do that which is good, and you will have praise from the same.

Romans 13:4
For he is a servant of God to you for good. But if you do that which is evil, be afraid, for he doesn't bear the sword in vain; for he is a servant of God, an avenger for wrath to him who does evil.

1 Peter 2:14
Or to governors, as sent by him for vengeance on evildoers and for praise to those who do well.

The Greek word translated "evil" is not the word for the moral evil and sin we see in many passages. Instead, it is a general word which speaks of the temporal, Earthly evil acts we might commit (like breaking a law). It can also refer in other contexts to afflictions that come upon us.

The term is used by Pilate to ask exactly what kind of evil the Lord Jesus Christ had done that could possibly warrant a crucifixion, which was reserved for the worst of criminals. What could He have done?

Matthew 27:23
But the governor said, "Why? What evil has he done?" But they cried out exceedingly, saying, "Let him be crucified!"

Jesus uses it to refer to evil remarks that He did not make and yet was hit in the face.

John 18:23
Jesus answered him, "If I have spoken evil, testify of the evil; but if well, why do you beat me?"

Also, it is used of Paul's evil persecutions of the Christians.

Acts 9:13
But Ananias answered, "Lord [Jesus], I have heard from many about this man, how much evil he did to your saints at Jerusalem.

Paul uses the word to speak of the objects of lust.

1 Corinthians 10:6
Now these things were our examples, to the intent we should not lust after evil things, as they also lusted.

Also, in 1 Timothy, the apostle utilizes the word to describe the *evil* that comes from the love of money.

1 Timothy 6:10
For the love of money is a root of all kinds of evil. Some have been led astray from the faith in their greed and have pierced themselves through with many sorrows.

A final example is Paul's use of the word to refer to the "bad things" that evil Alexander did in order to completely disrupt his ministry.

2 Timothy 4:14
Alexander, the coppersmith, did much evil to me. The Lord will repay him according to his deeds.

In Romans 13:3, Paul explains that rulers bring terror to those who do temporal, earthy wickedness one of which is breaking the law. Therefore, we must be unwilling to do evil to avoid their terror.

Romans 13:3
For rulers are not a terror to the good work, but to the evil. Do you desire to have no fear of the authority? Do that which is good, and you will have praise from the same.

In 1 Peter 2, Peter asserts that evil such as breaking the law brings vengeance upon us. As a result, Christians must be unwilling to do evil to avoid their vengeance.

1 Peter 2:14
Or to governors, as sent by him for vengeance on evildoers and for praise to those who do well.

In Romans 13:4, Paul uses two different verbs with the adjective "evil." The first one is the verb "do" as in "you do that which is *evil*. This is the usual word for "do" in English. The second verb is in the phrase "does evil." This verb "do" refers to "practicing" something.

Romans 13:4
For he is a servant of God to you for good. But if you do that which is evil, be afraid, for he doesn't bear the sword in vain; for he is a servant of God, an avenger for wrath to him who does evil.

Here, the apostle indicates that doing evil by not submitting to authorities incites them to use their swords [or weapons] against us. Their divine responsibility is to take the Lord's vengeance out on those who are practicing evil. Therefore, as we commit acts that are against the law, we will receive the vengeance of God through them. These authorities also administer God's wrath to those who practice evil. We do not want their weapons pointed at us because their authority is from God and He is pointing them at us. This truth is a key to obedience.

In all three passages, the implication is the same. If we are unwilling to do evil in general. Then, we will be unwilling to do evil by breaking the law in particular. Then the legal authorities with not have to be a terror to us, make us afraid, and become the instruments of God's vengeance in His wrath.

Our Willingness to Do Good

In the same way, believers should be willing to "do good" by submitting themselves to the governing authorities. It is through being willing to do good that we will submit fully to the numerous rulers and ordinances. Those unwilling to do good break their laws and thus the command of God.

Romans 13:3
For rulers are not a terror to the good work, but to the evil. Do you desire to have no fear [terror] of the authority? Do that which is good, and you will have praise from the same.

1 Peter 2:14-15
Or to governors, as sent by him for vengeance on evildoers and for praise to those who do well [good]. For this is the will of God, that by well-doing [doing of good] you should put to silence the ignorance of foolish men.

In these two passages, the words translated "good, well, well-doing" have all the same root but are used in various grammatical forms. As in the unwillingness we should have to resist, withstand, and do evil, we must also be willing to do good. In this way, we will then be willing to submit to all governmental authorities.

The Greek word translated "good" refers to someone who is intrinsically good or to something which is good in and of itself. This is opposed to another Greek word which refers to the extrinsic: something noble or someone beautiful. It was used many times in this sense.

In these first three verses, the word "good" refers to words or actions proceeding from the inner person that will edify or build someone up.

Romans 15:2
Let each one of us please his neighbor for that which is good, to be building him up.

Ephesians 4:28
Let him who stole steal no more; but rather let him labor, producing with his hands something that is good, that he may have something to give to him who has need.

Ephesians 4:29
Let no corrupt speech proceed out of your mouth, but only what is good for building others up as the need may be, that it may give grace to those who hear.

In the passage below, Paul refers to the "works" that are intrinsically "good" that Christians are to engage in.

Ephesians 2:10
For we are his workmanship, created in Christ Jesus for good works, which God prepared before that we would walk in them.

The apostle uses the term "good" to speak of any "good" that we would do for one another.

1 Thessalonians 5:15
See that no one returns evil for evil to anyone, but always follow after that which is good, for one another, and for all.

As we can see, all of these examples refer to the intrinsic good of words and actions. If we are continually willing to speak "good things" and act in "good ways," we will submit to governing authorities. Then, we will receive praise from them. It will also silence the foolish criticisms of the unsaved as we obey and demonstrate our "doing of good." They will not be able to criticize us for doing evil and acting just like them. Here is another important underlying motivation for submission to the authorities.

Our Desire to Fear Authority

Another indirect way that will help in our submission to authorities is to develop a healthy fear of them. Therefore, as Christians we should develop a healthy fear of government and their many emissaries of justice.

Romans 13:3
For rulers are not a terror to the good work, but to the evil. Do you desire to have no fear of the authority? Do that which is good, and you will have praise from the same.

THE PERSECUTION OF THE SAINTS AND HOW TO OVERCOME IT

Romans 13:4
For he is a servant of God to you for good. But if you do that which is evil, be afraid, for he doesn't bear the sword in vain; for he is a servant of God, an avenger for wrath to him who does evil.

The apostle Paul was concerned the Christians in Rome and elsewhere would not follow the laws and lose their fear of authority. This is implied in his question, "Do you desire to have no fear of the authority?" This "fear" we have is important because our fear encourages us to fully submit. If we fear reprisal for disobedience to the law, then we will obey. We must always desire this fear and not allow ourselves to be hardened to it.

The words that are translated "terror, fear, afraid" in the two passages are different forms of the same word. It had the original meaning of "flight." So, it came to mean "a fear that causes flight." Our English word "phobia" is derived from this word. So, it refers to "great fear, dread or terror." This word translated "fear" is used in numerous places in the New Testament with this very idea.

In Matthew 14, it is used of the terror of the disciples when they saw Jesus walking on the water during the great wind that had blown them into the middle of the sea. The word "cried out" means to "scream at the top of your lungs."

Matthew 14:26
When...disciples saw him walking on the sea, they were troubled, saying, "It's a ghost!" and they cried out for fear.

It was used to describe the terror and fear that comes over someone in the midst of an angelic appearance.

Luke 1:12
Zacharias was troubled when he saw him, and fear fell upon him.

Matthew 28:4
For fear of him [angel at the tomb], the guards shook, and became like dead men.

When Ananias was struck dead by the Lord, it was used to speak of the fear that gripped the people.

Acts 5:5
Ananias, hearing these words, fell down and died. Great fear came on all who heard these things.

It can also describe the respect and the awestruck feeling of one's fear of God.

2 Corinthians 5:11
Knowing therefore the fear of the Lord, we persuade men, but we are revealed to God; and I hope that we are revealed also in your consciences.

2 Corinthians 7:1
Having therefore these promises, beloved, let us cleanse ourselves from all defilement of flesh and spirit, perfecting holiness in the fear of God.

The word describes Joseph of Arimathea's reason for not revealing his belief in Jesus. He was fearful of the Jews.

John 19:38
After these things, Joseph of Arimathea, being a disciple of Jesus, but secretly for fear of the Jews, asked of Pilate that he might take away Jesus' body. Pilate gave him permission. He came therefore and took away his body.

This is not just a little fear, but a deep and terrifying fear of the authorities. The point that the apostle Paul is making is that we need to fear governmental authorities. This keeps us obeying the law. If we allow ourselves to disobey, then this will lead to less fear and more disobedience which will create a vicious and very painful cycle. Then we will become people who are not fearful of the laws of the land and will be at a great disadvantage.

Our Payment of Taxes

Submitting to the governing authorities involves paying taxes to support their existence. This is always a part of our obedience to the authorities. Paul uses two different verbs in the same passage. The first verb focuses on the finishing of a task or accomplishment of a purpose.

Romans 13:6
For this reason you also pay taxes, for they are servants of God's service, attending continually on this very thing.

The Greek word translated "pay" means "to finish, perform, or do as commanded."

Here are several examples where this Greek word is used in other contexts.

Matthew 7:28
When Jesus had finished saying these things, the multitudes were astonished at his teaching,

Luke 12:50
But I have a baptism to be baptized with, and how distressed I am until it is accomplished!

Acts 13:29
When they had fulfilled all things that were written about him, they took him down...and laid him in a tomb.

When we pay our taxes, we finish or accomplish a critical and important God given task.

In the same passage, the apostle Paul uses a different verb to emphasize a different aspect of the truth.

Romans 13:7
Therefore give [render] everyone what you owe: if you owe taxes, pay taxes; if customs, then customs; if respect, then respect; if honor, then honor.

The Greek word translated "give [render]" means "to deliver, to give back." It can be used in a general sense to describe giving something to another. In the context of money, the word refers to "paying a debt." We will only look at this use of the Greek word.

It is used by in numerous parables to refer to payment of debts or wages.

Matthew 18:25
But because he couldn't pay, his lord commanded him to be sold, with his wife, his children, and all that he had, and payment to be made.

Matthew 20:8
When evening had come, the lord of the vineyard said to his manager, "Call the laborers and pay them [laborers] their wages, beginning from the last to the first."

Luke 7:42
When they couldn't pay, he forgave them both. Which of them therefore will love him most?"

We can see this Greek word used to speak of the payment of the debt by the Good Samaritan.

Luke 10:35
On the next day, when he [the Samaritan] departed, he took...two denarii, and gave them to the host, and said to him, "Take care of him. Whatever you spend beyond that, I will repay you when I return."

It was used by Peter when he referred to the sale of the land by Ananias and Sapphira.

Acts 5:8
About three hours later, his wife, not knowing what had happened, came in. Peter answered her, "Tell me whether you sold the land for so much." She said, "Yes, for so much."

So, using this word concerning the payment of taxes, Paul reiterates his teaching by emphasizing the "debt" aspect. This debt is ours and paid because the Lord gave it to us. This is due to His establishment of these authorities regardless of what these authorities may even think.

The word translated "taxes" is "tribute to an authority." In Romans 13:7, he also mentions "customs." These refer more to "sales taxes." Therefore, Paul is speaking of "finishing the task of" or "paying our debt of" the numerous taxes from our local, state, regional, or national authorities.

This is the same principle that Jesus taught when He was confronted about His teaching and practice on handling His taxes. The Jewish Sanhedrin was always attempting to find a violation of Roman law so they could accuse Him and drag Him to the Romans for trial. Luke describes one occasion.

Luke 20:20-23
They watched him, and sent out spies, who pretended to be righteous, that they might trap him in something he [Jesus] said, so as to deliver him up to the power and authority of the governor.

They asked him, "Teacher, we know that you say and teach what is right, and aren't partial to anyone, but truly teach the way of God. Is it lawful for us to pay taxes to Caesar, or not?" But he perceived their craftiness, and said to them, "Why do you test me?

The Lord Jesus did not play into their hands but gave an astounding answer.

Luke 20:23-26
But he perceived their craftiness, and said to them, "Why do you test me? Show me a denarius [Roman coin]. Whose image and inscription are on it?" They answered, "Caesar's." He said to them, "Then give to Caesar the things that are Caesar's, and to God the things that are God's." They were not able to trap Him in His words before the people. They marveled at his answer and were silent.

Jesus clearly states that we are to pay all our taxes. This is giving to Caesar what is due him. We cannot let our feelings stand in our way. What is due is due.

The point is clear. When we submit to the Lord by paying our taxes, then we encourage ourselves to submit to the many authorities we are supporting. If we oppose the taxes, then our opposition will grow toward authorities.

Our Necessary Respect

We have another truth found in the same verse. Not only are we to pay our taxes, but we must give them respect.

Romans 13:7
Therefore give everyone what you owe: if you owe taxes, pay taxes; if customs, then customs; if respect, then respect; if honor, then honor.

Here is the same word "render" or "give" we just discussed. We must render the appropriate respect to the established authorities. Again, this is critical.

The word translated "respect" is the same word that is used in Romans 13:3-4 but is used in a different way. This can mean the recognition of another's authority and power and having a fearful respect toward them. It is used many places with this Scriptural concept of fearful respect.

This term is used to describe the fearful respect the crowd had for Christ when they saw Him heal the paralytic. Notice, they did not run away in terror but stood in the amazement with respectful fear.

Luke 5:26
Amazement took hold on all, and they glorified God. They were filled with fear, saying, "We have seen strange things today."

When Jesus raised the mother's dead son in Nain, this term is used to portray the recognition that someone was in their midst that was more than a man.

Luke 7:16
Fear took hold of all...they glorified God, saying, "A great prophet has arisen among us...God...visited his people!"

The people who encountered the apostles saw numerous miracles and a fearful respect came upon all.

Acts 2:43
Fear came on every soul, and many wonders and signs were done through the apostles.

The mandate to evangelize and the coming judgment made them fearfully respect God.

2 Corinthians 5:11
Knowing therefore the fear of the Lord, we persuade men, but we are revealed to God; and I hope that we are revealed also in your consciences.

So, this fearful respect is due governing authorities because they are God's avengers and wield the sword.

We do not just submit, but we respect their authority and power. This is an attitude which pours forth into respectful words and actions. This attitude accompanies obedience not a bitter, angry spirit.

Our Necessary Honor

A second attitude which accompanies our submission is honor. We must honor the authorities God has established.

Romans 13:7
Therefore give everyone what you owe: if you owe taxes, pay taxes; if customs, then customs; if respect, then respect; if honor, then honor.

1 Peter 2:17
Honor all men. Love the brotherhood. Fear God. Honor the king.

In these two passages, both Paul and Peter are speaking of the same truth: we must honor all men especially God's servants. The Greek word translated "honor" in its verb form means "to estimate or fix the value of a thing; thus, to value or honor a person."

First, it refers to the monetary value of a thing. Matthew utilizes the term to describe the real price of the coinage Judas requested to betray the Son.

Matthew 27:6
The chief priests took the pieces of silver, and said, "It's not lawful to put them into the treasury, since it is the price of blood."

Luke uses the word to explain the selling of property by the saints to provide for the needs of their own people who had recently come to know the Lord.

Acts 4:34
For neither was there among them any who lacked, for as many as were owners of lands or houses sold them...brought the proceeds of the things that were sold.

Below, the term is used for the price (value) of Christ's blood which was shed for our sins.

1 Corinthians 6:20
For you were bought with a price. Therefore glorify God in your body and in your spirit, which are God's.

    Second, it refers to the full recognition of one's value to another. It is the honor given because of the great value of someone. Here, it refers to the value of Christ.

Revelation 4:9
When the living creatures give glory, honor, and thanks to him...who lives forever and ever.

In this passage, the word is used to speak of divine honor.

John 5:23
That all may honor the Son, even as they honor the Father. He who doesn't honor the Son doesn't honor the Father who sent him.

To recognize the value of the Father, one must recognize the value of the Son. We cannot recognize one without the other.

It is used of the reputation (his value to others) of Gamaliel.

Acts 5:34
But one stood up in the council, a Pharisee named Gamaliel, a teacher of the law, honored by all the people, and commanded to put the apostles out for a little while.

In his letter to the Hebrews. the inspired author describes how the marriage bed must be valued; that is, sex within marriage must be recognized as the only sex to be honored.

Hebrews 13:4
Let marriage be held in honor among all...let the bed be undefiled: but God will judge the sexually immoral and adulterers.

So, we must recognize the value of the government and its structure God has put into place.

As we have seen, another response is to honor the people God has placed in the government. We must recognize their value to God, society, and ourselves. They prevent evil from happening. In our words or actions, we must show value.

Our Continual Readiness

Another indirect action we can engage in as we submit to the governing authorities is to prepare for good works.

Titus 3:1
Remind them to be in subjection to rulers and to authorities, to be obedient [to rulers], to be ready for every good work.

The word translated "to be ready" refers to "being ready or prepared" to do something. In the New Testament, it is used to speak of "preparation" in a variety of situations.

It is used to describe the preparation of a meal.

Matthew 22:4
Again he sent out other servants, saying, 'Tell those who are invited, "Behold, I have prepared my dinner. My cattle and my fatlings are killed, and all things are ready. Come to the marriage feast!"

It refers to being prepared to join a wedding celebration.

Matthew 25:10
While they went away to buy, the bridegroom came, and those who were ready went in with him to the marriage feast, and the door was shut.

The word describes the preparation of the upper room for the Lord's arrival.

Mark 14:15
He will himself show you a large upper room furnished and ready. Get ready for us there.

Peter used it to demonstrate his readiness to die for the lord Jesus Christ.

Luke 22:33
He said to him, "Lord, I am ready to go with you both to prison and to death!"

Luke uses the word to speak of those who had prepared and were ready to assassinate Paul.

Acts 23:21
Therefore don't yield to them, for more than forty men lie in wait for him, who have bound themselves under a curse neither to eat nor to drink until they have killed him. Now they are ready, looking for the promise from you."

The verb "ready" is in the present tense which indicates a continual readiness for good deeds. So, Paul's point is to be ready for good deeds which will help us in being ready for the good deed of obedience to the law.

Our Confident Affirmation

To be in subjection to governing authorities, we must be affirming confidently how important this submission is as a good work. Paul begins his discussion with obedience to authorities and shows how that obedience is a good work. He finishes his discussion by charging Titus to confidently affirm the importance of good works, one of which is to submit to government.

Titus 3:8
This saying is faithful, and concerning these things I desire that you affirm confidently, so that those who have believed God may be careful to maintain good works. These things are good and profitable to men.

This word comes from a root word which means "to make firm, establish, confirm, or make sure." This word refers to verifying the truth. The Greek term was used by Mark and the author of Hebrews to describe the confirmation of the truth with great miracles.

Mark 16:20
They went out, and preached everywhere, the Lord working with them, and confirming the word by the signs that followed. Amen.

Hebrews 2:3
How will we escape if we neglect so great a salvation — which at the first having been spoken through the Lord, was confirmed to us by those who heard.

If we affirm confidently to each other that good works is important, then those "good works" must include obedience to authorities.

Our Careful Maintenance

Finally, we must be careful to maintain good works. If we do this, then obedience will flow from this because it also is a good work.

Titus 1:8
This saying is faithful, and concerning these things I desire that you affirm confidently, so that those who have believed God may be careful to maintain good works. These things are good and profitable to men.

The words translated "be careful" means "be thoughtful." It comes from a root word meaning "the mind." It is used to describe the thinking process. This is used in Paul's letter to the Corinthians in this way.

1 Corinthians 14:20
Brothers, don't be children in thoughts, yet in malice be babies, but in thoughts be mature.

The word translated "maintain" means "to set into place, set over, or to place before." We see this word used by Paul in his writings.

1 Thessalonians 5:12
But we beg you, brothers, to know those who labor among you, and are over you in the Lord, and admonish you.

1 Timothy 3:4
One who rules his own house well, having children in subjection with all reverence.

1 Timothy 3:12
Let servants be husbands of one wife, ruling their children and their own houses well.

1 Timothy 5:17
Let the elders who rule well be counted worthy of double honor, especially those who labor in the word and in teaching.

So, Paul says we are to be thinking of putting good works in its proper place in our lives. If we do this, then the good work of submitting to authorities will flow from that.

Our Commitment to God's Structure

Since our subjection to the governing authorities is the main issue in this discussion concerning persecution, I will only touch on the many reasons given for our obedience without elaborating on them since that is for another book.

First, we are to be subject to authorities because they are divinely authorized.

Romans 13:1
Let every soul be in subjection to the higher authorities, for there is no authority except from God, and those who exist are ordained by God.

The critical word in this passage is the verb "is." This is in the present tense and should be properly interpreted "for there is 'continually existing' no authority except from God." If there is an authority that is currently in place, it is from God.

Second, we must submit to the authorities because they are established by God. Though they appear as if they have established themselves, they have not. It is the Lord's work.

THE PERSECUTION OF THE SAINTS AND HOW TO OVERCOME IT

Romans 13:1
Let every soul be in subjection to the higher authorities, for there is no authority except from God... who exist are ordained by God.

The verb "ordained" is in the perfect tense. This refers to past actions with continuing results. If a governing authority was established in the past and continues to exist, it is divinely established and must be obeyed.

Third, we submit because God is continuing the existence of the authorities.

Romans 13:1
Let every soul be in subjection to the higher authorities, for there is no authority except from God, and those who exist are ordained by God.

If they are continuing to exist, we can be fully assured that His power is allowing this, and we should and must fully obey the authorities.

Four, we submit to authorities because government is God's divine structure in society. It is part of God's blueprint to keep order.

Romans 13:2
Therefore he who resists the authority, withstands the ordinance of God; and those who withstand will receive to themselves judgment.

Five, we should submit to the government because they are to administer God's divine judgment in His behalf. They are his arm of power in judgment.

Romans 13:2
Therefore he who resists the authority, withstands the ordinance of God; and those who withstand will receive to themselves judgment.

Here, Paul explains that if we do not submit, then they will render a judgment and punishment. This is God's judgment.

Six, we obey so we will continue to possess the proper fear of doing evil. We must be afraid of punishment.

Romans 13:3
For rulers are not a terror to the good work, but to the evil. Do you desire to have no fear of the authority? Do that which is good, and you will have praise from the same.

This word translated "fear" means intense dread or terror.

Seven, Believers must remain fearful of the authorities themselves.

Romans 13:3
For rulers are not a terror to the good work, but to the evil. Do you desire to have no fear of the authority? Do that which is good, and you will have praise from the same.

This question implies that Christians must desire the fear of authorities. If we are not submitting to authorities, we will eventually not fear them, and it will get worst.

Eight, for God to give us the necessary praise, we must obey.

Romans 13:3
For rulers are not a terror to the good work, but to the evil. Do you desire to have no fear of the authority? Do that which is good, and you will have praise from the same.

1 Peter 2:14
Or to governors, as sent by him for vengeance on evildoers and for praise to those who do well.

They provide praise to the saints for their good behavior. This is God's praise.

Nine, we obey because they provide a divine service for God.

Romans 13:4
For he is a servant of God to you for good. But if you do that which is evil, be afraid, for he doesn't bear the sword in vain; for he is a servant of God, an avenger for wrath to him who does evil.

These are servants of God even though they may not even know it.

Ten, Christians must understand these authorities bear a sword even against Christians and should be obeyed.

Romans 13:4
For he is a servant of God to you for good. But if you do that which is evil, be afraid, for he doesn't bear the sword in vain; for he is a servant of God, an avenger for wrath to him who does evil.

These authorities are armed, and we must be afraid of their weapons that may be used against us.

Eleven, we obey all authorities because these officials are God's divine avengers and instruments of His justice.

Romans 13:4
For he is a servant of God to you for good. But if you do that which is evil, be afraid, for he doesn't bear the sword in vain; for he is a servant of God, an avenger for wrath to him who does evil.

1 Peter 2:14
Or to governors, as sent by him for vengeance on evildoers and for praise to those who do well.

They bring God's vengeance upon man when they refuse to follow the laws.

Twelve, we submit for the sake of our consciences. This means that God has put within us moral conscience that instructs and guides us into appropriate behavior. It will tell us to submit to the government. If we do not listen our consciences will become callous to obedience.

Romans 13:5
Therefore you need to be in subjection, not only because of the wrath, but also for conscience' sake.

This callousness will cause us to refuse to submit over and over. This "callousness" will bring nothing but sorrow upon sorrow on us as Christians.

Thirteen, we obey because they are always on call. They are continually in service for God.

Romans 13:6
For this reason you also pay taxes, for they are servants of God's service, attending continually on this very thing.

We must remember they are continually in service to God for His sake and ours.

Fourteen, we are to submit to governmental authorities for the Lord's sake.

1 Peter 2:13
Therefore subject yourselves to every ordinance of man for the Lord's sake: whether to the king, as supreme.

The Greek word "Lord" means "master." Our Master desires that we obey His servants.

Fifteen, we are to obey the government because they have a divine sender.

1 Peter 2:14
Or to governors, as sent by him for vengeance on evildoers and for praise to those who do well.

These authorities do not send themselves; they are sent by God.

Sixteen, another reason to submit to authorities is that this subjection is the will of God. This is something we do not have to figure out. It is crystal clear.

1 Peter 2:15
For this is the will of God, that by well-doing you should put to silence the ignorance of foolish men.

As we do good which includes submitting to authorities in this context, we are in line with the will of God.

Seventeen, we obey all authorities because God does not want unbelievers to criticize us due to disobedience to the law. He wants to silence the foolish scoffing of the unsaved.

1 Peter 2:15
For this is the will of God, that by well-doing you should put to silence the ignorance of foolish men.

Our good behavior in obeying the government will silence unbelievers because they will not have anything bad to say about us. They will not be able to point their fingers at any believer and say, "That Christian is a lawbreaker."

Eighteen, we must obey authorities because disobedience to is an improper use of our Christian liberty.

1 Peter 2:16
As free, and not using your freedom for a cloak of wickedness, but as bondservants of God.

We cannot say to authorities that we do not have to obey them because we are citizens of heaven.

Nineteen, as bondservants of God, we must obey His servants who are in authority.

1 Peter 2:16
As free...not using your freedom for a cloak of wickedness, but as bondservants of God.

As bondservants of God, we are to obey our master which is to obey the government.

Twenty, the support of authorities through prayer is please God and is acceptable to Him.

1 Timothy 2:3-4
For this is good [noble] and acceptable in the sight of God our Savior; who desires all...to be saved and come to full knowledge of the truth.

Essentially, when we pray for authorities, we please our Lord because he deems it as one of the actions that are "good and acceptable" to Him.

As it can be so clearly seen, obedience to all governing authorities is the normal, regular course of action for us, as Christians. This will become important as we contrast this with our behavior when those same governing authorities overstep the divine boundaries. This will be a powerful and clear testimony to them when these submissive believers are suddenly defiant and willing to stand their ground!

Chapter 8

Restrain with Deliberate Action

As we consider the first set of responses to persecution which are legal ones, we now come to the second action we may take. With our fundamental reaction being obedience, then Christians may permeate, penetrate, and infiltrate local, regional, or national governments in order to advance God's message and protect God's people. While they do this, they serve for the good of all relying on the wisdom of God. We see in both Testaments God raising up believers to restrain persecution with deliberate action. Sometimes, it was not a direct governmental position but a position of influence in a society.

In the Old Testament, it was to testify that He was the true God and to protect the nation of Israel from extinction (Israel was the light of the world). In the New Testament, it was the gospel of Jesus Christ and the protection of His saints (the church is the light of the world). In some of these situations, defiance of the law was also involved. In these cases, we will only consider them briefly here. In a later chapter, it will be dealt with extensively in our chapter on believers defying the law to obey a divine command.

The Difficult Rise of Joseph

God was going to bring a famine on the land and desired to protect the entire nation of Israel who were in the loins of Jacob and His sons from death. Without His nation, He would have no one to testify of Him to the world and there would be no Messiah. Due to Joseph's boasting, he was sold into slavery by his other brothers. A very wealthy Egyptian purchased him, discovered God was with him, and gave him charge over all his affairs which he wisely handled.

Genesis 39:1-6
Joseph was brought...to Egypt. Potiphar, an officer of Pharaoh's, the captain of the guard, an Egyptian, bought him from the hand of the Ishmaelites...Yahweh was with Joseph, and he was a prosperous man. He was in the house of his master the Egyptian. His master saw that Yahweh was with him, and that Yahweh made all that he did prosper in his hand. Joseph found favor in his sight. He ministered to him, and he made him overseer over his house, and all that he had he put into his hand. From the time that he made him overseer in his house, and over all that he had, Yahweh blessed the Egyptian's house for Joseph's sake. Yahweh's blessing was on all that he had, in the house and in the field. He left all that he had in Joseph's hand. He didn't concern himself with anything, except for the food which he ate.

Unfortunately, Potiphar's wife was attracted to him, and he refused her advances. She accused him of rape, and he was thrown into prison. He was where God wanted him.

Genesis 39:20
Joseph's master took him, and put him into the prison, the place where the king's prisoners were bound, and he was there in custody.

Once again, God worked in his life, and he rose again to a position of power and influence.

Genesis 39:21-23
But Yahweh was with Joseph, and showed kindness to him, and gave him favor in the sight of the keeper of the prison. The keeper of the prison committed to Joseph's hand all the prisoners who were in the prison. Whatever they did there, he was responsible for it.

The keeper of the prison didn't look after anything that was under his hand, because Yahweh was with him; and that which he did, Yahweh made it prosper.

This position allowed Joseph to meet the prisoners that God wanted him to meet for his next rise to power. He had to interpret the dreams of the two prisoners from Pharaoh's court in order to demonstrate that God was with him. This would eventually bring him to Pharaoh's court.

Genesis 40:12-14
Joseph said..., "This is its interpretation: the three branches are three days. Within three more days, Pharaoh will lift up your head, and restore you....You will give Pharaoh's cup into his hand...But remember me when it will be well with you, and please show kindness to me, and make mention of me to Pharaoh, and bring me out of this house.

Then Pharaoh had a dream and the cupbearer remembered him and told the emperor. He sent for Joseph and God's man was able to interpret the dream. Then Pharaoh put Joseph over the whole land to prepare for the famine that was predicted.

Genesis 40:38-43
Pharaoh said to his servants, "Can we find such a one as this, a man in whom is the Spirit of God?" Pharaoh said to Joseph, "Because God has shown you all of this, there is no one so discreet and wise...You shall be over my house...according to your word will all my people be ruled. Only in the throne I will be greater than you."

As a result, when the famine came, Joseph was able to save the entire nation of Israel that were in the loins of Jacob and his sons. Joseph attributed his rise to power to God and to God alone.

Genesis 50:20-21
As for you, you meant evil against me, but God meant it for good, to bring to pass, as it is today, to save many people alive. Now therefore don't be afraid. I will nourish you and your little ones." He comforted them...spoke kindly to them.

This is the reason the people of Israel found themselves in Egyptian slavery for seventy years and paved the way for the most dramatic event of the Old Testament: the Passover (by the angel of death).

The Return of Moses

As we look at the rise of Moses, we will discuss it through the eyes of Stephen in the book of Acts rather than Moses in the book of Exodus. The Lord God protected Moses from the being killed after his birth.

Acts 7:19-21
The same took advantage of our race, and mistreated our fathers, and forced them to throw out their babies, so that they wouldn't stay alive. At that time Moses was born, and was exceedingly handsome. He was nourished three months in his father's house. When he was thrown out, Pharaoh's daughter took him up, and reared him as her own son.

So, Moses was raised by the daughter of Pharaoh and instructed in the great knowledge and learning at that time. He was placed in a powerful position in this great nation which God would use later.

Acts 7:21-22
When he was thrown out, Pharaoh's daughter took him up and reared him as her own son. Moses was instructed in all the wisdom of the Egyptians. He was mighty in his words and works.

When Moses felt the time had come for him to deliver Israel from bondage, this prince attempted to defend a Hebrew.

Acts 7:23-25
But when he was forty years old, it came into his heart to visit his brothers, the children of Israel. Seeing one of them suffer wrong, he defended him, and avenged him who was oppressed, striking the Egyptian. He [Moses] supposed that his brothers understood that God, by his hand, was giving them deliverance; but they didn't understand.

Afterward, he discovered that their hearts were hardened, and they rejected him.

Acts 7:26-29
The day following, he appeared to them as they fought, and urged them to be at peace...saying, "Sirs, you are brothers. Why do you wrong one another?" But he...pushed him away, saying, "Who made you a ruler and a judge over us? Do you want to kill me, as you killed the Egyptian...." Moses fled...and became a stranger in the land of Midian, where he became the father of two sons.

After forty years hiding in the wilderness, the time had come for deliverance. So, God spoke to Moses in a burning bush.

Acts 7:34
"I [Yahweh] have surely seen the affliction of my people that is in Egypt, and have heard their groaning. I have come down to deliver them...I will send you into Egypt."

When Moses entered Pharaoh's court, he was not a stranger. He knew and understood the ways of Pharaoh and would been able to navigate the many the many procedures of the court. The once rejected leader had returned. God was able to protect His people and proclaim His deity to all nations.

The Diet of Daniel and the Three

It was common practice for a nation to conquer lands and move the inhabitants to other areas to separate them from their land and each other. They would take the leaders and reeducate them if they were willing. Daniel and three others (Hananiah, Mishael, and Azariah) were some of the leaders who were taken when Judah was conquered by Babylon. As they were being prepared for their positions of authority, they took a stand for their God and proclaimed His message.

Daniel 1:8-16
But Daniel purposed in his heart that he would not defile himself with the king's dainties, nor with the wine which he drank: therefore he requested of the prince of the eunuchs that he might not defile himself....Then Daniel said to the steward whom the prince of the eunuchs had appointed... "Test your servants, I beg you, ten days; and let them give us vegetables to eat, and water to drink. Then let our faces be looked on before you, and the face of the youths who eat of the king's dainties; and as you see, deal with your servants." So he listened to them in this matter, and proved them ten days. At the end of ten days their faces appeared fairer, and they were fatter in flesh, than all the youths who ate of the king's dainties. So the steward took away their dainties, and the wine that they should drink, and gave them pulse.

These four penetrated deep into Babylon and provided a clear testimony for their God. This God separated His people from the other nations and their idolatry to show He existed.

The Dream Interpretation of Daniel

God placed Daniel into the highest ranks of the kingdom of Babylon in order to proclaim His message and protect His people by providing the interpretation of king's dreams.

Daniel 2:36-39
This is the dream; and we will tell its interpretation before the king. You, O king, are king of kings, to whom the God of heaven has given the kingdom, the power, and the strength, and the glory...has he given into your hand, and has made you to rule over them all: you are the head of gold. After you shall arise another kingdom....

When Daniel concluded his interpretation, the king knew it had come from God.

Daniel 2:47
The king answered to Daniel, and said, "Of a truth your God is the God of gods, and the Lord of kings, and a revealer of secrets, since you have been able to reveal this secret."

As a result, Daniel was promoted and then brought the three others with him.

Daniel 2:48-49
Then the king made Daniel great, and gave him many great gifts, and made him to rule over the whole province...and to be chief governor over all the wise men of Babylon. Daniel requested of the king, and he appointed Shadrach, Meshach, and Abednego, over the affairs of the province of Babylon: but Daniel was in the gate....

The people of Israel in captivity would be fully protected so a remnant could return at God's time. Their message could be proclaimed then and even now as we are reading these words.

The Unwillingness to Bend the Knee

The Lord raised Shadrach, Meshach, and Abednego (their Babylonian names) to positions of authority due to Daniel's rise. God desired for them to demonstrate His power and to declare His message as He delivered them from the fiery furnace. The story begins with officials in the palace desiring to remove their authority and Jewish God from their midst. It was not uncommon for ancient emperors to create images of themselves and require their subjects to bow down to them. When this happened, the officials sprang into action. They wanted them dead.

Daniel 3:13-14
Then Nebuchadnezzar in rage and fury commanded to bring Shadrach, Meshach, and Abednego. Then they brought these men before the king. Nebuchadnezzar answered them, "Is it on purpose, Shadrach, Meshach, and Abednego, that you don't serve my god, nor worship the golden image which I have set up? Now if you are ready whenever you hear the sound of the horn, flute, zither, lyre, harp, pipe, and all kinds of music to fall down and worship the image which I have made, good: but if you don't worship, you shall be cast the same hour into the middle of a burning fiery furnace; and who is that god that shall deliver you out of my hands?"

These great men of faith defied the emperor and refused to worship his image.

Daniel 3:18-19
But if not, let it be known to you, O king, that we will not serve your gods, nor worship the golden image which you have set up. Then was Nebuchadnezzar full of fury, and the form of his appearance was changed.... He...commanded that they should heat the furnace seven times more than it was usually heated.

Once they were thrown into the fiery furnace, God delivered them.

Daniel 3:25
He answered, Look, I see four men loose, walking in the middle of

the fire, and they are unharmed; and the aspect of the fourth is like a son of the gods. Then Nebuchadnezzar came near to the mouth of the burning fiery furnace: he spoke and said, Shadrach, Meshach, and Abednego, you servants of the Most High God, come out, and come here. Then Shadrach, Meshach, and Abednego came out of the middle of the fire.

Then the emperor honored them and their God.

Daniel 3:28
Nebuchadnezzar spoke and said, Blessed be the God of Shadrach, Meshach, and Abednego, who has sent his angel, and delivered his servants who trusted in him, and have changed the king's word, and have yielded their bodies, that they might not serve nor worship any god, except their own God.

The message was announced and then he made a decree to protect God's people.

Daniel 3:29
Therefore I make a decree, that every people, nation, and language, which speak anything evil against the God of Shadrach, Meshach, and Abednego, shall be cut in pieces, and their houses shall be made a dunghill; because there is no other god who is able to deliver after this sort.

Once again, God placed these men in high places to advance His message and protect His people.

The Interpretation Leading to Madness

Though Nebuchadnezzar had seen the mighty works of God, he still thought that all he had possessed in dominion, status, and treasures were from his own hand. It was time for the Lord God to show him who was in control. So, God gave him a dream which Daniel interpreted. It symbolized God striking the king with madness in order to show not only him but the whole world who the true God was.

Daniel 4:33
This was fulfilled the same hour on Nebuchadnezzar. He was driven from men, and ate grass as oxen, and his body was wet with the dew of the sky, until his hair had grown like eagles' feathers, and his nails like birds' claws.

For seven years, the Nebuchadnezzar lived with the mind of an animal and then God lifted the curse in order for the king to give Him glory.

Daniel 4:34-35
At the end of the days I, Nebuchadnezzar, lifted up my eyes to heaven, and my understanding returned...and I blessed the Most High, and I praised and honored him who lives forever; for his dominion is an everlasting dominion, and his kingdom from generation to generation.....the inhabitants of the Earth are reputed as nothing; and he does according to his will in the army of heaven, and among the inhabitants of the Earth; and no one can stay his hand, or ask him, What are you doing?

Nebuchadnezzar now knew that it was Daniel's God who was supreme over all. Again, God used Daniel to protect His people and advance His gospel.

The Declaration from Belshazzar's Judgment

Though Nebuchadnezzar's son knew what had happened to his father and the declaration he had made concerning the God of Israel, He refused to acknowledge the Lord. Then the son, Belshazzar hosted a great banquet with a thousand of his lords. Belshazzar, his wives, and concubines drank wine out of gold and silver vessels which were taken by his father from the temple of Israel's God in front of their guests. Then, they praised all their idols made of gold, silver, brass, iron, wood, and stone.

This made the Lord God angry, and He responded with a terrifying vision.

Daniel 5:5-6
In the same hour, the fingers of a man's hand came out and wrote near the lamp stand on the plaster of the wall of the king's palace. The king saw the part of the hand that wrote. 6 Then the king's face was changed in him, and his thoughts troubled him; and the joints of his thighs were loosened, and his knees struck one against another.

None of his enchanters, Chaldeans, or soothsayers could interpret the vision, then Daniel was remembered.

Daniel 5:13-14
Then was Daniel brought in before the king. The king spoke and said to Daniel, "Are you that Daniel, who are of the children of the captivity of Judah, whom the king my father brought out of Judah? I have heard of you, that the spirit of the gods is in you, and that light...understanding...excellent wisdom are found in you."

God had given Daniel great wisdom, and the king knew it.

Now, Daniel could proclaim the message that his own father had proclaimed but his son had ignored.

Daniel 5:18-21
You, king, the Most High God gave Nebuchadnezzar your father the kingdom, and greatness, and glory, and majesty: and because of the greatness that he gave him, all the peoples, nations, and languages trembled and feared before him...But when his heart was

lifted up, and his spirit was hardened so that he dealt proudly...He was driven from the sons of men, and his heart was made like the animals'...until he knew that the Most High God rules in the kingdom of men, and that he sets up over it whomever he will.*

Then, Daniel declared that God would take the kingdom from him and give it to the Medes and Persians. The son's response was to raise Daniel's position and stature in his own kingdom.

*Daniel 5:29
Then commanded Belshazzar, and they clothed Daniel with purple, and put a chain of gold about his neck, and made proclamation concerning him, that he should be the third ruler in the kingdom.*

The Lord God used this to put Daniel in a major position in the new Persian kingdom. Of course, this would allow him to protect God's people and advance His gospel.

The Announcement After the Lion's Den

Darius, the new emperor, respected Daniel deeply and wanted to place him over the entire realm.

*Daniel 6:1-4
It pleased Darius to set over the kingdom of [Persia] one hundred twenty satraps...and over them three presidents, of whom Daniel was one; that these satraps might give account to them, and that the king should have no damage. Then this Daniel was distinguished above the presidents and the satraps, because an excellent spirit was in him; and the king thought to set him over the whole realm.*

God gave Daniel great wisdom and the Satraps wanted to destroy him, but they could not entrap him.

Daniel 6:4-5
Then the presidents and the satraps sought to find occasion against Daniel as touching the kingdom; but they could find no occasion nor fault, because he was faithful, neither was there any error or fault found in him. Then these men said, "We shall not find any occasion against this Daniel, except we find it against him concerning the law of his God."

So, these officials decided to convince Darius to make a proclamation.

Daniel 6:7
All the presidents...deputies...and the satraps, the counselors and the governors, have consulted together to establish a royal statute, and to make a strong decree, that whoever shall ask a petition of any god or man for thirty days, except of you, O king, he shall be cast into the den of lions.

Of course, Daniel defied the authorities.

Daniel 6:10
When Daniel knew that the writing was signed, he went into his house (now his windows were open in his room toward Jerusalem) and he kneeled on his knees three times a day, and prayed...gave thanks before his God, as he did before.

When the king discovered what Daniel had done, he had no choice but to throw him in the lion's den. This is not what he wanted at all but was compelled to follow the law.

Daniel 6:19
Then the king arose very early in the morning, and went in haste to the den of lions. When he came near to the den to Daniel, he cried with a lamentable voice; the king spoke and said to Daniel, Daniel, servant of the living God, is your God, whom you serve continually, able to deliver you from the lions?

The result was an advancement of God's message and the protection of God's people under a new regime.

Daniel 6:25
Then king Darius wrote to all the peoples, nations, and languages, who dwell in all the Earth...I make a decree, that in all the dominion of my kingdom men tremble and fear before the God of Daniel; for he is the living God, and steadfast forever, His kingdom that which shall not be destroyed; and his dominion shall be even to the end. He delivers and rescues, and he works signs and wonders in heaven and in Earth, who has delivered Daniel from the power of the lions.

This also prepared Daniel for an exalted position under the next ruler after Darius so he would protect God's people and advance His gospel.

Daniel 6:28
So this Daniel prospered in the reign of Darius, and in the reign of Cyrus the Persian.

The Identification of The Magi

We cannot leave the life and witness of Daniel without mentioning the important influence He obviously had on the Magi who eventually came to honor the newborn king of the Jews. In His book, Daniel identified several court officials that he worked with using specific titles for their positions. Though Daniel does not distinguish the differences in these specific positions, the translators of the Septuagint (Greek translation of the Hebrew Bible at the time of Christ) were able to They used the Greek term "Magi" for the exact same Aramaic word. For our study here, we need to simply note that these were high officials that Daniel influenced in the official court. The Satraps were governors of regions.

Daniel 1:20
In every matter of wisdom and understanding, concerning which the king inquired of them, he found them ten times better than all the magicians and enchanters [Magi] who were in all his realm.

Daniel 2:2
Then the king commanded to call...magicians, and the enchanters [Magi], and the sorcerers, and the Chaldeans, to tell the king his dreams. So, they came in and stood before the king.

Daniel 2:10
The Chaldeans answered before the king, and said, There is not a man on the Earth who can show the king's matter, because no king, lord, or ruler, has asked such a thing of any magician, or enchanter [Magi], or Chaldean.

Daniel 2:27
Daniel...said...secret which...king has demanded can neither wise men, enchanters [Magi], magicians, nor soothsayers, show....

Daniel 4:6-7
Therefore I made a decree to bring in all the wise men of Babylon before me, that they might make known to me the interpretation... dream....magicians...enchanters [Magi]...Chaldeans...soothsayers came in; and I told the dream before them; but they didn't make known to me its interpretation.

Daniel 5:7
The king cried...to bring in the enchanters [Magi], the Chaldeans, and the soothsayers. The king spoke and said to the wise men of Babylon, Whoever shall read this writing, and show me its interpretation, shall be clothed with purple, and have a chain of gold about his neck, and shall be the third ruler in the kingdom.

Daniel 5:11
There is a man in your kingdom, in whom is the spirit of the holy gods; and in the days of your father light and understanding and

wisdom, like the wisdom of the gods, were found in him; and the king Nebuchadnezzar...the king, your father, made him master of the magicians, enchanters [Magi], Chaldeans, and soothsayers.

So, it was Daniel who provided the "Magi" in both the Babylonian and then Persian courts with the knowledge that the a "star" would signal the birth of the King of the Jews." This would lead these court officials on a long journey from the East to identify the newborn Jesus.

Matthew 2:1-2
Now when Jesus was born in Bethlehem of Judea in the days of King Herod, behold, wise men [Magi] from the east came to Jerusalem, saying, "Where is he who is born King of the Jews? For we saw his star in the east, and have come to worship him."

Matthew 2:9-11
They, having heard the king, went their way; and behold, the star, which they saw in the east, went before them, until it came and stood over where the young child was. When they saw the star, they rejoiced with exceedingly great joy. They came into the house [one to two years later] and saw the young child with Mary, his mother, and they fell down and worshiped him. Opening their treasures, they offered to him gifts: gold, frankincense, and myrrh.

The verification of the kingship and deity of the newborn Son of God occurred because these Magi were influenced by Daniel and were able to identify the Christ due to their high position.

The Restoration of The Nation as Light

While in captivity, Nehemiah was the cupbearer to the King. He functioned perfectly in this important position but remained religiously distinct. He was placed in power by

God to rebuild and restore the nation of Israel when they returned from captivity.

Nehemiah 2:1-6
In the month Nisan, in the twentieth year of Artaxerxes the king, when wine was before him, I took up the wine, and gave it to the king. Now I had not been sad before in his presence. The king said to me, "Why is your face sad, since you are not sick? This is nothing else but sorrow of heart." Then I was very much afraid. I said to the king, "Let the king live forever! Why shouldn't my face be sad, when the city, the place of my fathers' tombs, lies waste, and its gates have been consumed with fire?" Then the king said to me, "For what do you make request?" So I prayed to the God of heaven. I said to the king, "If it pleases the king, and if your servant has found favor in your sight, that you would send me to Judah, to the city of my fathers' tombs, that I may build it." The king said to me (the queen was also sitting by him), "For how long shall your journey be? And when will you return?" So it pleased the king to send me; and I set him a time.

So, Nehemiah was able to return to the land and rebuild the walls of Jerusalem.

The Preservation by Esther

The story of Queen Esther is a powerful example of God placing someone into a key position in a secular kingdom to advance His message and protect His people. The Jews had been taken into Babylon for a long captivity for their idolatry against God, but they were still His people. The Persians had taken over under Daniel's prophetic rise. Now, Ahasuerus was on the throne and became angry with his queen because she would not parade herself before his drunken lords. To replace her, he called for the most beautiful women to be brought to his palace. Then, Esther, the Jewess, was chosen.

When her uncle Mordechai refused to bow down before Haman, a newly appointed high official, he sought revenge upon this Jew and his people who bowed only to their God.

Esther 3:5
When Haman saw that Mordecai didn't bow down, nor pay him homage, Haman was full of wrath. But he scorned the thought of laying hands on Mordecai alone, for they had made known to him Mordecai's people. Therefore Haman sought to destroy all the Jews who were throughout the whole kingdom of Ahasuerus, even Mordecai's people.

As Haman's influence over the king rose, the danger for Mordechai and the Jewish people grew. So, Mordechai begged Esther to speak to the king. She told him that she risked death by asking to be in the presence of the emperor without his request. Her uncle urged her saying that she may be in her position for "such a time as this."

Esther 4:14
For if you remain silent now, then relief and deliverance will come to the Jews from another place, but you and your father's house will perish. Who knows if you haven't come to the kingdom for such a time as this?"

So, Esther decided to take the risk of death because she knew that God must have placed her as queen to save her people.

Esther sent an urgent message to her uncle explaining that she had decided to intervene and desired prayer and fasting for the Lord's protection.

Esther 4:15-17
Then Esther asked them to answer Mordecai, "Go, gather together all the Jews who are present in Susa, and fast for me, and neither eat nor drink three days, night or day. I and my maidens will also

fast the same way. Then I will go in to the king, which is against the law; and if I perish, I perish." So Mordecai went his way, and did according to all that Esther had commanded him.

Esther, the Jewish queen, met with the king and revealed all of Haman's plans to destroy her people.

Esther 7:4-6
"For we are sold, I [Esther] and my people, to be destroyed, to be slain, and to perish. But if we had been sold for male and female slaves, I would have held my peace, although the adversary could not have compensated for the king's loss." Then King Ahasuerus said to Esther the queen, "Who is he, and where is he who dared presume in his heart to do so?" Esther said, "An adversary and an enemy...wicked Haman!"

Eventually, Haman was hanged on the gallows that he had built for Mordechai.

Then, the king made an edict declaring that the Jewish people could defend themselves if his people attacked them.

Esther 8:11
In those letters, the king granted the Jews who were in every city to gather themselves together, and to defend their life, to destroy, to kill, and to cause to perish, all the power of the people and province that would assault them, their little ones little ones and women, and to plunder... possessions.

This led to the salvation message of the Jews concerning their God being heard by the people in the empire. Then, many came to believe in Yahweh.

Esther 8:17
In every province...every city, wherever the king's commandment and his decree came, the Jews had gladness, joy, a feast, and a good

day. Many...of the land became Jews; for the fear of the Jews had fallen on them.

God had indeed placed Esther in a high position for "such as time as this." The queen was able to protect God's people and in so doing promote His message.

The Miracle Muting of a Prominent Priest

As we move into the New Testament, we will find that God brought influential people to His glorious Son in order to advance the gospel and protect His saints. The first begins with the muting of Zacharias, a prominent priest.

Luke 1:5-7
There was in the days of Herod...a certain priest...Zacharias, of the priestly division.... He had a wife of the daughters of Aaron...her name was Elizabeth. They were both righteous before God, walking blamelessly in all the...and ordinances of the Lord. But they had no child, because Elizabeth was barren, and they both were well advanced in years.

When a multitude were gathered just outside the temple, the angel Gabriel appeared to him with a message from God of a future son.

Luke 1:10
The whole multitude of the people were praying outside at the hour of incense.

The angel announced the conception of the forerunner, John the Baptist. Their child would prepare God's people for the Messiah. Because Zacharias did not believe the angel, he was struck mute for the duration of the pregnancy. This would draw attention to not only Zacharias but to John and Jesus.

Luke 1:11-13
An angel of the Lord appeared to him, standing on the right side of the altar of incense.... But the angel said to him, "Don't be afraid, Zacharias...your request has been heard. Your wife, Elizabeth, will bear you a son...John."

Luke 1:14-16
You will have joy and gladness, and many will rejoice at his birth. For he will be great in the sight of the Lord, and he will drink no wine nor strong drink. He will be filled with the Holy Spirit, even from his mother's womb. He will turn many of the children of Israel to the Lord their God.

The people marveled when he left the temple.

Luke 1:21-22
The people were waiting for Zacharias, and they marveled that he delayed in the temple. When he came out, he could not speak to them. They perceived that he had seen a vision in the temple. He continued making signs...and remained mute.

Then, the people marveled when he named his son John.

Luke 1:61-63
They said to her, "There is no one among your relatives who is called by this name." They made signs to his father, what he would have him called. He asked for a writing tablet, and wrote, "His name is John." They all marveled. Again, the people marveled at the restoration of his speech.

Luke 1:64-66
His mouth was opened immediately and his tongue freed, and he spoke, blessing God. Fear came on all who lived around them, and all these sayings were talked about throughout all the hill country of Judea. All who heard them laid them up in their heart, saying, "What then will this child be?" The hand of the Lord was with him.

Finally, people marveled when he prophesied that salvation was on its way through the line of David as promised.

Luke 1:67-69
His [John the Baptist's] father Zacharias was filled with the Holy Spirit...prophesied, saying, "Blessed be the Lord, the God of Israel, for he...visited and redeemed his people; and has raised up a horn of salvation for us in the house of his servant David.

This influential priest was able to advance the good news by proclaiming the forerunner of the Messiah.

The Wealthy Women's Support of Christ

From the beginning of the Jesus' ministry, the Lord had wealthy, influential women supporting Him financially.

Luke 8:1-3
Soon afterwards, he [Jesus] went about through cities and villages, preaching and bringing the good news of God's Kingdom. With him were the twelve, and certain women who had been healed of evil spirits and infirmities: Mary who was called Magdalene, from whom seven demons had gone out; and Joanna, the wife of Chuzas, Herod's steward [manager]; Susanna; and many others; who served them from their possessions.

Though not much is known about these women and the "many others," they were influential since they had enough wealth to fund his ministry. In a strict patriarchal society, women did not have possessions and material goods to sell unless they had an income like Lydia or a husband who had owned them. We know that Joanna's husband, Chuza, was a high-ranking official as manager of Herod's household. These are mentioned to demonstrate that these influential believers advanced the gospel through financial support.

The Preservation of The Body for Resurrection

Two influential and wealthy men who came to Christ and became pivotal in advancing the gospel and protecting the saints was Nicodemus and Joseph of Arimathea. Because they were members of the Sanhedrin and secret disciples, they secured the physical body of Jesus for burial.

John 19:38-40
After these things, Joseph of Arimathea, being a disciple of Jesus, but secretly for fear of the Jews, asked of Pilate that he might take away Jesus' body. Pilate gave him permission. He came therefore and took away his body. Nicodemus, who at first came to Jesus by night, also came bringing a mixture of myrrh and aloes, about a hundred Roman pounds. So they took Jesus' body, and bound it in linen cloths with the spices, as the custom of the Jews is to bury.

First it was critical that the body of Jesus be taken down from the cross and buried before the Sabbath and within the three-day time frame, He had prophesied.

John 2:18-19
The Jews therefore answered him, "What sign do you show us, seeing that you do these things?" Jesus answered them, "Destroy this temple, and in three days I will raise it up."

Matthew 12:39-40
But he answered them, "An evil and adulterous generation seeks after a sign, but no sign will be given to it but the sign of Jonah the prophet. For as Jonah was three days and three nights in the belly of the huge fish, so will the Son of Man be three days and three nights in the heart of the earth.

Second, they provided a necessary witness to believers and unbelievers then and now that Jesus truly died before they claimed He resurrected.

Joseph provided the tomb that Jesus was buried in. The other secret disciple, Nicodemus, brought spices to prepare the Lord's body.

Matthew 27:57-61
When evening had come, a rich man from Arimathea named Joseph, who himself was also Jesus' disciple, came. This man went to Pilate and asked for Jesus' body.... Pilate commanded the body to be given up. Joseph took the body and wrapped it in a clean linen cloth and laid it in his own new tomb, which he had cut out in the rock. Then, he rolled a large stone against the door of the [his] tomb, and departed. Mary Magdalene was there, and the other Mary, sitting opposite the tomb.

This also allowed the disciples to know exactly where Jesus was buried so the events of the resurrection could take place in their sight. Though not usually noticed, this was a critical sovereign act of God.

These men became a critical part of establishing the "fact" of the resurrection which is central to the gospel message. This fact was instrumental in its advancement.

The Veiled Influence on the Jewish Council

Perhaps, another important part these two men played in the advancement of the good news and the protection of the saints involved their participation in the Jewish Council. It was this body of men that instigated the crucifixion of Jesus by the Romans. We know that when the time that had been determined by the Father, Jesus made his ultimate sacrifice.

John 7:30
They sought therefore to take him; but no one laid a hand on him, because his hour had not yet come.

We also understand that the Jews began plotting Jesus' demise from the beginning of His three-year ministry. After Jesus healed the lame man at the pool of Bethesda and claimed that God was His Father, the Jews were already so angered they began to plot His death.

John 5:16-18
For this cause the Jews persecuted Jesus, and sought to kill him, because he did these things on the Sabbath. But Jesus answered them, "My Father is still working, so I am working, too." For this cause therefore the Jews sought all the more to kill him, because he not only broke the Sabbath, but...called God his...Father, making himself equal with God.

The Lord continually controlled the spread of information about His miracles to slow the rise of His fame. This kept a restraint on the devious actions of the Sanhedrin to silence Him until God's time.

Mark 7:32-36
They brought to him one who was deaf...had an impediment in his speech. They begged him to lay his hand on him.... that is, "Be opened!" Immediately his ears were opened...the impediment...of his tongue was released, and he spoke clearly. He commanded them that they should tell no one, but the more he commanded...the more they proclaimed it.

These two men received Christ during their tenure on the Jewish council but kept it secret out of fear. We do not know exactly what they may have done to protect the Lord and restrain the actions against Him, but we receive a glimpse.

It was the great Feast of Booths and Jesus was teaching in the temple. His preaching and miracles were so powerful that it was having an impact on the people which upset the leaders. A group of Pharisees began to challenge Jesus and rebuke the people who were listening to him. They blamed this on the people's ignorance of the law.

John 7:47-49
The Pharisees therefore answered them, "You aren't also led astray, are you? Have any of the rulers believed in him, or of the Pharisees? But this multitude that doesn't know the law is cursed."

Their strategy was to make the people believe that following Jesus was against the correct interpretation of the law, and they would be cursed. Second, the leaders who know the law unlike them have not followed Jesus.

Nicodemus intervened with a powerful legal challenge from the law that he knew very well. He also knew they would know exactly what he was talking about.

John 7:50-53
Nicodemus (he...came to him by night, being one of them) said to them, "Does our law judge a man, unless it first hears from him personally and knows what he does?" They [the Jewish leaders] answered him, "Are you also from Galilee? Search, and see that no prophet has arisen out of Galilee." Everyone went to his own house.

Nicodemus asserted that they could not possibly judge Jesus according to the law unless they had heard Him themselves and watched him long enough to discern what He actually said and did. Of course, they had not yet done that, and he silenced their accusations.

So, they attempted to make it look as if Nicodemus was defending him because he was also from Galilee. They did not expect any prophet to come from Galilee because it was considered a worthless region.

THE PERSECUTION OF THE SAINTS AND HOW TO OVERCOME IT

John 7:52
They answered him, "Are you also from Galilee? Search, and see that no prophet has arisen out of Galilee."

Of course, this was a lie because they would have known the prophecy of Isaiah.

Isaiah 9:1
But there shall be no more gloom for her who was in anguish. In the former time, he brought into contempt the land of Zebulun and the land of Naphtali; but in the latter time he has made it glorious, by the way of the sea, beyond the Jordan, Galilee of the nations.

In his gospel, Matthew refers to this very statement.

Matthew 4:13-16
Leaving Nazareth, he came and lived in Capernaum, which is by the sea, in the region of Zebulun and Naphtali, that it might be fulfilled which was spoken through Isaiah...saying, "The land of Zebulun and the land of Naphtali, toward the sea, beyond the Jordan, Galilee of the Gentiles, the people who sat in darkness saw a great light; to those who sat in the region and shadow of death, to them light has dawned."

Nevertheless, they were silenced, and then afterward the crowd departed.

John 7:53
Everyone went to his own house.

Through this glimpse of Nicodemus' effort to defend Jesus, we can infer that this may have continued in the Sanhedrin.

It is reasonable to assume the Joseph would have done the same. He was also a member of the same Jewish council. Why? Notice, how Luke describes him.

Luke 23:50-56
Behold, a man named Joseph, who was a member of the council, a good and righteous man (he had not consented to their counsel and deed), from Arimathea, a city of the Jews, who was also waiting for God's Kingdom.

It is easy to assume that this good and righteous man who was not willing to consent with the murder of Jesus, had some influence in at least stalling the arrest of Jesus through questions, objections, or discussing the interpretation of the law? Therefore, it is what Nicodemus and Joseph did that would have aided Jesus in His efforts to advance the good news and protect Him from being seized.

The Centurion's Confirmation of The Gospel

Cornelius was a Centurion and a religiously devout God-fearing Gentile. He was deeply respected in the community in which he lived and worked. His testimony for the Lord would have been well respected.

Acts 10:1-2
Now there was a certain man in Caesarea, Cornelius by name, a centurion of what was called the Italian Regiment, a devout man, and one who feared God with all his house, who gave gifts for the needy generously to the people, and always prayed to God.

The Lord Jesus told Cornelius to send for Peter and He told Peter to preach the gospel to Cornelius.

Acts 10:4-5
He [Cornelius], fastening his eyes on him [angel], and being frightened, said, "What is it, Lord?" He said to him, "Your prayers and your gifts to the needy have gone up for a memorial before God. Now send men to Joppa, and get Simon...called Peter.

Acts 10:15
A voice came to him [Peter] again the second time, "What God has cleansed, you must not call unclean."

Acts 10:19
While Peter was pondering the vision, the Spirit said to him, "Behold, three men [from Cornelius] seek you. But arise, get down, and go with them, doubting nothing; for I have sent them."

Then, Peter went to Cornelius and preached the gospel to him and his entire household. To confirm to Peter that God desired to save the Gentiles, the Spirit came upon them.

Acts 10:44-48
While Peter was still speaking these words, the...Spirit fell on all those who heard the word. They of the circumcision who believed were amazed, as many as came with Peter, because the gift of the...Spirit was also poured out on the Gentiles. For they heard them...languages...magnifying God. Then Peter answered, "Can anyone forbid these people from being baptized with water? They...received the Holy Spirit just like us." He commanded them to be baptized in the name of Jesus Christ....

As a result, Cornelius would have had some kind of impact in the advancement of the good news and perhaps even in the protection of the saints.

The Ministry and Confirmation of Two Brothers

During the life of Jesus, his brothers and sisters did not appear to believe that He was the Messiah.

John 7:2-9
Now the feast of the Jews, the Feast of Booths, was at hand. His brothers therefore said to him, "[Jesus] Depart from here and go

into Judea, that your disciples also may see your works which you do. For no one does anything in secret while he seeks to be known openly. If you do these things, reveal yourself to the world." For even his brothers didn't believe in him. Jesus therefore said to them, "My time has not yet come, but your time is always ready. The world can't hate you, but it hates me, because I testify about it, that its works are evil. You go up to the feast. I am not yet going up to this feast, because my time is not yet fulfilled." Having said these things to them, he stayed in Galilee.

In this passage, they accuse Him of trying to become popular and encourage Him to stop doing things in secret and go up to the feast and demonstrate in public who He thinks He is.

After the resurrection, we not only see two of His half-brothers saved but both wrote inspired epistles.

Galatians 1:18-19
Then after three years I went up to Jerusalem to visit Peter, and stayed with him fifteen days. But of the other apostles I saw no one except James, the Lord's brother.

Jude 1:1
Jude, a servant of Jesus Christ, and brother of James, to those who are called, sanctified by God the Father, and kept for Jesus Christ.

James was the half-brother of Jesus and the chief elder or pastor the Jerusalem church.

Acts 12:17
But he...declared to them how the Lord had brought him out of the prison. He said, "Tell these things to James and to the brothers." Then he departed and went to another place.

Acts 15:13
After they were silent, James answered, "Brothers, listen to me."

Acts 21:18
The day following, Paul went in with us to James; and all the elders were present.

The assembly at Jerusalem was the central church for the spread of the gospel to the Jews, the affirmation of Paul, the confirmation of the gospel to the Gentiles without Jewish restrictions, and the demonstration of how God protects His saints in persecution. This church was important to verifying God's truth to not only the Jews but also the Gentiles as He brought His gospel to all.

Acts 5:28
Saying, "Didn't we strictly command you not to teach in this name? Behold, you have filled Jerusalem with your teaching, and intend to bring this man's blood on us."

Acts 6:7
The word of God increased and the number of the disciples greatly multiplied in Jerusalem. A great company of the priests were obedient to the faith.

Galatians 2:9
And when they perceived the grace that was given to me, James and Cephas and John...who were reputed to be pillars, gave to Barnabas and me the right hand of fellowship, that we should go to the Gentiles, and they to the circumcision.

Acts 15:19
Therefore my judgment is that we don't trouble those from among the Gentiles who turn to God.

Acts 12:7
And behold, an angel of the Lord stood by him, and a light shone in the cell. He struck Peter on the side, and woke him up, saying, "Stand up quickly!" His chains fell off his hands.

As we can see the two brothers of Jesus were an amazing testimony of those who were averse to Jesus and then came to believe in Him. This influenced the advance of the gospel and the protection of the people of God.

The Influence of a Successful Businesswoman

Lydia was a successful businesswoman who would have had a powerful influence on believers and unbelievers alike. Though we do not know many of the details, it seems very appropriate that she should be mentioned here.

In Philippi, Paul went to the river to see if there was a prayer meeting among the ladies. This was the custom when a town didn't have ten Jewish men to form a synagogue.

Acts 16:13
On the Sabbath we went outside the city gate to the river, where we expected to find a place of prayer. We sat down and began to speak to the women who had gathered there.

So, Paul began to preach the gospel to the women. He met a woman named Lydia.

Acts 16:14
A certain woman named Lydia, a seller of purple, of the city of Thyatira, one who worshiped God, heard us; whose heart the Lord opened to listen to the things which were spoken by Paul.

The Lord opened the heart of this woman, and she received Christ as Savior and Lord.

The author of Acts, Luke, mentioned that she sold purple fabrics from Thyatira. Those kinds of fabrics were for the rich not the commoner. She "worshiped God" which meant she was a God-fearing Gentile. This would give her access to the Jewish and the Gentile worlds.

Then she believed, took Paul to her home, and he shared the gospel with whoever was in her house: mother, father, and servants. They received Jesus Christ as Savior and Lord.

Acts 16:15
When she and her household were baptized, she begged us, saying, "If you have judged me to be faithful to the Lord, come into my house, and stay." So she persuaded us.

Then, she asked Paul and the others to stay in her house. First, her success in business allowed her to offer her home as a base for Paul's ministry in Philippi. This was important to the advancement of the gospel and the protection of the Paul and his companions.

Second, after winning the Philippians jailor to Christ, her home became the location of the new church in town. Luke's account of Paul's ministry in Philippi ends with a description of her home church.

Acts 16:40
They went out of the prison, and entered into Lydia's house. When they had seen the brothers, they encouraged them, then departed.

The Slave Owner's Release of a Runaway

Perhaps another important person who might have been a powerful influence on the advance of the Gospel and the protection of the saints was Philemon, the slave owner, who welcomed his runaway slave back as a Christian brother. This is found in Paul's letter to Philemon. When Paul arrived in Rome, he met a runaway slave named Onesimus.

After Onesimus came to Christ, Paul discovered that his owner was a dear friend of his in the city of Colossae named Philemon. For a time, both Paul and Onesimus ministered together, but it came time to return him to his master so he could face his crime. This was a serious offense.

Rather than just let Onesimus return and face it alone, he decided to use the opportunity to teach both Onesimus and Philemon some important truths concerning forgiveness, the true fellowship between followers of Christ, and obeying the law. Paul sent a letter on behalf of this new believer which recommended that Philemon should forgive him. Then, he should be welcomed as a new brother in Christ rather than as a fugitive slave who deserved severe punishment.

Philemon 1:10-16
I beg you for my child, whom I have become the father of in my chains, Onesimus, who once was useless to you, but now is useful to you and to me. I am sending him back. Therefore receive him, that is, my own heart, whom I desired to keep with me, that on your behalf he might serve me in my chains for the Good News. But I was willing to do nothing without your consent, that your goodness would not be...of necessity, but of free will. For perhaps he was therefore separated from you for a while, that you would have him forever, no longer as a slave, but more....a beloved brother, especially to me, but how much rather to you, both in the flesh and in the Lord.

Paul asserts that God really had a purpose in this slave running away, and it was for his salvation. Now, Philemon has Onesimus back as a beloved brother in the flesh and in the Lord. He is especially a beloved brother to the apostle. His wish is that Onesimus should now be embraced as the beloved brother he has become in Christ. Rather than taking his time to punish this runaway, he should be cherished as a spiritual sibling.

Philemon 1:17-18
If then you count me a partner, receive him as you would receive me. But if he has wronged you at all, or owes you anything, put that to my account. I, Paul, write this with my own hand: I will repay it (not to mention to you that you owe to me even your own self besides). Yes, brother, let me have joy...in the Lord. Refresh my heart in the Lord. Having confidence in your obedience, I write to you, knowing that you will do even beyond what I say.

Though we are not told specifically what happens, we can be assured that Philemon welcomed Onesimus into his own household and church at Colossae. What else could he have done after such a powerful commendation from Paul?

Perhaps, once the letter was read completely, Philemon did the unthinkable to the unbelieving Roman world, he unchained and released Onesimus. Then Philemon reached out his hands and cried, "Welcome, my brother!" What an influence this might have been to all those in his community that saw how much his relationship with his slave Onesimus had changed through Christ.

The Affirmation of a Jailor

In Philippi, the apostle Paul won a jailor to Jesus Christ. This man would have had an influence on believers and unbelievers alike since he would be an unlikely candidate to depart from the Roman religion of gods.

After Paul cast the demon out of the fortune telling slave girl, her masters saw that the hope of their gain was gone. So, they seized Paul and Silas and dragged them into the marketplace before the rulers.

Acts 16:20-21
When they had brought them to the magistrates, they said, "These

men [Paul and Silas], being Jews, are agitating our city and advocate customs which it is not lawful for us to accept or to observe, being Romans."

Though these charges were false, the magistrates and crowd believed everything that was said. So, Paul and Silas were beaten and thrown into inner dungeon of this Roman prison.

Acts 16:22-23
The multitude rose up together against them, and the magistrates tore their clothes off of them, and commanded them to be beaten...When they had laid many stripes on them, they threw them into [the inner] prison, charging the jailer to keep them....

While in prison, they were praying and singing out loud for all to hear. This would include the prisoners and guards.

Acts 16:25
But about midnight Paul and Silas were praying and singing hymns to God, and the prisoners were listening to them.

They never forgot that they were unbelievers around who needed Christ and they would have to be the light even in their bruised, beaten half dead condition. And the reason actually came with an answer to their many prayers with a powerful earthquake.

Acts 16:26-27
Suddenly there was a great Earthquake...that the foundations of the prison were shaken; and immediately all the doors were opened...everyone's bonds were loosened. The jailer, being roused out of sleep and seeing the prison doors open, drew his sword and was about to kill himself, supposing that the prisoners had escaped.

In Roman times if any prisoner escaped one had to pay with his own life. Often, these guards would commit suicide rather than face the inevitable death at the hands of his fellow Romans. So, the distraught jailor took out his sword and prepared to kill himself when Paul stopped him.

Acts 16:28
But Paul cried...saying, "Don't harm yourself, for we are all here!" He called for lights, sprang in, fell down trembling before Paul and Silas, brought them out...said, "Sirs, what must I do to be saved?"

Paul had saved his life and now he would save his soul. Here again was another sovereign act of God.

Acts 16:31-32
They said, "Believe in the Lord Jesus Christ, and you will be saved, you and your household." They spoke the word of the Lord to him, and to all who were in his house.

The entire household received Jesus Christ and they became a part of the church in the city of Philippi. As these saints share their faith, what a testimony this would be! God works in these marvelous ways.

The jailor wasn't just some recluse who got stuck tending prisoners but was most likely an ex-Roman soldier with real status in the community. He and his household would have had a great Christian influence.

The Aid of Caesar's Household

We do not know much about those in Caesar's household but do know that they would have included all those in this palace not just his home. These people would be comprised of the servants, soldiers, and officers of the emperor. Paul won many of these to Jesus Christ while in his first Roman Imprisonment.

Philippians 4:22
All the saints greet you, especially those who are of Caesar's household.

Could they have aided in Paul's ability to not only dictate his letter, but have someone in his holding area to write them down, and then allow perhaps another to send them out to a church?

Romans 16:22-24
I, Tertius, who write the letter, greet you in the Lord. Gaius, my host and host of the whole assembly, greets you. Erastus, the treasurer of the city, greets you, as does Quartus....The grace of our Lord...be with you all! Amen.

The Support of The Praetorian Guards

While the apostle Paul was in the same imprisonment, he brought many guards to Christ.

Philippians 1:13
So that it became evident to the whole palace guard, and to all the rest, that my bonds are in Christ.

What might be the ramifications of believing guards? Could they have aided in the advancement of the gospel and the protection of the saints?

In Paul's first Roman imprisonment, he wrote four letters: Ephesians, Colossians, Philippians, and Philemon. In Paul's second and last Roman imprisonment, he wrote his second letter to Timothy.

2 Timothy 4:6
I am already being offered, and the time of my departure has come.

Prisoners in the ancient world were not incarcerated for long periods of time. Instead, prisons became holding tanks for death. Paul knew his end was coming but desperately wanted to see Timothy. How else would Paul have sent greetings and written this letter? As with the assumed aid of Caesar's household, we can reasonably conclude that the guards supported Paul in any way they could. As we can see from the Scriptures, our basic reaction to the law is obedience. Yet, there are other options we may take to deal with persecution. In this chapter, we saw that at times God will have His people permeate, penetrate, and infiltrate local, regional, or national governments in order to advance His message and protect His people while they serve for the good of all. Other times, God will bring to His Son people who are in positions of responsibility in order to do the same. Also, if those who are in a place of influence in society, God will use them to advance and protect. These are the other ways in which we, as Christians, stand our ground against persecution.

STANDING YOUR GROUND

Chapter 9

Apply with A Judicial Response

The third legal response would be adjudication. In most regions and nations of the world, people may not simply choose to do and say whatever they please. There are always laws for the common good and safety of all people. We learned in our chapter on subjecting ourselves to human government that God has placed authorities on Earth to organize and sustain societies and punish wrong doers in His behalf. This includes persecutors inside and outside the government.

We are not required to allow governmental officials or unbelieving citizens to mock, slander, libel, or harm us if it is against the law of the land. As Christians, we do not cease being citizens and may use the law to advance our message and protect God's people from persecution including by all governmental authorities. We will see that Paul often used his Roman citizenship and his knowledge of the law to advance the gospel and protect the saints. The apostle often appealed to his readers to follow his example as he lived and served the Lord.

1 Corinthians 4:16
I beg you therefore, be imitators of me.

1 Corinthians 11:1
Be imitators of me, even as I also am of Christ.

Galatians 4:12
I beg you, brothers, become as I am, for I also have become as you are. You did me no wrong.

Philippians 3:17
Brothers, be imitators together of me, and note those who walk this way, even as you have us for an example.

Philippians 4:9
The things which you learned, received, heard, and saw in me: do these things, and the God of peace will be with you.

1 Thessalonians 1:6
You became imitators of us, and of the Lord, having received the word in much affliction, with joy of the Holy Spirit,

2 Thessalonians 3:7
For you know how you ought to imitate us. For we didn't behave ourselves rebelliously among you,

2 Thessalonians 3:9
Not because we don't have the right, but to make ourselves an example to you, that you should imitate us.

Though not often noted, Paul continually used the laws of the land to advance the good news and protect himself, his companions, and the new churches that he established. It was his practice.

He exercised the rights that he possessed as both a Jewish and Roman citizen at critical times in his ministry. He stood before Jewish town officials, the Sanhedrin, and King Herod. Before the Romans he faced numerous local magistrates, regional governors, and eventually the emperor Himself. All of this was for the purpose of advancing the gospel and protecting Paul and other saints. Therefore, we not only can but ought to imitate him in his many judicial responses as he applied the laws of the land. These powerful examples of Paul's adjudication of both Jewish and Romans laws will be examined in their order of appearance in Acts.

The Roman Beating in Philippi

In Acts 16, Paul encountered persecution because he had removed a demon from a fortune telling slave girl. After losing their profit from her demonic skills, her legal masters dragged Paul before the city magistrates. Paul and Silas, his companion, were publicly accused of agitating the people and advocating customs that were illegal for Roman citizens to practice. In a great display of pomp and circumstance, the rulers tore their robes, ordered them to be beaten with rods, and secured in prison. The jailer threw them into the inner prison and locked them up in the stocks.

In Acts 16, the day arrived for their release.

Acts 16:35-40
But when it was day, the magistrates sent the sergeants, saying, "Let those men go." The jailer reported these words to Paul, saying, "The magistrates have sent to let you go; now therefore come out, and go in peace." But Paul said to them, "They have beaten us publicly, without a trial, men who are Romans, and have cast us into prison! Do they now release us secretly? No, most assuredly, but let them come themselves and bring us out!" The sergeants reported these words to the magistrates, and they were afraid when they heard that they were Romans, and they came and begged them. When they had brought them out, they asked them to depart from the city. They went out of the prison, and entered into Lydia's house. When they had seen the brothers, they comforted them, and departed.

So, the jailer declared that the rulers of the city had sent word that they could now go in peace. Rather than quietly leaving, Paul challenged the magistrates legally. He simply revealed what these rulers had forgotten to ask them. They were Roman citizens. As a result, they could not be beaten or imprisoned without a trial.

They would not leave secretly to hide what had been done. Instead, he demanded that the leaders escort them out of the city safely for all to see. After they saw the brethren, then he would leave. When the magistrates found out the two were Romans, they literally begged the two to leave quietly. They greatly feared the exposure of Paul's illegal imprisonment. Paul may also have been securing the safety of the little church in Philippi so it would be left alone.

Upon his arrival in Philippi, Paul did not disclose his true citizenship. Why? By faith, Paul knew God was at work. The Philippian jailer and all in his household would never have received Christ without his illegal imprisonment. Here, Paul chooses not to utilize the law to win the jailer to Christ. Yet later, Paul employs the same law for his own protection and the protection of all the saints in Philippi. This would allow all of them to freely share the gospel. The law was used to protect believers and advance the gospel as the Spirit led.

The Mob Action in Jerusalem

In Acts 21, Paul entered the Jewish temple area in the city of Jerusalem. Some irate Jews from Asia recognized Paul. Since they had seen him with a Gentile in the city, they supposed Paul had brought him into the temple. They stirred up the crowds because of this defilement. The mob grabbed Paul, dragged him out, and began beating him.

Acts 21:27-30
When the seven days were almost completed, the Jews from Asia, when they saw him in the temple, stirred up all the multitude and laid hands on him, crying out, "Men of Israel, help! This is the man who teaches all men everywhere against the people, and the law, and this place. Moreover, he also brought Greeks into the temple, and [he] has defiled this holy place!" For they had seen

Trophimus, the Ephesian, with him in the city...they supposed that Paul had brought him into the temple. All the city was moved, and the people ran together. They seized Paul and dragged him out of the temple. Immediately the doors were shut.

When the Roman cohort discovered that a mob murder was about to occur, they stormed into the crowd and rescued Paul.

Acts 21:31-33
As they were trying to kill him, news came up to the commanding officer of the regiment that all Jerusalem was in an uproar. Immediately he took soldiers and centurions and ran down to them. They, when they saw the chief captain and the soldiers, stopped beating Paul. Then the commanding officer came near, arrested him, commanded him to be bound with two chains, and inquired who he was and what he had done.

Here the government is protecting its citizens against harm even if it is of a religious nature. The Lord God protects his persecuted people through the government He creates.

The Interrogation by The Romans

Once Paul had been bound, the commanding officer attempted to find out from the crowd what Paul had done, but he received nothing of substance.

Acts 21:34
Some shouted one thing, and some another, among the crowd. When he couldn't find out the truth because of the noise, he commanded him to be brought into the barracks.

Then, Paul convinced the officer to let him speak to the crowd. This he did which only caused more chaos.

STANDING YOUR GROUND

After preaching the gospel, indicting the crowd for killing Stephen, and declaring that he was turning his attention to the Gentiles, the Jews went into a frenzy.

Acts 22:22
They listened to him until he said that; then they lifted up their voice and said, "Rid the earth of this fellow, for he isn't fit to live!"

Finally, in desperation, the commanding officer ordered his soldiers to question Paul through scourging. They would torture him to discover why he had incited such an uproar.

Acts 22:23-26
As they cried out, threw off their cloaks, and threw dust into the air, the commanding officer commanded him to be brought into the barracks, ordering him to be examined by scourging, that he might know for what crime they shouted against him like that. When they had tied him up with thongs, Paul asked the centurion who stood by, "Is it lawful for you to scourge a man who is a Roman, and not found guilty?" When the centurion heard it, he went to the commanding officer and told him, "Watch what you are about to do, for this man is a Roman!"

Paul allowed himself to be tied up in chains in preparation for the beating. Then, he casually inquired of the centurion near him as to whether any Roman citizen could be scourged without the ruling of a court. Of course, it was obvious. So, the soldier went and informed his superior. Paul gained the upper hand over his legal authority by not disclosing his Roman citizenship and allowing them to break the law.

Acts 22:27-28
The commanding officer came and asked him, "Tell me, are you a Roman?" He said, "Yes." The commanding officer answered, "I bought my citizenship for a great price." Paul said, "But I was born a Roman."

Then, he created a greater advantage over the superior by his birth as a citizen rather than paying for it. He was a true undeniable Roman and was mistreated.

Acts 22:29-30
Immediately those who were about to examine him departed from him, and the commanding officer also was afraid when he realized that he was a Roman, because he had bound him.

The commander was frightened because he had illegally bound Paul with chains. Consequently, Paul was released and now was a free man. Here again, Paul utilizes the law to protect himself from persecution. It is interesting to note that Paul manipulates the situation to place the commander in a difficult dilemma. This provided Paul with the advantage as this drama unfolds. They should have asked him if he was a Roman and they simply made a foolish assumption. From then on, the commander would be much more vigilant and careful as he handled Paul.

His Careful Handling by the Romans

After this, the commander brought Paul safely before the Jewish council.

Acts 22:30
But on the next day, desiring to know the truth about why he was accused by the Jews, he freed him from the bonds, and commanded the chief priests and all the council to come together, and brought Paul down and set him before them.

What did Paul do? He attempted to preach the gospel. The apostle Paul utilized the law to provide safe travel to the Jewish council so he could preach the good news to them. It is obvious that the crowds were still milling around to catch Paul if he was released. They were not finished with him yet.

As he began his testimony of salvation and his gospel presentation, he was slapped in the face. Paul rebuked them for breaking their own law.

Acts 23:1-4
Paul, looking steadfastly at the council, said, "Brothers, I have lived before God in all good conscience until today." The high priest, Ananias, commanded those who stood by him to strike him on the mouth. Then Paul said to him, "God will strike you, you whitewashed wall! Do you sit to judge me according to the law, and command me to be struck contrary to the law?" Those who stood by said, "Do you malign God's high priest?"

When they responded with a personal attack, he realized that would never listen made a shrewd move to tie up the court in endless debate.

Acts 23:5-9
Paul said, "I didn't know, brothers, that he was high priest. For it is written, 'You shall not speak evil of a ruler of your people.'" But when Paul perceived that the one part were Sadducees and the other Pharisees, he cried out in the council, "Men and brothers, I am a Pharisee, a son of Pharisees. Concerning the hope and resurrection of the dead I am being judged!" When he had said this, an argument arose between the Pharisees and Sadducees, and the crowd was divided. For the Sadducees say that there is no resurrection, nor angel, nor spirit; but the Pharisees confess all of these. A great clamor arose, and some of the scribes of the Pharisees' part stood up, and contended, saying, "We find no evil in this man. But if a spirit or angel has spoken to him, let's not fight against God!"

Paul splits the council wide open theologically.

Having made a mistake once with Paul, the Romans jumped in to protect him and treated him differently than before.

Acts 23:10
When a great argument arose, the commanding officer, fearing that Paul would be torn in pieces by them, commanded the soldiers to go down and take him by force from among them, and bring him into the barracks.

Paul was not bound and imprisoned but brought into their own living quarters. Once again, the apostle used the law to protect himself and advance the gospel.

The Plot to Assassinate Him

Since they could not convict Paul in their own courts nor in the Roman ones, all that was left was to assassinate him.

Acts 23:12-15
When it was day, some of the Jews banded together, and bound themselves under a curse, saying that they would neither eat nor drink until they had killed Paul. There were more than forty people who had made this conspiracy. They came to the chief priests and the elders, and said, "We have bound ourselves under a great curse, to taste nothing until we have killed Paul. Now therefore, you with the council inform the commanding officer that he should bring him down to you tomorrow, as though you were going to judge his case more exactly. We are ready to kill him before he comes near."

Paul was informed of this plot by his nephew.

Acts 23:16
But Paul's sister's son heard they were lying in wait, and he came and entered into the barracks and told Paul.

Knowing that the commander was being especially vigilant with him, Paul sent the boy to inform the commander.

Acts 23:17
Paul summoned one of the centurions, and said, "Bring this young man to the commanding officer, for he has something to tell him."

Paul did not summon one of the soldiers but a Centurion who had charge over a hundred men. The word translated "summon" refers to Paul calling the Centurion over to him. He did not go to the Centurion. He summoned him.

When his nephew was brought to this high ranked commander, he was treated with great respect and urgent concern.

Acts 23:18-22
So he took him, and brought him to the commanding officer, and [he] said, "Paul, the prisoner, summoned me and asked me to bring this young man [nephew] to you. He has something to tell you." The commanding officer took him by the hand, and going aside, asked him privately, "What is it that you have to tell me?" He said, "The Jews have agreed to ask you to bring Paul down to the council tomorrow, as though intending to inquire somewhat more accurately concerning him. Therefore don't yield to them, for more than forty men lie in wait for him, who have bound themselves under a curse to neither eat nor drink until they have killed him. Now they are ready, looking for the promise from you." So the commanding officer let the young man go, charging him, "Tell no one that you have revealed these things to me."

The commander took the nephew's hand and led him into a private place and had a conversation with the nephew. He doesn't question him or ask for evidence but believes him outright and then acts immediately on the belief. He will not take any chances with Paul.

Acts 23:23-24
He called to himself two of the centurions, and said, "Prepare two hundred soldiers to go as far as Caesarea, with seventy horsemen, and two hundred men armed with spears, at the third hour of the night." He asked them to provide animals, that they might set Paul on one, and bring him safely to Felix the governor.

Paul had a powerful section of the Roman army now at his disposal. he knew how to handle things legally.

The Delegation to Felix

In Acts 24, when Paul stood before Felix, the governor which constituted a court of law. He was there to defend himself and Tertullus came to prosecute him on behalf of the Jews.

Acts 24:1-8
After five days, the high priest, Ananias, came down with certain elders and an orator, one Tertullus. They informed the governor against Paul. When he was called, Tertullus began to accuse him, saying, "Seeing that by you we enjoy much peace, and that prosperity is coming to this nation by your foresight, we accept it in all ways and in all places, most excellent Felix, with all thankfulness. But that I don't delay you, I entreat you to bear with us and hear a few words. For we have found this man to be a plague...instigator of insurrections among all the Jews throughout the world, and a ringleader of the sect of the Nazarenes. He even tried to profane the temple, and we arrested him. By examining him yourself you may ascertain all these things of which we accuse him." The Jews also joined in the attack, affirming that these things were so.

Then, Paul took the opportunity to advance the gospel with a powerful testimony.

Acts 24:10
When the governor had beckoned to him to speak, Paul answered, "Because I know that you have been a judge of this nation for many years, I cheerfully make my defense."

Here again, the apostle Paul acknowledges the power of the government's authority to protect him from many kinds of persecution.

After his appeal, Felix does not imprison him but holds him until he can speak directly with the commander. Paul is able to advance the kingdom while he is protected from harm.

Acts 24:22-23
But Felix, having more exact knowledge concerning the Way [name for Christianity], deferred them, saying, "When Lysias, the commanding officer, comes down, I will decide your case." He ordered the centurion that Paul should be kept in custody, and should have some privileges, and not to forbid any of his friends to serve him or to visit him.

Though Felix protected him from the Jewish persecution, Paul was still in his custody for two years to appease these rebellious people. Two years Paul sat waiting. His advance of the gospel may have slowed, but Paul shared Christ with Felix, his wife, and all who visited him.

Acts 24:24-27
But after some days, Felix came with Drusilla, his wife, who was a Jewess, and sent for Paul, and heard him concerning the faith in Christ Jesus. As he reasoned about righteousness, self-control, and the judgment to come, Felix was terrified, and answered, "Go your way for this time, and when it is convenient for me, I will summon you." Meanwhile, he also hoped that money would be given to him by Paul, that he might release him. Therefore also he sent for him more often and talked with him. But when two years were fulfilled,

Felix was succeeded by Porcius Festus, and desiring to gain favor with the Jews, Felix left Paul in bonds.

Here, Paul was able to handle himself judicially and advanced the gospel and protect himself.

The Response to Festus

In Acts 25, after two years had passed, Festus succeeded Felix as governor. After only three days in office, the Jews were once again ready to come after Paul and so Festus convened his court.

Acts 25:6-8
When he had stayed among them more than ten days, he went down to Caesarea, and on the next day he sat on the judgment seat, and commanded Paul to be brought. When he had come, the Jews who had come down from Jerusalem stood around him, bringing against him many and grievous charges which they could not prove, while he said in his defense, "Neither against the law of the Jews, nor against the temple, nor against Caesar, have I sinned at all."

So, Paul made his judicial defense before Festus, the governor. He was innocent of all charges.

The Appeal to Caesar

Festus also wanted to appease the Jews and asked Paul if he was willing to go back to the Jewish council. He wanted essentially to get rid of Paul and avert a decision.

Acts 25:9
But Festus, desiring to gain favor with the Jews, answered Paul and said, "Are you willing to go up to Jerusalem, and be judged by me there concerning these things?"

Shouldn't this governor have known that he was sending Paul back into the mouth of the serpent? In his attempt to appease the Jews, Festus was about to send his prisoner to his death. Since Paul knew this would end in assassination, he took his final judicial action as a Roman citizen, he appealed to Caesar.

Acts 25:10-11
But Paul said, "I am standing before Caesar's judgment seat, where I ought to be tried. I have done no wrong to the Jews, as you also know very well. For if I have done wrong and have committed anything worthy of death, I don't refuse to die; but if none of those things is true that they accuse me of, no one can give me up to them. I appeal to Caesar!"

The apostle chose to invoke a Roman citizen's ultimate protection from the law and appealed to the emperor. This appeal to Caesar was irrevocable. Once declared by a Roman citizen, it could not be stopped. Every Roman citizen who felt he was not receiving justice could travel to Rome and present his case before the emperor. After conferring with his council, Festus agreed.

Acts 25:12
Then Festus, when he had conferred with the council, answered, "You have appealed to Caesar. To Caesar you shall go."

Paul was now under the full protection of the Romans as he advanced the gospel to the highest court in the land. This was Paul's judicial response to the illegal activity of the Jews primarily and the Romans secondarily.

The charges could now be answered face to face with the ruler of the entire Roman Empire. It had been continually revealed to the apostle by the Lord that he would preach the gospel to the emperor himself. How was a Christian Rabbi from Tarsus ever going to stand before the most powerful man in the world and proclaim the plan of redemption? It was done as a citizen using the law to advance and protect!

The Testimony to King Agrippa

Now, the apostle Paul made his appeal to Herod Agrippa, current King of Israel.

Acts 26:1-3
Agrippa said to Paul, "You may speak for yourself." Then Paul stretched out his hand, and made his defense. "I think myself happy, King Agrippa, that I am to make my defense before you today concerning all the things that I am accused by the Jews, especially because you are expert in all customs and questions which are among the Jews. Therefore I beg you...hear me patiently.

Acts 26:28-29
Agrippa said to Paul, "With a little persuasion are you trying to make me a Christian?" Paul said, "I pray to God, that whether with little or with much, not only you, but also all that hear me today, might become such as I am, except for these bonds."

Acts 26:30-32
The king rose up with the governor, and Bernice, and those who sat with them. When they had withdrawn, they spoke to one another, saying, "This man does nothing worthy of death or of bonds." Agrippa said to Festus, "This man might have been set free if he had not appealed to Caesar."

If Christians truly desire to advance the gospel or protect themselves from persecution, they should utilize the law as Paul did. This should be done as the Spirit leads. The Earthly citizenship of believers should not be left at the door of God's kingdom but instead should be used wisely and with great care in His name and for His sake.

The Bible indicates the saints may use the law and the courts to stand their ground against persecution. In most societies of the world, people may not simply choose to do and say whatever they please. There are always laws for the common good and safety of all people. As Christians, we do not cease being citizens. As a result, we should utilize the law to advance our message and protect ourselves and other saints from persecution. This would include authorities of the government. As we have learned, Paul often used his Roman citizenship and the law for the purpose of standing his ground against persecution and we may do the same.

We must remember the advice of Jesus as He sent the twelve out to preach and spoke to not only them but all his disciples in the generations to come.

Matthew 10:16-20
"Behold, I send you out as sheep among wolves. Therefore be wise as serpents and harmless as doves. But beware of men, for they will deliver you up to councils, and in their synagogues they will scourge you. Yes, and you will be brought before governors and kings for my sake, for a testimony to them and to the nations. But when they deliver you up, don't be anxious how or what you will say, for it will be given you in that hour what you will say. For it is not you who speak, but the Spirit of your Father who speaks in you.

The word translated wisdom refers to "being cautious, prudent, and mindful of one's own interests." In this case, we are to be mindful and cognizant of our own protection, the protection of His people, and God's advancement of the gospel. One of the things Jesus was speaking of was being wise as serpents in a court of law. Notice, Jesus mentions being brought before "governors and kings." We must utilize the law with great wisdom. It is important that Christians use the law to advance and protect wisely.

Chapter 10

Defy to Obey A Divine Command

So far, we have seen three legal responses Christians may take against persecution to advance the gospel and protect the saints. Now, we come to our last legal response that we could take when the government oversteps its authority. There might come a time where we, as Christians, may be asked to do or not to do something that the Bible commands. These would entail the essentials of the Christian life all believers must know. These divine commandments originate from the clear teaching of Scriptures. These encompass the important principles that Christians are to practice in order to grow in Christ and function in the kingdom of God. If we are asked to cease these practices, we may defy the law to obey the divine commands. In the last two chapters, we saw other legal responses we may take and, in the chapters, to come we will study non-legal responses we may engage in. This last legal response of defiance is perfectly acceptable to God and was utilized by His apostles and others.

The Divine Non-Negotiables

No matter what circumstances we find ourselves in are required by God to grow in our Christian faith and walk. Also, we must encourage others to do the same. These are givens. If we are told that we cannot think, speak, or act in the way that God desires by even a governing authority, it will become necessary to disobey that human command.

These divine commands involve growing in all areas of our lives to become like Christ. To grow spiritually is to be transformed into the likeness of Christ. The Father desires for His children to think, speak, and act more and more like His Son in their lives on this Earth. Being a Christian or a follower of Christ does not mean becoming the best of who we are, it means becoming the best of who He is in us. For it does not mean simply following Christ but becoming like Him in every way. It is growing into His image.

Galatians 2:20
I have been crucified with Christ, and it is no longer I that live, but Christ living in me. That life which I now live in the flesh, I live by faith in the Son of God, who loved me, and gave himself up for me.

In Ephesians 4, the apostle Paul describes a key purpose of the Pastor's work in our lives as teaching, preaching, and shepherding.

Ephesians 4:12-13
For the perfecting [maturing] of the saints, to the work of serving, to the building up of the body of Christ; until we all [individually and corporately] attain to the unity of the faith, and of the knowledge of the Son of God, to a full grown man, to the measure of the stature of the fullness of Christ.

Without endeavoring to unpack every part of this passage, we need to simply note that the goal of every believer is to measure up to the "stature of the fullness of Christ."

This would be like a brother who was standing next to his older brother and desiring to grow into his image. He would be checking his height, weight, and build. From a spiritual perspective, we are standing next to Christ and growing into his spiritual image checking our supernatural character, holy attitudes, and Christian lifestyle. As this younger brother desired to think, speak, and act like his older brother, so we do the same regarding Christ.

What does this really mean? If Christ was dependent on God, we learn to be dependent on God. If Christ was patient, we learn to be patient. If Christ obeyed God's commands, we learn to obey God's commands. The essentials of the living our lives as Christians that cannot be stopped by any human authority revolves around the principles by which we must live and act like Christ.

The Sharing of The Gospel

The first aspect of the Christian life that no government on earth has a right to stop any Christian from practicing is sharing the gospel. In Matthew 28, Jesus gave a divine and powerful command.

Matthew 28:18-19
Jesus came to them and spoke to them, saying, "All authority has been given to me in heaven and on Earth. Go, and make disciples of all nations, baptizing them in the name of the Father and of the Son and of the Holy Spirit. teaching them to observe all things that I commanded you. Behold, I am with you always, even to the end of the age." Amen.

The main verb is the command: make disciples. This occurs by "going, baptizing, and teaching." These three are non-negotiables in the Christian life. The "going" and "baptizing" means to go places, share the good news, and baptize. The sharing of the gospel is implicit in these terms.

In Acts 1, Jesus made clear where this "going" was to be.

Acts 1:8
But you will receive power when the Holy Spirit has come upon you. You will be witnesses to me in Jerusalem, in all Judea and Samaria, and to the uttermost parts of the Earth.

We are to "go" to our local city, region, country, and the ends of the Earth. So, wherever we are and wherever we go we are to share the gospel. If everyone has heard the gospel, we are to take it to the ends of the Earth.

When the persecution of Saul [Paul] erupted in full force, the saints were scattered. Where did they go and what did they do? They shared the gospel.

Acts 8:3-4
But Saul ravaged the assembly, entering into every house and dragged both men and women off to prison. Therefore those who were scattered abroad went around preaching the word.

When the apostles were commanded to no longer preach the gospel, they defied the law to obey a divine command.

In Acts 4, after Peter and John healed the lame man, they preached Christ and won saved many souls.

Acts 4:1-3
As they spoke to the people, the priests and the captain of the temple and the Sadducees came to them, being upset because they taught the people and proclaimed in Jesus the resurrection from the dead. They laid hands on them, and put them in custody until the next day, for it was now evening.

This upset the Jewish leaders, so the apostles were arrested and brought before their council, the Sanhedrin. Then, they gave them a serious command.

Acts 4:17-18
But so that this spreads no further among the people, let's threaten them, that from now on they don't speak to anyone in this name. They called them, and charged them not to speak at all nor teach in the name of Jesus.

The Sanhedrin ordered Peter and John to stop sharing the gospel.

Acts 4:19-20
But Peter and John answered them, "Whether it is right in the sight of God to listen to you rather than to God, judge for yourselves, for we can't help telling the things which we saw and heard."

The response of the apostles was immediate. They would obey God in defiance of man. They declared to the council that they would not obey them. Since it was not right in the sight of God, they would continue preaching the gospel. No one had the authority to stop the spread of the good news of Jesus Christ.

When the Sanhedrin dragged all the apostles before their council in Acts 5, this body of men asked the apostles again for a reason for their disobedience. In verse 29, they repeated themselves.

Acts 5:29
But Peter and the apostles answered, "We must obey God rather than men."

This statement could not be clearer. The gospel is to be preached by the saints even if they defy the legal authorities by doing it. Why? No government or institution can forbid any Christian from sharing the good news of salvation in Jesus Christ. If a government body, individual official, or a law forbids the proclaiming of the gospel of the Lord Jesus, they are to be disobeyed.

The sharing of the gospel must be done both individually and together with other Christians. Jesus preached with His disciples and sent them out two by two.

The Baptism in Water

The second principle that cannot be compromised is the confirmation of faith through water baptism. In Matthew 28, this is found in the phrase "baptizing." Jesus commanded his disciples "to make disciples" by "baptizing." As we saw, this implies saving faith first.

Christians must immediately respond to their salvation by being baptized. Baptism in water does not save. God desires new believers to proclaim their new faith in Christ to the world through water baptism. It must become the initial response a believer makes in His obedience to Christ as Lord of his life. It is an act of faith which places us in the eyes of angels, believers, demons, and unbelievers squarely into life in the kingdom of God.

Water baptism was continually declared and practiced as the initial response after someone became a Christian. One believes, and then one is baptized. This was the pattern of Christ and the apostles in their proclamation of the gospel.

First, they proclaimed His kingdom.

Luke 8:1
Soon...he went about through cities...preaching...the good news of God's Kingdom. With him were the twelve. Then, they baptized those who received Christ.

John 3:22
After these things, Jesus came with his disciples into the land of Judea. He stayed there with them, and baptized.

Here is the sequence and pattern the Lord God desires. Once we come to faith in Christ, then he baptized in water for all to see.

In Acts 2, after the people heard the gospel, they cried out asking Peter what they should do. Notice His answer.

Acts 2:38
Peter said to them, "Repent, and be baptized, every one of you, in the name of Jesus Christ for the forgiveness of sins, and you will receive the gift of the Holy Spirit."

Peter so identified baptism with a believer's salvation that he simply mentions it rather than belief in Christ alone. Though baptism does not save a soul, but it is seen as the first step in obedience and identification with the body of Christ.

Acts 2:41
Then those who gladly received his word [the gospel] were [water] baptized. There were added that day about three thousand souls.

They received Christ and then were baptized. This would have been a momentous undertaking because at least three thousand people were saved that day. Yet, they baptized all of them. Why? Water baptism after salvation was God's desired pattern and an important command.

In Acts 8, Luke clearly records that after the citizens of Samaria believed in the good news of the kingdom and Jesus Christ preached by Philip, they were being baptized.

Acts 8:12-13
But...they believed Philip preaching good news concerning God's Kingdom and the name of Jesus...they were baptized, both men and women. Simon himself also believed. Being baptized, he continued with Philip. Seeing signs...miracles occurring, he was amazed.

In verses 35-36, Philip was sent to the Ethiopian eunuch, and he shared the gospel with him. As soon as the eunuch believed, he asked Philip to be baptized.

Acts 8:35-36
Philip opened his mouth...beginning from this Scripture, preached to him Jesus. As they went on the way, they came to some water, and the eunuch said, "Behold, here is water. What is keeping me from being baptized?"

The eunuch felt that he should be baptized right then. How did the eunuch know this? Philip must have explained this during his presentation of the gospel.

In Acts 10, once the God's Holy Spirit had entered into Cornelius, his household, relatives, and friends indicating belief in the Lord Jesus Christ, the apostle Peter ordered them to be baptized. We see here salvation and then baptism that confirmed their faith to both unbelievers and believers alike.

Acts 10:44-48
While Peter was still speaking these words, the Holy Spirit fell on all those who heard the word. They [Jews] of the circumcision who believed were amazed, as many as came with Peter, because the gift of the Holy Spirit was also poured out on the Gentiles. For they heard them speaking in other languages and magnifying God. Then Peter answered, "Can anyone forbid these people from being baptized with water? They have received the Holy Spirit just like us." He commanded them to be baptized in the name of Jesus Christ. Then they asked him to stay some days.

In his ministry, Paul evangelized and then baptized those who received Christ. In Acts 16, Lydia and her household believed and were baptized.

Acts 16:14-15
A certain woman named Lydia, a seller of purple, of the city of Thyatira, one who worshiped God, heard us; whose heart the Lord opened to listen to the things which were spoken by Paul. When

she and her household were baptized, she begged us, saying, "If you have judged me to be faithful to the Lord, come into my house, and stay." So, she persuaded us.

Then a short time later, the jailer and his household believed and were baptized. Why? He thought an Earthquake had released all the prisoners and was going to take his own life. Paul stopped him and presumably kept the prisoners from leaving. He responded with a question.

Acts 16:29-33
He called for lights, sprang in, fell down trembling before Paul and Silas, brought them out, and said, "Sirs, what must I do to be saved?" They said, "Believe in the Lord Jesus Christ, and you will be saved, you and your household." They spoke the word of the Lord to him, and to all who were in his house. He took them the same hour of the night and washed their stripes, and was immediately baptized, he and all his household.

Paul's reaction to the question was preaching the gospel and baptism. They go hand in hand.

In Acts 18, Luke described the salvation of Crispus and his whole household (family and servants). Then, they were immediately baptized.

Acts 18:8
Crispus...ruler of the synagogue, believed in the Lord [Jesus] with all his house. Many...Corinthians...believed and were baptized.

In Acts 22, Paul describes his baptism by Ananias which came right after his salvation.

Acts 22:16
Now why do you wait? Arise, be baptized, and wash away your sins, calling on the name of the Lord.

As soon as Paul's blindness was removed by the prophet, he demanded that Paul rise and be baptized. In fact, he asked Paul why he was delaying. Here this prophet proclaimed the baptism that was to proceed immediately after faith in Jesus Christ. Baptism follows but does not save.

Water baptism is to occur almost immediately after one is saved, because it is the outward sign of the believer's inward faith. It was always proclaimed in the gospel as the initial act of obedience after salvation. As a result, the saints should proclaim the gospel and explain baptism within it. Then, they should urge the new Christian to be baptized as soon as possible for the world to see.

When the apostles were reprimanded for preaching the gospel and commanded to stop, we saw that they refused. This would have been a refusal to also discontinue baptism!

When the Jewish leaders ordered Peter and John to stop sharing the gospel, this would have included baptism.

Acts 4:19-20
But Peter and John answered them, "Whether it is right in the sight of God to listen to you rather than to God, judge for yourselves, for we can't help telling the things which we saw and heard."

The "things that they saw and heard" would have included the truth of baptism. As a result, no government has God's authority to forbid us to baptize the newly saved. If it does attempt to prevent us from baptizing them, we may defy these authorities. Notice, it is both an individual activity and one that is done together. The individual gets baptized but must be immersed in water by someone else and must have an audience for the declaration of their newfound faith and identification with the church.

The Use of The Scriptures

The Word of God is essential for not only coming into the kingdom of God but living and growing in the kingdom. It has knowledge and power to transform believers into the image of Christ. The last part of the command of Jesus in Matthew 28 was to go, baptize, and "teach." Teaching and learning the Word of God is essential to our growth.

In 3 John 3, the apostle calls it "walking in truth." We are to live according to the truth.

3 John 3
For I rejoiced greatly, when brothers came and testified about your truth, even as you walk in truth.

This "walking" consists of knowing and obeying the truth. The truth energizes and transforms us into Christlikeness.

In 1 Thessalonians 2, Paul explains how the Word worked in the lives of these new believers.

1 Thessalonians 2:13
For this cause we also thank God without ceasing, that, when you received from us the word of the message of God, you accepted it not as the word of men, but, as it is in truth, the word of God, which also works in you who believe.

This work that the Word of God performs in our lives is the changing of our old unrighteous thoughts and ways to God's righteous thoughts and ways. God requires us, as Christians, to live supernaturally upon this Earth, not naturally.

He sometimes asks us to think and behave in ways that seem contrary to everything we hold true, such as loving our enemies as in Matthew 5.

Matthew 5:44
But I tell you, love your enemies, bless those who curse you, do good to those who hate you, and pray for those who mistreat you and persecute you.

Another way in which we are to behave that is contrary to human reason is to forgive people over and over again as in Matthew 18.

Matthew 18:21-22
Then Peter came and said to him, "Lord, how often shall my brother sin against me, and I forgive him? Until seven times?" Jesus said to him, "I don't tell you until seven times, but, until seventy times seven.

Who can do that? The saints can do it as the Holy Spirit works through His Word as we read it and study it. This is a crucial understanding for believers.

In 2 Peter 1, Peter explains that through the knowledge of God we have all the things we need that pertain to life and godliness. With this knowledge is granted the divine power to live it.

2 Peter 1:2-4
Grace to you and peace be multiplied in the knowledge of God and of Jesus our Lord, seeing that his divine power has granted to us all things that pertain to life and godliness, through the knowledge of him who called us by his own glory and virtue. by which he has granted to us his precious and exceedingly great promises; that through these you may become partakers of the divine nature, having escaped from the corruption that is in the world by lust.

Where do we find this knowledge of Him? The answer to this question is found in Hebrews chapter one. Here, the author describes how this knowledge was revealed.

THE PERSECUTION OF THE SAINTS AND HOW TO OVERCOME IT

Hebrews 1:1-2
God, having in the past spoken to the fathers through the prophets at many times and in various ways, has at the end of these days spoken to us by his Son, whom he appointed heir of all things, through whom also he made the worlds.

God has been revealing Himself throughout human history through the nation of Israel and now through His Son in the Holy Scriptures. With the knowledge of God found in His Word comes the actual spiritual power to act on it.

In 1 Thessalonians 1:5, Paul describes this supernatural phenomenon when he claims that the gospel came to them in power, the Holy Spirit, and full assurance.

1 Thessalonians 1:4-6
We know, brothers loved by God, that you are chosen, and that our Good News came to you not in word only, but also in power, and in the Holy Spirit, and with much assurance. You know what kind of men we showed ourselves to be among you for your sake. You became imitators of us and of the Lord, having received the word in much affliction, with joy of the Holy Spirit.

When they heard God's Word, power was unleashed by the Spirit to believe it and assure them of its truth. This will not occur unless we are consistently in the Word of God. This is why God's Word speaks to so many areas of life, because so many areas have to change to become like Christ.

And the Word provides everything we need for life and godliness. The Word can provide us with God's thoughts and ways concerning the knowledge of Him, His Son, and Spirit. So, we need to read, study, and teach the Word. This is not a negotiable item concerning the law. We must have access to the Bible so we can individually study it. Yet, this is not enough. We must study with others also.

In Colossians 3, Paul outlines how Christians must share the Word with others.

Colossians 3:16
Let the word of Christ dwell in you richly; in all wisdom teaching and admonishing one another with psalms, hymns, and spiritual songs, singing with grace in your heart to the Lord.

This is just one of the many verses which indicate Christians must be sharing and studying the Word together with other Christians. No government can order us to no longer fulfill this important function in the Body.

The Prayer of Christians

Another command given in Scripture that is absolutely necessary for living the Christian life is prayer. We are to be praying for ourselves, other believers, and the unsaved.

In many of Paul's letters, he asks for prayer and asks the saints to pray for others.

Romans 15:30-32
Now I beg you, brothers, by our Lord Jesus Christ, and by the love of the Spirit, that you strive together with me in your prayers to God for me, that I may be delivered from those who are disobedient in Judea, and that my service which I have for Jerusalem may be acceptable to the saints; that I may come to you in joy through the will of God, and together with you, find rest. Now the God of peace be with you all.

Ephesians 6:18
With all prayer and requests, praying at all times in the Spirit, and being watchful to this end in all perseverance and requests for all the saints.

In fact, in 1 Thessalonians 5, Paul encourages Christians to never stop praying. This can involve both a specific prayer time and casually throughout the day. This is essential to the proper living of the Christian life and growth in Him.

1 Thessalonians 5:16-20
Always rejoice. Pray without ceasing. In everything give thanks, for this is the will of God in Christ Jesus toward you.
Don't quench the Spirit. Don't despise prophecies.

Prayer is essential in living the Christian life. We are told in many places that we are to give our burdens to the Lord in prayer. This is so important.

1 Peter 5:6-7
Humble yourselves therefore under the mighty hand of God, that he may exalt you in due time; casting all your worries on him, because he cares for you.

Philippians 4:6-7
Be anxious for nothing, but in everything by prayer and supplication with thanksgiving let your requests be made known to God. And the peace of God, which surpasses all comprehension, will guard your hearts and your minds in Christ Jesus.

Prayer teaches us dependence on God. When we pray, share our needs with Him, and ask for help, we depend on Him for our needs.

Psalm 4:1
Answer me when I call, God of my righteousness. Give me relief from my distress. Have mercy on me, and hear my prayer.

Prayer brings about obedience. We ask God to help us to obey his law, and He will answer us. He will provide the strength through the Spirit as we pray to Him when each and every occasion arrives. Life brings many of these times in our lives. The Lord desires for us to rely on Him in prayer throughout our journey with Him.

Psalm 119:34
Give me understanding, and I will keep your law. Yes, I will obey it with my whole heart.

Prayer can provide relief from many sinful patterns in our lives. When we conquer sinful habits, we grow in Him.

Psalm 119:133
Establish my footsteps in your word. Don't let any iniquity have dominion over me.

Prayer can help us resist temptation. Though our flesh easily stumbles into sin, we can ask the Lord God to help us watch for temptations to avoid or help us withstand them.

Matthew 26:41
Watch and pray, that you don't enter into temptation. The spirit indeed is willing, but the flesh is weak.

Prayer can bring spiritual renewal in confession. Believers constantly confess their sins and their hearts through prayer. After this, we can ask God for a renewed commitment.

Psalm 51:2
Wash me thoroughly from my iniquity. Cleanse me from my sin.

Psalm 51:10
Create in me [a believer] a clean heart, O God. Renew a right spirit within me.

Prayer can bring divine wisdom. Of course, it is provided through His Word. We search His Word and pray. Then, the

Spirit will help us apply His truths to the specific situations that we encounter in our lives.

James 1:5
But if any of you lacks wisdom, let him ask...God, who gives to all liberally and without reproach; and it will be given to him.

Not only is prayer important in our lives and the lives of other Christians but also in the lives of the unsaved. Why? We are to pray for their salvation. People come to Christ through the prayers of others. As the Gospel of Jesus Christ is being proclaimed throughout the world giving life eternal, we are to be a part of that through prayer. Oftentimes, we are told we need to share the gospel, but there is another very important piece to that message and that is praying for those who might be saved and those who share the gospel with them, including ourselves.

In Romans 9, Paul is discussing our salvation in Christ and the Spirit's resultant work which suddenly prompts him to share his great burden for his fellow Jews. Paul exposes his deepest feelings and longings for his unsaved kinsmen and brethren. Seeing them perish, burdens his heart.

Romans 9:1-3
I [Paul] tell the truth in Christ. I am not lying, my conscience testifying with me in the Holy Spirit...I have great sorrow and unceasing pain in my heart. For I... wish that I myself were accursed from Christ for my brothers' sake [Jews] my relatives according to the flesh.

Instead, he takes all that sorrow, grief, and burden to God in prayer.

Romans 10:1-2
Brothers, my heart's desire and my prayer to God is for Israel, that

they may be saved. For I testify about them that they have a zeal for God, but not according to knowledge.

His deep burden for them has led him straight to the throne before an all-powerful God pleading for their salvation.

In the same way, we can participate in those we know in attaining eternal life through our prayers. We can give life through prayer. The salvation of souls begins on our knees.

We can also pray for those who may share Christ with them, including ourselves. The Bible gives several aspects of sharing Christ for which we can pray.

First, we can pray for opportunities to share. Paul exhorts the Colossians to devote themselves to prayer and then asks them to pray for him.

Colossians 4:3
Praying together for us also, that God may open to us a door for the word, to speak the mystery of Christ, for which I am also in bonds.

Christians may request of the Lord to open a door for us to share the gospel with those who do not know Christ.

Second, we can pray that those sharing the gospel will make a clear presentation.

Colossians 4:4
That I may reveal it as I ought to speak.

Third, we can pray for boldness in sharing the gospel. Evangelism is not necessarily an easy task. Christians do not always know how people will react, and it can be a fearful experience.

Ephesians 6:19
On my behalf, that utterance may be given to me in opening my mouth, to make known with boldness the mystery of the Good News.

When the Babylonians took the Jews into captivity, Daniel was among them. Since he was an exceptional man, the emperor raised him up to be a part of his council. The other Gentiles did not like Daniel's Jewish faith in God so they convinced the king to make an edict that no one could make a petition to God of man for 30 days except to the emperor himself.

The penalty would be death by being cast alive into the lion's den. These wicked officials knew Daniel would defy this and Daniel actually did.

Daniel 6:10
When Daniel knew that the writing was signed, he went into his house (now his windows were open in his chamber toward Jerusalem) and he kneeled on his knees three times a day, and prayed, and gave thanks before his God, as he did before.

Notice, Daniel went to his house and began praying three times a day in front of his window in full view of the city. He did this because no man can require a believer to stop praying to God. Prayer is a non-negotiable command.

In the passages studied, there was a mutual exchange of prayer requests together. James sums it up in James 5 when he discusses confessing and praying for one another.

James 5:16
Confess your offenses to one another, and pray for one another, that you may be healed. The insistent prayer of a righteous person is powerfully effective.

So, we must pray individually and together as believers. No governmental authority of command us to never do this important supernatural activity.

The Living of a Righteous Life

God desires us to live righteously as His Son Jesus did. We cannot live anyway we desire; instead, we must live like our Savior and Lord. This is what the Christian life entails: obedience. This is accomplished by walking like Him. Over and over the apostles describe the Christian life as a walk.

The Greek word translated "walk" means simply to walk about in one's life.

1 John 2:6
He who says he remains in him [a believer] ought himself also to walk just like he walked.

Colossians 2:6-7
As therefore you received Christ Jesus, the Lord, walk in him, rooted and built up in him, and established in the faith, even as you were taught, abounding in it [faith] in thanksgiving. Be careful that you don't let anyone rob you through his philosophy and vain deceit, after the tradition of men, after the elements of the world, and not after Christ.

Colossians 1:10
So that you will walk in a manner worthy of the Lord, to please Him in all respects, bearing fruit in every good work and increasing in the knowledge of God.

We are to walk about in our lives moment by moment in a manner that is worthy of Jesus. It simply refers to thinking, speaking, and acting in the normal ways of life.

We are to live to please Him in every area of our lives (in all respects). A walk involves one step at a time. Wherever we go, whatever we think, say, and do, we must behave as Christians. We must conduct our lives fully and completely as believers in the Lord Jesus Christ. We cannot compromise on this holy walk.

This Christian walk involves doing good works. Paul explains in Ephesians 2 that we were created to for this very purpose.

Ephesians 2:10
For we are His [the Lord's] workmanship, created in Christ Jesus for good works, which God prepared beforehand so that we would walk in them.

We are to walk about living righteously and doing good deeds as His workmanship. We display God's creative work in our lives as He transforms us into the image of His Son.

In Ephesians 4, Paul begs his readers to live for Christ.

Ephesians 4:1
He cries out, "I therefore, the prisoner in the Lord, beg you to walk worthily of the calling with which you were called. We were called out of the world into eternal life and out to walk worthy of that calling. Paul was in prison waiting for a trial before Caesar for the persecution he had experienced because he himself walked worthy of the Lord.

In 1 Thessalonians 2, he instructs the new believers to live worthy of their Father.

1 Thessalonians 2:12
As you know, we exhorted, comforted, and implored every one of you, as a father does his own children, to the end that you should

walk worthily of God, who calls you into his own Kingdom and glory.

We are members of the kingdom and recipients of His glory and blessings and must walk worthy of this honor.

This is not the earning of salvation, but the display of it. In 1 John 1, the apostle calls it "walking in the light."

1 John 1:7
But if we walk in the light, as he is in... the light, we [believers] have fellowship with one another, and the blood of Jesus Christ, his Son, cleanses us from all sin.

Paul gives the same encouragement in 1 Thessalonians 4.

1 Thessalonians 4:1
Finally then, brothers, we beg and exhort you in the Lord Jesus, that as you received from us how you ought to walk and to please God, that you abound more and more.

Our goal is to continually walk and please God. How do we do this? We walk according to the commandments, and they are found in God's Word.

2 John 1:6
This is love, that we should walk according to his commandments.

The Lord Jesus expected those who loved Him to keep His commandments. This was the way to demonstrate our love not to earn His love.

John 14:23
Jesus answered him, "If a man loves me, he will keep my word. My Father will love him, and we will come to him, and make our home with him.

The keeping of the commandments is the way to love Christ. This is also called living righteously. We have been saved to live this life righteously. It's not just a set of rules we obey but more living in His image.

Titus 2:11-15
For the grace of God has appeared, bringing salvation to all men, instructing us to the intent that, denying ungodliness and worldly lusts, we would live soberly, righteously, and godly in this present world; looking...blessed hope and appearing of the glory of our... God and Savior, Jesus Christ; who gave himself for us...might redeem us from all iniquity, and purify for himself a people for his own possession, zealous for good works. Say these things and exhort and reprove with all authority. Let no man despise you.

No government can forbid believers to practice Christ's righteousness either individually or together. We saw in a previous discussion of Ephesians 4:13 that we are growing together into the stature of Christ.

Our Association with Sin

No government can require us to do the opposite of living righteous, which is accepting, participating in, or assisting in sinful attitudes, words, or actions. If a law is passed which states that people must sin in a particular way, we must deny the law to obey the divine command. We must refuse to sin. This is a part of our old lives in darkness and can never be a part of our new lives in the light.

The Lord Jesus Christ spent much time with unbelievers, but they never accepted, participated, or assisted in sin. How do we know this? The Bible states that Jesus never sinned in His earthly life. He never did anything that was against the commands of His Father.

We know this by the testimony of His disciples who had lived with Him throughout His ministry. The apostle Peter declared continually that Jesus Christ did not sin. This was the testimony of an eyewitness.

1 Peter 2:22
Who did not sin, "neither was deceit found in his mouth."

1 Peter 1:19
But with precious blood, as of a faultless and pure lamb, the blood of Christ.

1 Peter 3:18
Because Christ also suffered for sins once, the righteous for the unrighteous, that he might bring you to God; being put to death in the flesh, but made alive in the spirit.

Acts 3:14
But you denied the Holy and Righteous One, and asked for a murderer to be granted to you.

John, His beloved disciple, claimed also that He did not sin.

1 John 3:5
You know that he was revealed to take away our sins, and in him is no sin.

Even His enemies acknowledged His sinless character. Judas, the betrayer, felt remorse due to this.

Matthew 27:4
Saying, "I have sinned in that I betrayed innocent blood." But they said, "What is that to us? You see to it."

When they brought Him before Pilate, he could find nothing that Jesus had done wrong.

Matthew 27:24
So...Pilate [governor] saw that nothing was being gained, but rather that a disturbance was starting, he took water, and washed his hands before the multitude, saying, "I am innocent of the blood of this righteous person. You see to it."

John 19:4
Then Pilate went out again, and said to them, "Behold, I bring him out to you, that you may know that I find no basis for a charge against him."

Even the wife of Pilate acknowledged His righteousness.

Matthew 27:19-20
While he was sitting on the judgment seat, his wife sent to him, saying, "Have nothing to do with that righteous man, for I have suffered many things today in a dream because of him." Now the chief priests and the elders persuaded the multitudes to ask for Barabbas and destroy Jesus.

One of the thieves that were crucified alongside of Him chastised the other because it was common knowledge that there was no sin found in the Lord.

Luke 23:41
And we indeed justly, for we receive the due reward for our deeds, but this man has done nothing wrong.

Next, we will see that even demons were willing to proclaim His holiness and righteousness.

Luke 4:33-34
In the synagogue there was a man who had a spirit of an unclean demon, and he cried out with a loud voice, saying, "Ah! what have we to do with you, Jesus of Nazareth? Have you come to destroy us? I know you who you are: the Holy [sinless] One of God!"

God supernaturally testified to the fact that His Son was sinless. At His baptism, the Father testified of His holiness.

Matthew 3:17
Behold, a voice out of the heavens said, "This is my beloved Son, with whom I am well pleased."

The Holy Spirit continually testified that Jesus Christ was without sin through inspired men.

Isaiah 53:9
They made his grave with the wicked, and with a rich man in his death; although he had done no violence, nor was any deceit in his mouth.

2 Corinthians 5:21
For him who knew no sin he made to be sin on our behalf; so that in him we might become the righteousness of God.

Hebrews 4:15
For we don't have a high priest who can't be touched with the feeling of our infirmities, but one who has been in all points tempted like we are, yet without sin.

Hebrews 7:26
For such a high priest was fitting for us [as believers]: holy, guiltless, undefiled, separated from sinners...made higher than the heavens.

Luke 1:35
The angel answered her, "The Holy Spirit will come on you, and the power of the Most High will overshadow you. Therefore also the holy one who is born from you will be called the Son of God."

Jesus Himself claimed to be without sin. The Lord told the Pharisees that He always pleased the Father.

John 8:46
Which of you convicts me of sin? If I tell the truth, why do you not believe me?

Later, Jesus asked them the impossible which was to accuse Him of any sin.

John 8:29
He who sent me is with me. The Father hasn't left me alone, for I always do the things that are pleasing to him.

    Second, Jesus Christ confronted sin wherever He saw it. In John 8, when the adulterous woman was cast before Jesus for condemnation, He not only wrote the sins of the accusers on the ground but told the woman to sin no more.

John 8:8-11
Again he stooped down, and with his finger wrote on the ground. They, when they heard it, being convicted by their conscience, went out one by one, beginning from the oldest, even to the last. Jesus was left alone with the woman where she was, in the middle. Jesus, standing up, saw her and said, "Woman, where are your accusers? Did no one condemn you?" She said, "No one, Lord." Jesus said, "Neither do I condemn you. Go your way. From now on, sin no more."

    In John 4, when Jesus encountered the Samaritan woman, He accused her also of sin and offered eternal life.

John 4:15-17
The woman said to him, "Sir, give me this water, so that I don't get thirsty, neither come all the way here to draw." Jesus said to her, "Go, call your husband...come here." The woman answered, "I have no husband." Jesus said to her, "You said well, 'I have no husband,' for you have had five husbands; and he whom you now have is not your husband. This you have said truly."

Some have the mistaken notion that Jesus attended the many celebrations and drank with unbelievers. This is not true. Jesus was often invited for a meal and a presentation of His teachings which he gladly attended. The wine that He drank was regular drink of the Jews (the mixed beverage of water and a little wine to kill the germs). This is similar to the way we serve water at a meal. He did not have wine with His meal the way people today serve wine unmixed in a glass. This was considered "strong drink" in the Bible. We know this because Jesus was accused falsely of this very thing and denied it.

Matthew 11:18-19
For John came neither eating nor drinking, and they say, "He has a demon." The Son of Man came eating and drinking, and they say, "Behold, a gluttonous man and a drunkard, a friend of tax collectors and sinners!" But wisdom is justified by her children.

Luke 7:3-35
For John the Baptizer came neither eating bread nor drinking wine, and you say, "He has a demon." The Son of Man [the [Lord] has come eating and drinking, and you say, "Behold, a gluttonous man, and a drunkard; a friend of tax collectors and sinners!" Wisdom is justified by all her children.

Jesus denies their accusation by stating that they should look at the fruit that came out of the wisdom of His actions.

Though this is obvious, we should never associate ourselves together with sin. When Corinth was involved in false doctrine and tolerating sin, the apostle Paul asked them to test themselves to see if they were even Christians.

2 Corinthians 13:5
Examine your own selves, whether you are in the faith. Test your own selves... know...that Jesus Christ is in you....

No government or institution can force us to sin or assist in their sin. If governmental authorities want us to assist in their evil deeds either individually or together, we must defy these authorities. This would include words and actions against the Ten Commandments. We cannot bow to idols, take the Lord's name in vain, steal, lie, murder, or covet our neighbor's families or goods. We cannot participate in any activities that assist the authorities in committing these sins.

The Gathering of The Saints

The Christian life was never meant to be lived as a group of individuals in a kingdom but together with others. In Acts 2, when Luke described the functioning of the church, he spoke of participating in spiritual things together in houses and general assemblies.

Acts 2:42-47
They continued steadfastly in the apostles' teaching...fellowship, in the breaking of bread, and prayer. Fear came on every soul, and many wonders and signs were done through the apostles. All who believed were together, and had all things in common. They sold their possessions and goods, and distributed them to all, according as anyone had need. Day by day, continuing steadfastly with one accord in the temple, and breaking bread at home, they took their food with gladness and singleness of heart, praising God, and having favor with all the people. The Lord added to the assembly day by day those who were being saved.

So, all of the spiritual non-negotiables are to be participated in individually and together. What is also important is the focus of our gatherings.

The focus is on meeting the spiritual needs of others rather than ourselves. We come to an assembly of believers to meet their needs while they meet ours. In Hebrews 10, the inspired author explains this truth.

Hebrews 10:24-25
Let us consider how to provoke one another to love and good works, not forsaking our own assembling together, as the custom of some is, but exhorting one another; and so much the more, as you see the Day approaching.

The Greek word translated "forsake" means "to abandon, forsake, desert, leave in straits, leave helpless." It carries the idea of totally abandoning, utterly forsaking, or leaving somebody behind to survive on their own.

In 2 Timothy 4, Paul speaks of a man who left him in the midst of his second imprisonment in Rome. Why? He loved this present world and did not want to lose access to it by supporting Paul.

2 Timothy 4:10
For Demas left me, having loved this present world, and went to Thessalonica; Crescens to Galatia, and Titus to Dalmatia.

Then Paul uses the word again to refer to everyone who should have come to his defense did not. This was most likely his preliminary hearing. The faithful ones had not yet come and the faithless never showed up.

2 Timothy 4:16
At my first defense, no one came to help me, but all left me. May it not be held against them.

So, in the same way as Paul was completely abandoned in dire circumstances, we, as Christians, are not to abandon the church. Why? The author explains the reason in the context prior to this command.

THE PERSECUTION OF THE SAINTS AND HOW TO OVERCOME IT

Hebrews 10:22-23
Let's draw near with a true heart in fullness of faith, having our hearts sprinkled from an evil conscience, and having our body washed with pure water, let us hold fast the confession of our hope without wavering; for he who promised is faithful.

The readers of these words were wavering in their faith toward God as they struggled with the temptations of the lusts of the flesh and the world. In the midst of this, they needed to remain strong and encourage each other to stand firm in the faith.

In the midst of this, the "Day of the Lord" was drawing near, and they had to be ready.

Hebrews 10:24-25
Let us consider how to provoke one another to love and good works, not forsaking our own assembling together, as the custom of some is, but exhorting one another; and so much the more, as you see the Day approaching.

The emphasis on the "Day of the Lord" was the concept of being ready at any time for the Lord to come! We saw in an earlier chapter that evil would increase on the Earth and the saints would face greater and greater temptations to sin and persecution for Christ. These are the dire circumstances that the Greek word implies.

As this occurred, they were to provoke and exhort each other to love and good works. This emphasis is not on being provoked and exhorted but provoking and exhorting. It is other focused. We are to be gathering with others regularly and consistently not for the sake of ourselves but for what we can do in the lives of other believers. We need each other to live the lives God desires and to mature into His image until He comes.

This need that others have for us is disclosed in the first and last part of the passage.

Hebrews 10:24-25
Let us consider how to provoke one another to love and good works, not forsaking our own assembling together, as the custom of some is, but exhorting one another; and so much the more, as you see the Day approaching.

The Greek word "consider" means "to think something through." The author exhorts his readers to seriously think through how they could provoke each other to love and good works. The Greek word "provoke" refers to "inciting or irritating someone into action." In this case, it is for love and good. Christians need to gather together either in one on one, in small groups, or as a whole in order to do this. We cannot do all that God desires for His children alone. Also, we need to exhort others in this direction. This word in the Greek has the idea of coming alongside someone to encourage them to action.

How do we do this? It is through the "one anothers" in the New Testament. We are to show love and honor to each other which is so important in building the Body of Christ.

Romans 12:10
In love of the brothers [and sisters] be tenderly affectionate to one another; in honor preferring one another. We should build up one another in the faith.

Romans 14:19
So then, let us follow after things which make for peace, and things by which we may build one another up.

Christians must bear the burdens of one another which will help all grow stronger in the Christian life.

Galatians 6:2
Bear one another's burdens, and so fulfill the law of Christ.

Also, we ought to teach and warn one another.

Colossians 3:16
Let the word of Christ dwell in you richly; in all wisdom teaching and admonishing one another with psalms, hymns, and spiritual songs, singing with grace in your heart to the Lord.

Believers should comfort one another.

1 Thessalonians 4:18
Therefore comfort one another with these words.

They should also serve one another.

1 Peter 4:10
As each has received a gift, employ it in serving one another, as good managers of the grace of God in its various forms.

Christians must pray for one another.

Ephesians 6:18-19
With all prayer and requests, praying at all times in the Spirit, and being watchful to this end in all perseverance and requests for all the saints: on my behalf, that utterance may be given to me in opening my mouth, to make known with boldness the mystery of the Good News.

Also, believers must partake of communion together. At the last supper, Jesus gave this command.

1 Corinthians 11:23-26
For I received from the Lord that which...I delivered to you, that the Lord Jesus on the night in which he was betrayed took bread.

When he had given thanks, he broke it and said, "Take, eat. This is my body, which is broken for you. Do this in memory of me." In the same way he [Christ] also took the cup, after supper, saying, "This cup is the new covenant in my blood. Do this, as often as you drink, in memory of me." For as often as you eat this bread and drink this cup, you proclaim the Lord's death until he comes.

We must be breaking bread in communion with believers until the Lord comes.

These are a few of the descriptions of what is to be done in the gathering of the saints. This requires training and maturity. It is accomplished by those who have been given as gifts to the church. God has placed within the church many evangelists and pastor-teachers. The responsibility of the evangelist is to equip the saints to share the gospel of Christ and build the body up numerically. The responsibility of the pastor-teacher is to instruct the saints in doctrine. This will build the church up spiritually. In Ephesians 4, the apostle Paul describes this principle.

Ephesians 4:11
He gave some to be apostles; and some, prophets; [these saints laid the foundation and have now passed away] and some, evangelists; and some, shepherds and teachers [these saints remain today].

The terms "shepherds and teachers" refers to one person. These shepherd-teachers "shepherd" the flock by "teaching" them. They are absolutely essential to spiritual growth.

Paul continues to explain their purpose in the next part of the passage.

Ephesians 4:12
For the perfecting of the saints, to the work of serving, to the building up of the body of Christ.

This perfecting and building are designed to equip all the saints to serve. This serving involves the provoking to love and good works through the "one anothers." These push the local church toward spiritual maturity both individually and together.

In the next verse, Paul explains that their goal is for the flock to become fully mature to the point that they measure up to Christ's stature.

Ephesians 4:13
Until we all attain to the unity of the faith, and of the knowledge of the Son of God, to a full grown man, to the measure of the stature of the fullness of Christ.

In the next verse, he contrasts this maturity to immaturity or their child-like behavior.

Ephesians 4:14
That we may no longer be children, tossed back and forth... carried about with every wind of doctrine, by the trickery of men, in craftiness, after the wiles of error.

He describes spiritual children (those who are not shepherd-taught) as ones who go from spiritual fad to spiritual fad. They cannot land on settled doctrine because they do not know the truth. The pastor-teachers job is to study the Word diligently and to teach it to the flock of God by presenting it to them clearly and fully.

The evangelist is to equip the saints to share the gospel. This is also critical for the kingdom of God, the church, to grow numerically. As Christians live their lives in the midst of persecution, they will need to have the tools necessary to answer the questions of those seeking Christ. This is critical so the Holy Spirit to be able to use them.

No government or institution can forbid us to gather and assemble together. If the government attempts to prevent us from gathering, we must defy these authorities.

These are the necessary clear divine commands that must be followed by Christians regardless of what governmental authorities dictate. When any command of a governmental authority is at odds with these direct commands of God, then without any reservation in the full knowledge of what they are doing Christians may defy the law. This is never done in self-righteous indignation, anger, spite, or pride, or.

This is simply done to obey the commands of God in His Holy Word. It should reflect a firm, but humble and gentle spirit. We have numerous examples in the Scriptures of this defiance. Christians must understand that this is one option they have to defy the law. In upcoming chapters, we will see that we can choose to avoid the authorities. We will begin in the Old Testament and then move to the New.

A Divine Defiance

In Daniel 1:1-7, the prophet Daniel writes that the king of Babylon conquered Judah and brought over to their country some of the best the Jewish nation had to offer. Three of these important people were Meshach, Shadrach, and Abed-Nego. After time and training, they became high officials of Babylon.

In Daniel 3:1-11, the emperor, Nebuchadnezzar, created a large golden image of himself and asked the entire kingdom to bow down to it in worship. If they refused, they would be thrown into a fiery furnace.

In verse 12, Daniel records the men's response.

THE PERSECUTION OF THE SAINTS AND HOW TO OVERCOME IT

Daniel 3:12
There are certain Jews whom you have appointed over the affairs of the province of Babylon: Shadrach, Meshach, and Abednego; these men, O king, have not respected you. They don't serve your gods, nor worship the golden image which you have set up.

The king's reaction was immediate and predictable for the emperor.

Daniel 3:13
Then Nebuchadnezzar in [his] rage and fury commanded to bring Shadrach, Meshach, and Abed-nego. Then they [his officials] brought these men before the king.

Then, the king of Babylon provides them with one more chance to worship his image and warns them that he will throw them into the fiery furnace that day. They defy the law to obey a divine command.

Daniel 3:16-17
Shadrach, Meshach, and Abed-nego [Babylonian names] answered the king, "Nebuchadnezzar, we have no need to answer you in this matter. If it be [so], our God whom we serve is able to deliver us from the burning fiery furnace; and he will deliver us out of your hand, O king. But if not, be it known to you, O king, that we will not serve your gods, nor worship the golden image which you have set up."

They told the Emperor that they would not serve his gods, nor would they bow down to his image in worship.

This would be a violation of God's first commandment.

Exodus 20:3-6
You shall have no other gods before me. You shall not make for yourselves an idol, nor...image of anything that is in the heavens

above, or that is in the Earth beneath, or that is in the water under the Earth: you shall not bow yourself down to them, nor serve them, for I, Yahweh your God, am a jealous God, visiting the iniquity of the fathers on the children, on the third and...the fourth generation of those who hate me, and showing lovingkindness to thousands of those who love me and keep my commandments.*

Notice, this is a clear and direct commandment from God.

As a result, they were thrown into the fiery furnace and delivered by God.

Daniel 3:27
The satraps, the deputies, and the governors, and the king's counselors, being gathered together, saw these men, that the fire had no power on their bodies, nor was the hair of their head singed, neither were their pants changed, nor had the smell of fire passed on them.

They defied the law of the land and were delivered by God.

In Daniel 6, Daniel defied Darius, Emperor of the Medes and Persians. His evil Satraps, who were in the court of the emperor with Daniel, were jealous of him. As a result, they tried to trap him by convincing Darius to make an edict. The edict stated that no man in the land could make a petition to a god or man for 30 days, except to the emperor himself. The penalty would be death by being cast alive into the lion's den. These wicked officials knew Daniel would defy this.

Daniel 6:10-12
When Daniel knew that the writing was signed, he went into his house (now his windows were open in his room toward Jerusalem) and he kneeled on his knees three times a day, and prayed, and gave thanks before his God, as he did before....assembled together, and found Daniel making petition and supplication before his God.

Notice, Daniel defied the law to obey a divine command. He went to his house and began praying three times a day in full view of the city. He did not do it out of pride or anger.

As a result, he was thrown into the den of lions.

Daniel 6:16
Then the king commanded, and they brought Daniel, and cast him into the den of lions. The king spoke and said to Daniel, Your God whom you serve continually, he will deliver you.

As with the others, God rescued him.

Daniel 6:20
When he came near to the den to Daniel, he cried with a lamentable voice; the king spoke and said to Daniel, "Daniel, servant of the living God, is your God, whom you serve continually, able to deliver you from the lions?" Then Daniel said to the king, "O king, live forever. My God has sent his angel, and has shut the lions' mouths, and they have not hurt me; because as before him innocence was found in me; and also before you, O king, have I done no hurt." Then was the king exceeding glad, and commanded that they should take Daniel up out of the den. So Daniel was taken up out of the den, and no kind of harm was found on him, because he had trusted in his God.

God's divine commands are a higher authority than man's laws. When man's ordinances oppose God's clear precepts, obedience to God prevails.

In every example, there was no disrespect, anger, harsh language, or violence. There was a straightforward defiance of the law. When asked, they gave a simple, clear answer.

We have already seen that the apostles defied the Jewish leaders because God was a higher authority than man.

Acts 5:29-32
But Peter and the apostles answered, "We must obey God rather than men." The God of our fathers raised up Jesus, whom you killed, hanging him on a tree. God exalted him with his right hand to be a Prince and a Savior, to give repentance to Israel, and remission of sins. We are His witnesses of these things; and so also is the Holy Spirit, whom God has given to those who obey him.

One day, Christians might find themselves being asked to do something or not do something that is clearly contrary to the Scriptures by the government. Believers must obey their God, rather than man. The only caution that should be taken by Christians is that they must be certain they are obeying a clear, direct principle of Scripture.

A Humble Acceptance

When Christians decide to defy the law in order to obey a divine command and are arrested, they must be willing to accept the punishment the law provides. They may avoid the punishment or even use the laws to protect themselves as citizens. The saints do not have to wave their legal rights or surrender their day in court. This is still acceptance. Yet, they must realize that a direct defiance of the law may lead to arrest and imprisonment or even death.

To choose the option of direct legal defiance, we must be willing to humbly accept the consequences if caught. This is what Meshach, Shadrach, and Abed-Nego experienced with the fiery furnace.

Daniel 3:16-18
Shadrach, Meshach, and Abed-nego [Babylonian names] answered the king, Nebuchadnezzar, we have no need to answer you in this matter. If it be [so], our God whom we serve is able to deliver us

from the burning fiery furnace; and he will deliver us out of your hand, O king. But if not, be it known to you, O king, that we will not serve your gods, nor worship the golden image which you have set up.

Daniel humbly accepted the lion's den. He knew when he had made his original decision, this would follow.

Daniel 6:16-18
Then the king commanded, and they brought Daniel, and cast him into the den of lions. [Now] the king spoke and said to Daniel, Your God whom you serve continually, he will deliver you. A stone was brought, and laid on the mouth of the den; and the king sealed it with his own signet, and with the signet of his lords; that nothing might be changed concerning Daniel. Then the king went to his palace...passed the night fasting; neither were instruments of music brought before him: and his sleep fled from him.

Peter, John, and the apostles accepted their imprisonment, beatings, and death.

Acts 5:40-42
They agreed with him. When they had called the apostles to them, they beat them and charged them not to speak in the name of Jesus, and let them go. They therefore departed from the presence of the council, rejoicing that they were counted worthy to suffer dishonor for Jesus' name. Every day, in the temple and at home, they never stopped teaching and preaching Jesus, the Christ.

They never pulled back, but instead, continued to preach. They knew the Lord God had the power to protect them from physical death or deliver them into heaven. In either case, they would be fully delivered. Paul explained to the Philippians, that to remain would produce fruitful ministry, but to depart would send him to Christ. Both were good; the second was better.

Philippians 1:20-24
According to my earnest expectation and hope, that I will in no way be disappointed, but with all boldness, as always, now also Christ will be magnified in my body, whether by life or by death. For to me to live is Christ, and to die is gain. But if to live in the flesh, this will bring fruit from my work; then I don't make known what I will choose. But I am in a dilemma between the two, having the desire to depart and be with Christ, which is far better. Yet, to remain in the flesh is more needful for your sake.

The normal practice of believers is to obey the law. We have discovered there may come a time when the governing authorities require us to disobey a clear command of God. This we can never do; instead, we must defy the law to obey a divine command. This is the final legal response found in the Scriptures. This defiance to order to stand our ground is perfectly acceptable to God and was utilized by His apostles and others.

Chapter 11

Mislead to Prevent Harm

As we look at the responses to persecution, we have seen the legal responses we may take against those who desire to stop the advance of the gospel and harm God's people. The second kind of response is to avoid the persecution. This appears to be the normal response by those in both the Old and New Testaments. The third kind of response is simply to face the persecution with great courage and boldness when surrounded, seized, captured, or arrested. The final response is to physically defend ourselves or others, when lives are threatened, there is no escape, and death is at our door. In the next three chapters we will address this second response, then the other two kinds of responses will be discussed in the chapters after these. As mentioned earlier, it is critical that we understand these four different kinds of biblical responses. Otherwise, the many words and actions God's people took when facing harm or death will be confusing and leave us in a state of immobility when persecution comes.

Before we proceed, we must make a connection between the previous study of our responsibilities to the established governing authorities with these new principles from God's Word. When persecution in the form of laws and policies from governing authorities which restrict us from practicing the non-negotiables of the faith, we learned that we may defy them in order to obey a divine command. This defiance of ours is included in the next three kinds of responses we are about to discuss. Therefore, in the chapters ahead, when we use the term persecutors, we will be referring to those who are vigilantes (citizens acting outside the law), or the governmental authorities who may be enforcing the law which is contrary to God's commands. It will also include those citizens who are following these improper laws who want us to obey them also. If we will not, then they attempt to coerce us into obedience or inform the authorities when we do not.

In this chapter, we will discuss the biblical principles that govern our avoidance reactions to persecution. The chapters following will describe the numerous examples of avoidance both verbally and behaviorally. With each illustration, the evidence that supports these principles will be explained. So, the reader will need to keep this in mind as we proceed. The three chapters should be read together before any personal conclusions should be drawn.

When we think of persecution, our thoughts immediately go to the Lord Jesus and how He stood up to those who were condemning Him. Our minds will focus on the apostles in Jerusalem and how they yelled, "We will obey God rather than men." Yet was this the normal response of believers throughout the Old and New Testaments? Was it even the normal response of Jesus and the apostles, including Paul? It was not. Instead, avoidance which included some type of deception was the norm.

To understand the many ways in which we can "avoid" persecution, we must consider the issue of deception. Why? The various words and actions that are taken is always some form of what is considered by most people as "deception." If we withdraw, escape, hide, we are deceiving those searching to harm us. If we have others tell persecutors that we are somewhere else, we are deceiving them. Even if they remain silent, this is a type of deception since the "truth" is not being told. If we disguise ourselves or others, we are deceiving them. If we defy the law by assembling as true Christians in secret to practice the many non-negotiables of the faith, we are deceiving the authorities.

The question arises, "Is this deception wrong according to God's standards? Then, another question comes immediately after, "Is it acceptable to God?" We will discover that not only is this "deception" right but acceptable to God and is seen as a great act of faith.

In the next chapters, we will study numerous examples from both Testaments concerning the apparent deception of key biblical characters such as Rahab, Jacob, David and others in words and actions. We will discover that these real-life illustrations that portray Gods' righteous holy people apparently doing wicked deeds of deception leading to His will being accomplished are not "unrighteous deeds" at all. In fact, they were powerful acts of faith.

Their Deceptive Words and Actions to Harm

When we think of lying or deception, the first thing that comes to our minds is the telling of a falsehood or making a statement that is not true under any circumstances. We have come to believe that the saying, "A lie is a lie no matter what the motives or circumstances are" is always correct. Many believe that the Lord God will intervene if we never "lie." For example, if we are carrying banned Bibles in our luggage as we enter a nation, we should reveal that we have them when asked. If they don't ask, we will not tell. Then, we leave the issue up to God. Yet, the fact that we are breaking their law by bringing Bibles into their nation and deceiving them by not revealing the fact really defeats their position. Anything short of entering a country with the Bibles sitting on top of our luggage is deceptive. Yet is this wrong? Is hiding them in luggage "lying?"

The reason this seems like an odd dilemma is due to our misunderstanding of "lying" and "deception" which is bound up in human wisdom. The idea that "all falsehoods are sinful" is not the biblical perspective on these terms. Allow me to explain. There are hundreds of words and passages in the Scriptures that speak directly to the topic of "lying" or provide examples of "deceptions" by people. If one analyzes these passages, it will be discovered that the biblical definition of "lying" is not "making a false statement or giving a false impression anytime and in any circumstance." Instead, it is "a deliberate deception for the purpose of evil or harm."

Passages that use terms such as "lying, liars, or deceivers" which are not explained in the context should be seen in the light of passages which clearly define, explain, illustrate, or apply them. When a word or idea is translated from one language to another, something may be added or subtracted to the meaning of the word by the new word used. Why? It is because words have all kinds of understandings, nuances, and connotations from one language to another. The most common example is "love." There is one word in the English language with many meanings in numerous contexts, but several words in the Greek language. So, how should the exact meaning of a word be determined? We must study it in its numerous contexts.

When the concepts of "lying" and "deception" are studied in light of their contexts, we discover that the sinful act of "lying" or "deception" is always deliberate and with an evil or harmful purpose in mind. Even in secular life, we know that "lying" is always deliberate and comes with some kind of evil motive. In the light of this, let us consider the many passages on lying and deception in the Scriptures and see if this definition is the best fit for understanding the numerous truths taught.

First, let us consider God's character. When the Scriptures state that the Lord God does not "lie," it means God does not deliberately deceive or make a false statement to us for the express purpose of doing evil or harm. It is not in His divine character. He does not behave like man who cannot always be trusted that his motives are pure.

Numbers 23:19
God is not a man, that he should lie, nor the son of man, that he should repent. Has he said, and will he not do it? Or has he spoken, and will he not make it good?

Titus 1:2
In hope of eternal life, which God, who can't lie, promised before time began.

Hebrews 6:18
That by two immutable things, in which it is impossible for God to lie, we may have a strong encouragement, who have fled for refuge to take hold of the hope set before us.

What are these passages revealing about God? If He says something, it will happen. If He makes a promise, it will be fulfilled. If He makes a covenant, He will absolutely abide by it. God will never deliberately deceive us for evil or harm. His motives will always be pure.

Several passages teach that God condemns all "lying" and "deceiving." Using our definition, this means God condemns deception of any kind which is done for the purpose of evil or harm.

Proverbs 6:16-19
There are six things which Yahweh hates; yes, seven which are an abomination to him: haughty eyes, a lying tongue [for evil], hands that shed innocent blood; a heart that devises wicked schemes, feet

that are swift in running to mischief, a false witness who utters lies [for the harm of others], and he who sows discord among [his] brothers.

Proverbs 12:22
Lying lips [for evil] are an abomination to Yahweh, but those who do the truth are his delight.

Exodus 20:16
You shall not give false testimony against your neighbor.

All of these can easily be interpreted as deliberate "lying" or "deceiving" for evil or harm. The lying tongue or lying lips and the false testimony against our neighbor refers to "any deliberate words which provide falsehoods for evil or harm."

We are told not to deceive others in the New Testament.

Ephesians 4:25
Therefore putting away falsehood, speak truth each one with his neighbor. For we are members of one another.

Colossians 3:9
Don't lie to one another, seeing that you have put off the old man with his doings.

According to our definition, Paul is saying that we should not be making deliberately false statements for evil or harm.

In Acts chapter five, we can clearly see God disciplining two members of the church when they deliberately lied for evil or harm.

Acts 5:1-10
But a certain man named Ananias, with Sapphira, his wife, sold a possession, and kept back part of the price, his wife also being

aware of it, then brought a certain part and laid it at the apostles' feet. But Peter said, "Ananias, why has Satan filled your heart to lie to the Holy Spirit and to keep back part of the price of the land....You haven't lied to men, but to God." Ananias...fell down and died [just as Peter said] .... About three hours later, his wife, not knowing what had happened, came in. Peter answered her, "Tell me whether you sold the land for so much." She said, "Yes, for so much." But Peter asked her, "How is it that you have agreed together to tempt the Spirit of the Lord? Behold, the feet of those who have buried your husband are at the door, and they will carry you out." She fell down immediately at his feet and die...

With our definition of "lying," this fits perfectly. These two people sold a piece of property, kept back some of the money, and lied about it. They wanted people to think that they had given all the money to the church. Because of this evil motive of pride, God disciplined them unto death. Evil and wickedness is always around "lying."

Deliberate falsehoods for the purpose of evil and harm come from the darkness of Satan. He is the father of lies.

John 8:44
You are of your father, the devil, and you want to do the desires of your father [Satan]. He was a murderer from the beginning, and doesn't stand in the truth, because there is no truth in him. When he speaks a lie, he speaks on his own; for he is a liar, and its father.

The deliberate telling of falsehoods for the purpose of evil and harm is the characteristic of the unsaved who are judged by God for it. This makes sense because their father is the devil, and this is in his character as we just saw.

Psalm 10:7
His mouth is full of cursing, deceit, and oppression. Under his tongue is mischief and iniquity.

Ephesians 4:22
That you put away, as concerning your former way of life, the old man, that grows corrupt after the lusts of deceit.

Psalm 5:6
You will destroy those who speak lies. Yahweh [God] abhors the bloodthirsty and deceitful man.

Revelation 21:7-8
He who overcomes...I will be his God...he will be my son. But for the cowardly, and unbelieving, sinners, abominable, murderers, sexually immoral, sorcerers, idolaters, and all liars, their part is in the lake that burns with fire and sulfur, which is the second death (DEJ).

Unbelievers deliberately deceive for the purpose of evil or harm to satisfy their own lusts.

As we can this definition fits perfectly with the concept of deliberately making false statements for the purpose of evil or harm. Now, we will look at what "telling the truth" is in light of this definition. It is very similar.

Our Truthful Words and Actions for Good

Now, what about "telling the truth?" Aren't we supposed to be honest in everything? Are we? Does the Bible teach this directly? Could "speaking the truth" also have a much more specific definition in its contexts just like lying? Wouldn't a simple definition that is similar to ours for lying be much more fitting? Let us consider a similar definition for telling the truth: "a deliberate true statement for good."

Again, as in lying, when we are telling the truth, it is seen as righteous as long as our motives are good. What if we tell a truth to harm someone? It this righteous? No! Here are a few secular examples, we will consider several biblical ones in the following section. If a parent wraps a present for her daughter and her brother tells her what it is in order to ruin the surprise, would this be truly righteous? Well, he told the truth, didn't he?

If two high school students were determined to fight two other students at school and we knew this, wouldn't it be wrong to tell them that the two they wanted to fight were hiding in the restroom so we could watch the fight? In this case, wouldn't it be wrong to tell the truth? Or would we be applauded by the school authorities for our truthfulness? We would not; instead, we would be in much trouble.

Though this will be slightly tedious, we will now consider the same or similar passages we just studied concerning our definition of lying. Usually, the Bible deals with the negative concerning telling the truth. It will teach that we should not lie with the implication that we should tell the truth instead. Sometimes, it will contrast the two. We will consider both. To begin, we again will focus on God's character. When the Scriptures state that God does not "lie," it means that God always tells the truth for good.

Numbers 23:19
God is not a man, that he should lie, nor the son of man, that he should repent. Has he said, and will he not do it? Or has he spoken, and will he not make it good?

Titus 1:2
In hope of eternal life, which God, who can't lie, promised before time began.

Hebrews 6:18
That by two immutable things, in which it is impossible for God to

lie, we may have a strong encouragement, who have fled for refuge to take hold of the hope set before us.

What are these passages revealing about God? If He says something, it will happen. If He makes a promise, it will be fulfilled. If He makes a covenant, He will absolutely abide by it because He intends good toward us. We can fully rely on Him because His motive is pure. This means that He tells the truth for the purpose of good. Honesty pours out of good intentions.

Several passages teach that God condemns all "lying" and "deceiving." Using our definition, this means God approves the telling of truths for the purpose of good.

Proverbs 6:16-19
There are six things which Yahweh hates; yes, seven which are an abomination to him: haughty eyes, a lying tongue [for evil], hands that shed innocent blood; a heart that devises wicked schemes, feet that are swift in running to mischief, a false witness who utters lies [for the harm of others], and he who sows discord among brothers.

Proverbs 12:22
Lying lips [for evil] are an abomination to Yahweh, but those who do the truth are his delight.

Exodus 20:16
You shall not give false testimony against your neighbor.

All of these can easily be assumed to say that God desires we tell the truth for good. It can be implied that God loves a "truthful tongue." He looks favorably on a truthful witness with good intentions. Also, "truthful lips with good motives" pleases the Lord. We should provide a truthful testimony on behalf of our neighbor for his good.

If we take a look at the New Testament commands, we will see that the same definition fits again perfectly. When we are commanded to tell the truth, it really means to make accurate statements for good.

Ephesians 4:25
Therefore putting away falsehood, speak truth each one with his neighbor. For we are members of one another.

Colossians 3:9
Don't lie to one another, seeing that you have put off the old man with his doings.

Here, Paul is saying do not make deliberate false statements for evil or harm but rather tell the truth for good.

God disciplines His own children when they deliberately lie for evil or harm and do not tell the truth.

Acts 5:3-4
But Peter said, "Ananias, why has Satan filled your heart to lie to the Holy Spirit, and to keep back part of the price of the land? While you kept it, didn't it remain your own? After it was sold, wasn't it in your power? How is it that you have conceived this thing in your heart? You haven't lied to men, but to God."

Ananias and Sapphira had the freedom to keep back come of the money and tell the truth for good; instead, they lied out of pride.

Falsehoods for the purpose of evil and harm come from the darkness that is in Satan. He does not "tell the truth for the purpose of good."

John 8:44
You are of your father, the devil, and you want to do the desires of

your father [Satan]. He was a murderer from the beginning, and doesn't stand in the truth, because there is no truth in him. When he speaks a lie, he speaks on his own; for he is a liar, and its father.

Lying is the characteristic of the unsaved who are judged by God. Telling the truth for the purpose of good is a quality of the truly saved.

Psalm 10:7
His mouth is full of cursing, deceit, and oppression. Under his tongue is mischief and iniquity.

Ephesians 4:24
And put on the new man, who in the likeness of God has been created in righteousness and holiness of truth.

Revelation 21:7-8
He who overcomes, I will give him these things. I will be his God...he...my son....for the cowardly, and unbelieving, sinners, abominable, murderers, sexually immoral, sorcerers, idolaters, and all liars, their part is in the lake that burns with fire and sulfur, which is the second death.

Unbelievers deliberately deceive for the purpose of evil to satisfy their own lusts and believers tell the truth to do good.

It is interesting to note of the numerous times that the Greek word is used for truth it is almost always referring to the truth revealed in the Scriptures as opposed to the errors and lies of false teachers. This was a bigger concern than just being honest. These false teachers told lies that condemned men to hell. In fact, some of the passages we just considered could have this meaning also. Some have interpreted Paul's description of "the belt of truth" as "the belt of honesty" in his description of our spiritual armor in Ephesians chapter six. But this cannot be the case.

The weapons of our warfare and the armor of light have such concepts as faith, hope, love, righteousness, gospel, peace, the Word, and salvation. Therefore "the truth" of the Bible fits better as the belt that holds up the sword of the Spirit (specific Scriptures used) and the lower (skirt-like) garment which had to be tucked in to fight. Honesty is not seen among the many times these words are found together. It was important but in no way as critical as the God's truth revealed by the apostles. This truth is the focus of the Word.

Ephesians 6:13-17
Therefore put on the whole armor of God, that you may be able to withstand in the evil day, and having done all, to stand. Stand therefore, having the utility belt of truth buckled around your waist...the breastplate of righteousness, and having fitted your feet with the preparation of the Good News of peace, above all, taking up the shield of faith, with which you will be able to quench all the fiery darts of the evil one. And take the helmet of salvation, and the sword of the Spirit, which is the Word of God.

Here, he mentions the "truth" of the Word, not honesty.

2 Corinthians 6:7
In the Word of truth, in the power of God; by the armor of righteousness on the right hand and on the left.

So, what we have seen is the definition of "telling the truth" means "telling the truth for good." Though it seems we are a long way from our topic, the groundwork is almost laid.

Their Betraying Words and Actions for Harm

Now, let us consider the opposite of telling the truth for good which we briefly mentioned in the few examples we provided from the home and school yard. This is referred to as "betrayal." I am using this word because it comes from the words and actions of Judas who betrayed the Lord. We will use this word "betrayal" for "telling the truth for the purpose of evil or harm."

We will look at a couple of examples of "telling the truth in order to harm." The first is Doeg the Edomite who was a foreigner in the land of Israel. Saul became jealous of David when he began winning battle after battle and the women of Israel began singing his praises.

1 Samuel 18
As they came, when David returned from the slaughter of the Philistine, the women came out of all the cities of Israel, singing and dancing, to meet king Saul with tambourines, with joy, and with instruments of music. The women sang to one another as they played, and said, "Saul has slain his thousands, and David his ten thousands." Saul was very angry, and this saying displeased him. He said, "They have credited David with ten thousands, and they have only credited me with thousands. What can he have more but the kingdom?" Saul watched David from that day and forward.

When Saul became jealous enough to attempt to kill him, David ran for his life. When he arrived in Nob, he went to the tabernacle and asked Ahimelech the priest to give him some food and weapons. One of Saul's men was there.

1 Samuel 21:7
Now a certain man of the servants of Saul was there that day, detained before Yahweh; and his name was Doeg the Edomite, the best of the herdsmen who belonged to Saul.

Later, Doeg the Edomite, who was in charge of Saul's shepherds, discloses to Saul that he saw Ahimelech helping David. Though Saul's enemy was long gone, the High Priest Ahimelech had helped him, nevertheless.

THE PERSECUTION OF THE SAINTS AND HOW TO OVERCOME IT

1 Samuel 22:9
Then Doeg the Edomite, who stood by the servants of Saul, answered and said, "I saw the son of Jesse [David] coming to Nob, to Ahimelech the son of Ahitub.

This was the "truth." Obviously, Doeg mentioned it to gain some favor in Saul's eyes. He would have known that Saul would retaliate against the priest.

Saul ordered the high priest and eighty-five other priests to be killed almost eliminating the entire lineage of Eli. Since his men would not do such a treacherous and horrendous thing as take their swords against God's priests, he ordered Doeg to do it. Not only did Doeg kill them but went to Nob and killed their families and their animals.

1 Samuel 22:18-19
The king said to Doeg, "Turn and attack the priests!" Doeg the Edomite turned, and he attacked the priests, and he killed on that day eighty-five people who wore a linen ephod. He struck Nob, the city of the priests, with the edge of the sword, both men and women, children and nursing babies, and cattle and donkeys and sheep, with the edge of the sword.

In David's psalm about this incident, he mentions this treacherous betrayal of Doeg. I have retranslated the Hebrew words to best fit the meaning of the text.

The inscription at the beginning of Psalm 52 attributes it to the actual situation we are discussing concerning Doeg the Edomite.

Psalm 52
For the Chief Musician. A contemplation by David, when Doeg the Edomite came and told Saul, "David has come to Ahimelech's house."

Why a Psalm written about him? He became one of the great betrayers in the Old Testament. What did he do? He told the truth for evil and harm.

Psalm 52
Why do you boast of evil, mighty man [Doeg]? God's loving kindness endures continually. Your tongue [Doeg] plots calamity like a sharp razor, working treachery [betrayal]. You love evil [Doeg] more than good, deceit rather than speaking the truth. Selah. You love all words that devour [people], your crafty tongue. God will likewise destroy you forever. He will take you up, and pluck you out of your tent, and root you out of the land of the living...The righteous also will see it, and fear, and laugh at him, saying, "Behold, this is the man who didn't make God his strength, but trusted in the abundance of his riches, and strengthened himself in his wickedness (DEJ)."

Though Doeg told the exact truth about Ahimelech helping David, he had evil, treacherous intentions that betrayed both Ahimelech and David. The was such a sin that David provides a harsh prophecy of his demise. So, we can see that telling the truth with evil or harmful intentions is wrong. It usually involves a betrayal and should have this word used to describe it.

Please note that Doeg told the "truth" to the legal authority who was Saul. Yet, King Saul was acting outside of God's commands by seeking David's death without cause. Now, we have a second example similar to Doeg's betrayal.

This one involved Judas who told the "truth" to the legal Jewish authorities who were seeking the death of Jesus, who was innocent of any wrong. What was Judas' sin? It was telling the truth to do evil or harm Jesus. Judas told the exact truth concerning the location and identity of Jesus at the time the Jewish authorities wanted it.

THE PERSECUTION OF THE SAINTS AND HOW TO OVERCOME IT

After the triumphal entry of Jesus and his teaching and preaching against the Pharisees and other Jewish leaders, they decided it was time to kill Him.

Matthew 26:3-5
Then the chief priests, the scribes, and the elders of the people were gathered together in the court of the high priest, who was called Caiaphas. They took counsel together that they might take Jesus by deceit and kill him. But they said, "Not during the feast, lest a riot occur among the people."

They had to do it night away from the crowds. To do this, they would need the Lord's exact location. Judas provided this for a price.

Matthew 26:14-16
Then one of the twelve, who was called Judas Iscariot, went to the chief priests and said, "What are you willing to give me if I deliver him to you?" So they weighed out for him thirty pieces of silver. From that time he sought opportunity to betray him.

When Judas realized that Jesus would be alone that very evening with His disciples away from the crowds, he went and told the priests.

Mark 14:10
Judas Iscariot, who was one of the twelve, went away to the chief priests, that he might deliver him to them.

After Jesus had prayed in the garden of Gethsemane, the time the Father had appointed for His demise had come.

Matthew 26:46
Arise, let's be going. Behold, he who betrays me is at hand."

How did Judas know where Jesus would be that night?

John 18:2
Now Judas, who betrayed him, also knew the place, for Jesus often met there with his disciples.

Judas guided the authorities to the exact location where Jesus was and identified him with a kiss. Once they knew it was the man they were seeking, they immediately arrested the Lord.

Matthew 26:47-49
While he was still speaking, behold, Judas, one of the twelve, came...with...a great multitude with swords and clubs, from the chief priests and elders of the people. Now he [Judas] who betrayed him had given them a sign, saying, "Whoever I kiss, he is the one. Seize him." Immediately he came to Jesus, and said, "Greetings, Rabbi!" and kissed him.

Matthew 26:50
Jesus said to him [Judas], "Friend, why are you here?" Then they came and laid hands on Jesus, and took him.

Acts 1:16
"Brothers [Christians], it was necessary that this Scripture should be fulfilled, which the Holy Spirit spoke before by the mouth of David concerning Judas, who was guide to those who took Jesus.

Now, let us consider the situation for a moment. Judas simply told the exact truth to the authorities. He told "the truth, the whole truth, and nothing but the truth." He told no lies about words or actions of sedition as some of the false witnesses who would stand before Jesus did. He just told the truth. Yet, terrible things are said about Judas.

Mark 3:19
and Judas Iscariot, who also betrayed him. Then he came into a house.

Matthew 10:4
Simon the Zealot; and Judas Iscariot, who also betrayed him.

Matthew 26:23
He answered, "He who dipped his hand with me in the dish will betray me."

Matthew 26:24
The Son of Man goes even as it is written of him, but woe to that man through whom the Son of Man is betrayed! It would be better for that man if he had not been born.

Matthew 26:25
Judas, who betrayed him, answered, "It isn't me, is it, Rabbi?" He said to him, "You said it."

Luke 6:16
Judas the son of James; and Judas Iscariot, who also became a traitor.

Luke 22:48
But Jesus said to him, "Judas, do you betray the Son of Man with a kiss?"

John 6:71
Now he spoke of Judas, the son of Simon Iscariot, for it was he who would betray him, being one of the twelve.

John 12:4
Then Judas Iscariot, Simon's son, one of his disciples, who would betray him, said.

John 18:5-6
They answered him, "Jesus of Nazareth." Jesus said to them, "I am he." Judas also, who betrayed him, was standing with them. As soon then as he had said unto them, I am he, they went backward, and fell to the ground.

Notice, Judas is called a betrayer and a traitor. It would have been better had he never been born. Jesus even told Pilate that Judas had committed a greater sin.

John 19:11
Jesus answered, "You would have no power at all against me, unless it were given to you from above. Therefore he who delivered me to you has greater sin."

But what was his evil deed? What was the sin that was so great that he would wish he had never been born? What was worse than what Pilate did who actually condemned Him to death? The answer is found in the combination of the truth telling and the motive of evil or harm. The intent of Judas was only half the story, it would not have been complete without the truth being said. It was the truth and the intent for evil or harm that made the betrayal. Judas spent many days with Jesus and was part of the twelve. He was His friend. For money, He was willing to put Jesus in danger of death. His heart was full of evil for He was possessed by the Devil when He told them the "truth."

Luke 22:3
Satan entered into Judas, who was also called Iscariot, who was counted with the twelve.

John 13:2
During supper, the devil having already put into the heart of Judas Iscariot, Simon's son, to betray him.

Second, Judas cooperated fully with the authorities. This is exactly what we are told to do by Jesus, Paul, and Peter when they command our submission to government. So, what was wrong with what Judas did? He told the truth knowing that the officials were acting beyond their authority and violating the sixth commandment. We must remember that the Jewish Council had authority and they brought the Roman soldiers to verify that authority on this occasion.

Matthew 26:47
While he was still speaking, behold, Judas, one of the twelve, came, and with him a great multitude with swords and clubs, from the chief priests and elders of the people [from the Jewish Council].

John 18:3
Judas then, having taken a detachment of soldiers [Roman] and officers [Temple guards] from the chief priests and the Pharisees, came there with lanterns, torches, and weapons.

To make it worse, Judas came to realize the gravity of his betrayal. Perhaps, at first, he justified his actions by telling himself that he was cooperating with the authorities, and they were taking the actions. Nevertheless, he knew what he had done and returned the "blood money." Rather than repent, he killed himself.

Matthew 27:3-5
Then Judas, who betrayed him, when he saw that Jesus was condemned, felt remorse, and brought back the thirty pieces of silver to the chief priests and elders. saying, "I have sinned in that I betrayed innocent blood." But they said, "What is that to us? You see to it." He threw down the pieces of silver in the sanctuary and departed. Then he went away and hanged himself.

Paul's calls this a sorrow onto death.

2 Corinthians 7:10
For godly sorrow produces repentance to salvation, which brings no regret. But the sorrow of the world...death.

According to those who believe in "telling the truth" at all times and letting the Lord do a divine miracle, Judas should have been applauded for his righteous deed. Yet, he was not. So, by implication, if we tell the truth in order to allow evil or harm to innocent Christians, are we not betrayers? These two instances will suffice for our discussion because the evidence for the next point is overwhelming.

Our Misleading Words and Actions to Protect

Finally, we come to the fourth possibility in our topic of lying and honesty, which is deceiving persecutors to protect from evil or harm. Since the words "deceive" or "lie" have powerful negative connotations in the English language, let us use the term "mislead" for situations where God's people will deceive in words or actions to protect themselves or others from evil or harm. The study in this chapter and the next two will establish the fact that the Bible absolutely teaches that we can mislead persecutors in order to protect ourselves or others from evil or harm.

This would also include those who seek to harm us even if it is not for our faith. I make this statement with one caveat in mind by way of reminder, we may not mislead if a crime was committed against a law that does not deny us a non-negotiable of our Christian lives. For example, if several people had stolen jewelry from a store, we could not protect them from authorities. Instead, we would have to turn them into God's established authorities administering His wrath upon evil doers whether they are believers or not. One last thing, since this book addresses only persecution, I cannot take up the issue of "illegitimate laws" against human dignity and whether they can be disobeyed because of the extensive nature of the subject.

In our discussion of misleading of persecutors, we will include not only making false statements but also providing only part of the truth or none of the truth to mislead. It is with this aspect that we will begin our study. The belief that Christians must always "tell the truth, the whole truth, and nothing but the truth" must be challenged. Though in many courtrooms this is necessary and valued, Christians are not required by any Scriptural passages to "give the truth, whole truth, and nothing but the truth so help me God" to anyone including authorities at all times under all conditions. Why? It is because there are no Bible passages which support this understanding. In fact, we see something very different not only in word and actions of righteous people in God's Word but in the words and actions of God Himself.

Here is an important question, "Does the Almighty tell truth, the whole truth, and nothing but the truth so help Himself?" Initially, our response might be in the affirmative, but upon reflection this simply is not true. God certainly did not tell us "the whole truth" in His revelations throughout human history in Scripture; instead, the Lord God gave us only part of the truth with more and more revealed as time went on.

Though God does not lie, He is not compelled to explain to us "the whole truth." Let us consider His revelation to the prophets.

1 Peter 1:10-12
Concerning this salvation, the prophets sought and searched diligently, who prophesied of the grace that would come to you, searching for who or what kind of time the Spirit of Christ, which was in them, pointed to, when he predicted the sufferings of Christ, and the glories that would follow them. To them it was revealed, that not to themselves, but to you, they ministered these things, which now have been announced to you through those who preached the Good News to you by the Holy Spirit sent out from heaven; which things angels desire to look into.

Matthew 13:17
For most certainly I tell you that many prophets and righteous men desired to see the things which you see, and didn't see them; and to hear the things which you hear, and didn't hear them.

Jeremiah 33:3
Call to me, and I will answer you, and will show you great things, and difficult, which you don't know.

In God's redemptive plan, other parts of "the whole truth" would be revealed later and remained a mystery for many years. Then, the mystery was revealed through the Son of God and delivered to the apostles who were to present it to mankind in the New Testament age.

Ephesians 3:3-5
How that by revelation the mystery was made known to me, as I wrote before in few words, by which, when you read, you can perceive my understanding in the mystery of Christ, which in other generations was not made known to the children of men, as it has now been revealed to his...apostles and prophets in the Spirit.

We must understand that we will not have "the whole truth" about ourselves until He comes.

1 Corinthians 13:12-13
For now we see in a mirror, dimly, but then face to face. Now I know in part, but then I will know fully, even as I was also fully known. But now faith, hope, and love remain — these three. The greatest of these is love.

Some parts of the Second Coming are not known. We do not possess "the whole truth" concerning the exact time Jesus will return and every detail that is involved. We only know that He will come like thief in the night, and we will be in a moment changed among other things.

THE PERSECUTION OF THE SAINTS AND HOW TO OVERCOME IT

Matthew 24:36
But no one knows of that day and hour, not even the angels of heaven, but my Father only.

When Job cried out to God, the Lord refused to provide "the whole truth" of what happened in the heavenly places. In fact, he acknowledged that Job did not have the authority to know the truth.

Job 38:1-3
Then Yahweh answered Job out of the whirlwind, "Who is this who darkens counsel by words without knowledge? Brace yourself like a man, for I will question you, then you answer me!

Job 40:4
Then Job answered Yahweh, "Behold, I am of small account. What shall I answer you? I lay my hand on my mouth.

Sometimes, the Lord God does not desire for us to know "the whole truth" and He does not feel as if He must disclose all about Himself and His intentions.

Perhaps, there will be truth that will never be revealed to us because we could not understand it. How could our finite minds comprehend all that is in in the divine mind?

Deuteronomy 29:29
The secret things belong to Yahweh our God; but the things that are revealed belong to us and to our children forever, that we may do all the words of this law.

Some of the things of God may forever remain secret and there will be no concern over it.

There are times when we are not allowed to reveal "the whole truth" for a variety of reasons. In Matthew 18, Jesus commands us not to tell "the whole truth" to everyone when a brother is sinning against us. We must go to him privately.

Matthew 18:15
If your brother sins against you, go, show him his fault between you and him alone [privately]. If he listens to you, you have gained back your brother.

When the apostle Paul had his encounter in the heavenly places, he heard words which could not be revealed.

2 Corinthians 12:1-4
It is doubtless not profitable for me to boast. For I will come to visions and revelations of the Lord. I know a man in Christ, fourteen years ago (whether in the body, I don't know...whether out of the body, I don't know; God knows), such a one caught up into the third heaven. I know such a man (whether in the body, or outside of the body, I don't know; God knows), how he was caught up [went to] into Paradise, and heard unspeakable words, which it is not lawful for a man to utter.

Some of the people that Jesus healed were not to tell "the whole truth" concerning who had miraculously healed them. The time was not right. For example, Jesus told the blind man at Bethsaida to tell no one who had healed him.

Mark 8:25
Then again.... He looked intently, and was restored, and saw everyone clearly. He sent him away to his house, saying, "Don't enter into the village, nor tell anyone in the village."

Another consideration is how God deals with unbelievers for judgment. Is not "the hardening of men's hearts" a form of deception? The "hardened heart" is essentially man taking the knowledge of God and suppressing it in his heart for the purpose of continuing his sin. God does this to men also.

Romans 1:18
For the wrath [anger] of God is revealed from heaven against all ungodliness and unrighteousness of men, who suppress the truth in unrighteousness.

Here, people do not want to repent and turn from sin, so they deceive themselves. They tell themselves that what they are seeing, hearing, and sensing about the knowledge of God is not true.

One of God's responses to this is to further harden their hearts to advance His agenda and for judgment. When God hardens their hearts, then He himself suppresses the truth so they will not respond. This way they will continue to lie to themselves about who He is. He does this in order to fulfill some good and to bring judgment into people's lives at His appointed time. It is not for evil or the senseless harming of others. Often, these two purposes are found together. This is exactly what happened in the case of Israel's leader Moses with his confrontation and Pharaoh.

When God hardened Pharaoh's heart against Moses, He did it in order for all the nations to observe through miracles and a powerful deliverance that He was Israel's God, and He was the only true deity. They needed to put their trust in Him. To Israel, God wanted to not only show them the same but also to proclaim His future deliverance by His Passover lamb (His Son).

Exodus 9:12
Yahweh hardened the heart of Pharaoh, and he didn't listen to them, as Yahweh had spoken to Moses.

Exodus 10:20
But Yahweh hardened Pharaoh's heart, and he didn't let the children of Israel go.

Some may say that many innocent people were harmed in Egypt, but we know that no one is innocent, and all deserve punishment and judgment at any time God desires.

Romans 3:23
For all have sinned, and fall short of the glory of God.

When Jesus was asked about a group of apparently innocent people who had died, His response different than expected.

Luke 13:1-5
Now there were some...who told him about the Galileans, whose blood [Pontius] Pilate had mixed with their sacrifices. Jesus answered them, "Do you think that these Galileans were worse sinners than all the other Galileans, because they suffered such things? I tell you, no, but unless you repent, you will all perish in the same way. Or those eighteen, on whom the tower in Siloam fell, and killed them; do you think that they were worse offenders than all the men who dwell in Jerusalem? I tell you, no, but, unless you repent, you will all perish in the same way."

Jesus simply illustrated the fact that no one is innocent, and all deserve judgment at any time. This is explained by the author of Hebrews.

Hebrews 9:27
Inasmuch as it is appointed for men to die once, and after this, judgment.

So, God used the judgment day of some of the Egyptians to bring the knowledge of Him to the world.

When the Son of God came to the Jews and offered them the kingdom, their hearts had already been hardened by His Father. Though individually, some were able to see, such as the disciples, but most could not.

THE PERSECUTION OF THE SAINTS AND HOW TO OVERCOME IT

John 12:40
He has blinded their eyes and he hardened their heart, lest they should see with their eyes, and perceive with their heart, and would turn, and I would heal them.

Romans 11:7
What then? That which Israel seeks for, that he didn't obtain, but the chosen ones obtained it, and the rest were hardened.

2 Corinthians 3:14
But their minds were hardened, for until this very day at the reading of the old covenant the same veil remains, because in Christ it passes away.

This was not for the purpose of evil or harm but for Jesus to die on the cross and graft in the Gentiles.

This is the mystery of which Paul spoke. He wanted both the Jews and Gentiles to understand this powerful mystery, which was hidden (truth not disclosed) for centuries before it was revealed.

Ephesians 3:4-6
By which, when you read, you can perceive...the mystery of Christ; which in other generations was not made known to the children of men, as it has now been revealed to his holy apostles and prophets in the Spirit; that the Gentiles are fellow heirs, and fellow members of the body, and fellow partakers of his promise in Christ Jesus through the Good News.

Romans 11:17-18
But if some of the branches were broken off, and you, being a wild olive [that is a Gentile], were grafted in among them, and became partakers...of the olive tree; don't boast over the branches. But if you boast, it is not you [the Gentiles] who support the root, but the root [the Jews] supports you.

Jesus referred to the Gentiles receiving His gospel as His sheep from another pasture. This was a critical truth.

John 10:14-16
I am the good shepherd. I know my own, and I'm known by my own; even as the Father knows me, and I know the Father. I lay down my life for the sheep. I have other sheep, which are not of this fold. I must bring them also, and they will hear my voice. They will become one flock [church] with one shepherd [Christ].

Notice again, this truth had not been revealed. When it was, God deliberately veiled the eyes of the Jews in judgment.

The Lord Jesus spoke in parables to cloak the truth as an indictment to the Jews. This was also a form of misleading in order to judge them.

Matthew 13:10-11
The disciples came, and said to him, "Why do you speak to them in parables?" He answered them, "To you it is given to know the mysteries of the Kingdom of Heaven, but it is not given to them."

Matthew 13:12
For whoever has, to him will be given, and he will have abundance, but whoever doesn't have, from him will be taken away even that which he has.

Matthew 13:13-14
Therefore I speak to them in parables, because seeing they [the Jews] don't see, and hearing, they don't hear, neither do they understand. In them the prophecy of Isaiah is fulfilled, which says, "By hearing you will hear, and will in no way understand...you will see, and will in no way perceive."

Jesus as a judgment did not provide to them "the truth, the whole truth, and nothing but the truth."

The distinctions we are discussing are important as we begin our study of the kinds of words and actions, we may use in responding to our persecutors or those of others. In the next two chapters, we will see God's people mislead to protect themselves or others from evil or harm by providing only part of the truth or even providing false statements. In fact, these saints are lauded as acting in great faith.

As a result, we will discover that the saints can mislead their persecutors in order to protect themselves or others from harm. We are allowed to mislead them in words or actions or both. We absolutely may mislead those who are intending to harm us by simply hiding, escaping, avoiding, withdrawing, or disguising ourselves or others. Believers can withdraw to a place where no one can find them to avoid persecutors. Christians do not have to tell those who intend to harm them, all the information they desire when those they are protecting have done nothing wrong. Also, believers are not required to step forward in the name of Christ when someone is attempting to arrest or kill them for their faith.

Once this definition accepted, the passages that involve Rahab, Jacob, Michal (David's wife), David and many others that appear as if they had sinned and been blessed in spite of it can now be easily understood. They were not sinning at all. No "lying" occurred. In fact, they were accomplishing the Lord's purposes. This is the reason the Lord God did not chastise them for what they had done. He blessed them instead. We will see that these were powerful acts of faith which involved great risks. We will study the words and actions of Rahab, Rebekah, Abraham, and Samuel here and leave the rest for the next two chapters.

Let's begin with the clearest example of this principle in action which is Rahab. When Joshua and the twelve tribes entered the Promised Land, they were commanded by the Lord God to conquer it. Jericho was the first city on their path. So, Joshua decided that he must get a closer look at the people, soldiers, and fortifications of the city. To do this, he sent out spies to infiltrate it and find the information needed.

Joshua 2:1
Joshua the son of Nun secretly sent two men out of Shittim as spies, saying, "Go, view the land, including Jericho." They went and came into the house of a prostitute whose name was Rahab, and slept there.

Here, the two spies stopped at "Rahab's place" because her profession would allow them to stay without much attention or retribution. Also, most likely, her home was on the wall and could provide a way of escape if needed.

Nevertheless, the King of Jericho discovered that the spies were there and immediately sent word to Rahab.

Joshua 2:3
Jericho's king sent to Rahab, saying, "Bring out the men who have come to you, who have entered into your house; for they have come to spy out all the land."

Rather than exposing the two, Rahab made a false statement to the king because she knew harm would come to them.

Joshua 2:4-6
The woman took the two men and hid them. Then she said, "Yes, the men came to me, but I didn't know where they came from. About the time of the shutting of the gate, when it was dark, the men went out. Where the men went, I don't know. Pursue them quickly. You may catch up with them." But she had brought them up to the roof, and hidden them under the stalks of flax...she had laid in order on the roof.

So, Rahab "misled" the king in order to protect the spies from "evil and harm." The next two chapters will discuss the particulars but notice this: she deceived the king in both her words and her actions. This deception occurred to protect from evil and harm the innocent and is not "lying."

After the king's men left and the city's gate was shut, she spoke to the men and declared her faith in their God.

Joshua 2:7-11
The men pursued them along the way to the fords of the Jordan River. As soon as those who pursued them had gone out, they shut the gate. Before they had lain down, she came up to them on the roof. She said to the men, "I know that Yahweh has given you the land, and that the fear of you has fallen upon us, and that all the inhabitants of the land melt away before you. For we have heard how Yahweh dried up the water of the Red Sea before you, when you came out of Egypt; and what you did to the two kings of the Amorites, who were beyond the Jordan, to Sihon and to Og, whom you utterly destroyed. As soon as we had heard it, our hearts melted, and there wasn't any more spirit in... man, because of you: for Yahweh your God, he is God in heaven above, and on Earth beneath.

She explains to Israel's spies that she hid them because she believed in their God and that He was leading Israel to conquer their city.

Then, Rahab asks them to save her and her family.

Joshua 2:12-13
Now therefore, please swear to me by Yahweh, since I have dealt kindly with you, that you also will deal kindly with my father's house, and give me a true sign; and that you will save alive my father...mother...brothers...sisters, and all that they have, and will deliver our lives from death.

Here, Rahab misled the king to protect the spies from harm. Now, she wanted protection for herself and her family from the harm their army would do to them when the city was taken.

The spies were willing to save them all.

Joshua 2:14
The men said to her, "Our life for yours, if you don't talk about this business of ours; and it shall be, when Yahweh gives us the land, that we will deal kindly and truly with you."

She then tells the two spies how they could mislead the king's men to protect themselves by hiding in the mountains for three days and then escaping.

Joshua 2:15-16
Then she let them down by a cord through the window; for her house was on the side of the wall, and she lived on the wall. She said..., "Go to the mountain, lest the pursuers find you. Hide yourselves there three days, until the pursuers have returned. Afterward, you may go your way."

Though the king's men searched for the two spies, they were not able to find them.

Joshua 2:22-23
They went and came to the mountain, and stayed there three days, until the pursuers had returned. The pursuers sought them all along the way, but didn't find them. Then the two men returned, descended from the mountain, crossed the river, and came to Joshua the son of Nun. They told him all that had happened to them.

Finally, they told her if she kept their business to herself, gathered her family into her house, and tied a scarlet cord on the window, they would rescue all of them. No one would be harmed in any way.

Joshua 2:18
Behold, when we come into the land, tie this line of scarlet thread in the window which you used to let us down. Gather to yourself into the house your father, your mother, your brothers, and all your father's household.

Joshua 2:20-21
But if you talk about this business of ours, then we shall be guiltless of your oath which you've made us to swear." She said, "Let it be as you have said." She sent them away, and they departed. Then she tied the scarlet line in the window.

This fits perfectly with our definition of misleading. Rahab deceived the king because she was protecting the spies and then her and her family from evil or harm. It also fits with our biblical principle that one may "defy the law to obey a divine command." Rahab was defying the king of Jericho to obey a divine commandment (the sixth).

Now, let us take a look at this situation more closely and how it is described by various people in the Bible. First, Rahab described it as a "work of faith." She did not see it as wrong or a violation of God's law.

Joshua 2:11
As soon as we had heard it, our hearts melted, and there wasn't any more spirit in... man, because of you: for Yahweh your God, he is God in heaven above, and on Earth beneath.

She explains that she hid the two men because she believed in their God and that He was leading Israel to conquer their city. She knew this act of war was an act of God who was the true deity of the universe.

Second, Rahab called her words and actions an "act of kindness" and desired one in return.

Joshua 2:12
Now therefore, please swear to me by Yahweh, since I have dealt kindly with you, that you also will deal kindly with my father's house, and give me a true sign."

The misleading of the king and protection of the spies was an act of kindness. Also, the Hebrew spies agreed with her assessment by protecting her in a similarly kind way from their own army invasion.

Third, Joshua agreed with Rahab's analysis by protecting her family when the attack began.

Joshua 6:17
The city shall be devoted ...to Yahweh [God]. Only Rahab the prostitute shall live, she and all who are with her in the house, because she hid the messengers that we sent.

Joshua 6:25
But Rahab the prostitute, her father's household, and all that she had, Joshua saved alive. She lives in the middle of Israel to this day, because she hid the messengers whom Joshua sent to spy out Jericho.

Here, we see the mentioning of the central aspect of Rahab's "misleading" of the king: she "hid" the messengers. This is powerful testimony to Rahab's actions since God was with Joshua as He was with Moses.

Joshua 3:7
Yahweh said to Joshua, "Today I will begin to magnify you in the sight of all Israel, that they may know that as I was with Moses, so I will be with you."

This act of hiding must be accompanied by her deception of the king or there would have been no survival. So, they are speaking of both the verbal and physical deceptions that belong together in "her hiding of the spies."

So powerful and faithful were her words and actions that she is found in the Messianic line.

Matthew 1:5
Salmon became the father of Boaz by Rahab. Boaz became the father of Obed by Ruth.

She is also found in the list of the great people of faith in Hebrews chapter eleven.

Hebrews 11:31
By faith, Rahab the prostitute didn't perish with those who were disobedient, having received the spies in peace.

The author states that it was faith in God that caused her to receive the spies in "peace." She was not disobedient as the rest of the city was. Because of her belief in the true God (her obedience), she protected the spies. The phrase "received the spies in peace" refers to the entire act of misleading. The opposite of this would have been to expose the spies to the king in betrayal.

Rahab committed righteous acts with righteous words. In his letter, James utilizes her words and actions as a perfect example of faith being demonstrated by good works.

James 2:25-26
In the same way, wasn't Rahab the prostitute also justified by works, in that she received the messengers and sent them out another way? For as the body apart from the spirit is dead, even so faith apart from works is dead.

He explains that her act of faith was "receiving the spies." This means welcoming them and not exposing them to the king. Then, Rahab "sent them out another way" absolutely involves the misleading of king and his men. These two actions are called "works of faith." It would be foolish to think that both the author of Hebrews and James carefully excluded her "lies" and focused on her heart of faith.

Now, some say that she lied and should have exposed the spies and God would have done something supernatural to rescue them. Yet isn't it obvious that the inspired writers have commended her for these righteous acts; that is, this is exactly how God miraculously worked. Then, God blessed her for taking the grave risk in faith by not allowing her to be found out and then commending her by key people in the Bible. This was the miraculous rescue.

A similar situation occurs with Abraham and Sarah twice. Abraham misleads two leaders on two different occasions to protect himself from harm. The first incident occurred with Pharaoh and his travels through Egypt. He was frightened that Pharaoh would take Sarah into his own harem and then without a thought kill him.

Genesis 12:10-15
There was a famine in the land. Abram went down into Egypt to live as a foreigner there, for the famine was severe in the land. When he had come near to enter Egypt, he said to Sarai his wife, "See now, I know that you are a beautiful woman to look at. It will happen, when the Egyptians see you, that they will say, 'This is his wife.' They will kill me, but they will save you alive. Please say that you are my sister, that it may be well with me for your sake, and that my soul may live because of you." When Abram had come into Egypt, Egyptians saw that the woman was very beautiful. The princes of Pharaoh saw her, and praised her to Pharaoh; and the woman was taken into Pharaoh's house.

Though Pharaoh blessed Abraham with many servants and livestock because he thought Abraham was her brother, God stepped in.

Genesis 12:17-19
Yahweh afflicted Pharaoh and his house with great plagues because of Sarai, Abram's wife. Pharaoh called Abram and said, "What is this that you have done to me? Why didn't you tell me that she was your wife? Why did you say, 'She is my sister,' so that I took her to be my wife? Now therefore, see your wife, take her, and go your way."

Abraham was not punished by God for misleading Pharaoh. The question arises, "Why not?"

Then, it happened again when he was travelling in the region of Gerar.

Genesis 20:1-3
Abraham traveled from there toward the land of the South, and lived between Kadesh and Shur. He lived as a foreigner in Gerar. Abraham said about Sarah his wife, "She is my sister." Abimelech king of Gerar sent, and took Sarah.

The Lord God spoke to the king in a dream and told him to that He had closed up all the wombs in his country because he had Abraham's wife.

Genesis 20:18
For Yahweh had closed up tight all the wombs of the house of Abimelech, because of Sarah, Abraham's wife.

King Abimelech had to humbly request Abraham to pray for him to be released from God's curse, which he did. When the king asked Abraham the reason for misleading him, he told him it was out of fear.

Genesis 20:11
Abraham said, "Because I thought, 'Surely the fear of God is not in this place. They will kill me for my wife's sake.'"

Then, Abraham explained that he did not withhold the whole truth from him and only told him a part of it.

Genesis 20:12
Besides, she is indeed my sister, the daughter of my father, but not the daughter of my mother; and she [Sarah] became my wife.

Once again, Abraham was not punished, the king was.

The story of Jacob and Esau is another illustration. The tale begins with Esau selling his birthright for soup.

Genesis 25:30-34
Esau said to Jacob, "Please feed me with that same red stew, for I am famished." Therefore his name was called Edom. Jacob said, "First, sell me your birthright." [His twin] Esau said, "Behold, I am about to die. What good is the birthright to me?" Jacob said, "Swear to me first." He swore to him. He sold his birthright to Jacob. Jacob gave Esau bread and stew of lentils. He ate and drank, rose up, and went his way. So Esau despised his birthright. Jacob gave Esau bread and stew of lentils. He ate and drank, rose up, and went his way. So Esau despised his birthright.

Later, their mother Rebekah and Jacob conspired to seize the blessing also. Isaac decided that it was time to bless Esau and asked him to hunt and prepare a meal for him and then he would be blessed.

Genesis 27:2-4
He said, "See...I am old. I don't know the day of my death. Now therefore, please take your weapons, your quiver and your bow, and go out to the field, and get me venison. Make me savory food,

such as I love, and bring it to me, that I may eat, and that my soul may bless you before I die."

When Rebekah found out that Isaac had decided to bless Esau after he had prepared a meal, this righteous woman swung into action.

Genesis 27:5-10
Rebekah heard when Isaac spoke to Esau his son. Esau went to the field to hunt for venison, and to bring it. Rebekah spoke to Jacob her son, saying, "Behold, I heard your father speak to Esau your brother, saying, 'Bring me venison, and make me savory food, that I may eat, and bless you before Yahweh before my death.' Now therefore, my son, obey my voice according to that which I command you. Go now to the flock, and get me from there two good young goats. I will make them savory food for your father, such as he loves. You shall bring it to your father, that he may eat, so that he may bless you before his death."

After this, Rebecca put the skins of the lambs on Jacob's hands and arms to simulate Esau's hairy flesh and sent him to be blessed by his father. Though Isaac was suspicious of his voice, he was convinced by the skins. So, he passed his blessing onto him.

Genesis 27:26-29
His father Isaac said to him, "Come near now, and kiss me, my son." He came near...and blessed him, and said, "Behold, the smell of my son is as the smell of a field which Yahweh has blessed....Let peoples serve you, and nations bow down to you. Be lord over your brothers. Let your mother's sons bow down to you...."

So, Jacob received the blessing rather than Esau. When Esau came in and discovered what had occurred, he was angry and tearful and begged his father for the blessing. Isaac refused and cursed him instead.

Genesis 27:37-41
Isaac answered Esau, "Behold, I have made him your lord, and all his brothers I have given to him for servants. I have sustained him with grain and new wine. What then will I do for you, my son?" Esau said to his father, "Do you have just one blessing, my father? Bless me, even me also, my father." Esau lifted up his voice, and wept. Isaac his father answered him, "Behold, your dwelling will be of the fatness of the Earth, and of the dew of the sky from above. You will live by your sword, and you will serve your brother...."

After this Esau hated Jacob and sought to kill him.

Genesis 27:41
Esau hated Jacob...said in his heart, "The days of mourning for my father are at hand. Then I will kill my brother Jacob."

Most people when reading this account, assume that these were two young boys who didn't like each other and were tricksters. This could not be further from the truth.

First, Rebekah had received a prophecy when the twins were in her womb that gave the blessing and birthright to Jacob, the second born son.

Genesis 25:21-20
Isaac entreated Yahweh for his wife, because she was barren. Yahweh was entreated by him, and Rebekah his wife conceived. The children struggled together within her. She said, "If it is like this, why do I live?" She went to inquire of Yahweh. Yahweh said to her, "Two nations are in your womb. Two peoples will be separated from your body. The one people will be stronger than the other people. The elder will serve the younger." When her days to be delivered were fulfilled, behold, there were twins in her womb.

They knew this prophecy and understood that the promise given to Abraham and then Isaac had to go to Jacob even though he was not the first-born son. Both Jacob and Esau would have also known this as they were growing up. Why would she keep this from them? She fully expected when the time came for Isaac to follow God's holy prophecy about the promise.

Both siblings were men when these events occurred not young boys or even young men. We know this because Esau was forty when he took two non-Jewish wives.

Genesis 26:41
Esau hated Jacob because of the blessing...which his father blessed him. Esau said in his heart, "The days of mourning for my father are at hand. Then I will kill my brother Jacob."

This incident in Genesis 26 was sandwiched in between the selling of the birthright (Genesis 25) and the taking of the blessing (Genesis 27). This means that they were living with their parents, which was common at that time, into middle age. Some estimate the ages of the men at the selling of the blessing near the age of forty and the taking of the blessing at the age of seventy.

Second, the selling of his birthright was not the trick of two boys but the demonstration of how Esau did not see the value of his birthright as first-born son and all it entailed. This was the custom of ancient man at the time and was articulated later by Moses for the passing down of land, possessions, and animals within a family line. It had to be regulated or chaos would ensue.

Deuteronomy 21:15-17
If a man has two wives, the one beloved and the other hated, and they have borne him children, both the beloved and the hated, and if the firstborn son is hers who was hated, then it shall be, in the day that he causes his sons to inherit that which he has...he shall

acknowledge the firstborn, the son of the hated, by giving him a double portion of all that he has... The right of the firstborn is his.

Esau knew this custom and commandment but did not care. Why? The author of Hebrews gives us the answer.

Hebrews 12:16
Lest there be...sexually immoral...or profane [no religion] person, like Esau, who sold his birthright for one meal.

Esau was immoral and had no faith; that is, he was living by the lusts of his flesh without regard for God or His laws.

Jacob, on the other hand, was a prophet and man of God.

Luke 13:28
There will be weeping...gnashing of teeth, when you see Abraham, Isaac, Jacob...all the prophets, in God's Kingdom, and yourselves being thrown outside.

Matthew 8:11
I tell you that many will come from the east and the west, and will sit down with Abraham, Isaac...Jacob in the Kingdom of Heaven.

Matthew 22:32
I am the God of Abraham, and the God of Isaac, and the God of Jacob?' God is not the God of the dead, but of the living.

He knew God and understood that He had received the promise from Abraham and was in the line of promise. This is why he did not object to disguising himself due to sin but instead he did not want to incur his father's wrath.

Matthew 1:2
Abraham became the father of Isaac. Isaac became the father of Jacob. Jacob became the father of Judah and his brothers.

There was one unfortunate problem: Esau was his father Isaac's favored son, and he knew it. The promise was his by birth, but it meant nothing to him. Jacob would deal with this himself. It was his promise by prophecy. The Lord had intervened. He would wait for an opportunity to acquire the birthright and expose Esau's true callous heart.

Genesis 25:30
Esau said to Jacob, "Please feed me with some of that red stew, for I am famished." Therefore his name was called Edom. Jacob said, "First, sell me your birthright." Esau said, "Behold, I am about to die. What good is the birthright to me?" Jacob said, "Swear to me first." He swore to him. He sold his birthright to Jacob. Jacob gave Esau bread and lentil stew. He ate and drank, rose up, and went his way. So Esau despised his birthright.

The needs of the flesh at any moment were worth more than his future and the future of his descendants. What did he care about his birthright, or some promise given to his father and grandfather?

Jacob did care. We see him mentioned in Hebrews when Abraham was living in tents by faith in the promise. The grandfather, father, and son all believed in the same God and the same promise. There is no Esau here. Why? He was not interested in "religious" things.

Hebrews 11:9
By faith, he lived...an alien in the land of promise, as in a land not his own, dwelling in tents, with Isaac and Jacob, the heirs with him of the same promise.

Most likely, once Jacob had the birthright, it would have only been a matter of time before he had the blessing. Isaac would have known about Esau and the disdain he had for God's commandments and prophecies which governed his birthright and blessing. Yet, Isaac was determined to give it to Esau anyway because he favored him and that is what he wanted.

Here is the critical point. Isaac's decision to bless Esau in spite of the promise would do untold evil as He disobeyed God and untold harm in disrupting the Messianic line. This is the line Jesus would and must come from in order to fulfill numerous prophecies. He must descend from the kingly line of David which would also identify Him as the Son of God. It was in line with God's promise to Abraham.

So, Rebekah acted quickly, and Jacob followed. Jacob's only reservation was that Isaac may retaliate and curse him. He did not object to the action because it was a sin. Isaac was already rebelling against God, so the risk was higher. In this case, Rebekah having the prophecy given directly to her had enough strength for the both of them.

In Hebrews, the inspired author speaks of Isaac's faith demonstrated by this blessing.

Hebrews 11:20
By faith, Isaac blessed Jacob and Esau...concerning things to come.

Here he speaks of the blessing he gave by faith even though at the time he thought he was blessing Esau. How can this be reconciled? Isaac gave the blessing by faith and God through the righteous misleading of Rebekah and Jacob took care of the rest. When he realized what had happened, he did not rescind the blessing because "by faith" he knew God's chosen person had been blessed.

Isaac had Esau's godlessness and contempt confirmed to him by the unrepentant tears of his son Esau and the placing of the blame for what happened on his righteous brother.

Genesis 27:36
He said, "Isn't he rightly named Jacob? For he has supplanted me these two times. He took away my birthright. See...he has taken away my blessing." He said, "Haven't you reserved a blessing for me?"

Esau should have repented of his contempt for all that they believed: the prophecy, birthright, blessing, and faith in the God of his grandfather, father, and brother. He did not. This is affirmed by the author of Hebrews.

Hebrews 12:17
For you know that even when he afterward desired to inherit the blessing, he was rejected, for he found no place for a change of mind though he sought it diligently with tears.

He had no place for God in his heart and God had no place for him in his plan.

Concerning Isaac's hard-hearted stubbornness which led to Jacob's misleading him, we will see an identical situation with Tamar. She was another deeply faithful woman in the Messianic line who had to mislead a disobedient Judah to protect the promise.

An additional reason is the sovereign choice of the Lord God in this incident was to demonstrate a powerful example of election. God chooses who God chooses. This is seen in several passages by inspired authors who returned to this historic incident to demonstrate this truth.

Malachi 1:1-3
A revelation, Yahweh's word to Israel by Malachi. "I have loved you," says Yahweh. Yet you say, "How have you loved us?" "Wasn't Esau Jacob's brother?" says Yahweh, "Yet I loved Jacob; but Esau I hated, and made his mountains a desolation...."

Romans 9:10-13
Not only so, but Rebekah also conceived by one, by our father Isaac. For being not yet born, neither having done anything good or bad, that the purpose of God according to election might stand, not of works, but of him who calls, it was said to her, "The elder will serve the younger." Even as it is written, "Jacob I loved, but Esau I hated.

God chooses whom He chooses was not demonstrated by the sin of lying but by a righteous misleading.

Now, let us consider the similar incident with Judah and Tamar. Judah was not the first-born son of Jacob and had no birthright or blessing. The first-born son was Reuben, but he committed a grievous sin by sleeping with Bilhah, who was his father's concubine.

Genesis 35:21-22
Israel traveled, and spread his tent beyond the tower of Eder. While Israel lived in that land, Reuben went and lay with Bilhah, his father's concubine, and Israel heard of it.

As a result, Reuben had lost both his birthright and blessing. Jacob describes this on the day of his transfer of all that he had and all his prophecies concerning his children.

Genesis 49:3-4
Reuben, you are my firstborn, my might, and the beginning of my strength, excelling in dignity, and excelling in power. Boiling over like water, you shall not excel, because you went up to your father's bed, then defiled it. He went up to my couch.

The authors of Chronicles as they wrote the history of Israel after the Jews returned from captivity in the Medo-Persian empire mentions this same critical incident. This change in the line was important.

1 Chronicles 5:1-2
The sons of Reuben the firstborn of Israel (for he was the firstborn; but, because he defiled his father's couch, his birthright was given to the sons of Joseph the son of Israel; and the genealogy is not to be listed according to the birthright. For Judah prevailed above his brothers, and from him came the prince; but the birthright was Joseph's).

According to this chronicle, Joseph received the birthright, but Judah was given the blessing. It was the blessing that determined the line of the Messiah. It states that the "prince" will come from him.

This is confirmed also by blessing of Judah.

Genesis 49:8-12
Judah, your brothers will praise you. Your hand will be on the neck of your enemies. Your father's sons will bow down before you. Judah is a lion's cub. From the prey, my son, you have gone up. He stooped down, he crouched as a lion, as a lioness. Who will rouse him up? The scepter will not depart from Judah, nor the ruler's staff from between his feet, until he comes to whom it belongs. The obedience of the peoples will be to him. Binding his foal to the vine, his donkey's colt to the choice vine, he has washed his garments in wine, his robes in the blood of grapes. His eyes will be red with wine, his teeth white with milk.

With Judah in the line of the promise, how does Tamar fit in? In Genesis 38, we are provided with another illustration of misleading to protect from evil or harm.

Genesis 38:1-4
At that time, Judah...visited a certain Adullamite...There, Judah saw the daughter of a certain Canaanite man named Shua. He took her, and went into her. She conceived, and bore a son; and he named him Er.

Judah marries a Canaanite (non-Jew). She bears him three sons whose names were Er, Onan, and Shelah.

Genesis 38:6
Judah took a wife for Er, his firstborn...her name was Tamar.

So, Tamar was the daughter-in-law of Judah having married his first-born son. This would put their children in the line of the Messiah.

Genesis 38:7
Er, Judah's firstborn, was wicked in Yahweh's sight. So Yahweh killed him.

God disciplined her husband Er knowing that Judah would have to provide a kinsmen redeemer according to Moses to raise up seed for Er's line.

Deuteronomy 25:5-6
If brothers dwell together, and one of them dies and has no son, the wife of the dead shall not be married outside to a stranger. Her husband's brother shall go in to her, and take her as his wife, and perform the duty of a husband's brother to her. It shall be that the firstborn whom she bears shall succeed in the name of his brother who is dead, that his name not be blotted out of Israel.

Judah then commanded Onan, Er's brother to do his duty for Tamar and he too was killed by God.

Genesis 38:8-10
Judah said to Onan, "Go in to your brother's wife, and perform the duty of a husband's brother to her, and raise up offspring for your brother." Onan knew that the offspring wouldn't be his; and when he went in to his brother's wife, he [Onan] spilled his semen on the ground, lest he should give offspring to his brother. The thing which he did was evil in Yahweh's sight, and he killed him also.

Judah's solution was for Tamar to return to her family and wait for his youngest son, Shelah, to grow up. This she did.

Tamar followed God's law given through Moses though it was at great personal sacrifice.

Genesis 38:11
Then Judah said to Tamar, his daughter-in-law, "Remain a widow in your father's house, until Shelah, my son, is grown up;" for he said, "Lest he also die, like his brothers." Tamar went and lived in her father's house.

Judah did not want Shelah to die like his brothers, so he sent Tamar away. He was not about to command his last son to raise up offspring for his dead brother and take the chance that Shelah would be killed by God also. This was a grievous sin against God's law.

We do not know how long Tamar had waited but it became obvious that Judah would not fulfill his promise or follow God's commandments. So, when she discovered that Judah was going to be shearing sheep in Timnah, she decided to mislead Judah and force him to follow God's law.

Genesis 38:14
She took off the garments of her widowhood, and covered herself with her veil, and wrapped herself, and sat in the gate of Enaim, which is on the way to Timnah; for she saw that Shelah was grown up, and she wasn't given to him as a wife.

She put on the disguise of a prostitute to entice him to take the responsibility he had.

Genesis 38:15
When Judah saw her, he thought that she was a prostitute, for she had covered her face. He turned to her...and said, "Please come, let

me come in to you," for he didn't know that she was his daughter-in-law. She said, "What will you give me, that you may come in to me?" He said, "I will send you a young goat from the flock." She said, "Will you give me a pledge, until you send it?" He said, "What pledge will I give you?" She said, "Your signet and your cord, and your staff that is in your hand." He gave them to her, and came in to her, and she conceived by him.

Unwittingly, Judah fulfilled his responsibility and Tamar hers. She was now going to produce the offspring promised to her by God through the commands of Moses.

When Judah searched for the prostitute, the man could not locate her. Then, he found out that Tamar was pregnant and was angry until he discovered it was his.

Genesis 38:24-25
About three months later, Judah was told, "Tamar, your daughter-in-law, has played the prostitute. Moreover, behold, she is with child by prostitution." Judah said, "Bring her out, and let her be burned." When she was brought out, she sent to her father-in-law, saying, "I am with child by the man who owns these." She also said, "Please discern whose these are – the signet, and the cords, and the staff."

Notice, how Judah describes Tamar when he discovers what she had done. He does not rebuke her but lauds her for her righteousness.

Genesis 38:26
Judah acknowledged them, and said, "She is more righteous than I, because I didn't give her to Shelah, my son." He knew her again no more.

Judah recognizes the righteous action of Tamar. Yet, that righteous action involved misleading Judah with a disguise.

Second, we know that from this misleading, which was a righteous act, the messianic line came from her son Perez.

Genesis 38:27
In the time of her travail, behold, twins were in her womb. When she travailed, one put out a hand, and the midwife took and tied a scarlet thread on his hand, saying, "This [Zerah] came out first." As he drew back his hand, behold, his brother came out, and she said, "Why have you made a breach for yourself?" Therefore his name was called Perez. Afterward his brother came out, who had the scarlet thread on his hand, and his name was called Zerah.

Though she most likely did not know this, she was obeying God's commands in faith.

Matthew 1:3
Judah became the father of Perez and Zerah by Tamar. Perez became the father of Hezron. Hezron became the father of Ram.

Luke 3:33
The son of Amminadab, the son of Aram, the son of Hezron, the son of Perez, the son of Judah.

Third, a sovereign God killed both sons knowing exactly what every person would do in this situation in order to have Tamar conceive by Judah to preserve the Messianic line. This is the reason the Lord blessed Tamar. She had done nothing wrong before God. Her misleading of Judah had prevented evil and harm to occur.

Fourth, Tamar's act of faith is mentioned in Ruth. Here, Boaz secures the kinsmen redeemer rights to marry Ruth.

Ruth 4:10
Moreover, Ruth the Moabitess, the wife of Mahlon, I [Boaz] have purchased to be my wife, to raise up the name of the dead on his

inheritance, that the name of the dead may not be cut off from among his brothers and from the gate of his place. You are witnesses today."

In the blessing of the elders, they mention Tamar.

Ruth 4:12
Let your house be like the house of Perez, whom Tamar bore to Judah, of the offspring which Yahweh will give you by this young woman.

What Tamar had done was common knowledge among the people. Her righteous act brought Tamar the blessing of offspring and they wish the same on Boaz. Would they have known that Judah, Tamar, and Perez were Boaz's ancestors and that he was also in the line of promise? Yes, of course. The Jews were meticulous in tracking genealogies.

Tamar's actions to preserve the line according to the kinsmen redeemer was well known and applauded. Her deceit was not overlooked, it was part of it and not a sin.

Another incident involves God giving direct permission to "mislead." In 1 Samuel 16, God commands Samuel to go and anoint a new king over Israel unbeknownst to Saul who was king. Saul had offered a sacrifice without waiting for Samuel, the priest, and God was done with him.

1 Samuel 16:1
Yahweh said to Samuel, "How long will you mourn for Saul, since I have rejected him from being king over Israel? Fill your horn with oil, and go. I will send you to Jesse...for I have provided a king for myself among his sons."

Samuel protested for fear that Saul will retaliate, so the Lord God told Samuel to provide a partial truth to King Saul.

THE PERSECUTION OF THE SAINTS AND HOW TO OVERCOME IT

1 Samuel 16:2
Samuel said, "How can I go? If Saul hears it, he will kill me." Yahweh said, "Take a heifer with you, and say, I have come to sacrifice to Yahweh. Call Jesse to the sacrifice, and I will show you what you shall do. You shall anoint to me him whom I [God] name to you." Samuel did that which Yahweh spoke, and came to Bethlehem. The elders of the city came to meet him trembling, and said, "Do you come peaceably?" He said, "Peaceably; I have come to sacrifice to Yahweh. Sanctify yourselves, and come with me to the sacrifice."

Samuel sanctified Jesse and his sons and called them to the sacrifice. Samuel did not tell the elders, nor David's father Jesse. He just invited him to the sacrifice.

When Saul invited David to his own court to soothe his spirit with music, he did not know that David had already been anointed king in his place. This partial truth was kept from him. Why? He would murder David if He found out.

1 Samuel 16:23
When the [evil] spirit...was on Saul, David took the harp, and played with his hand; so Saul was refreshed..."

This incident is mentioned to once again demonstrate the truth that misleading persecutors or enemies to protect from evil or harm is not only a righteous act but is an acceptable way to avoid persecution. Also, it should be noted that Saul was the governing authority at the time. Samuel defied him by keeping this important truth from him to obey a divine command.

Our final argument concerning whether we may mislead or not is based on the idea that God usually disciplined his servants when they sinned. He pointed out their sin, so it was clear to all. For example, when David sinned against

God with Bathsheba, the prophet Nathan was sent to expose the evil he had done. Then he lost his firstborn son.

2 Samuel 12:7-10
Nathan said to David, "You are the man.... Why have you despised Yahweh's word, to do that which is evil in his sight? You have struck Uriah the Hittite with the sword, and have taken his wife to be your wife, and have slain him with the sword of the children of Ammon. Now therefore the sword will never depart from your house, because you have despised me, and have taken Uriah the Hittite's wife to be your wife."

2 Samuel 12:14-15
"However, because by this deed you have given great occasion to Yahweh's enemies to blaspheme, the child also who is born to you will surely die." Nathan departed to his house.

We just learned how the Lord God responded when Saul had offered the sacrifice without Samuel.

1 Samuel 13:4-9
All Israel heard...Saul...struck the garrison of the Philistines...The people were gathered together after Saul to Gilgal...Philistines assembled themselves together to fight with Israel...When the men of Israel saw that they were in trouble (for the people were distressed), then the people hid themselves in caves, in thickets, in rocks, in tombs, and in pits. Now some of the Hebrews had gone over the Jordan to the land of Gad and Gilead; but as for Saul, he was yet in Gilgal, and all the people followed him trembling. He stayed seven days, according to the time set by Samuel; but Samuel didn't come to Gilgal, and the people were scattering from him. Saul said, "Bring the burnt offering to me here, and the peace offerings." He offered the burnt offering.

Once King Saul had sinned, the Lord God sent Samuel to rebuke and punish him.

THE PERSECUTION OF THE SAINTS AND HOW TO OVERCOME IT

1 Samuel 13:10-13
It came to pass that as soon as he had finished offering the burnt offering, behold, Samuel came; and [King] Saul went out to meet him...Samuel said to Saul, "You have done foolishly. You [Saul] have not kept the commandment of Yahweh your God, which he commanded you; for now Yahweh would have established your kingdom on Israel forever. But now your kingdom will not continue. Yahweh has sought for himself a man after his own heart, and Yahweh has appointed him to be prince over his people, because you have not kept that which Yahweh commanded you."

Once again, sin was confronted.

We have learned that we may mislead our persecutors to avoid persecution. This means that we may false statements or give false impressions to protect ourselves or others from harm. This may be done also to governmental authorities if they are acting against God's commandments or asking us to violate them. We may not lie by telling a falsehood in order to do evil or harm. In the next two chapters, we will learn the practical application of this misleading of persecutors to avoid evil or harm and the biblical examples and evidence of its acceptability to God.

STANDING YOUR GROUND

Chapter 12

Avoid to Protect the Saints

In this chapter, we will continue discussing the important avoidance responses we can make toward our persecutors in order to protect the saints. We have learned that avoidance often leads to some form of deception. When this deception occurs to protect from evil or harm, it is perfectly acceptable to God. We called this kind of deception "misleading" to distinguish this principle from the sin of "lying" which is "deceiving for the purpose of evil or harm." We discovered that Christians may mislead in words or actions as long as it does not involve committing a crime where the authorities are searching for them or others. This means a crime other than a Christian non-negotiable. If a non-negotiable becomes a crime, then the saints by supernatural necessity ought to defy the law to obey the Lord God's divine command. This may involve misleading the authorities.

Therefore, as a reminder, when we say "persecutors," we will be speaking of persecutors who are vigilantes (citizens acting outside the law) or governmental authorities who are acting against God's direct commands. Now, we come to the study of the numerous options we may take in our actions to avoid persecution. If misleading is involved, I will provide a discussion of it and the biblical support that demonstrates it is acceptable to God. The last chapter, this one, and the next should be read together to understand these principles. As we study these biblical stories of avoidance, we will consider in this chapter avoidance actions which mislead and then in the next chapter we will discuss the verbal avoidances and our misleading persecutors in words. Usually these are done in tandem, but we will separate them for clarity.

As we begin this study, it must be noted that we never see Jesus or any apostle turning themselves over to the Jewish authorities when they were sought even though they were given the power of arrest by the Romans (though capital punishment was not allowed). The betrayal by Judas was allowed because it was Christ's time to die. If it had not been, Jesus would have avoided it.

Mark 14:41
He came the third time, and said to them, "Sleep on now, and take your rest. It is enough. The hour has come. Behold, the Son of Man is betrayed into the hands of sinners."

Matthew 26:45-46
Then he came to his disciples, and said to them, "Sleep on now, and take your rest. Behold, the hour is at hand, and the Son of Man is betrayed into the hands of sinners. Arise, let's be going. Behold, he who betrays me is at hand."

The avoidance of Jesus and His followers took many forms of action in order to mislead persecutors in order to protect themselves from evil or harm. Some of these avoidance behaviors will appear very similar but will have subtle distinctions. I place them all here so all options can be seen.

A Quick Escape

Christians may find themselves in a situation where they must quickly escape the possibility of harm. In Matthew 2, Matthew describes the urgent departure of Joseph and Mary from the clutches of Herod. The king ordered all the babies in Bethlehem from two years old and younger to be killed.

Matthew 2:13-15
Now when they [the Magi] had departed, behold, an angel of the

Lord appeared to Joseph in a dream, saying, "Arise and take the young child and his mother, and flee into Egypt, and stay there until I tell you, for Herod will seek the young child to destroy him." He arose and took the young child and his mother by night, and departed into Egypt, and was there until the death of Herod; that it might be fulfilled which was spoken by the Lord through the prophet, saying, "Out of Egypt I called my son."*

In this instance, an angel from God assisted the couple in misleading their persecutor. If they quickly escaped, those attempting evil or harm upon them would not know where they were. This was the very point of escaping. Also, they were defying the governmental authority of Herod who was king at the time. He was hindering the sharing of the gospel (in the person of the Messiah) and breaking God's command against murder. The angel is the divine confirmation that this kind of avoidance is acceptable.

In Acts 5, an angel rescued the apostles when they were imprisoned. God was providing them with a quick escape. It was not a loud confrontation and spectacular defense but a swift departure.

Acts 5:17-21
But the high priest rose up, and all those who were with him (which is the sect of the Sadducees), and they...laid hands on the apostles, and put them in public custody. But an angel of the Lord opened the prison doors by night, and brought them out, and said, "Go stand and speak in the temple to the people all the words of this life." When they heard this, they entered into the temple about daybreak, and taught. But the high priest came, and those who were with him, and called the council together, and all the senate of the children of Israel, and sent to the prison to have them brought.

In this situation, an angel assisted them in misleading their persecutors. Once again, if they quickly escaped, those who were attempting evil or harm against them would not know at first where they were. These persecutors were legitimate governmental authorities who were being defied. This was God's doing and His acceptance.

In another incident, Jesus claimed to be the Messiah in the synagogue at Nazareth and indicted them for their hardness of hearts.

Luke 4:28-30
They were all filled with wrath in the synagogue, as they heard these things. They rose up, threw him out of the city, and led him to the brow of the hill that their city was built non, that they might throw him off the cliff. But he, passing through the middle of them, went his way with God.

Here, the Lord escaped by walking invisibly through their midst.

On another occasion, it was the Feast of the Dedication in Jerusalem and Jesus was again in the temple and claimed to be one with God the father. This sent the Jews in a rage.

John 10:39-42
They sought again to seize him, and he went out of their hand. He went away again beyond the Jordan into the place where John was baptizing at first, and he stayed there. Many came to him. They said, "John indeed did no sign, but everything that John said about this man is true." Many believed in him there.

Again, the Lord God made a quick supernatural escape from their grasp.

In these two instances, Jesus quickly escaped most likely through supernatural means so they could not grab Him and harm Him. They could not lay hands on Him because they were misled. These Jews attempted to provide a vigilante justice in their rage. This violated God's law against murder. Since the good news was embodied in and proclaimed by the Lord, they had no right to stop Him. The Son of God confirmed God's acceptance of escape by His own behavior.

An Alternate Route

The Magi were warned in a dream about the danger of returning to Herod in order to provide the location of the newborn "King of The Jews."

Matthew 2:11
They came into the house and saw the young child with Mary, his mother, and they fell down and worshiped him. Opening their treasures, they offered to him gifts: gold, frankincense, and myrrh. Being warned in a dream not to return to Herod, they went...to their...country another way.

Here, the warning in the dream would have been from God confirming the acceptance of an alternate route when we desire to avoid persecution. Again, Herod, as a governing authority, had no right to stop the gospel in the person of Christ or murder the innocent. He could be defied by going another way.

We saw the same situation with the spies that Rahab had protected. She sent the King's men in one direction and told the spies to avoid harm by going in a different direction.

Joshua 2:15-17
Then she let them down by a cord through the window; for her house was on the side of the wall, and she lived on the wall. She [Rahab] said to them, "Go to the mountain, lest the pursuers find you. Hide yourselves there three days, until the pursuers have

returned. *Afterward, you may go your way." The men said to her, "We will be guiltless of this your oath which you've made us to swear."*

So, if needed, Christians can avoid persecution by taking an alternate route from their pursuers. Since the King knew that the God of Israel had given Jericho into their hands, they were to submit but were disobedient.

Hebrews 11:31
By faith, Rahab the prostitute didn't perish with those who were disobedient, having received the spies in peace.

The king and his men were disobedient to the Lord God by attempting to capture the spies. Rahab welcomed them in peace and kept them in peace. This was great act of faith. They would have no right to kill the spies. Her misleading was justified in the eyes of God.

A Different Location

When persecution comes, we might travel to a different location from where our potential or actual persecutors are not able to find us. When Herod had died, Mary and Joseph were told to return to Israel. They were warned in a dream to go to Nazareth to avoid His successor. They had to find a different location with the Lord's help to avoid harm.

Matthew 2:18-23
"A voice was heard in Ramah, lamentation, weeping and great mourning, Rachel weeping for her children; because they are no more." But when Herod was dead, behold, an angel...appeared in a dream to Joseph in Egypt, saying, "Arise...go into the land of Israel, for those who sought the young child's life are dead." He arose and took the young child and his mother, and came into the

land of Israel. But when he heard that Archelaus was reigning over Judea in the place of his father, Herod, he was afraid to go there. Being warned in a dream, he [Joseph] withdrew into the region of Galilee, and came and lived in a city called Nazareth; that it might be fulfilled which was spoken through the prophets...he will be called a Nazarene.

In this circumstance, an angel assisted the couple again in misleading a potential persecutor. The angelic assistance and prophetic identification of Jesus as the "Nazarene," shows an acceptance from the Lord. We may do the same.

A Public Presence

Saints who have a public persona may avoid persecution by staying in public if this would avoid harm. They should stay in the public eye as much as possible. Jesus did this very thing on numerous occasions.

For the most part, the ministry of Jesus was in public.

Matthew 9:35
Jesus went about all the cities and the villages, teaching in their synagogues...preaching...Good News of the Kingdom, and healing every disease and every sickness among the people.

One of the results of this open ministry was protection from being arrested or harmed by the Jewish leaders. They could not seize Jesus because He was most often in public view and the people admired Him. So, they attempted to trick Him into saying something blasphemous.

After the Lord cleansed the temple a second time, He was teaching in the temple and Luke comments on the intentions of the Jewish leaders.

STANDING YOUR GROUND

Luke 19:47-48
He was teaching daily in the temple, but the chief priests and the scribes and the leading men among the people sought to destroy him. They couldn't find what they might do, for all the people hung on to every word that he said.

His ministry was public, and He was seen as a prophet and the people were mesmerized by His words. They could not possibly seize Him without a riot.

Later, he was teaching in parables, and it began to dawn on the Jewish leaders that He was speaking against them. Though they greatly desired to seize Him, they could not because He was in the public eye.

Matthew 21:45-46
When the chief priests and the Pharisees heard his parables, they perceived that he spoke about them. When they sought to seize him, they feared the multitudes...they considered him [Jesus] to be a prophet.

Mark's account also demonstrates this public protection that Jesus enjoyed.

Mark 12:12
They tried to seize him, but they feared the multitude; for they perceived that he spoke the parable against them. They left him, and went away.

As we can see, His public ministry kept Him from any harm. One of the options Christians have to avoid persecution is to continually remain in the public eye. This was also to avoid the persecution of authorities (Jewish leaders) behaving in an illegitimate way by trying to stop the gospel embodied in Christ's person and message and kill an innocent man. Is this not a confirmation of this holy method to avoid persecution?

A Reclusive Existence

As Jesus waited for the time allotted by the Father for His crucifixion, the Lord had to eventually become much more reclusive because the Jews were becoming more brazen in their questioning and attempts to seize Him. Christians may have to do the same. They may have to avoid persecution by staying out of the public eye depending on the intensity of the pursuit of their persecutors.

After Jesus performed the spectacular miracle of raising Lazarus from the dead, the Jews conspired to kill Him. They could not allow any more of these powerful miracles.

John 11:47-48
The chief priests therefore and the Pharisees gathered a council, and said, "What are we doing? For this man does many signs. If we leave him alone like this, everyone will believe in him, and the Romans will come and take away both our place and our nation."

The Lord responded by ending His very public ministry and became more reclusive.

John 11:53-54
So from that day forward they took counsel that they might put him to death. Jesus therefore walked no more openly among the Jews, but departed from there into the country near the wilderness, to a city called Ephraim. He [the Lord] stayed there with his disciples.

The betrayal of Judas involved him disclosing to the Jews exactly where Jesus was at a given time so they could arrest Him in the night. He would lead the leaders of Israel with their army and mob to Jesus and identify Him with a kiss. This way the general population would not know until later what was happening.

John 18:2
Now Judas, who betrayed him, also knew the place, for Jesus often met there with his disciples.

In this situation, Jesus was misleading a governmental body with authority. The Jewish Council was recognized by the Romans and the nation as legitimate. Why didn't Jesus turn Himself in? Not only was it not His time, but these leaders were plotting an action against the sixth commandment. He absolutely could defy them. Jesus' actions confirm that this is acceptable.

Herein lies and option for all believers when persecution comes. We might have to cease our public ministries and become more reclusive. This does not mean we necessarily stop all sharing of the gospel or service to the saints; instead, we will have to be more careful where we show ourselves.

A Demanded Silence

Out of the many ways in which we, as saints, can respond to persecution is to avoid it by asking others to not reveal our location or activities to those to whom we interact. Once again, Jesus often asked those He had healed not to mention what He had done to anyone. One incident occurred when He healed the leprous man. The Lord told him not to reveal what he had done. Though the man disregarded what the Lord had requested, Jesus still asked.

Mark 1:43-45
He strictly warned him, and immediately sent him out, and said to him, "See you say nothing to anybody, but go show yourself to the priest, and offer for your cleansing...for a testimony to them." But he went out, and began to proclaim it much, and to spread about the matter, so that Jesus could no more openly enter into a city....

After the Lord Jesus was transfigured and His glory was displayed, He asked His three disciples to tell no one what they had seen and heard at that time.

Mark 9:9-10
As they were coming down from the mountain, he [Jesus] commanded them that they should tell no one what things they had seen, until after the Son of Man had risen from the dead. They kept this saying to themselves, questioning what the "rising from the dead" meant.

Again, after the raising of Jairus' daughter in Galilee, he ordered all the onlookers to not reveal what He had done.

Mark 5:40-43
They ridiculed him. But he, having put them all out, took the father of the child, her mother, and those who were with him, and went in where the child was lying. Taking the child by the hand, he said to her, "Talitha cumi!" which means, being interpreted, "Girl, I tell you, get up!" Immediately...girl rose up....they were amazed....He [Jesus] strictly ordered them [all who had seen it} that no one should know this, and commanded that something should be given to her to eat.

Once again, after the Lord healed the two blind men of their disabilities, Jesus requested that these two seeing men tell nobody what had happened to them.

Matthew 9:27-30
As Jesus passed by from there, two blind men followed him, calling out and saying, "Have mercy on us, son of David!" When he had come into the house, the blind men came to him. Jesus said to them, "Do you believe that I am able to do this?" They told him, "Yes, Lord." Then he touched their eyes, saying, "According to your faith be it done to you." Their eyes were opened. Jesus strictly commanded them, saying, "See that no one knows about this."

Again, the two healed men did not heed the instructions of the Lord.

Matthew 9:31
But they went out and spread abroad his fame in... that land.

When Jesus had departed from the borders of Tyre and Sidon, He arrived at the Sea of Galilee. After healing a mute and deaf man, Jesus commanded him to keep silent about it. he did not want anyone to know.

Mark 7:32-37
They brought to him one who was deaf and had an impediment in his speech. They begged him to lay his hand on him. He took him aside from the multitude, privately, and put his fingers into his ears, and he spat...touched his tongue. Looking up...he sighed, and said to him, "Ephphatha!" that is, "Be opened!" Immediately his ears were opened...the impediment of his tongue was released, and he spoke clearly. He commanded them that they should tell no one, but the more he commanded them, so much the more widely they proclaimed it.

As with many others, he would not remain quiet about it, but the Lord did request that he not share what happened with anyone.

Even following Peter's proclamation that Jesus was the true Messiah, they were to tell no one.

Matthew 16:15-16
He said to them, "But who do you say that I am?" Simon Peter answered, "You are the Christ, the Son of the living God."

Matthew 16:20
Then he commanded the disciples that they should tell no one that he was Jesus the Christ.

Mark 8:30
He commanded...that they should tell no one about him.

Luke 9:21
But he warned...commanded them to tell this to no one.

In these many instances, Jesus was not telling the people the truth about who He was. This is a form of misleading. As a result, some would think He was someone else. Just before Peter's declaration, Peter described some misconceptions that the people had of his identity.

Matthew 16:13-14
Now when Jesus came into the parts of Caesarea Philippi, he asked his disciples, saying, "Who do men say that I, the Son of Man, am?" They said, "Some say John the Baptizer, some, Elijah, and others, Jeremiah or one of the prophets."

Jesus did this to stall His persecution, so they did not lay hands on Him until the time the Father had designated. This is a confirmation that this is acceptable to God because His Son practiced this method of avoiding persecution. Also, this applied to the governing authorities.

An Immediate Withdrawal

At times, we might immediately withdraw from an event that may bring persecution. We can simply leave as fast as we can. In the synagogue, when the Lord Jesus healed a man's withered hand on the Sabbath in Galilee, the response of the Pharisees was cold and harsh because they believed there was to be no healing (work) on the Sabbath. This led to the devising of a plan to destroy Him and Jesus immediately withdrew from there to avoid His own destruction. He was not about to turn Himself over to them. It was not the time.

Matthew 12:13-15
Then he told the man, "Stretch out your hand." He stretched it out...it was restored whole, just like the other. But the Pharisees went out...took counsel...how they might destroy him. Jesus, perceiving that, withdrew from there. Great multitudes followed him; and he healed them all.

So, another avoidance response Christians may choose is to immediately withdraw from those attempting to persecute them. They simply leave the premises. Again, His time had not come but Jesus still withdrew to avoid persecution. As a result, this method is acceptable to God. Also, the Pharisees would have involved the Jewish Council, therefore He misled governing authorities as to His whereabouts.

A Hidden Presence

Jesus clearly proclaimed that He was the "I AM" of the Old Testament in the temple. When they attempted to lay hands on Him, He hid and then escaped by supernaturally passing through their midst.

John 8:58-59
Jesus said to them [the Jews], "Most certainly, I tell you, before Abraham came into existence, I AM." Therefore they took up stones to throw at him, but Jesus was hidden, and went out of the temple, having gone through the middle of them, and so passed by.

Sometime after the second cleansing of the temple, Jesus preached to the unbelieving multitudes. As He finished, He felt the necessity to quickly depart and hide Himself. The crowd was becoming agitated by His claims.

John 12:35-37
Jesus...said to them, "Yet a little while the light is with you. Walk

while you have the light, that darkness doesn't overtake you. He who walks in the darkness doesn't know where he is going. While you have the light, believe in the light, that you may become children of light." Jesus said these things and he departed and hid himself from them. But though he [Christ] had done so many signs in their presence, yet they didn't believe in him.

In Exodus 1, the new Pharaoh commanded that all the male Hebrew babies must be killed by the midwives. In Exodus 2, the parents of Moses hid him in defiance of the king.

Exodus 2:1-2
A man of the house of Levi went and took a daughter of Levi as his wife. The woman conceived and bore a son. When she saw that he was a fine child, she hid him three months.

This great act of misleading governmental authorities by the parents of Moses is referred to as a powerful act of faith by the inspired author of Hebrews.

Hebrews 11:23
By faith, Moses, when he was born, was hidden for three months by his parents, because they saw that he [Moses] was a beautiful child...were not afraid of...king's commandment.

Of course, we have already described the hiding of the spies by Rahab in defiance of the King of Jericho.

Joshua 2:6
But she had brought them up to the roof, and hidden them under the stalks of flax which she had laid in order on the roof.

We have already discovered that this action on Rahab's part was referred to as a "work of faith" by James in his letter to the scattered saints.

James 2:25
In the same way, wasn't Rahab the prostitute...justified by works, in that she received the messengers...sent them out another way?

In all these different circumstances, we see our Lord Jesus and others misleading those who were potential or actual persecutors including the defiance of some authorities. As is obvious from our Lord's actions and the writings of James and Hebrews this hiding from the presence of persecutors is acceptable to God in order to avoid evil or harm.

An Assisted Avoidance

As Christians avoid persecution, they may enlist help to do this. They themselves may have to assist others also. On his way to persecute the Christians, Paul became a believer on the road to Damascus. Afterward, he proclaimed the gospel, and the Jewish people were outraged by the total reversal in his commitment to Judaism and the words that he spoke.

In Acts 9, Paul went into the city that he had originally intended to search for Christians to harm and preached the gospel instead. These Jews immediately sought to kill him. His Lord and His message were hated.

Acts 9:23-25
When many days were fulfilled, the Jews conspired together to kill him, but their plot became known to Saul [now Paul]. They watched the gates both day and night that they might kill him, but his disciples took him by night, and let him down through the wall, lowering him in a basket.

Paul described this incident of avoidance in his letter to the Corinthians.

THE PERSECUTION OF THE SAINTS AND HOW TO OVERCOME IT

2 Corinthians 11:32-33
In Damascus the governor under King Aretas guarded the city of the Damascenes desiring to arrest me. Through a window I was let down in a basket by the wall, and escaped his hands.

Neither Paul nor the Christians wanted to turn him over to his persecutors; instead, the Damascus followers of Christ assisted him in escaping and avoiding the persecution. Notice, Paul was evading the governing authorities.

After this, the apostle Paul journeyed to Jerusalem and shared the gospel. The Hellenists he debated against also sought to murder him, but Barnabas intervened. This "son of encouragement" took Paul immediately to the apostles so he could describe what had happened in his life. Afterward, Paul went back to proclaiming the gospel.

Acts 9:27-30
But Barnabas took him and brought him to the apostles, and declared to them how he had seen the Lord on the way, and that he had spoken to him, and how at Damascus he had preached boldly in the name of Jesus. He was with them entering into Jerusalem, preaching boldly in the name of the Lord Jesus. He spoke and disputed against the Hellenists, but they were seeking to kill him [Paul]. When the brothers [in Christ] knew it, they [Christians] brought him down to Caesarea, and sent him off to Tarsus.

His aggressive behavior caused such a stir that the Jews tried to lay their hands on him in order to kill him but the came to his rescue and responded by assisting the apostle in his avoidance of persecution.

Of course, we have seen Rahab and others assist believers in avoiding persecution. We will see Michal assist David as well. Since this assistance involved verbal misleading, we will discuss it in the next chapter.

In these instances, we see Paul having no problem with escaping persecution with the assistance of other Christians. This would include his defiance of the legitimate authority in Damascus. Therefore, it is acceptable to God. Perhaps, there will be times that the brethren will insist that we leave the situation rather than take a stand. This can always be an option when persecution comes.

A Different Destination

At times, believers can avoid persecution by traveling to a different destination or location other than the one either the persecutors are expecting or may have influence over.

Matthew 2:21-23
He arose and took the young child and his mother, and came into the land of Israel. But when he heard that Archelaus was reigning over Judea in the place of his father, Herod, he was afraid to go there. Being warned in a dream, he withdrew into the region of Galilee, and came and lived in a city called Nazareth; that it [the prophecy] might be fulfilled which was spoken through the prophets that he [Jesus] will be called a Nazarene.

Also, the misleading was to a governmental authority. He most likely would have killed the child Jesus in violation of the sixth commandment. Since they received the assistance of angels, this approach is acceptable to God.

A Deliberate Avoidance

One of the defensive responses Christians can make is to deliberately avoid the confrontation all together. We simply do not put ourselves into a difficult situation where physical violence can occur.

First, in Acts 19, Luke records an incident in which Paul chooses to separate himself from a situation to avoid the evil and harm of persecution.

Acts 19:8-10
He entered into the synagogue, and spoke boldly for a period of three months, reasoning and persuading about the things concerning the kingdom of God. But when some were hardened and disobedient, speaking evil of the Way before the multitude, he [Paul] departed from them, and separated the disciples, reasoning daily in the school of Tyrannus. This continued for the space of two years, so that all those who lived in Asia heard the word of the Lord Jesus, both Jews and Greeks.

He changed his location to avoid the potential confrontation and the resultant persecution.

At another time, the apostle changed his traveling plans to avoid persecution.

Acts 20:3
When he had spent three months there, and a plot was made against him by Jews as he was about to set sail for Syria, he determined to return through Macedonia.

Paul's use of this option demonstrates its legitimacy before God. Paul averted his persecution by changing course. We are not required to boldly walk into a dangerous situation if it can be avoided. We rarely see this occur unless the Lord has given direct revelation as with Agabus (Acts 21:10-11).

A Nightly Voyage

There might be times that we, as Christians, will have to avoid some kind persecution by making a run for it at night.

We might have to escape their notice by leaving in the cloak of darkness so we cannot be seen.

In Acts 17, Paul's sharing of the gospel was met with many different reactions. Yet, at the same time, many people were saved.

Acts 17:1-4
Now when they [Paul and others] had passed through... they came to Thessalonica...there was a Jewish synagogue. Paul, as was his custom, went in...and for three Sabbath days reasoned with them from the Scriptures, explaining and demonstrating that the Christ had to suffer and rise again from the dead, and saying, "This Jesus, whom I proclaim to you, is the Christ." Some of them were persuaded [implies saved], and joined Paul and Silas, of the devout Greeks a great multitude, and not a few of the chief women.

Others responded negatively and caused quite a stir in the city to the point that Paul needed to avoid persecution by doing something drastic.

Acts 17:5-9
But the unpersuaded Jews took along...wicked men from the marketplace...set the city in an uproar....When they didn't find them, they dragged Jason and certain brothers before the rulers of the city, crying, "These who have turned the world upside down have come here also, whom Jason has received. These all act contrary to the decrees of Caesar, saying that there is another king, Jesus!" The multitude and the rulers of the city were troubled when they heard these things. When they had taken security from Jason and the rest, they let them go.

As a result, Paul had to flee in the dead of night. It was the only way in which he could avoid this angry mob from seizing him. Otherwise, the history of the early church may have been quite different.

Acts 17:10
The brothers immediately sent Paul and Silas away by night to Berea. When they arrived...went into the...synagogue.

Paul demonstrates in his actions that the behavior is pleasing to God since He engaged in it. Here again is an example of avoiding persecution. Paul did not turn himself over to the Jews but left at night. We may choose to do this also.

A Brethren Escort

There are times when the brethren must become active and protect a Christian from persecution. There is strength in numbers. The brethren may use their numbers to escort another brother or sister to a location to protect him or her.

In Acts 17, Paul had a powerful ministry in Berea with the gospel. When the Jewish mob who had persecuted Paul in Thessalonica heard that he was there, they came down from that city to stir the Berean Jews up to harm him again.

Acts 17:11-13
Now these were more noble than those in Thessalonica, in that they received the word with all readiness of the mind, examining the Scriptures daily to see whether these things were so. Many of them therefore believed...and not a few men. But when the Jews of Thessalonica had knowledge that the word of God was proclaimed by Paul at Berea also, they came there likewise, agitating the multitudes.

The Berean Christians wanted Paul avoid persecution, so they escorted him out of the city to a safe location.

Acts 17:14-15
Then the brothers immediately sent out Paul to go as far as to the

sea...Silas and Timothy still stayed there. But those who escorted Paul brought him as far as Athens. Receiving a commandment to Silas and Timothy that they should come to him very quickly, they departed.

The Greek word translated "escorted" means "to set, put, place, set one over a thing (in charge of it), to appoint one to administer an office, or to conduct or to bring to a certain place." This word is not a casual walking with a person but more of an appointed or official escort.

In Matthew 24, it is used to describe a slave who has been put in charge of his master's household.

Matthew 24:45
Who then is the faithful and wise servant, whom his lord has set over his household, to give them their food in due season?

In Acts 6, the apostles use the term to describe the seven men put in charge of the distribution of food when a dispute arose among the widows.

Acts 6:3
Therefore select from among you, brothers, seven men of good report, full of the Holy Spirit and of wisdom, whom we may appoint over this business.

In Acts 7, in Stephen's powerful sermon before the Jewish Sanhedrin, this spiritual man described Joseph's position over Egypt as appointed by Pharaoh, the ruler of the land of Egypt.

Acts 7:10
And delivered him out of all his afflictions, and gave him favor and wisdom before Pharaoh, king of Egypt. He made him governor over Egypt and all his house.

In Titus 1, Paul writes to Titus and commands him to appoint elders in the cities of Crete.

Titus 1:5-6
I left you in Crete for this reason, that you would set in order the things that were lacking and appoint elders in every city, as I directed you, if anyone is blameless, the husband of one wife, having children who believe, who are not accused of loose or unruly behavior.

All of these uses indicate an official appointment for a task or position. These brethren were appointed to escort Paul out of the area. The reason is obvious: to avoid any persecution. As believers, we may do the same. Once Paul took this action, we can be assured it is acceptable to God.

A Familial Rescue

There may be times in which we must rely on family to avoid persecution. This might even involve those who do not know Christ. Family members will love us and want to protect us in spite of what they may think of our religion. Paul was informed by his nephew that there was a plot on his life. There is no description or indication whatsoever regarding his nephew's faith. The nephew cared for Paul.

We find this incredible story in Luke account. Paul was dragged before the Jewish Sanhedrin to explain his gospel. When he saw that he was not making any progress, he sought to divide the group by claiming that he believed in the resurrection from the dead. The Pharisees believed in it and their liberal counterparts, the Sadducees, did not.

Acts 23:6
But when Paul perceived that the one part were Sadducees and the other Pharisees, he cried out in the council, "Men and brothers, I

am a Pharisee....Concerning the hope and resurrection of the dead I am being judged!"

This great confusion in the midst of this confrontation led the Centurion in charge of Paul to immediately grab him and quickly leave.

Acts 23:10
When a great argument arose, the commanding officer, fearing that Paul would be torn in pieces...commanded the [Roman] soldiers to go down and take him by force from among them, and bring him into the barracks.

As a result, a plot involving Paul's assassination began to emerge among the Jews and was told to the Jewish Council who gave their approval.

Acts 23:12-15
When it was day, some of the Jews banded together, and bound themselves under a curse, saying that they would neither eat nor drink until they had killed Paul. There were more than forty people who had made this conspiracy. They came to the chief priests and the elders, and said, "We...bound ourselves under a great curse, to taste nothing until we have killed Paul. Now therefore, you with the council inform the commanding officer that he should bring him down to you tomorrow, as though you were going to judge his case more exactly. We are ready to kill him before he comes near."

Then, Paul discovered the plot through his nephew who came to tell him all that was going on behind his back.

Acts 23:16-17
But Paul's sister's son heard of their lying in wait, and he came and entered into the barracks and told Paul. Paul summoned one of the centurions...said, "Bring this young man to the commanding officer, for he has something to tell him.

As a result, Paul was able to avoid persecution and death by these assassins. Though Paul did not directly seek help from his nephew, he certainly welcomed the information and then acted on it. This should be considered apostolic validation for seeking help from our families.

In the Old Testament, David was on the run from Saul, and he received great assistance from his wife. Since we will discuss this at length in the next chapter, we will look at this incident briefly. David had just fled Saul's presence after the king's spear almost hit him.

1 Samuel 19:9-12
An evil spirit from Yahweh was on Saul, as he sat in his house with his spear in his hand; and David was playing with his hand. Saul sought to pin David to the wall with the spear; but he slipped away out of Saul's presence, and he stuck the spear into the wall. David fled, and escaped that night. Saul sent messengers to David's house, to watch him, and to kill him in the morning. Michal, David's wife, told him, saying, "If you don't save your life tonight, tomorrow you will be killed." So Michal let David down through the window. He went away, fled, and escaped.

Had Michal not assisted her husband, David would have been arrested and killed when Saul's men arrived. Without this misleading of the king and his men there would have been no Messianic line through David. So, we have another option in avoiding persecution which is help from the aid of family members.

A Brilliant Disguise

Rebekah had been promised that her older son would be serving her younger son contrary to Hebrew cultural norms. She knew that God was with her younger son Jacob and that he must receive the inheritance and the blessing. She knew that Esau despised the birthright (inheritance) and quickly traded it to Jacob for some soup. When Esau was sent to hunt for game to serve Isaac a meal and receive his blessing, Rebekah acted quickly to disguise Jacob as Esau to mislead a stubborn, rebellious Isaac.

Genesis 27:10
Go now to the flock and get me two good young goats from there. I will make them savory food for your father, such as he loves.

Genesis 27:15-16
Rebekah took the good clothes of Esau, her elder son, which were with her in the house, and put them on Jacob, her younger son. She put the skins of the young goats on his hands, and on…his neck.

Genesis 27:21-23
Isaac said to Jacob, "Please come near, that I may feel you, my son, whether you are really my son Esau or not." Jacob went near to Isaac his father. He felt him, and said, "The voice is Jacob's voice, but the hands are the hands of Esau." He didn't recognize him, because his hands were hairy, like his brother Esau's hands. So he blessed him.

    The disguise worked and Jacob was truly blessed. Also, the messianic line could continue as God had planned. This was not God being willing to overlook what Rebekah did. He knew her and worked through her. Isaac did not rescind the blessing because He knew that Rebekah had done the right thing. This was noted in Hebrews as an act of faith.

Hebrews 11:20-21
By faith, Isaac blessed Jacob and Esau…concerning things to come.

It is foolish to think that the "deception was sinful but never brought up by any inspired writer." If we are allowed to mislead then using a disguise is perfectly acceptable to avoid evil or harm. The harm that would have occurred would have been catastrophic.

A second illustration of a clever and brilliant disguise is Tamar's disguise as a prostitute. Though that may seem odd by today's standards, it would not have been to ancient man. Ancient man did not see multiple wives and prostitution with the same stigma as we do today. This does not condone the practice; I am merely describing the difficult situation woman have found themselves in.

By way of reminder, Tamar's husband was killed by God before she could conceive. His brother would not be her kinsmen redeemer and was also struck down by God. When their Father Judah promised his last son to her and refused to keep his promise, Tamar had to come up with a plan that involved a brilliant disguise.

Genesis 38:14-15
She took off the garments of her widowhood, and covered herself with her veil, and wrapped herself, and sat in the gate of Enaim, which is on the way to Timnah...When Judah saw her, he thought that she was a prostitute, for she had covered her face. He turned to her by the way, and said, "Please come, let me come in to you," for he didn't know that she was his daughter-in-law.

As we saw previously, the disguise was effective, and this righteous woman conceived Perez who would be in the line of promise from Judah. As a result, Judah made a statement concerning Tamar that revealed her true righteousness. This is critical.

Genesis 38:26
Judah acknowledged them, and said, "She is more righteous than I, because I didn't give her to Shelah, my son."

Judah, though "misled" through Tamar's disguise, praised her doing what she had to do to follow the commandment of Moses and therefore the will of God.

Sometimes, we may have to disguise ourselves to avoid persecution to protect ourselves or others from harm. This kind of misleading is only limited by our imaginations.

A Secret Signal

Another method Christians can avoid evil and harm from persecution is by creating a special secret signal that only those avoiding them will know. This is obvious but must be described so we know the options are available.

We continue the story of Rahab with the secret signal she gave to identify the home where her family would be when the Israelites attacked Jericho.

Joshua 2:17-21
The men said to her, "We will be guiltless of this your oath which you've made us to swear. Behold, when we come into the land, tie this line of scarlet thread in the window which you used to let us down. Gather to yourself into the house your father, your mother, your brothers, and all your father's household. It shall be that whoever goes out of the doors of your house into the street, his blood will be on his head, and we will be guiltless. Whoever is with you in the house, his blood shall be on our head, if any hand is on him. But if you talk about this business of ours, then we shall be guiltless of your oath which you've made us to swear." She said, "Let it be as you have said." She sent them away, and they departed. Then she tied the scarlet line in the window.

And Rahab was delivered and saved her whole family and relatives from harm.

THE PERSECUTION OF THE SAINTS AND HOW TO OVERCOME IT

Joshua 6:22
Joshua said to the two men who had spied out the land, "Go into the prostitute's house, and bring the woman and all that she has out from there, as you swore to her." The young men who were spies went in, and brought out Rahab with her father, her mother, her brothers, and all that she had. They also brought out...her relatives, and they set them outside of the camp of Israel.

Another example of a secret signal is in the true story of Jonathon's aid in David's escape from Saul's household. This protected David from the harm of his father, Saul. David ate meals at the king's table and became afraid after Saul attempted to kill him. Jonathon and David made a plan to avoid his evil and harm if needed. David would miss several days, and Jonathon would tell Saul that David was visiting relatives. Then he would watch for his father Saul's reaction. Once Jonathon determined whether Saul would repent of his wickedness toward David or not, he would give David a secret signal only they understood.

1 Samuel 20:18-23
Then Jonathan said to him, "Tomorrow is the new moon, and you will be missed, because your seat will be empty. When you have stayed three days, go down quickly, and come to the place where you hid yourself when this started, and remain by the stone Ezel. I will shoot three arrows on its side, as though I shot at a mark. Behold, I will send the boy, saying, 'Go, find the arrows!' If I tell the boy, 'Behold, the arrows are on this side of you. Take them;' then come; for there is peace to you and no danger, as Yahweh lives. But if I say this to the boy, 'Behold, the arrows are beyond you;' then go your way; for Yahweh has sent you away. Concerning the matter which you and I have spoken of, behold, Yahweh is between you and me forever."

Since the secret signal indicated a lack of repentance on Saul's part, then David had to flee.

1 Samuel 20:41-42
As soon as the boy was gone, David arose out of the south, and fell on his face to the ground, and bowed himself three times. They kissed one another, and wept with one another, and David wept the most. Jonathan said to David, "Go in peace, because we have both sworn in Yahweh's name, saying, 'Yahweh is between me and you, and between my offspring and your offspring, forever.'" He arose and departed; and Jonathan went into the city.

We see the same reasons for confirming that misleading is acceptable in these incidences. David was innocent, they were obeying the divine authorization of David's kingship, the king was acting outside God's boundaries for authorities, and no correction was given by the author. So, Christians may use secret signals in their avoidance of persecution.

A Secret Identity

Among the many methods Christians have utilized to avoid persecution was by simply not identifying themselves as believers when they were. This secret identity is perfectly acceptable to God.

In fact, had Nicodemus and Joseph of Arimathea had identified themselves, they would never have been able to take possession of the body of Christ to bury it.

John describes Joseph clearly as a secret disciple who did not want his identity as a Christian known.

John 19:38
After these things, Joseph of Arimathea, being a disciple of Jesus, but secretly for fear of the Jews, asked of Pilate that he might take away Jesus' body. Pilate gave him permission. He came therefore and took away his body.

Then, he explains that Nicodemus was the one who came to Jesus at night. This implies that he also was a secret disciple.

John 19:39
Nicodemus, who at first came to Jesus by night, also came bringing a mixture of myrrh and aloes, about a hundred Roman pounds.

They both were fearful of the reprisal of the Jews, but it did allow them to take possession of the Lord's body for the reasons we discussed in a previous chapter.

John 19:40-42
So they took Jesus' body, and bound it in linen cloths with the spices, as the custom of the Jews is to bury. Now in the place where he was crucified there was a garden. In the garden was a new tomb in which no man had ever yet been laid. Then because of the Jews' Preparation Day (for the tomb was near at hand) they laid Jesus there.

When these pivotal men are discussed, nothing is said about the secrecy of the identity. It is stated as a matter of fact. This misleading of the legitimate authorities was used powerfully by God.

A Secretive Movement

Another strategy for avoiding persecution is traveling in secret and then appearing wherever one was needed for evangelism and ministry. This was one of the strategies the Lord used.

Jesus knew that the Jews wanted to seize Him near the time of the Feast of Booths being celebrated in Jerusalem. So, Jesus traveled in secret and then also separately from His family. He knew they would be watching for them.

John 7:1-2
After these things, Jesus was walking in Galilee, for he wouldn't walk in Judea, because the Jews sought to kill him. Now the feast of the Jews, the Feast of Booths, was at hand. So, He let His family go up to Jerusalem before Him and He traveled secretly.

The Jews were watching for Him in the city.

John 7:10-15
But when his brothers had gone up to the feast, then he also went up, not publicly, but as it were in secret. The Jews therefore sought him at the feast, and said, "Where is he?"

Finally, He appeared in public to proclaim the kingdom where the Jews could not lay hands on Him.

John 7:13-14
Yet no one spoke openly...fear of the Jews. But when it was now the middle of the feast, Jesus went up into the temple and taught.

This is similar to other strategies we have discussed and can be used in junction with some of the others. It is acceptable to God because His Son used it.

A Stealth Practice

This last technique involving misleading is obvious and implied in the other avoidance actions but should at least be mentioned. It is the practicing of all aspects of the Christian faith individually and together in secret. We might say in "stealth mode." This may occur when the government turns against the church and bans Christians assembling together and all the other non-negotiables. At this point, we are given a choice. We can become a Daniel standing publicly against the laws or a Nicodemus living secretly for the Lord.

Joseph of Arimathea and Nicodemus practiced their faith in secret.

John 19:38
After these things, Joseph of Arimathea, being a disciple of Jesus, but secretly for fear of the Jews, asked of Pilate that he might take away Jesus' body. Pilate gave him permission. He came therefore and took away his body.

John 7:50
Nicodemus (he who came to him by night, being one of them) said to them.

Neither of these men were chastised by the Lord and as we have seen did some important "stealth" work for Jesus.

Most likely, when Jesus held the last supper in the upper room it was essentially in secret. He went to the Garden of Gethsemane with the disciples in secret. How do we know this? Judas' betrayal involved telling the Jewish authorities where Jesus was located so they could arrest him.

Luke 22:6
He [Judas] consented, and sought an opportunity to deliver him [Jesus] to them in the absence of the multitude.

John 18:2
Now Judas, who betrayed him, also knew the place, for Jesus often met there with his disciples.

So, we do have the option as Christians to live secret lives for the Lord and meet, study the Scriptures, pray, partake of communion, and practice the other non-negotiables in secret.

In this chapter, we discussed action-oriented responses of avoidance in order to protect ourselves and others from evil or harm. If this involves the misleading of persecutors, this is acceptable to God. So, to stand our ground, we may have to avoid the persecution ourselves or help others to do the same.

Chapter 13

Evade with a Careful Rhetoric

As we continue to address the second kind of responses, we may make to avoid persecution, we will now consider what can be said. So far, we have learned that avoidance often leads to some form of deception. When this deception occurs to protect from evil or harm, it is perfectly acceptable to God. We called this kind of deception "misleading" to distinguish it from "lying" which is "deceiving for the purpose of evil or harm." It was discovered that Christians may mislead in words or actions as long as it does not involve committing a crime in which the legal authorities are searching for them or others unless it involves the non-negotiables of the Christian life. By way of reminder, when we use the term persecutors, we will be speaking of persecutors who are vigilantes (citizens acting outside the law), or governmental authorities who are following the law but acting against God's direct commands.

Now, we will consider the numerous verbal options we may take. This will require evading with a careful rhetoric. If "misleading" is involved, I will provide a discussion of it and the biblical support that demonstrates it is acceptable to God. The two chapters and this one must be read together to understand the important principle of "misleading to protect from evil or harm." By way of reminder, we do not have to tell "the truth, the whole truth, and nothing but the truth" in every situation. This concept of "telling the whole truth" is simply not found in every instance where questions are asked in the Bible. It is not seen in every single discourse by the Lord Jesus, the apostles, and other Christians in the New Testament nor is this displayed in the Old Testament.

It is also important to note, we are not required to stand up and face a shooter and declare we are Christians. Though some godless or idol worshipping terrorist may ask all those in a crowd to stand up if they believe in God or if they are Christians, we do not have to obey them. Though it may seem noble, God does not require it. His only requirement is to "not deny Him." This would be worshipping false gods. If a gun was to our head and to stay alive, we would have to deny Christ, then we must die for Him. Yet, as we know with Peter's denial, it is forgiven. Though there will come some consequences from it.

Here is a short sketch of what happened with Peter.

Luke 22:60-62
But Peter said, "Man, I don't know what you are talking about!" Immediately, while he was still speaking, a rooster crowed. The Lord turned and looked at Peter. Then Peter remembered the Lord's word, how he said to him, "Before the rooster crows you will deny me three times." He went out, and wept bitterly.

John 21:15
So when they had eaten their breakfast, Jesus said to Simon Peter, "Simon, son of Jonah, do you love me [Jesus] more than these?" He [Peter] said to him, "Yes, Lord; you know that I have affection for you."

In these passages, we see the disapproval of the Lord Jesus, the horrific mourning over what He had done, and the fact that all of the gospels record this denial. Though Peter went on to become a great apostle for the Lord and even die for Him, this stain of denial was always a part of His life.

Some may be wondering about Paul words in 2 Timothy concerning the denial of the Lord and what he really meant as he wrote to Timothy.

2 Timothy 2:12
If we endure, we will also reign with him. If we deny him, he also will deny us.

Here, Paul uses verbs that are in the tense that indicates "continuous action." If we are continually denying Him, He will continually deny us. This could not possibly refer to the denying of Him out of such fear and weakness that we fall.

It is easy to judge what we might do when there is no threat, but we should take to heart the words of Paul in two of his letters.

1 Corinthians 10:12
Therefore let him who thinks he stands be careful that he doesn't fall.

Galatians 6:1
Brothers, even if a man is caught in some fault, you who are spiritual must restore such a one in a spirit of gentleness; looking to yourself so that you also aren't tempted.

So, outside of this specific situation, we have a variety of options when using a careful rhetoric.

A majority of the time, we could make numerous kinds of verbal responses. We will now look at many illustrations of Old and New Testament saints who proceeded to avoid persecution and protect themselves and others from evil and harm. This involved some thought in regard to the words they should use. So, we now learn the options we may take as we evade persecution utilizing a careful rhetoric. We must provide thoughtful and well-considered responses.

Some of these avoidance scenarios we have studied have a "careful rhetoric" component and must be looked at again in the light of the misleading of persecutors by different saints in Scriptures. As we discuss these, we will continue to find evidence that words which mislead when evil or harm is intended is perfectly acceptable to God.

A Fake Identity

As we have seen, Rebekah was concerned that Esau would receive the blessing rather than Jacob whom God promised to receive it. So, she created a fake identity for him. Since we have looked extensively at this story, we will consider only the change of identity as an acceptable option for misleading persecutors. We also saw how she created a brilliant disguise with the animal skins to simulate the hairy hands and arms of his brother. Now, we will study the actual words that he said as he misled his father who was unwilling to follow God's promise.

When Jacob had the game, Isaac desired on the plate and the animal skins on his hands and arms, he approached Isaac.

Genesis 27:18-21
He came to his father, and said, "My father?" He said, "Here I am. Who are you, my son?" Jacob said to his father, "I am Esau your firstborn. I have done what you asked me to do. Please arise, sit and eat of my venison, that your soul may bless me." Isaac said to his son, "How is it that you have found it so quickly, my son?" He said, "Because Yahweh your God gave me success."

Here, Jacob takes on the identity of his brother and states falsely that he is Esau. Yet, Isaac was suspicious. Could he be suspicious because he knew Jacob was supposed to receive the blessing. He must have known about the birthright being sold to Jacob for a bowl of soup. He must have known that Jacob already had God's approval and that he was acting outside God's will. Yet, Esau was his favorite, and he was determined to give Esau something.

Genesis 27:21
Isaac said to Jacob, "Please come near, that I may feel you, my son, whether you are really my son Esau or not." Jacob went near to Isaac his father. He felt him, and said, "The voice is Jacob's voice, but the hands are the hands of Esau." He didn't recognize him, because his hands were hairy, like his brother Esau's hands. So he blessed him.

One more time, Isaac's asks Jacob to identify himself and Jacob misleads him again.

Genesis 27:24-27
He said, "Are you really my son Esau?" He said, "I am." He said, "Bring it near to me, and I will eat of my son's venison, that my soul may bless you." He brought it near to him, and he ate. He brought him wine, and he drank. His father Isaac said to him, "Come near now, and kiss me, my son." He came near, and kissed him. He smelled the smell of his clothing, and blessed him, and said, "Behold, the smell of my son is as the smell of a field which Yahweh has blessed."

The blessing went to the exact person that the Lord God had chosen despite Isaac's stubborn and sinful rebellion. So, if persecutors come to harm us or others, they may have to be misled as to our true identities or the identities of others.

A Possible Scenario

One of the options for avoiding persecution is a careful rhetoric involving a possible scenario which is false. This scenario would not be the real scenario because if it were, the persecutors would do us or others much harm. Instead, we may mislead them by providing a fake scenario which is within the realm of possibility but not the correct one.

In the first chapter of Exodus, the Hebrew midwives were told that they were to kill all the Hebrew males.

Exodus 1:15-16
The king of Egypt spoke to the Hebrew midwives, of whom the name of the one was Shiphrah, and the name of the other Puah, and he [Pharaoh] said, "When you perform the duty of a midwife to the Hebrew women, and see them on the birth stool; if it is a son...you shall kill [against God's law] him; but if it is a daughter, then she shall live."

The midwives refused to do it.

Exodus 1:17
But the midwives feared God, and didn't do what the king of Egypt commanded them, but saved the baby boys alive.

When these women were asked by Pharaoh himself the reason for the survival of the male babies, they created a possible scenario which misled them.

Exodus 1:19
The midwives said [misled]...Pharaoh, "Because the Hebrew women aren't like the Egyptian...for they are vigorous, and give birth before the midwife comes to them."

As a result, rather than punishing the two midwives for misleading the authorities, the Lord blessed them.

Exodus 1:20-21
God dealt well with the midwives...the people multiplied, and grew very mighty. Because the midwives feared God, he [God] gave them families.

Pharaoh had no right to kill the baby boys. This was against the sixth commandment. They had every right to defy the law to obey a divine command. The divine command is not to harm others. This governing authority went way beyond his God-given powers to be an avenger for God's wrath. Two statements demonstrate God's approval of the possible scenario. First, God blessed them. Second, their act was due to their fear of God. These were acts of faith. Third, Moses God did not qualify their behavior with, "Though they sinned by not "obeying Pharaoh..." This indicates that we may mislead with a possible scenario when legal authorities, vigilantes, or whomever are attempting to harm us or others.

Ignorant Pretense

There may be times when persecution comes and we will have to choose to act as if we do not know where someone is located or other information, they might otherwise desire. This ignorant pretense is acceptable to God.

We come to the incident involving Rahab again and her great act of faith. Here, we will concentrate on the words Rahab used to mislead the enemies of the Hebrews. By way of reminder, Joshua had entered the promised land and sent spies to Jericho to view the situation from the perspective of a battle perspective. When Joshua's spies came to Jericho, Rahab hit them and then mislead the authorities to protect them from any harm. Why did she do this? She knew that their God was the true God. When they came to destroy her city, Rahab wanted to honor God and protect her family.

Joshua 2:3
Jericho's king sent to Rahab, saying, "Bring out the men who have come to you, who have entered into your house; for they have come to spy out all the land."

Here, the king demanded that Rahab bring out the spies. He knew where they were and wanted to seize them. So, Rahab put on an ignorant pretense. She said that she did not know who they were.

Joshua 2:4-5
The woman took the two men and hid them. Then she said, "Yes, the men came to me, but I didn't know where they came from. About the time of the shutting of the gate, when it was dark, the men went out. Where the men went, I don't know. Pursue them quickly. You may catch up with them."

As we can see, another option for avoiding persecution is an ignorant pretense. We can simply say that we do not know the information they need. This is acceptable to God.

A Kept Secret

Another way, we can avoid the evil and harm that persecutors may bring to ourselves or others is to keep the information that they desire, and we possess a secret. This is found in another aspect of Rahab's story. For the spies to protect her, she was required to keep secret what happened.

Joshua 2:14-16
The men said to her, "Our life for yours, if you don't talk about this business of ours; and it shall be, when Yahweh gives us the land, that we will deal kindly and truly with you." Then she let them down...for her house was on the side of the wall, and she lived on the wall. She said to them, "Go to the mountain, lest the pursuers find you.... Afterward, you may go your way."

And Rahab kept the secret. This means that she continued to mislead the king. This led to her family being protected and unharmed by the Israelites.

Joshua 6:17
The city shall be devoted...to Yahweh [our God]. Only Rahab the prostitute shall live, she and all who are with her in the house, because she hid the messengers that we sent.

God did not chastise her; instead, her and her family were protected from harm.

The author of Hebrews states that Rahab's faith in God was demonstrated in her receiving the spies in peace.

Hebrews 11
By faith, Rahab the prostitute didn't perish with those who were disobedient, having received the spies in peace.

We should recognize that this keeping of the secret must be included in the "welcoming of the spies in peace."

Then the author of this sacred history explains that Rahab and her family survived and was welcomed and lives in Israel still in the day of his writing.

Joshua 6:23
The young men who were spies went in, and brought out Rahab with her father, her mother, her brothers, and all that she had. They also brought out all of her relatives, and they set them outside of the camp of Israel.

Then he explains the reason she was spared. Rahab hid the messengers.

Joshua 6:25
But Rahab the prostitute, her father's household, and all that she had, Joshua saved alive. She lives in the middle of Israel to this day, because she hid the messengers whom Joshua sent to spy out Jericho.

In this instance, Rahab kept the secret of helping the spies and their impending attack for quite some time. We see this misleading of persecutors was an intricate part of the entire event. Therefore, Rahab keeping the secret to protect her, the spies, and her family had to have been viewed as part of her act of faith by both the author of Hebrews and James. This indicates that it is an option when persecution comes.

A Simulated Illness

Sometimes, we may have to pretend we or others are sick to avoid persecution and protect ourselves or others from evil or harm. This is so beautifully seen in Michal's solution in her misleading of Saul's men when they came to kill her husband, David.

David was on the run from Saul. David was becoming more and more famous for his many victories and Saul was becoming more and more worried about his crown. David had married Saul's daughter Michal. After one of Saul's rages, he sought to arrest David.

1 Samuel 19:9-10
An evil spirit from Yahweh was on Saul, as he sat in his house with his spear in his hand; and David was playing with his hand. 10 Saul sought to pin David to the wall with the spear; but he slipped away out of Saul's presence, and he stuck the spear into the wall. David fled, and escaped that night.

After David fled, Saul sent soldiers to David and Michal's house, and she decided to mislead them to protect David from evil and harm.

1 Samuel 19:10-12
Saul sent messengers to David's house, to watch him, and to kill

him [David] in the morning. Michal, David's wife, told him, saying, "If you don't save your life tonight, tomorrow you will be killed." So Michal let David down through the window. He went away, fled, and escaped.*

After David escaped, his wife took the household idols and placed them on his bed and covered them over to resemble a sick David.

1 Samuel 19:13
Michal took the teraphim, and laid it in the bed, and put a pillow of goats' hair at its head, and covered it with clothes.

When Michal was asked, she clearly mislead them with her words.

1 Samuel 19:14
When Saul sent messengers to take David, she said, "He is sick."

Though the simulated sickness of David did not fool Saul, it gave David enough time to escape.

1 Samuel 19:15-16
Saul sent the messengers to see David, saying, "Bring him up to me in the bed, that I may kill him." When the messengers came in, behold, the teraphim was in the bed, with...pillow of goats' hair at its head.

When confronted with her misleading, she continued to mislead her father by telling him that David had threatened her now to protect herself from evil and harm.

1 Samuel 19:17
Saul said to Michal, "Why have you deceived me like this and let my enemy go, so...he has escaped?" Michal answered Saul, "He said to me, 'Let me go! Why should I kill you?'"

As a result of this, the Messianic line was preserved through her misleading words.

A Special Mission

Sometimes, we may find it necessary to pretend as if we are on a mission for someone when we are not. This careful rhetoric has God's approval when some come to do evil or harm to us and others.

You may remember Saul's jealously toward David made him rage in anger. When it turned into attempted murder, David fled to the city of Nob. [King] Saul had moved the Tabernacle to this city and placed Ahimelech a descendent of Eli as High Priest. Ahimelech was a supporter of Saul, so David had to mislead the High Priest into helping him. It was the only way.

1 Samuel 21:1-5
Then David came to Nob to Ahimelech the priest. Ahimelech came to meet David trembling, and said to him, "Why are you alone, and no man with you?" David said to Ahimelech the priest, "The king has commanded me to do something, and has said to me, 'Let no one know anything about the business about which I send you...what I have commanded you. I have sent the young men to a certain place.' Now therefore what is under your hand? Please give me five loaves of bread in my hand, or whatever is available." The priest answered David, and said, "I have no common bread, but there is holy bread; if only the young men have kept themselves from women." David answered the priest, and said to him, "Truly, women have been kept from us as usual these three days....

David affirmed that the men had met the purity standards for consuming the bread. In his mind, this was the only real issue.

THE PERSECUTION OF THE SAINTS AND HOW TO OVERCOME IT

1 Samuel 21:6
So the priest gave him holy bread; for there was no bread there but the show bread that was taken from before Yahweh, to put hot bread in the day when it was taken away.

After David had received the bread, the warrior continued his misleading to obtain a weapon from Ahimelech.

1 Samuel 21:8-10
David said to Ahimelech, "Isn't there here under your hand spear or sword? For I haven't brought my sword or my weapons with me, because the king's business required haste." The priest said, "Behold, the sword of Goliath the Philistine...is here wrapped in a cloth behind the ephod. If you would like to take that, take it; for there is no other except that here." David said, "There is none like that. Give it to me." David arose, and fled that day for fear of Saul, and went to Achish the king of Gath.

So, David fled that very day having misled Ahimelech to obtain food and a weapon to protect himself and his men from the evil and harm Saul was attempting. Also, David was defying the legal authority (the king) to obey the Lord God's sixth commandment which was not to kill. He had to keep himself alive because he had already anointed king.

This is acceptable to God. Why? First, David attributed his help to God in his psalm about this incident.

Psalm 52:8-9
But as for me, I am like a green olive tree in God's house. I trust in God's loving kindness forever and ever. I will give you thanks forever, because you have done it. I will hope in your name, for it is good, in the presence of your saints.

How could David have said this if he knew he had sinned against God? He would have written that he had sinned, repented, and was now trusting the Lord. This is how he handled his sin in Psalm 32.

Psalm 32:5-7
I acknowledged my sin to you. I didn't hide my iniquity. I said, I will confess my transgressions to Yahweh, and you forgave the iniquity of my sin. Selah....You are my hiding place. You will preserve me from trouble. You will surround me with songs of deliverance. Selah.

Second, Jesus refers to this incident in His teaching without comment on the misleading that occurred. We see this reference in three of the gospels.

Luke 6:1-5
Now on the second Sabbath after the first, he was going through the grain fields. His disciples plucked the heads of grain and ate, rubbing them in their hands. But some of the Pharisees said to them, "Why do you do that which is not lawful to do on the Sabbath day?" Jesus, answering them, said, "Haven't you read what David did when he was hungry, he, and those who were with him; how he entered into God's house, and took and ate the show bread, and gave also to those who were with him, which is not lawful to eat except for the priests alone?" He said to them, "The Son of Man is lord of the Sabbath."

Mark 2:25
He said to them, "Did you never read what David did when he had need and was hungry – he, and those who were with him? How he entered into God's house at the time of Abiathar the high priest, and ate the show bread, which is not lawful to eat except for the priests, and gave also to those who were with him?"

Matthew 12:3-4
But he said to them, "Haven't you read what David did when he was hungry, and those who were with him: how he entered into

God's house and ate the show bread, which was not lawful for him to eat, nor for those who were with him, but only for the priests?"

David could not have eaten the bread without his pretense of a second mission. Would not the Lord have made some distinction between what was right and what was wrong?

So, an option we may take when protecting the innocent from evil or harm is to pretend to be on a secret mission or something similar. This is acceptable to God.

A Sensible Fabrication

At times, we might have to fabricate a sensible story to avoid persecution and protect ourselves and others from evil or harm. This is an acceptable option for God. Just after the incident concerning Michal and David's misleading of Saul, Jonathon who was David's best friend and companion was compelled to mislead also.

Since David normally ate at the king's table, the two of them concocted a scheme to determine whether his father Saul would repent and turn away from his determination to kill David or not.

1 Samuel 20:5-9
David said to Jonathan, "Behold, tomorrow is the new moon, and I should not fail to dine with the king; but let me go, that I may hide myself in the field to the third day at evening. If your father misses me at all, then say, 'David earnestly asked leave of me that he might run to Bethlehem his city; for it is the yearly sacrifice there for all the family.' If he says, 'It is well,' your servant shall have peace; but if he is angry, then know that evil is determined by him. Therefore deal kindly with your servant; for you have brought your servant into a covenant of Yahweh with you...."

And this is exactly what happened. To protect David's life, Jonathon had to mislead Saul with a sensible fabrication as to the reason David was not at the king's table.

Once again, this was acceptable. David was in the Messianic line and would provide the claim to David's throne that the Messiah would use to identify Himself, take the throne, and fulfill the promises by God to Israel.

Another option to evade and avoid persecution in our careful rhetoric is to simply fabricate a sensible story, which will mislead vigilantes or even lawful authorities disobeying a command of God.

A Feigned Condition

Another way to protect ourselves and others from the evil and harm of persecution is to feign a mental illness. This was the solution that David engaged in to avoid being arrested and possibly killed by the King of Gath as he ran from his real enemy which was Saul.

1 Samuel 21:10-15
David arose, and fled that day for fear of Saul, and went to Achish the king of Gath. The servants of Achish said to him, "Isn't this David the king of the land? Didn't they sing to one another about him in dances, saying, 'Saul has slain his thousands, David his ten thousands?'" David laid up these words in his heart, and was very afraid of Achish the king of Gath. He changed his behavior before them, and pretended to be insane in their hands, and scribbled on the doors of the gate, and let his spittle fall down on his beard. Then Achish said to his servants, "Look, you see the man is insane. Why then have you brought him to me? Do I lack madmen, that you have brought this fellow to play the madman in my presence? Should this fellow come into my house?"

Because David mislead Achish, his own life was spared, and he was able to escape.

1 Samuel 22:1
David therefore departed from there, and escaped [fled] to the cave of Adullam.

Was this acceptable to God? For the answer, we turn to a psalm attributed David which was written with this incident in mind.

Here is the inscription of Psalm 34.

Psalm 34
By David...when he pretended to be insane [mislead] before Abimelech [Achish], who drove him away, and he departed.

Though this is not considered an inspired inscription, it most likely was written right after this incident.

David conceived of a clever way to avoid being murdered or imprisoned and attributed it to the Lord God.

Psalm 34:1-4
I will bless Yahweh at all times. His praise will always be in my mouth. My soul shall boast in Yahweh. The humble shall hear of it, and be glad. Oh magnify Yahweh with me. Let us exalt his name together. I sought Yahweh, and he answered me, and delivered me from all my fears.

David refers to himself as a poor man in that he was in a lot of trouble and had nowhere to turn.

Psalm 34:6
This poor man cried, and Yahweh heard him, and saved him out of all his troubles.

David praises God for what he knew was angelic help as he misled his way out of this terrifying incident.

Psalm 34:7
Yahweh's angel encamps around those who fear him, and delivers them.

David would have taken refuge in Him and trusted God that the clever scheme would work; and it did.

Psalm 34:8
Oh taste and see that Yahweh is good. Blessed is the man who takes refuge in him.

While David was thinking up the plan, he would have been crying out to the Lord to save him from these troubles.

Psalm 34:17
The righteous cry, and Yahweh hears, and delivers them out of all their troubles.

This fits our principle perfectly. Achish would have had no right to put David to death or imprison him but he would have. Why? David would have been seen as a threat to himself and his kingdom. Therefore, David had the right to mislead this king who intended harm.

The beauty of this true story in David's life is that we can easily put ourselves in David's place. Remember, God does not chastise David for what he did nor is it dealt with as the Lord did in his sin with Bathsheba. Some may say, "David repented from his deception and then wrote this psalm." Yet, nothing in the context of the psalm indicates that this could possibly be the case. Why not let David speak? Therefore, an option to avoid persecution is to feign mental illness which is perfectly acceptable to God.

A Specific Refusal

Another response to our persecutors (including those in authority) is to refuse to answer their questions and instead respond differently. Asking a question does not necessarily imply that it must be answered.

At the trial of Jesus, Annas asked Him about His disciples and His teachings, and the Lord refused to answer any of their questions. As a result, He was slapped in the face.

John 18:19-22
The high priest therefore asked Jesus about his disciples, and about his teaching. Jesus answered him, "I spoke openly to the world. I always taught in synagogues, and in the temple, where the Jews always meet. I said nothing in secret. Why do you ask me? Ask those who have heard me.... When he had said this, one of the officers standing by slapped Jesus with his hand, saying, "Do you answer the high priest like that?"

When Jesus was questioned by the Sanhedrin, He not only refused to answer but gave them a warning.

Luke 22:66-71
As soon as it was day, the assembly of the elders of the people was gathered together, both chief priests and scribes, and they led him away into their council, saying, "If you are the Christ, tell us." But he said to them, "If I tell you, you won't believe, and if I ask, you will in no way answer me or let me go. From now on, the Son of Man will be seated at the right hand of the power of God."

Then they asked Him the question that He desired to answer and so He responded.

Luke 22:70-71
They all said, "Are you then the Son of God?" He [Jesus] said to

them, *"You say it, because I am."* They said, *"Why do we need any more witness? For we ourselves have heard from his own mouth!"*

As can be seen, our Lord Jesus engaged in this powerful option. So, we, as followers of Him, could refuse to verbally respond to a question by those intending harm. Instead, we can respond to a different question that they may not have asked, issue a veiled warning, or respond verbally in some other way. Here, we can let the Spirit of God inside us lead. If nothing immediately comes to mind, then the next option can be utilized.

An Absolute Silence

When He was asked about the false testimony that was given concerning Him, at first Jesus remained silent.

Mark 14:57-61
Some stood up, and gave false testimony against him, saying, "We heard him say, 'I will destroy this temple that is made with hands, and in three days I will build another made without hands.'" Even so, their testimony didn't agree. The high priest stood up in the middle, and asked Jesus, "Have you no answer? What is it which these testify against you?" But he stayed quiet, and answered nothing. Again the high priest asked him, "Are you the Christ, the Son of the Blessed?"

When the high priest gave the Lord Jesus a question that He desired to answer, He responded.

Mark 14:62-64
Again the high priest asked him, "Are you the Christ, the Son of the Blessed?" Jesus said, "I am. You will see the Son of Man [He is referring to Himself] sitting at the right hand of Power, and coming with the clouds of the sky." The high priest tore his clothes,

and said, "What further need have we of witnesses? You have heard the blasphemy! What do you think?" They all condemned him to be worthy of death.

When Jesus stood before Pilate, He used this strategy for questions He did not want to answer. In Matthew 27, Pilate asked a question and the Lord remained silent.

Matthew 27:13-14
Then Pilate said to him, "Don't you hear how many things they testify against you?" He gave him no answer, not even one word, so that the governor marveled greatly.

When Pilate, the governor, sent the Lord to King Herod, Jesus was accused by the Jews and questioned by Herod and remained silent.

Luke 23:6-10
But when Pilate heard Galilee...he asked if the man [Jesus] was a Galilean. When he found out that he was in Herod's jurisdiction, he sent him [Jesus] to Herod, who was also in Jerusalem during those days. Now when Herod saw Jesus, he was exceedingly glad, for he had wanted to see him for a long time, because he had heard many things about him. He hoped to see some miracle done by him. He questioned him with many words, but he gave no answers. The chief priests and the scribes stood, vehemently accusing him.

So, once again Jesus refused to speak.

As we can see, when a question is asked, we may remain in absolute silence. This is perfectly acceptable to God since His own Son engaged in absolute silence. It is important to realize that every question does not deserve an answer nor are we required to give one in every single circumstance. This includes any questions which may be presented to us by governing authorities acting outside God's commands.

A Clever Answer

Sometimes, Christians avert impending persecution with a clever answer. Jesus used this technique often. In Luke 20, we see the Lord answer a question with another question which inevitably silenced them.

Luke 20:1-8
On one of those days, as he was teaching the people in the temple and preaching...the priests and scribes came to him with the elders. They asked him [Jesus], "Tell us: by what authority do you do these things? Or who is giving you this authority?" He [Jesus] answered them, "I also will ask you one question. Tell me: the baptism of John, was it from heaven, or from men?" They reasoned...saying, "If we say, 'From heaven,' he will say, 'Why didn't you believe him?' But if we say, 'From men' all the people will stone us, for they are persuaded that John was a prophet." They answered that they didn't know where it was from. Jesus said to them, "Neither will I tell you by what authority I do these things."

Later in the chapter, a similar incident occurs.

Luke 20:19-26
The chief priests and the scribes sought to lay hands on him that very hour, but they feared the people—for they knew he had spoken this parable against them. They watched him, and sent out spies, who pretended to be righteous, that they might trap him in something he said...to deliver him up to the power and authority of the governor. They asked him, "Teacher, we know that you say and teach what is right, and aren't partial to anyone, but truly teach the way of God. Is it lawful for us [the Jews] to pay taxes to Caesar, or not?" But he perceived their craftiness, and said to them, "Why do you test me? Show me a denarius. Whose image and inscription are on it?" They answered, "Caesar's." He said..."Then give to Caesar the things that are Caesar's...to God the things that are

God's." They weren't able to trap him in his words before the people. They marveled at his answer, and were silent.

Here Jesus provides such a clever reply that He was able to avoid a possible confrontation leading to His demise before the time designated by the Father.

Some Sadducees asked the Lord Jesus who would a man be married to in the resurrection if he had been married to several wives. This was done to trap Him. The Lord Jesus was always prepared for their many tricks. He often had a would respond to their devious questions with a clever reply that would silence them.

Luke 20:34-40
Jesus said to them, "The children of this age marry, and are given in marriage. But those who are considered worthy to attain to that age and the resurrection from the dead, neither marry, nor are given in marriage. For they can't die any more, for they are like the angels, and are children of God, being children of the resurrection. But that the dead are raised, even Moses showed at the bush, when he called the Lord 'The God of Abraham, the God of Isaac, and the God of Jacob.' Now he is not the God of the dead, but of the living, for all are alive to him [God]." Some of the scribes answered, "Teacher, you speak well." They didn't dare to ask him any more questions.

If we find ourselves in a situation that could develop into persecution and need a clever response, we need to ask God and he will provide the wisdom necessary to respond and we can count on this.

James 1:5
But if any of you lacks wisdom, let him ask of God, who gives to all liberally and without reproach; and it will be given to him." Also, wisdom is found in the Scriptures.

Since God almighty is sovereign, if He does not provide a clever answer, He will provide another alternative. If He does not, then perhaps it may be His will to experience the persecution we are trying to avoid.

Believers in Jesus may avoid persecution by providing a clever response to any questions that may be asked. As Jesus used this technique, so may we.

A Perplexing Reply

In the event of imminent persecution, we might respond to a question with a perplexing answer. This would be an answer which would confuse or trap them into silence. This response is similar to the one just discussed.

In this passage, the Jews ask the Lord Jesus to identify the authority by which He spoke and acted. Jesus responded with a question that would trap them and force them to be silent.

Mark 11:27-33
They came again to Jerusalem, and as he was walking in the temple, the chief priests, and the scribes, and the elders came to him, and they began saying to him, "By what authority do you do these things? Or who gave you this authority to do these things?" [The Lord] Jesus said to them, "I will ask you one question. Answer me, and I [Jesus] will tell you by what authority I do these things. The baptism of In John – was it from heaven, or from men? Answer me." They reasoned with themselves, saying, "If we should say, 'From heaven;' he will say, 'Why then did you not believe him?' If we should say, 'From men'" – they feared the people, for all held In John to really be a prophet. They answered Jesus, "We don't know." Jesus said to them, "Neither do I tell you by what authority I do these things."

Paul, the apostle, was mobbed in the temple area because the Jews thought he had brought a Gentile into their sacred space and seized him. When the Romans intervened, he was brought before the Sanhedrin and questioned. Paul gave an interesting response.

Acts 23:6-9
But when Paul perceived that the one part were Sadducees and the other Pharisees, he cried out in the council, "Men and brothers, I am a Pharisee, a son of Pharisees. Concerning the hope and resurrection of the dead I am being judged!" When he [Paul] had said this, an argument arose between the Pharisees and Sadducees, and the assembly was divided. For the Sadducees [liberals] say that there is no resurrection, nor angel, nor spirit; but the Pharisees confess all of these. A great clamor arose, and some of the scribes of the Pharisees part stood up, and contended, saying, "We find no evil in this man. But if a spirit or angel has spoken to him, let's not fight against God!"

Notice, Paul responded to their question by dividing the council in half over his reply. As we can clearly see, at times to avoid imminent persecution, we may give a completely different reply that could throw everyone into confusion or even silence them. This could only come from the wisdom of the Spirit.

Another method for evading persecution with a careful rhetoric is to respond with a perplexing reply. Jesus and Paul both used this option and so may we.

A Planned Silence

Another way to avoid persecution is to keep our saving knowledge of Christ between us and a select few when the persecution might become acute.

STANDING YOUR GROUND

Joseph of Arimathea and Nicodemus were two Christians who planned their silence. In John 3, Nicodemus came to the Lord Jesus by night to question him.

John 3:1-2
Now there was a man of the Pharisees named Nicodemus, a ruler of the Jews. The same came to him by night, and said to him, "Rabbi, we know that you are a teacher come from God, for no one can do these signs that you do, unless God is with him."

When the Pharisees found out that the officials, they sent did not arrest Jesus because no one had ever spoken with such authority, they were fuming. Nicodemus came to the Lord's defense.

John 7:46-53
The officers answered, "No man ever spoke like this man!" The Pharisees therefore answered them, "You aren't also led astray, are you? Have any of the rulers believed in him, or of the Pharisees? But this multitude that doesn't know the law is accursed." Nicodemus (he who came to him by night, being one of them) said to them, "Does our law judge a man, unless it first hears from him personally and knows what he does?" They answered him, "Are you also from Galilee? Search, and see that no prophet has arisen out of Galilee." Everyone went to his own house.

Finally, had Joseph and Nicodemus not been silent to avoid persecution from the Jews, they would not have been able to obtain the body of Jesus in order to bury Him in a time and place that met the numerous requirements of the law and fulfilled prophecy.

John 19:38-40
After these things, Joseph of Arimathea, being a disciple of Jesus, but secretly for fear of the Jews, asked of Pilate that he might take away Jesus' body. Pilate gave him permission. He came therefore

and took away his body. Nicodemus, who at first came to Jesus by night, also came bringing a mixture of myrrh and aloes, about a hundred Roman pounds. So they took Jesus' body, and bound it in linen cloths with the spices, as the custom of the Jews is to bury.

There is no commentary indicting these men for sinful behavior in their silence. If the persecution gets particularly harsh, we may choose to become secret disciples for a while. As a result, we might only share our faith in Christ with a select group.

We considered the numerous verbal options we may take when facing persecution. If misleading was involved, we found that it was acceptable to God. When persecution does come and information is requested that is intended to do evil or harm to innocent Christians, we should utilize all of the careful rhetoric options explained to evade the answer. This standing of our ground will protect ourselves and others.

STANDING YOUR GROUND

Chapter 14

Answer with a Strong Presentation

In the last two sections of the book, we discussed the legal and avoidance responses to persecution. Now, we come to the last two responses Christians may take as they stand their ground amid persecution. This chapter will discuss the third response to vigilantes (citizens acting outside the law), or even those citizens or governmental authorities who may be following the law but acting against God's commands. It is to answer with a strong presentation of the gospel. The next chapter will address the final response to persecution which is the physical defense of ourselves and others when threatened. Often, Christians fled the danger they faced but at other times they stood up, faced their accusers, and shared the gospel. This often occurred when they were surrounded, seized, captured, or arrested. Then, with great courage and boldness they spoke.

In this chapter, we will learn how to respond when arrested. We can no longer avoid our persecutors, whether vigilantes or governing authorities, and now must answer with a strong defense. They will bring up various charges against us and we must be prepared to answer them. In this chapter, we will discuss the appropriate answer to charges concerning our words and actions which they may deem illegal, unethical, or prejudiced and God sees as holy and righteous.

If Christians are arrested by legal authorities or seized by vigilantes for preaching the gospel or standing for the non-negotiables of the Christian faith (discussed in a previous chapter), what should we say? How shall we answer their questions? We must always respond by preaching the good news again! Over and over, the disciples were persecuted and then brought before their persecutors to speak. These evangelizing Christians had to stand trial for their denial of certain religious beliefs, defend their message and actions, and explain the good news that they were preaching. How did they respond?

These emboldened believers simply preached the gospel again. These courageous Christians refused to discuss every detail of their beliefs in contrast to the beliefs or laws of their persecutors. Instead, they continued to proclaim the basic message of salvation in Christ Jesus. These brave individuals focused on the message that men must repent, believe that Jesus is the Son of God and only Savior of the world, and receive Him as their Savior and Lord.

Paul described this strategy as the apostle contrasted his method of proclamation with the different methods of those who were wise in the world. In 1 Corinthians 2, the apostle Paul indicates that he always preached the simple message of salvation and nothing else. Those who were worldly wise depended on their speaking skills, logical argumentation, and persuasive manipulation.

1 Corinthians 2:2
For I determined not to know anything among you, except Jesus Christ, and him crucified.

He goes on to speak of his dependence on the Spirit of God to change hearts.

1 Corinthians 2:1-5
When I came to you, brothers, I did not come with excellence of speech or of wisdom, proclaiming to you the testimony of God. For I determined not to know anything among you, except Jesus

Christ, and him crucified. I was with you in weakness, in fear, and in much trembling. My speech and my preaching were not in persuasive words of human wisdom, but in demonstration of the Spirit and of power, that your faith wouldn't stand in the wisdom of men, but in the power of God.

In Matthew 10, Jesus sent His disciples out to preach as sheep among wolves. He warned them about these men who would deliver them up and scourge them.

Matthew 10:16
Behold, I send you forth as sheep in the midst of wolves. Therefore be wise as serpents, and harmless as doves.

Then, in verses 19-20, the Lord told them not to be anxious concerning how or what they would say. In that hour, the Holy Spirit would guide them as they spoke.

Matthew 10:19-20
But when they deliver you up, don't be anxious how or what you will say, for it will be given you in that hour what you will say. For it is not you who speak, but the Spirit of your Father who speaks in you.

These words can certainly apply to any saint who shares the good news and experiences persecution from enemies. Why shouldn't it? We have the same Holy Spirit in us who can guide our minds to respond biblically.

In 1 Thessalonians 1, Paul recognizes the work of the Holy Spirit in the lives of the Thessalonians who not only received God's Word but proclaimed it in much affliction.

1 Thessalonians 1:6-9
You became imitators of us, and of the Lord, having received the word in much affliction, with joy of the Holy Spirit, so that you

became an example to all who believe in Macedonia and in Achaia. For from you has sounded forth the word of the Lord, not only in Macedonia and Achaia, but also in every place your faith toward God has gone forth; so that we need not to say anything [at all]. For they themselves report concerning us what kind of a reception we had from you; and how you turned to God from idols, to serve a living and true God.

The Holy Spirit guided Paul in his proclamation and their salvation. Now, the apostle was guiding the church in their proclamation and the salvation of many in their region. God, through the Spirit of Christ, will superintend every aspect of the proclamation of His redemptive plan, as has been noted in the discussion of God's role in evangelism.

This does not preclude the Spirit providing principles that should be followed. As He guides His children, the Bible prescribes a pattern to follow or a structure to frame their presentations. The following principles will help Christians structure their thinking as the Spirit leads them in the development of their gospel response to their persecutors and enemies. Any believer, who expects to be persecuted, should learn these important principles.

A Beginning with a Simple Declaration

In the Book of Acts, wherever the apostles and the other followers of Jesus traveled, whether they encountered Jews, Greeks, philosophers, men, women, slaves, or government officials, the gospel was simply declared. No matter how negative the reactions they heard the gospel.

In 2 Timothy 3:16, Paul indicates that one of the important ways in which the Scriptures can be utilized is for teaching. The preaching of the gospel is a part of that teaching.

THE PERSECUTION OF THE SAINTS AND HOW TO OVERCOME IT

2 Timothy 3:16
Every writing inspired by God is profitable for teaching, for reproof [conviction of sin], for correction, and for instruction which is in righteousness.

In Acts 4:1-9, the apostles were in Jerusalem proclaiming the resurrection of Jesus (the gospel). The Sanhedrin arrested them and held them in custody until the next evening. They were brought before the high priests, rulers, and scribes and interrogated. They wanted to know in whose name or by what power enabled them to heal the lame and crippled man and speak to their people.

In Acts 4, Peter began with the death and resurrection of Jesus Christ and proclaimed the gospel. This same gospel they had already heard from Jesus with the addition of the now risen Savior. They did not seek to argue or reason with them; instead, they proclaimed the good news again!

Acts 4:10
Be it known to you all, and to all the people of Israel, that in the name of Jesus Christ of Nazareth, whom you crucified, whom God raised from the dead, in him does this man stand here before you whole.

When told to cease their preaching, the apostles refused and went out and preached the gospel again. Continuing to proclaim the gospel in the midst of persecution is the biblical pattern. It is God's way when it comes time to speak.

In Acts 5, when Peter and John found themselves before the Sanhedrin, they proclaimed Christ.

Acts 5:28-32
Saying, "Didn't we strictly charge you not to teach in this name? Behold, you have filled Jerusalem with your teaching, and intend

to bring this man's blood on us." But Peter and the apostles answered, "We must obey God rather than men. The God of our fathers raised up Jesus, whom you killed, hanging him on a tree. God exalted him with his right hand to be a Prince and a Savior, to give repentance to Israel, and remission of sins. We are His witnesses of these things; and so also is the Holy Spirit, whom God has given to those who obey him."

In Acts 6, Stephen was hauled before the same council, because the Jews had been overcome by the Spirit and wisdom of his preaching and he declared the gospel. Then in Acts 7, when Stephen spoke to these hostile and angry religious men, he declared the good news of Jesus Christ. In the rest of Luke's account, Paul declared the gospel before the angry crowd of Jews (Acts 22), the Sanhedrin (Acts 23), Felix (Acts 24), Festus (Acts 25), King Herod Agrippa (Acts 26), and before Caesar (Philippians 1).

All of these people responded negatively. They were cold, contentious, and hardened of heart, but all heard a simple declaration of the good news. The goal in every evangelistic encounter, whether persecution comes or not, is to share the gospel. When the persecution comes, Christians are to share the gospel again. Why? Salvation is the ultimate goal of the saints. No amount of argumentation, criticism, or persuasion will diminish their opposition. Their only responsibility is to share the gospel. God's responsibility is to open the heart and provide the faith to believe through His love, mercy, and grace.

Ephesians 2:4-10
But God, being rich in mercy, for his great love with which he loved us, even when we were [spiritually] dead through our trespasses, made us alive together with Christ (by grace have you been saved), and raised us up with him, and made us to sit with him in the heavenly places in Christ Jesus, that in the ages to come

he might show the exceeding riches of his grace in kindness toward us in Christ Jesus; for by grace you have been saved through faith [alone], and that not of yourselves; it is the gift of God, not of works, that no one would boast. For we are his workmanship, created in Christ Jesus for good works, which God prepared before that we would walk in them.

Here, Paul attested to the fact that we are to share the gospel clearly and God will do the rest.

An Ending with a Careful Admonition

In many of the presentations recorded in the gospels, after a negative reaction occurred, there was a careful admonition or warning. This admonishment was a caution that danger was ahead. There could be a warning of the judgment of sin and resultant condemnation in hell if they refused to believe.

When Paul preached to the Jews in Pisidian Antioch, he ended with a careful warning.

Acts 13:37-41
But he whom God raised up saw no decay. Be it known to you therefore, brothers, that through this man is proclaimed to you remission of sins, and by him everyone who believes is justified [declared righteous] from all things, from which you could not be justified by the law of Moses. Beware... lest that come on you which is spoken in the prophets: "Behold, you scoffers, and wonder, and perish; For I work a work in your days, A work which you will in no way believe, if one declares it to you."

He knew that he had received a great deal of resistance in his missionary journey from the Jews, so he cautioned them not to become scoffers who perish. He did not want them to mock his gospel and Savior which would lead to hell.

In 2 Timothy 3, Paul indicates that one of the important ways in which the Scriptures can be utilized is for reproof. This careful admonition is a part of that reproof.

2 Timothy 3:16
Every writing inspired by God is profitable for teaching, for reproof [conviction of sin], for correction, and for instruction which is in righteousness.

In Acts 28, Paul was imprisoned in Rome and sent for the Jewish leaders. For what purpose did he do this?

Acts 28:23
When they had appointed him a day, they [the Jews] came to him into his lodging in great number. He explained to them, testifying about the kingdom of God, and persuading them concerning Jesus, both from the law of Moses and from the prophets, from morning until evening.

He desired to explain his chains and proclaim the gospel to them. Some believed in the gospel and others would not. To those who did not believe he admonished them from the prophet Isaiah. He asserted that these Jewish leaders would continue to hear but would not understand. They would continue to see but would not perceive. Their hearts will become dull. If they closed their eyes and ears, they would perish in their sins.

There might be times in which the Holy Spirit will lead a Christian to issue a warning of judgment if the unbeliever refuses to embrace Christ. Christians should not shy away from this warning. All throughout the Old Testament, God sent His prophets to issue severe warnings to people and many responded. The reluctant preaching of Jonah and how more than 120,000 Ninevites believed in the God of Israel is a prime biblical example of this.

A Discussion with a Gentle Correction

Sometimes, as Christians proclaim the gospel again, there may be a need for a gentle correction. When one is sharing the good news, confusion, perplexity, or misunderstandings may occur, which needs correction, for the true gospel to be understood and believed. We see again in 2 Timothy 3, Paul indicates that the Bible can be utilized for correction.

2 Timothy 3:16
Every writing the [Scriptures] inspired by God is profitable for teaching, for reproof [conviction of sin], for correction, and for instruction which is in righteousness.

This correction can be observed in the book of Acts in the midst of sharing the gospel with those who are antagonistic.

In Acts 6, Luke, records that some from other regions were discussing God with Stephen but they could not stand up to his wisdom and the Holy Spirit working inside him.

Acts 6:9-10
But some of those... of the synagogue called "The Libertines," and of the Cyrenians, of the Alexandrians, and of those of Cilicia and Asia arose, disputing with Stephen....They...not able to withstand the wisdom and the Spirit by which he spoke.

The word in the Greek translated "disputing" means "to seek or examine together, to discuss or question." It doesn't carry the idea of quarreling. Stephen was answering questions, discussing their differences in beliefs, and clearing up their misunderstandings. Within this discussion would have been correction.

The same word is used to describe Paul's interaction with the Jews in Jerusalem in Acts 9.

Acts 9:29
Preaching boldly in the name of the Lord. He spoke and disputed against the Grecian Jews, but they were seeking to kill him.

After Paul fled from Damascus, he landed in Jerusalem. Immediately, he began preaching the gospel of Jesus Christ courageously to everyone who wanted to listen. Though, he was bold in his persecution, he was bolder in his preaching.

Luke portrays the apostle as talking and arguing with the Hellenistic Jews. The desire of these Jews was to put Paul to death because of the gospel. Yet, Paul tried to answer their questions, clear up any misunderstandings, and discuss the many differences between his beliefs and theirs. Within this verbal interaction was correction.

In Acts 14, when Paul returned to Antioch after his first missionary journey, he reported to the church how God had brought the gospel to the Gentiles. Everyone was elated because of this good news, but it was short lived because others came among them with mistaken notions of salvation thinking Gentiles had to be circumcised as Jews first.

Acts 14:24-28
They passed through Pisidia, and came to Pamphylia. When they had spoken the word in Perga, they went down to Attalia. From there they sailed to Antioch, from where they had been committed to the grace of God for the work which they had fulfilled. When they had arrived, and had gathered the assembly together, they reported all the things that God had done with them, and that he had opened a door of faith to the Gentiles. They stayed there with the disciples for a long time.

In Acts 15, some Jews came from Judea and claimed that the Gentiles had to be circumcised according to Moses. This caused quite a stir in the church.

THE PERSECUTION OF THE SAINTS AND HOW TO OVERCOME IT

Acts 15:1-2
Some men came down from Judea and taught the brothers, "Unless you are circumcised after the custom of Moses, you can't be saved." Therefore when Paul and Barnabas had no small discord and discussion with them, they appointed Paul and Barnabas, and some others of them, to go up to Jerusalem to the apostles and elders about this question.

To Paul, these Judeans were obviously confused. They might have misunderstood how Gentiles were saved. Paul and Barnabas began a discussion with them.

Luke recounts the incident using the words "discord and discussion." In this context, the first word in the Greek has the meaning of taking a stand on an issue. The second word means a seeking, an inquiry, questioning back and forth, or a debate about a controversy. Both sides took their stand and there was a debate. Since Paul was ultimately right, from his perspective he was simply correcting them. Remember, the Jewish believers were adamant that new Gentile Christians should be circumcised for salvation. Though these were not his enemies, they did oppose Paul's position.

In Acts 17, Luke details Paul's close encounter with the Epicurean and Stoic philosophers of Athens as "conversing."

Acts 17:18
Some of the Epicurean and Stoic philosophers [in Athens] also "conversing with" him. Some said, "What does this babbler want to say? [to us]" Others said, "He seems to be advocating foreign demons," because he [Paul] preached Jesus and the resurrection (DEJ).

In this context, the Greek word means "to bring together in the mind." These pompous pundits were attempting to piece together Paul's teachings with theirs. The apostle was trying to correct their false worldly wisdom and set them straight on God's divine wisdom.

These intellectuals displayed much hostility toward Paul and his message, and one of them ventured to wonder what this "babbler" wanted to say. The Greek word for "babbler" meant seed picker. Paul was picking up seeds from many different religions and philosophies. This implies he wasn't really smart enough to possess a logical, coherent, organized philosophy or religion. So, Paul attempted to correct these mistaken notions of this antagonistic group of sages who had challenged him.

In Acts 18, Luke records the meeting of both Aquila and Priscilla with Apollos, a powerful preacher of Jesus. He was an Alexandrian Jew who had come to Ephesus to share the gospel. Since he was only acquainted with John's baptism, this husband-and-wife team corrected him theologically.

Acts 18:26
He began to speak boldly in the synagogue. But when Priscilla and Aquila heard him, they took him aside, and explained to him the way of God more accurately.

After his gentle correction, he went on to correct others. In verses 27-28, Apollos traveled to the region of Achaia and powerfully refuted the Jews in public. These would not be Jews who supported his beliefs but opposed them.

Acts 18:27-28
When he [Apollos] had determined to pass over into Achaia, the brothers encouraged him, and wrote to the disciples to receive him. When he had come, he helped them much, who had believed through grace; for he powerfully refuted the Jews, publicly showing by the Scriptures that Jesus was the Christ.

The term translated "refuted" comes from a Greek root word that means to convict, call to account, or correct. It has the sense of a competition as people are exchanging ideas. It does not mean to quarrel or be contentious. When people respond negatively to the gospel, even bent on persecution, Christians might have to engage in a powerful discussion. This may entail a gentle correction.

Timothy encountered this very issue in his congregation. As a young Pastor, Timothy had involved himself in arguing and quarreling. In 2 Timothy 2, Paul encouraged him instead to gently teach and correct them with patience. This was critical in Timothy's approach to these instigators.

2 Timothy 2:24-25
The Lord's servant must not quarrel, but be gentle toward all, able to teach, patient, in gentleness correcting those who oppose him: perhaps God may give them repentance leading to a full knowledge of the truth,

The pastor's congregation had a cluster of contentious people who loved to speculate and discuss peripheral issues within the church. This could only lead to ungodliness and ultimate ruin for the hearers of these controversies. Instead, the Lord's servant must not quarrel but patiently and gently correct those who oppose him. Their hope should be that God may give them repentance and full knowledge of His truth. Through gentle correction, the Lord would retrieve them from this snare of the Devil since they have been taken captive by him to do his will.

Christians who attempt to fight, argue, and quarrel with their enemies or persecutors will not lead them to salvation. The gentle correction of their false beliefs compared to the truth may clear up their doctrinal confusion. As the Spirit leads, this may direct them to the narrow path of salvation.

A Rebuke with a Strong Exhortation

In the New Testament, sometimes the believers provided careful admonitions. Yet, at other times, believers gave very strong exhortations. As we have seen in 2 Timothy 3, the Scriptures should be utilized for reproof. This reproof may involve a "strong exhortation" also.

2 Timothy 3:16
Every writing inspired by God is profitable for teaching, for reproof [conviction of sin], for correction, and for instruction which is in righteousness.

This is not just a warning of judgment, but an indictment for the hardness of their hearts, sinful stubbornness, or other extreme sinful attitudes. Why? These men were blocking others from the gospel. The word translated "rebuke" comes from a root which means "to convict." It has the sense of shaming, reprimanding severely, or chastening. It suggests a rebuke for error or a reproof for opposition to the truth.

In Titus 1, Paul describes certain empty talking, rebellious men from the circumcision who were continually deceiving believers and had disrupted whole households for shameful gain. In verse 13, Paul commanded Titus, his companion, to rebuke or "reprove" these liars severely.

Titus 1:13
This testimony is true. For this cause, reprove them sharply, that they may be sound in the faith.

His purpose was so they help them become sound in their faith and doctrine.

In Acts 7, Stephen preached the gospel and defended the faith to a hard-hearted Jewish Sanhedrin then he concluded his sermon with a strong exhortation. In verses 51-53, he termed them stiff-necked and uncircumcised in the heart and ears. He designated them as resisters of the Holy Spirit. He condemned them as acting just like their fathers who persecuted the prophets and became betrayers and killers of the righteous. This was foretold by the prophets. Stephen then accused them of receiving the law as if ordained by angels, and then disregarding it.

Acts 7:51-53
"You stiff-necked and uncircumcised in heart and ears, you always resist the Holy Spirit! As your fathers did, so you do. Which of the prophets didn't your fathers persecute? They killed those who foretold the coming of the Righteous One, of whom you have now become betrayers and murderers. You received the law as it was ordained by angels, and didn't keep it!"

These were fiery words for this group of persecutors and enemies of the gospel.

In Acts 8, Philip traveled into the region of Samaria and baptized a magician named Simon. Peter and John arrived to lay hands on these new converts, in order to baptize them in the Spirit. When Simon saw the power they possessed, he attempted to purchase it from them. In verses 18-23, Peter rebuked Simon. He exclaimed that Simon would perish with the silver he wanted to use to buy the Spirit's power. He condemned him for having an impure heart before God.

Acts 8:18-23
Now when Simon saw that the Holy Spirit was given through the laying on of the apostles' hands, he offered them money, saying, "Give me also this power, that whoever I lay my hands on may receive the Holy Spirit." But Peter said to him, "May your silver perish with you, because you thought you could obtain the gift of God with money! You have neither part nor lot in this matter, for

your heart isn't right before God. Repent therefore of this, your wickedness, and ask God if perhaps the thought of your heart may be forgiven you. For I see that you are in the gall of bitterness and in the bondage of iniquity."

As Peter told Simon to repent, Simon was so shaken up by Peter's strong exhortation, he begged for prayer.

A similar strong exhortation can be seen by Paul when he encountered opposition from Elymas. In Acts 13, Luke, the historian, describes what happened.

Acts 13:9-12
But Saul, who is also called Paul, filled with the Holy Spirit, fastened his eyes on him, and said, "Full of all deceit and all cunning, you son of the devil [his offspring], you enemy of all righteousness, will you not cease to pervert the right ways of the Lord? Now, behold, the hand of the Lord is on you, and you will be blind [physically], not seeing the sun for a season!" Immediately a mist and darkness fell on him. He went around seeking someone to lead him by the hand. Then the proconsul, when he saw what was done, believed, being astonished at the teaching of the Lord.

Here, Paul strongly exhorted and rebuked Elymas, who was keeping him from preaching to Sergius Paulus. In addition to his rebuke, he struck him with blindness.

On several occasions, Jesus rebuked the Pharisees with a strong exhortation. Over and over, the Lord Jesus warned them that judgment and condemnation would come due to their hypocrisy. Jesus called these leaders strong names.

Matthew 23:15-17
Woe to you, scribes and Pharisees, hypocrites! For you...make one proselyte... "Woe to you, you blind guides, who say, 'Whoever swears by the temple, it is nothing; but whoever swears by the gold

of the temple, he is obligated.' You blind fools! For which is greater, the gold or the temple that sanctifies the gold?

Then, He condemns them to judgment.

Matthew 23:33
You serpents, you offspring of vipers, how will you escape the judgment of Gehenna [hell]?

If the Spirit leads Christians to make strong exhortations, it should not be presented in sinful anger, but in righteous rebuke. It should be done to turn them to the Lord. When all else has failed a rebuke may be necessary.

A Termination with an Obvious Avoidance

There will be times when Christians share the gospel and people will not listen. They might be so spiritually dead, so controlled by their lusts and sin, so prideful, so ignorant and blind, so hardened and calloused that believers simply end up going around and around in their preaching or sharing of the gospel with no result, but more opposition. Eventually, the presentation must end. All that can be said is said.

In Acts 13, Paul and Barnabas entered Pisidian Antioch and preached to the Jews and God-fearing Gentiles in the synagogue. The preaching was so powerful that they asked them to come back the next Sabbath. This time almost the whole town turned out. But when the Jews saw the crowds, they went into a jealous rage and began interrupting and contradicting the apostle as he was speaking.

As a result, he rebuked them with the strong exhortation by declaring that they were unworthy of God's eternal life. Then the apostle Paul terminated his presentation with an obvious avoidance by exclaiming he was now going to the Gentiles. It was time to start avoiding them. This also is not done in anger but righteous passion.

Acts 13:46-49
Paul and Barnabas spoke out boldly, and said, "It was necessary that God's word should be spoken to you first. Since indeed you thrust it from you, and judge yourselves unworthy of eternal life, behold, we turn to the Gentiles. For so has the Lord commanded us, saying, 'I have set you as a light of the Gentiles, That you should be for salvation to the uttermost parts of the Earth.'" As the Gentiles heard this, they were glad, and glorified the word of God. As many as were appointed to eternal life believed. The Lord's word was spread abroad throughout all the region.

A similar incident occurred in Acts 18. In Corinth, Paul preached the gospel, and they kept resisting his gospel and blaspheming. In verses 4-6, as a result, he rebuked them with a strong exhortation by declaring their blood was now on their own heads.

Acts 18:4-6
He [Paul] reasoned in the synagogue every Sabbath, and persuaded Jews and Greeks. But when Silas and Timothy came down from Macedonia, Paul was compelled by the Spirit, testifying to the Jews that Jesus was the Christ. When they opposed him and blasphemed, he [Paul] shook out his clothing [symbol of his passion] and said to them, "Your blood be on your own heads! I am clean. From now on, I will go to the Gentiles!"

These hardened people would receive the condemnation and judgment that they deserved. Then, the apostle simply terminated his presentation with an obvious avoidance by exclaiming that he was now going to the Gentiles. These words were strong words of condemnation indicating that termination of his gospel presentations was over.

As has been examined, in the church Timothy pastored, He had a group of contentious people who argued, debated, quarreled, and bickered about theological issues. Yet, these were not legitimate theological problems causing them to be legitimately confused and perplexed, which required gentle correction. These were speculative and controversial subjects not addressed in the Bible and provided no spiritual gain.

1 Timothy 1:3-7
As I exhorted you to stay at Ephesus, when I was going into Macedonia, that you might charge certain men not to teach a different doctrine [than theirs], neither to pay attention to myths and endless genealogies, which cause disputes, rather than God's stewardship, which is in faith -- But the end of the charge is love, out of a pure heart and a good conscience and unfeigned faith; from which things some, having missed the mark, have turned aside to vain talking; desiring to be teachers of the law, though they understand neither what they say, nor about what they strongly affirm.

Timothy was also to avoid this empty chatter.

1 Timothy 6:20
Timothy, guard [protect] that which is committed to you, turning away from the empty chatter and oppositions of the knowledge which is falsely so called.

2 Timothy 2:16
But shun empty chatter...proceed further in ungodliness.

In 2 Timothy 3, Paul warns this minister to also avoid the contentious people propagating this false knowledge.

2 Timothy 3:5
Holding a form of godliness, but having denied the power thereof. Turn away from these, also.

Paul continues by describing these religious antagonists as having a form of godliness without any power. Though they appeared, sounded, and acted godly and devout, it was all outward. Why? It had no true spiritual power to change lives, only destroy them.

This principle is perfectly applicable to the persecutors of Christians. They may also want to debate and debate about minor issues without any end in sight and no real progress toward their salvation. So, Christians should terminate the discussion and avoid these persecutors.

Is this not how Christ behaved when they finally arrested Him? He had preached and they had heard over and over. There was nothing else He could say. All had been said and done. Jesus had answered all of the questions, performed all the miracles, and fulfilled all the prophecies needed.

Once He was arrested, He was questioned by numerous officials but did not give an answer. Many charges were brought against Him; yet he did not answer.

Matthew 27:12-14
When he was accused by the chief priests and elders, he answered nothing. Then Pilate said to him, "Don't you hear how many things they testify against you?" He gave him no answer, not even one word, so that the governor marveled greatly.

Mark 14:60-61
The high priest stood up in the midst, and asked Jesus, "Have you no answer? What is it which these testify against you?" But he stayed quiet, and answered nothing. Again the high priest asked him, "Are you the Christ, the Son of the Blessed?"

Christians may have to refuse to get involved in endless discussions with believers who oppose them or unbelievers who persecute them. There comes a time when everything has been said that needs to be said. Christians must rely on the Holy Spirit to guide them in this important area.

In this chapter, we discussed the third response to any and all vigilantes (citizens acting outside the law), or even citizens or governmental authorities who may be following the law but acting against God's commands. We learned that we must answer with a strong presentation of the gospel. Most of the time, Christians fled the danger they faced but at other times they stood up, faced their accusers, and shared the gospel. This often occurred when they were surrounded, seized, captured, or arrested. Then, with great courage and boldness they spoke. Our persecutors will bring up various charges against us and we must always be prepared to answer them. In this chapter, we also discussed the proper answer to charges concerning our words and actions which they may deem illegal, unethical, or prejudiced but our God sees as holy and righteous. Our answer to persecutors with a strong presentation is another way we stand our ground.

STANDING YOUR GROUND

Chapter 15

Defend as God Directs

We have discussed the many responses to persecution and come to our final response which involves a physical defense of ourselves and others to advance the gospel and protect God's people. In this particular case, the protection of God's people will advance the gospel. We are discussing the truth concerning physical self-defense and the defense of others. It is important to distinguish between this and other religions who have attempted to advance their "false gospel" through conquering peoples and imposing their beliefs on the conquered populace. If we, as Christians, are attacked may we defend ourselves and others if we cannot avoid the persecutors?

In an earlier part of the book, we considered the growing evil in the last days. This evil may and will turn into violent actions leveled against ourselves, family, friends, and fellow-Christians. Vigilantes may come and attempt to harm us and even the government will overstep it bounds and persecute us. When this becomes the case, our first response should be to deal with them by adjudication. The second might be to avoid them all together. If we are captured, then we should make a bold presentation of the gospel. Instead, what if they decide to kill us? If we are not able to escape or verbally confront them because of their intention to kill us, what should we do? The answer is to physically defend ourselves.

As this chapter was being written, it dawned on me that this subject was so important that it could not be dealt with in a single chapter of a book. There is so much confusion, and ignorance on the subject that it must be dealt with in a careful and systematic way considering all that the Bible says on the subject. This issue cannot be explained by simply quoting the words of Christ such as "turn the other cheek" or some other passage. Instead, the entire teaching of Scripture must be studied.

We as Christians cannot depend on a Pastor's word, or our consciences, or even what the government may say. If we decide to "pull the trigger" or not, lives will be on the line, and we will give an account to the Lord. Will we blame a book we read, a person we heard, or our own hearts? The answer is no, we must study the Bible and see what God has to say. If I gave the answer in one chapter, then all would rely on me! This responsibility I do not want nor can I bear it. Instead, I can study the Scripture, carefully unpack it for all to see, and then they can decide for themselves through the work of the Spirit. He gives the understanding of all things from His Scriptures.

Though this would normally be written in an epilogue, I feel that it may be missed so I include it here. The answer to this question is found in the companion book to this which is entitled

Defending Your Life

How Christians May Defend Themselves Against Attack

A Biblical Handbook.

By

Donald E. Jones, PhD

Chapter 16

Persist in Watchful Prayer

In Paul's first letter to Timothy, the apostle outlines ways in which believers can pray in the midst of persecution. This exhortation to pray involves our prayers for all men as well as those in authority.

1 Timothy 2:1-4
I exhort [beseech, entreat] therefore, first of all, that petitions, prayers, intercessions, and givings of thanks, be made for all men: for kings and all who are in high places; that we may lead a tranquil and quiet life in all godliness and reverence. For this is good and acceptable in the sight of God our Savior; who desires all...to be saved and come to...knowledge of...truth.

In Paul's words "tranquil and quiet life" are the important implication that these prayers are to involve the persecution of Christians. Why? The absence of persecution results in a peaceful life for believers. It is "all men" who can persecute, and it is a government that can prevent or stop it. Of course, they could also initiate a persecution against Christ's church. So, prayers must be offered up for them.

In this passage, Paul uses several terms to teach this truth. These different Greek words provide us with insight to the different aspects or elements of prayer. We will discuss these in the order of their appearance.

First, the apostle uses the term translated "petition" which is used to describe the prayer we are to have for all men and authorities in particular. This word focuses on the passion and emotion of seeking help from God.

We can almost feel the intensity, passion, and emotion in the many passages where this term is used. For example, Zacharias and Elizabeth were devastated because Elizabeth could not conceive. So, her husband cried out to his God and an angel brought the answer.

Luke 1:13
But the angel said to him, "Don't be afraid...because your request has been heard, and your wife, Elizabeth, will bear you a son, and you shall call his name John.

Paul desired his fellow Jews to come to salvation in Christ and prayed fervently for this.

Romans 10:1
Brothers, my heart's desire [passion] and my prayer to God is for Israel, that they may be saved.

Paul had just described the spiritual battle we face against the forces of evil and then asks the saints to pray fiercely.

Ephesians 6:18
With all prayer and requests, praying at all times in the Spirit, and being watchful to this end in all perseverance and requests for all the saints.

When Paul was under house arrest awaiting trial before the emperor, he was depending on the earnest prayers of the many believers in Philippi. Because they loved him so much, they not only supported him financially but sent ministers to help him. Now, they were praying for his deliverance.

Philippians 1:19
For I know...this will turn out to my salvation, through your supplication [earnest prayers] and...supply of the Spirit of Jesus Christ.

Timothy was Paul's son in the faith and Paul loved him. He prayed passionately for Timothy who was having so many problems in the church he was pastoring.

2 Timothy 1:3
I thank God, whom I [Paul] serve...with a pure conscience. How unceasing is my memory of you in my petitions, night and day.

The author of Hebrews describes the intense prayer of the Lord in the garden of Gethsemane using this word.

Hebrews 5:7
He, in the days of his flesh, having offered up prayers and petitions with strong crying and tears to him who was able to save him from death, and having been heard for his godly fear.

In these key passages, we learn the importance of pouring out our emotions as we pray for our governing authorities.

Second, after utilizing this word, the apostle uses a more general word for prayer. This is the usual word for prayer we see in the New Testament describing our worshipful communing with God. There are numerous examples. Luke portrays the time Jesus spent with the Father regularly using this term.

Luke 6:12
In these days, he went out to the mountain to pray, and he continued all night in prayer to God.

The ministry of the apostles involved this communion with God in prayer.

Acts 6:4
But we [the apostles] will continue steadfastly in prayer and in the ministry of the word.

So, we must be worshipfully communing with our Lord God on behalf of the governing authorities.

Third, the Greek word used to describe this prayer for all men and especially authorities are translated "intercessions." This word refers to a "conversation, meeting, or conference" between people.

Festus utilizes the word to describe the many conversations the Jews had with him against Paul.

Acts 25:24
Festus said, "King Agrippa [Herod], and all men who are here present with us, you see this man, about whom all the multitude of the Jews petitioned me, both at Jerusalem and here, crying that he ought not to live any longer.

In Romans 8, Paul speaks of the conversation the Spirit has inside of us with the Father. Then, a few verses later, he refers to Christ's conversation at the right hand of God.

Romans 8:27
He who searches the hearts knows what is on the Spirit's mind, because he makes intercession for the saints according to God.

Romans 8:34
Who is he who condemns? It is Christ who died, yes rather, who was raised from the dead, who is at the right hand of God, who also makes intercession for us.

Here, the apostle Paul describes Elijah's conversation with God to plead for Israel.

Romans 11:2-3
God didn't reject his people, which he foreknew. Or don't you know what the Scripture says about Elijah? How he pleads with

God against Israel: "Lord, they have killed your prophets, they have broken down your altars; and I am left alone, and they seek my life."

So, Christians are to be meeting and conversing with God concerning all men particularly the governing authorities He has established.

Lastly, we should be giving thanks to our God for these authorities. Thanksgiving was always a part of the prayers of Paul, and he urges us to do the same.

Ephesians 1:16
Don't cease to give thanks for you, making mention of you in my prayers.

Colossians 4:2
Continue steadfastly in prayer [communion with God], watching therein with thanksgiving.

For what are believers thanking God in our prayers? We are thanking Him for hearing us and answering us. We are grateful for how He answered our requests in the past and will now answer. We are so thankful that we can approach Him as His children and show the Lord our gratefulness for whatever answer He decides to provide in His wisdom and sovereignty. We are grateful for the opportunity to move His hand in power as He answers our prayers.

Then Paul continues to explain exactly what requests we should be making for all men and those authorities God has established.

1 Timothy 2:1-4
I exhort [beseech, entreat] therefore, first of all, that petitions, prayers, intercessions, and givings of thanks, be made for all men:

for kings and all who are in high places; that we may lead a tranquil and quiet life in all godliness and reverence. For this is good and acceptable in the sight of God our Savior; who desires all...to be saved and come to full knowledge of the truth.

We will now discuss these requests.

The Prevention of Persecution

According to this passage, we should ask that God would move the hearts of all men and the authorities to allow us to live peaceful lives as Christians in order to be able to practice our faith and share the gospel. This living of a peace-filled life is essentially praying for the prevention of persecution.

1 Timothy 2:2
For kings and all who are in high places; that we may lead a tranquil and quiet life in all godliness and reverence.

The word translated "lead" refers to "leading, sending, or passing through or across." It is a present subjunctive tense indicating a continual action that is desired. So, the prayer is for the passing of a life in continual peace. The Bible has many examples of this word being utilized for the course of one's life. In Luke 8, Jesus speaks of people who hear the gospel but the various pleasures of living then supplant it and they reject it.

Luke 8:14
That which fell among the thorns, these are those who have heard, and as they go on their way they are choked with cares, riches, and pleasures of life [living one's life], and bring no fruit to maturity.

Here, the word refers to the long period of her life when she was being seen by physicians.

THE PERSECUTION OF THE SAINTS AND HOW TO OVERCOME IT

Luke 8:43
A woman who had a flow of blood for twelve years, who had spent all her living on physicians, and could not be healed by any.

The word in this passage describes the "living" of one's life as a soldier.

2 Timothy 2:4
No soldier on duty entangles himself in the affairs of life, that he may please him who enrolled him as a soldier.

Here, the apostle John speaks of the pride of living our lives.

1 John 2:16
For all that is in the world, the lust of the flesh, the lust of the eyes, and the pride of life [living], isn't the Father's, but is the world's.

In all of these examples, the word "life" refers to the course of one's living. It describes the actual living of it. So, Paul is asserting that we are to pray for all men and the authorities allowing us to continually live peaceful lives as Christians.

Next, Paul describes the peaceful lives for which we must pray. These requests focus on preventing persecution.

1 Timothy 2:2
For kings and all who are in high places; that we may lead a tranquil and quiet life in all godliness and reverence.

It describes prayer for us to be left alone to do what we ought to do for God. The first description of our peaceful lives as we practice our faith is found in the word translated "tranquil." This word comes from a root that means "a wilderness or desert." So, it refers to having a life that is "still" or "quiet" as a wilderness is. Here are two simple examples of wilderness experiences that can illuminate our understanding of the word.

Mark 1:35
Early in the morning, while it was still dark, he rose up and went out, and departed into a deserted place [isolated], and prayed there.

Mark 6:31
He said to them, "You come apart into a deserted place, and rest awhile." For there were many coming and going, and they had no leisure so much as to eat.

As a wilderness is solitary and deserted, so we should pray for solitary living among unbelievers. They leave Christians alone and do not bother them.

The Greek word translated "quiet" is basically a synonym of the former word. It refers to "quiet, silent, still." A form of this word was used by Paul to describe how Christians are to "quietly" work and pay for their own provisions rather than sit around making noise and gossiping.

2 Thessalonians 3:12
Now those who are that way, we command and exhort in the Lord Jesus Christ, that with quietness they work...eat their own bread.

So, we must pray that all men and the governing authorities allow us to live quiet, still, and uninterrupted lives that are filled with peace in order to love and serve God.

The Practice of Our Faith

Now, the apostle Paul continues to elucidate what these peaceful lives without persecution are to accomplish. So, not only should we pray for peace in our lives but that we will take advantage of the solitary lives to practice our faith. This is such an important truth to understand.

1 Timothy 2:2
For kings and all who are in high places; that we may lead a tranquil and quiet life in all godliness and reverence.

The purpose of this is to be able to practice "godliness" and "reverence."

The first word Paul utilizes to explain this practice is the Greek word translated "godliness." We have seen this Greek word previously in our study of the coming oppression of Christians globally.

2 Timothy 3:12
Yes, and all who desire to live godly in Christ Jesus will suffer persecution.

You may remember that this word means "to be reverent by doing the things which demonstrate our deep respect for and honor of the God we have in our hearts." It conveys the idea of doing "religious or spiritual" things. This concept is different than righteousness (general good behavior) and holiness (being separate from the sinning of the world). The spiritual things Christians do are reading the Bible, praying, attending church services, fellowshipping with the saints, taking communion regularly, and giving to poor saints.

So, Paul is encouraging the believers to pray that all men and the authorities will allow us to participate in the many reverent activities of the Christian life just described.

The word translated "reverence" is the second aspect of the prayer to practice our faith. The word refers to "a quality of people which entitles them to respect and dignity."

It is used to describe the respect and dignity of a child of an elder in the church.

1 Timothy 3:4
One [the overseer] who rules [manages] his own house well, having children in subjection with all reverence.

Paul utilized the term to portray the example of respect and dignity Titus should be to his congregation.

Titus 2:7
In all things showing yourself an example of good works; in your teaching showing integrity [dignity], seriousness, incorruptibility.

In 1 Timothy 3, it is used to describe the lives of deacons.

1 Timothy 3:8
Servants, in the same way, must be reverent, not double-tongued, not addicted to much wine, not greedy for money.

It is also utilized to describe the qualifications of their wives which most likely were deaconesses in the churches.

1 Timothy 3:11
Their wives in the same way must be reverent, not slanderers, temperate, faithful in all things.

These church positions demand lifestyles that demonstrate respect of Christ, ourselves, and others. Also, we live in such a way that people will respect us. Therefore, we should pray that we can live quiet lives so we may also live with respect and dignity in the community.

The apostle Paul now moves on to his final thought which is to pray for the salvation of all men and especially those in authority.

1 Timothy 2:3-4
For this [prayer] is good and acceptable in the sight of God our Savior; who desires all people to be saved and come to full knowledge of the truth.

Here, he asserts that God desires all men to be saved. This either means that we are to pray for them to allow us to live in peace to share the gospel or to pray for their salvation.

The Salvation of All

In this passage concerning the prevention of persecution, we should be praying for all men and especially those who are governing authorities. If those who interact, influence, or even control us receive Christ as Savior and Lord, they will not persecute us but embrace us. We learned in a previous section concerning our holy actions toward persecutors that we are to pray for our enemies. We studied many examples of persecutors who had come to Christ. Therefore, if those who persecute us become true Christians, they will stop the persecution.

So, we must pray for the salvation of all others, those in a position of authority over us, and those who are persecuting us right now. Praying for the salvation of others is a critical part of prayer. Also, praying for the salvation of others is an essential part of evangelism. These are two sides of the same gospel coin. The personal and congregational prayers of the saints must involve the salvation of the unsaved including governmental authorities. To win others to Christ begins on one's knees.

In Matthew 6, the Lord's disciples approached Jesus and asked Him how they should pray. So, the Lord composed a prayer that included the salvation of the lost. Out of the many subjects for prayer Jesus could have chosen, He spoke of evangelism. In this prayer, Jesus commands them to pray that His Father's kingdom will come.

Matthew 6:10
Let your kingdom [of God] come. Let your will be done, as in Heaven, so on Earth.

According to Jesus, an essential element of one's prayer life is a request that the Lord God establish His kingdom. God will build His church on the Earth. How? The first way is through evangelism, so the church grows numerically.

In Romans 10:1, Paul cried out that his heart's true desire and prayer was for the Jews to be saved.

Romans 10:1
Brothers, my heart's desire and my prayer to God is for Israel, that they may be saved.

This prayer for the salvation of the Jews would be a prayer to advance the kingdom.

The Presentation of The Gospel

Not only are we to pray for the salvation of others which includes those in authority, but we should pray to have the peace necessary, and the real commitment needed to do it. In Luke 5, the author describes the ministry of Jesus as healing the people and proclaiming the kingdom of God. He was out teaching the multitudes and confronting Pharisees.

Luke 5:15-17
But the report concerning him spread much more, and great multitudes came together to hear, and to be healed by him of their

infirmities. But he withdrew himself into the desert, and prayed. On one of those days, he was teaching; and there were Pharisees and teachers of the law sitting by, who had come out of every village of Galilee, Judea, and Jerusalem. The power of the Lord was with him to heal them.

Then, in Mark 1, the author says Jesus would often slip away to pray.

Mark 1:35
Early in the morning, while it was still dark, he [Jesus] rose up and went out, and departed into a deserted place, and prayed there.

What would have been the subject of His prayers? I am sure it involves not only praying for those who were listening to be saved but also for the peace needed to speak. Certainly, He must have also prayed for the Jewish leaders to stay still long enough for Him to present the kingdom plan.

In Acts 6, Paul described the work of the apostles as the work of ministry and prayer.

Acts 6:4
But we will continue steadfastly in prayer and in the ministry of the word.

Since the apostles were always evangelizing, their praying would have involved not only entreaties for salvation but also the peaceful opportunity to present the good news. Preaching and praying always go hand in hand so Christians need to be constantly doing this.

In Colossians 4, the apostle Paul provides us insight into other requests we should bring to God in our prayers that relate to the presentation of the gospel. Paul requested the church in Colossae to ask God for opportunities.

Colossians 4:2-3
Continue steadfastly in prayer [communion with our God], watching therein with thanksgiving; praying together for us also, that God may open to us a door for the word, to speak the mystery of Christ, for which I am also in bonds.

As this peace abounds, we should pray for God to open up an opportunity for us to witness and that we would take it.

While we are praying for this quietness Paul speaks of, peace, we should be asking the Lord to give us wisdom in our witnessing. The apostle continues in his letter to exhort the saints at Colossae to pray for wisdom.

Colossians 4:4-5
[Pray] That I may reveal it [make it clear] as I ought to speak. Walk in wisdom toward those who are outside, redeeming the time.

Here, Paul asserts that we are to pray for wisdom from God which will guide us in what to say and how to say it. Then in verse 6, he describes what this looks like.

Colossians 4:6
Let your speech always be with grace, seasoned with salt, that you may know how you ought to answer each one.

Therefore, we must pray for wisdom to make our sharing of the gospel and other interactions with the unsaved seasoned as with salt.

As we constantly ask God to bring peace in order to live devoted lives to God which includes sharing the gospel, we ought to request that our gospel efforts will cause others to share the gospel and it will spread all over. Paul encourages the church in Thessalonica to pray that God would multiply the fruits of his evangelistic efforts quickly.

THE PERSECUTION OF THE SAINTS AND HOW TO OVERCOME IT

2 Thessalonians 3:1
Finally, brothers, pray for us, that the word of the Lord may spread rapidly and be glorified, even as also with you.

Here, we see that we should pray for the gospel to spread beyond our own locality to others as well as we share, win people to Christ, and they share and win people to Christ.

Now, once we find this peace, we are encouraged to pray for the boldness needed to share the gospel with all mankind and especially with governmental authorities.

Ephesians 6:19
On my behalf, that utterance may be given to me in opening my mouth, to make known with boldness the mystery of the Good News.

Here, Paul entreated the church to request God to give him courage in sharing the mystery of the gospel of Jesus Christ.

Finally, believers should pray for additional workers to share the gospel.

Matthew 9:37-38
Then he said to his disciples, 'The harvest indeed is plentiful, but the laborers are few. Pray therefore that the Lord of the harvest will send out laborers into his harvest."

The Lord gazed out at all the people and saw crops of souls ripe for harvest. He asked his disciples to pray that the Lord of the harvest would send out workers to share the gospel.

Once we have these quiet and tranquil lives, we must pray that God would motivate us to share His good news. Then, He would provide the boldness we need to present the gospel often in many locales.

The Prayer for Deliverance

Of course, when persecution comes upon us, we should automatically pray for protection and deliverance. In Acts 12, Luke records that it was the third time Peter had found himself in prison for preaching the gospel. It was the first time he was alone. One of his fellow apostles, James, the brother of John, had just suffered martyrdom at the hands of Herod, the king. Herod saw that this pleased the people so much that it was Peter's turn. Herod's intent was to parade him out in front of the people after the Passover feast, have a spectacular trial, and then slay him.

Knowing the apostles had escaped a secure prison before, Herod had two guards chained to Peter and placed two others in front of the cell door. For all outward or Earthly appearances all seemed hopeless this time. But, according to Acts 12, the saints began to pray, expecting to accomplish in the heavenly realm, what could not be done in the Earthly. They determined to ask God for a supernatural rescue from Herod's evil persecution.

Acts 12:3-5
When he saw that it pleased the Jews, he proceeded to seize Peter also. This was during the days of unleavened bread. When he had arrested him, he put him in prison...delivered him to four squads of four soldiers...to guard him, intending to bring him out to the people after the Passover. Peter therefore was kept in the prison, but constant prayer was made by the assembly to God for him.

Every minute Peter sat chained in that prison was met with a minute of intense crying out to God for his deliverance. And then the answer came, it could have been "no" as it had been with James, the brother of John, slain just days before. But God had other plans for Peter, his moment to glorify Him in martyrdom as James had done would have to come later.

Suddenly, an angel appeared in Peter's cell and the chains fell effortlessly to the ground without even awakening one of his unwanted companions. The chief apostle walked past the four guards and out of the prison. The large iron-gate which led into the city opened on its own accord, and he was free. After the angel disappeared and he came out of his daze, Peter found himself the participant in a mighty miracle. This was a miracle instigated or activated by prayer, intended by God's will, and provided by divine power. Peter went immediately to notify the praying saints.

Acts 12:12-16
Thinking about that, he came to the house of Mary...mother of John who was called Mark, where many were gathered together and were praying. When Peter knocked at the door of the gate, a maid named Rhoda came to answer. When she recognized Peter's voice, she didn't open the gate for joy, but ran in, and reported that Peter was standing in front of the gate. They said to her, "You are crazy!" But she insisted that it was so. They said, "It is his angel." But Peter continued knocking. When they had opened, they saw him, and were amazed.

No one could truly believe that God would answer in such a miraculous way. Yet, He did and will do again.

The Different Divine Answers

First, we see that God will deliver us or others who are being persecuted through our many prayers. In Paul's letter to the church in Philippi, he describes his dependence on the prayer of these saints for protection and deliverance.

Philippians 1:19-20
For I know that this will turn out to my salvation, through your supplication [passionate praying] and the supply of the Spirit of

Jesus Christ according to my earnest expectation and hope, that I will in no way be disappointed, but with all boldness, as always, now also Christ will be magnified in my body, whether by life or by death.

So, we should ask the Lord for a powerful deliverance. We must understand that sometimes our deliverance will come through death.

Second, we may see other answers that are different, but all will be for our good or even the good of others. Notice, what Paul says in Romans 8.

Romans 8:28
We know that all things work together for good for those who love God, to those [the saints] who are called according to his purpose.

This also includes answers to our prayers. The Lord was in the Garden of Gethsemane and in His humanity prayed for deliverance from the cross.

Matthew 28:39
He went forward a little, fell on his face, and prayed, saying, "My Father, if it is possible, let this cup pass...from me; nevertheless, not what I desire, but what you desire."

He knew God's will was for Him to save the world, so the Father could not answer His prayers in the exact way that He desired. The Lord would have to endure the persecution of the cross for the good of others.

Third, as with Christ on the cross, God sometimes desires us to endure for Him and perhaps for other reasons we may not yet know. Paul was not always delivered, in fact most of the time he had to persevere and endure his suffering, but God comforted Him.

THE PERSECUTION OF THE SAINTS AND HOW TO OVERCOME IT

2 Corinthians 4:8-10
We are pressed on every side, yet not crushed; perplexed, yet not to despair; pursued, yet not forsaken; struck down, yet not destroyed; always carrying in the body the putting to death of the Lord Jesus, that the life of Jesus may also be revealed in our body.

The apostle knew that persecution often had to be endured for the Lord's sake.

Fourth, we can be assured that all answers will be for the purpose of glorifying God's Son and advancing the kingdom either numerically or spiritually. The Philippians had prayed for Paul since the church was established. When he was arrested and sent to Rome, they were fearful and worried. They could not understand why the Lord God allowed him to be imprisoned in the first place and then to go on trial before the emperor. This often happens to us. We cannot understand what God is doing when he does not deliver us or a loved one from a physical malady or difficult situation. One reason is this: God wants the gospel shared to someone who may not have access to the gospel. In Philippians 1, Paul encourages them by explaining the "good" that was coming from his imprisonment.

Philippians 1:12-15
Now I want you to know, brothers and sisters, that what has happened to me has actually served to [pioneer] advance the gospel. As a result, it has become clear throughout the whole palace guard and to everyone else that I am in chains for Christ. And because of my chains, most of the brothers and sisters have become confident in the Lord and dare all the more to proclaim the gospel without fear. It is true that some preach Christ out of envy and rivalry, but others out of goodwill.

Paul was sharing the gospel with the household of Caesar (servants, family members, officials, and others employed in his palace), the guards he was chained to, and eventually even the emperor himself. Also, the Lord had awakened a sleeping church to become bolder in their advancement of the kingdom.

I inserted the kind of "advance" the word indicates in the Greek. The word translated "advance" in the English meant to make a pioneer advance where the gospel had not been. It was used by the Roman military to describe the soldiers who would cut away trees, plants, and shrubs to build a road for the army to advance in wartime.

Since the apostle Paul's imprisonment, the gospel of Jesus was making a pioneer advance into the capital city. God would not answer their prayers for deliverance, but He did give Paul the right perspective which brought peace.

Fifth, all answers will bring peace from God as we accept whatever He does according to His will.

Philippians 4:6-7
In nothing be anxious, but in everything, by prayer...petition with thanksgiving, let your requests be made known to God. And the peace of God, which surpasses all understanding, will guard your hearts and your thoughts in Christ Jesus."

Whatever issues that we face, struggles we have, hurdles we must overcome, we should bring them before the Lord in prayer. Then we should thank the Lord for the privilege of coming before the throne and the answer He will provide. This brings peace.

In 1 Peter 5, Peter explains that we can rest in His care.

1 Peter 5:6-7
Humble yourselves therefore under the mighty hand of God, that

he may exalt you in due time, casting all your worries on him, because he cares for you.

Sixth, God will not give us what we desire if it is sinful or from sinful motives. Among the readers of the letter James wrote, there were members of the church who were fighting among themselves over the satisfaction of their own lusts.

In James 4, the half-brother of Jesus gives this rebuke.

James 4:1-3
Where do wars and fightings among you come from? Don't they come from your pleasures that war in your members? You lust, and don't have. You murder and covet, and can't obtain. You fight and make war [with one another]. You don't have, because you don't ask [pray]. You ask, and don't receive, because you ask with wrong motives, so that you may spend it for your pleasures. As we can see, the Lord will not answer these kinds of prayers.

So, when we pray, God will answer. We must allow God to do this in the different ways he chooses based on His will.

The Prayer for Justice

When the Scriptures speak of "vengeance," they are really referring to our notion of "justice." In the Bible, the English words, "vengeance, avenge, judgment, judge, or justice" are the same words. In many cultures such as ours, when some see the word "vengeance," they immediately think of "acts of revenge" where people decide to punish others way beyond what is just with great bitterness and spite. This is not the biblical understanding. Though many translators may use the word "vengeance" the term comes closest to the English word "justice." We have already studied many truths about justice (vengeance) so far.

A short review of what we have learned in light of our persecutors is in order. We have learned that justice is God's responsibility, and we are not to take justice into our own hands even in regard to our persecutors.

Romans 12:19
Don't seek revenge yourselves, beloved, but give place to God's wrath. For it is written, "Vengeance belongs to me; I will repay, says the Lord."

We discovered that God will judge our persecutors at the Great White Throne judgment at the end of the world. Every evil that our persecutors have done against us will be fully judged.

Revelation 20:11-12
I saw a great white throne, and him who sat on it, from whose face the Earth and the heaven fled away. There was found no place for them. I saw the dead, the great and the small, standing before the throne, and they opened books. Another book was opened, which is the book of life. The dead were judged out of the things which were written in the books, according to their works.

We know that in God's wisdom and will, He can and does administer His justice directly on this Earth to evil doers which includes our persecutors. We studied the fact that God administers His justice on the Earth indirectly through the governmental authorities He has established.

Therefore, can Christians pray that God will administer His justice (vengeance) in their behalf to persecutors upon this Earth? The answer is yes. It will be up to God to decide whether He will administer His justice now or in the life to come but we may prey for this. We simply leave it at the throne for Him to decide. Remember this is not a prayer of "revenge" the way many think; instead, it is for justice.

We see these prayers for justice in the prayers and songs of the Old Testament Psalms.

Psalm 17:13
Arise, Yahweh, confront him. Cast him down. Deliver my soul from the wicked by your sword.

Psalm 35:1-4 (By David)
Contend, Yahweh, with those who contend with me. Fight against those who fight against me. Take hold of shield and buckler, and stand up for my help. Brandish the spear and block those who pursue me.... Let those who seek after my soul be disappointed and brought to dishonor. Let those who plot my ruin be turned back and confounded. Let them be as chaff before the wind, Yahweh's angel driving them on. Let their way be dark...slippery, Yahweh's angel pursuing them. For without cause they have hidden their net in a pit for me. Without cause they have dug a pit for my soul. Let destruction come on him unawares. Let his net that he has hidden catch himself. Let him fall into that destruction.

Psalm 43:1-2
Vindicate me, God, and plead my cause against an ungodly nation. Oh, deliver me from deceitful and wicked men. For you are the God of my strength. Why have you rejected me? Why do I go mourning because...oppression of the enemy?

Psalm 69:24-29
Pour out your indignation on them. Let the fierceness of your anger overtake them. Let their habitation be desolate. Let no one dwell in their tents. For they persecute him whom you have wounded. They tell of the sorrow of those whom you have hurt. Charge them with crime upon crime. Don't let them come into your righteousness.

Psalm 140:8-11
Yahweh, don't grant the desires of the wicked. Don't let their evil plans succeed, or they will become proud. Selah. As for the head of

those who surround me, let the mischief of their own lips cover them. Let burning coals fall on them. Let them be thrown into the fire, into miry pits, from where they never rise. An evil speaker won't be established...Evil will hunt...violent...to overthrow him.

Psalm 141:10
Let the wicked fall together into their own nets, while I pass by.

Psalm 55:1-15 (By David)
Listen to my prayer, God. Don't hide...from my supplication. Attend to me, and answer me. I am restless in my complaint, and moan...My heart is...pained...The terrors of death have fallen on me. Fearfulness and trembling have come on me. Horror has overwhelmed me.... Confuse them, Lord...confound their language, for I have seen violence and strife in the city....Let death come suddenly on them. Let them go...alive into Sheol. For wickedness is among them, in their dwelling.

Psalm 58:1-8 (By David)
Do you indeed speak righteousness, silent ones? Do you judge blamelessly, you sons of men? No, in your heart you plot injustice. You measure out the violence of your hands in the Earth....Their poison is like the poison of a snake; like a deaf cobra that stops its ear, which doesn't listen to the voice of charmers, no matter how skillful the charmer may be. Break their teeth, God, in their mouth. Break out the great teeth of the young lions, Yahweh. Let them vanish like water that flows away. When they draw the bow, let their arrows be made blunt. Let them be like a snail which melts and passes away, like the stillborn child, who has not seen the sun.

This last example has a heading that says, "For the Chief Musician....by David, when Saul sent, and they watched the house to kill him.

Psalm 59:1-14 (By David)
Deliver me from my enemies, my God. Set me on high from those who rise up against me. Deliver me from the workers of iniquity.

Save me from the bloodthirsty men. For, behold, they lie in wait for my soul. The mighty gather themselves together against me, not for my disobedience, nor for my sin, Yahweh. I have done no wrong, yet they are ready to attack me. Rise up, behold, and help me.... Don't kill them, or my people may forget. Scatter them by your power, and bring them down, Lord our shield. For the sin of their mouth, and the words of their lips, let them be caught in their pride, for the curses and lies which they utter. Consume them in wrath. Consume them, and they will be no more. Let them know that God rules in Jacob, to the ends of the Earth. Selah.

We can also see the saints beheaded during the tribulation crying out to God for justice.

Revelation 6:9-11
When he opened the fifth seal, I saw underneath the altar the souls of those who had been killed for the Word of God, and for the testimony of the Lamb which they had. They cried with a loud voice, saying, "How long, Master, the holy and true, until you judge and avenge our blood on those who dwell on the Earth?" A long white robe was given to each of them. They were told that they should rest yet for a while, until their fellow servants and their brothers, who would also be killed...should complete their course.

Therefore, believers may pray for the Lord God Almighty to immediately administer His justice upon persecutors. Isn't this what we do when anyone has committed crimes against us or others and are appearing before a court of law? There is no difference. Some might say, "How do we reconcile the commands to "to love, bless, do good to, pray for, not resist, and forgive their enemies" with a prayer for justice? First, we are told to love with knowledge and much discernment.

Philippians 1:9-11
This I pray, that your love may abound yet more and more in knowledge and all discernment...that you may approve the things

that are excellent, that you may be sincere and without offense to the day of Christ, being filled with the fruits of righteousness, which are through Jesus Christ, to the glory and praise of God.

Do we show greater love to people by letting them hurt and maim others or stopping these from doing harm? If they will be judged according to every deed done, then if the Lord God stops them, there will be less judgment for these people. Also, halting attacks upon other Christians shows greater love for those who are persecuted.

Second, what could be a greater blessing than stopping them from sinning against the name of Jesus Christ in their persecution? Third, what greater good can we do than stop their horrible aggressions through prayer? Fourth, who are we asking to resist them? It is not God? Fifth, can we forgive them and still ask God to stop their persecuting terror? Sixth, can we not pray for the Lord to stop them and then ask Him to open their hearts to receive Him? Didn't Paul have to be stopped on the road to Damascus before he could receive Jesus as Savior and Lord?

A Prayerful Observance

In the sixth chapter of his letter to the Ephesians, Paul speaks of the supernatural battle we find ourselves in and encourages us to pray for one another with a watchful and alert eye on each other. We are fellow warriors engaged in battle and communicating with the commander through our prayers.

Ephesians 6:18
With all prayer...requests, praying at all times in the Spirit, and being watchful to this end in... perseverance...requests for all the saints.

We are to be on the alert and praying. The word translated "watchful" in the Greek means "to be alert and keep watch." We are to be keeping watch over ourselves and all the saints praying as we see things happen.

Then Paul continues and asks the saints to pray for him as he battles spiritually the forces of evil as he faced the many persecutions that came his way.

Ephesians 6:19-20
On my behalf, that utterance may be given to me in opening my mouth, to make known with boldness the mystery of the Good News, for which I am an ambassador in chains; that in it I may speak boldly, as I ought to speak.

Notice, the apostle Paul asks for help in the midst of the persecution. This was Paul's regular practice and should become ours. When soldiers need help on the battlefield, they ask for it.

1 Thessalonians 5:24-26
He who calls you is faithful, who will also do it. Brothers, pray for us. Greet all the brothers with a holy kiss.

Colossians 4:3
Praying together for us also, that God may open to us a door for the word, to speak the mystery of Christ, for which I am also in bonds.

2 Thessalonians 3:1
Finally, brothers, pray for us, that the word of the Lord may spread rapidly and be glorified, even as also with you.

As the apostle Paul was battling and they were battling, they were praying for each other. They were spiritual warriors supporting each other.

A Prayerful Persistence

As we come before the throne of God and pray for these many requests, we must be consistent and persistent. Here, Paul describes his diligence in prayer for the many churches he founded.

Colossians 4:2
Devote yourselves to prayer, keeping alert in it with an attitude of thanksgiving.

Romans 12:12
Rejoicing in hope; enduring in troubles; continuing steadfastly in prayer.

2 Timothy 1:3
I thank God, whom I serve as my forefathers did, with a pure conscience. How unceasing is my memory of you in my petitions, night and day.

1 Thessalonians 3:10
Night and day praying exceedingly that we may see your face, and may perfect that which is lacking in your faith?

1 Thessalonians 5:17
Pray without ceasing.

Colossians 1:9:
"For this reason also, since the day we heard of it, we have not ceased to pray for you and to ask that you may be filled with the knowledge of His will in all spiritual wisdom and understanding."

The point isn't that we have to pray every minute of every day, but we must be persistent in prayer. It is the constant pursuit in prayer for our needs and the needs of others that God blesses.

At numerous times in King David's life, he needed God's power and prayed for it. He persisted in his requests and then watched for God to answer them.

Psalm 5:1-3
Give ear to my words, Yahweh. Consider my meditation. Listen to the voice of my cry, my King...my God; for to you do I pray. Yahweh, in the morning you shall hear my voice. In the morning I will lay my requests before you, and will watch expectantly.

Here, David describes his pattern of prayer. Every morning, he would go before the throne of God with his requests and eagerly watch for His divine work. He had persistence and watchfulness. Why? David knew His God and understood that His God responds to the prayers of His people in great power. We should do the same.

So, we see the numerous prayers that we may pray in the midst of persecution. These prayers will unleash the power of God in our lives and the lives of others.

STANDING YOUR GROUND

Chapter 17

Respond with a Courageous Persistence

As we have seen, the holy saints reacted to persecution in many ways. Yet, once they came face to face with it, they responded with real courageous persistence. As a result, the gospel was furthered. The more these enemies of the good news attempted to stamp out their enthusiasm and fire for Christ, the more it ignited them. Until the good news of the risen Jesus had spread all throughout the Roman Empire.

In Acts 8, after Stephen was martyred, Saul began his own persecution. The saints, who were scattered, shared the good news everywhere they went.

Acts 8:4
Therefore those who were scattered abroad went around preaching the word.

Though they were running for their lives with Saul in hot pursuit, these bold believers preached the good news. They proclaimed the gospel, even though their fellow Christians were imprisoned and murdered for the blessed Savior.

Then the mantel of martyrdom was passed down to one of the most unlikely characters in this drama of redemption: the protagonist of this persecution - Saul himself. Saul, now Paul, was miraculously converted by the resurrected Jesus Christ on the road to Damascus. After being blind for three days, Paul was baptized and began his own proclamation of the gospel that he had previously attempted to stamp out. He became the recipient of the very afflictions he had given for some time to those who were now his brethren.

In Acts 9, the prophet Ananias arrived in Damascus and declared that he would suffer much for His Lord.

Acts 9:16
For I will show him [Paul] how many things he must suffer for my name's sake.

Suffering was such a common experience that he began to welcome it as a great opportunity to enjoy a much deeper and more abiding relationship to Christ.

Philippians 3:10
That I may know him, and the power of his resurrection, and the fellowship of his sufferings, becoming conformed to his death.

The apostle explained that he desired to fully know Jesus Christ, the power of His resurrection as He worked in and through Him, and the fellowship of His sufferings as Paul partnered with Christ in suffering for Him.

If Christians share the gospel and it leads to persecution, they must seek to possess the following attitudes toward their suffering. The apostle experienced more persecution than most but possessed all of the following attitudes which allowed him to handle them in a divine way. Through these supernatural considerations, all Christians will find a deep fellowship with their Savior in their suffering for Him. The Spirit will provide the grace needed when the time arrives.

A Greater Boldness in Preaching

The Christian's response to persecution is to be even bolder and more courageous in preaching the gospel. In Acts 4, Peter and John appeared before the Jewish Sanhedrin with great courage and boldness.

THE PERSECUTION OF THE SAINTS AND HOW TO OVERCOME IT

Acts 4:15-20
But when they had commanded them to go aside out of the council, they conferred among themselves, saying, "What will we do to these men? Because indeed a notable miracle has been done through them, as can be plainly seen by all who dwell in Jerusalem, and we can't deny it. But so that this spreads no further among the people, let's threaten them, that from now on they don't speak to anyone in this name." They called them, and charged them not to speak at all...in the name of Jesus. But Peter and John answered them, "Whether it is right in the sight of God to listen to you rather than to God, judge for yourselves, for we can't help telling the things which we saw and heard."

These religious leaders had just crucified Christ a short time ago. So, they commanded Peter and John to stop all preaching and teaching in the name of Jesus or suffer the consequences from their wrath. These two apostles boldly told these men that they could not stop proclaiming Christ. These judges of God's people would have to decide for themselves whether it was right for Peter and John to give heed to them or to God. They would continue testifying to the people what they had seen and heard.

In Acts 4, when the two disciples were released, the two apostles went immediately to their own brethren. These saints praised God together for His sovereignty over their persecution. Then they prayed for the boldness, courage, and confidence they needed to continue preaching His good news. After the prayer, they proceeded back to the streets of Jerusalem to proclaim His Word again.

Acts 4:31-33
When they had prayed, the place was shaken where they were gathered together. They were all filled with the Holy Spirit, and they spoke the word of God with boldness. The multitude of those who believed were of one heart and soul. Not one of them [the

saints] *claimed that anything of the things which he possessed was his own, but they had all things in common. With great power, the apostles gave their testimony of the resurrection of the Lord Jesus. Great grace was on them all.*

Consequently, in Acts 5, all the apostles were imprisoned and brought before the Sanhedrin. Peter was asked why they did not obey their previous command not to preach. Once he said this, Peter proceeded to preach the gospel in the form of an indictment.

Acts 5:29-31
But Peter and the apostles answered, "We must obey God rather than men. The God of our fathers raised up Jesus, whom you killed, hanging him on a tree. God exalted him with his right hand to be a Prince and a Savior, to give repentance to Israel, and remission of sins."

Afterward, the council threatened them with the loss of their lives. To make sure the apostles understood the seriousness of their message to stop, they beat them and warned them again.

Once released, they went out and did the same thing again. They preached the good news with great boldness.

Acts 5:42
Every day, in the temple and at home, they never stopped teaching and preaching Jesus, the Christ.

The threat of their own deaths did not deter them from their evangelism. It only made them bolder. Their courage grew to greater and greater heights.

While Paul waited for his trial before Caesar, he wrote to the Philippians and explained his conviction as he prepared himself for his court appearance. Due to their prayers and the provision of the Holy Spirit, he was confident that he would not be put to shame. Instead, with great courage he would exalt Jesus Christ in his own body whether by life or death. Paul would demonstrate bravery in his evangelism.

Philippians 1:19-20
For I know that this will turn out to my salvation, through your supplication and the supply of the Spirit of Jesus Christ, according to my earnest expectation and hope, that I will in no way be put to shame...with all boldness, as always, now also Christ will be magnified in my body, whether by life, or by death.

Paul's fearlessness had even stirred up the Roman church to find the fortitude in the Holy Spirit to share the gospel.

Philippians 1:14
And that most of the brothers in the Lord, being confident through my bonds, are more abundantly bold to speak the word of God without fear.

Paul told the Thessalonians he boldly preached the gospel to them in the midst of great opposition.

1 Thessalonians 2:2
But having suffered before and been shamefully treated, as you know, at Philippi, we grew bold in our God to tell you the gospel of God in much conflict.

Here, Paul described the great boldness and courage that he experienced in proclaiming the gospel to them amid great conflict. He would courageously persist no matter what.

This supernatural courage and boldness come through prayer, the Word, and the Holy Spirit. It also proceeds from the support of other Christians and the believer's confidence in the sovereignty of God. Our Lord God is in control of all persecution. As was seen earlier, the knowledge that His persecuted followers are filling up what is lacking in Christ's afflictions and bearing the marks of His ownership through the partnership of their suffering for Him can greatly add to their boldness. They can walk into strife boldly proclaiming.

A Greater Commitment in Proclaiming

Persecution should only make Christians more committed to proclaiming the gospel. It should make them work that much harder at announcing the plan. Throughout the first century, the more effort the world exercised in squashing the gospel, the more energy Christians exercised in spreading it.

When real persecution began with Saul (who later became Paul), the good news of Christ rapidly spread through all of the region of Judea.

Acts 8:1
Saul was consenting to his [Stephen's] death. A great persecution arose against the assembly which was in Jerusalem in that day

It then spread to Samaria.

Acts 8:5
Philip went down to the city of Samaria, and proclaimed to them the Christ.

After this, the gospel of Christ spread into the regions of Phoenicia, Cyprus, and Antioch.

Acts 11:19-20
They [the believers] therefore who were scattered abroad by the oppression that arose about Stephen traveled as far as Phoenicia,

Cyprus, and Antioch, speaking the word to no one except...Jews. But there were some of them, men of Cyprus and Cyrene, who, when they had come to Antioch, spoke to the Greeks, preaching the Lord Jesus.

Then Saul was converted, and the gospel of Jesus literally exploded in the world. Why was Paul so persistent?

Philippians 3:12
Not that I have already obtained, or am already made perfect; but I press on, if it is so that I may take hold of that for which also I was laid hold of by Christ Jesus.

He was taken hold of by the Lord for his own salvation but also to spread the gospel. Paul was pressing on to take hold of this and spread the good news everywhere he could. This required immense tenacity.

The Sanhedrin did everything they could to stop Christ and eventually crucified him. Evil men did everything they could to destroy Paul also. This included stoning him.

Acts 14:19-20
But some Jews from Antioch and Iconium came there, and having persuaded the multitudes, they stoned Paul, and dragged him out of the city, supposing that he was dead. But as the disciples stood around him, he rose up, and entered into the city. On the next day he went out with Barnabas to Derbe.

It involved attempting to kill him by ambush, but they were unsuccessful.

Acts 23:12
When it was day, some of the Jews banded together, and bound themselves under a curse, saying that they would neither eat nor drink until they had killed Paul.

Imprisoning him did not help, because he simply shared Christ with those who visited him.

Acts 28:23
When they had appointed him a day, they came to him into his lodging in great number. He explained...testifying about the kingdom of God, and persuading them concerning Jesus, both from the law of Moses and from the prophets, from morning...evening.

The guards with whom he was chained heard the gospel from him.

Philippians 1:13
So that it became evident to the whole palace guard, and to all the rest, that my bonds are in Christ.

The gospel even reached into Caesar's very own household.

Philippians 4:22
All the saints greet you, especially those...of Caesar's household.

This was before Caesar would hear the gospel at Paul's trial.

Christians should have the exact same kind of persistence in suffering. As was previously discussed, the knowledge that their persecuted followers are filling up what is lacking in Christ's afflictions, and bearing the marks of ownership by Him through the partnership of their suffering for Him will increase their persistence. Regardless of the strife, they will proclaim Him.

A Greater Reliance on Judgment

Persecution might make Christians so angry they might want to become their own judge and jury in order to bring punishment upon their adversaries. As has been seen earlier, believers must always love their enemies and rely on God to avenge their suffering from the gospel. This does not mean that they cannot defend themselves. The believers from the tribulation cried out for our God to avenge their martyrdom because they relied on God for judgment.

Revelation 6:9-11
When he opened the fifth seal, I saw underneath the altar the souls of those who had been killed for the word of God, and for the testimony which they held. They cried with a loud voice, saying, "How long, Master, the holy and true, do you not judge and avenge our blood on those who dwell on the Earth?" There was given to each one of them a white robe. It was said to them that they should rest yet for a little time, until their fellow servants and their brothers, who would also be killed even as they were, had been fulfilled.

These saints relied on His power and His justice. When Christians are persecuted, they should do the same. God is the sole authority to judge the sins of unbelievers. Some of the judgment may occur upon the Earth but a day will come when all deeds will be judged, and everything will be made right before God.

The behavior of Jesus is the best example of this. As He stood before Annas, He was punched in the face and before Caiaphas, He was blindfolded, mocked, and beaten.

John 18:22
When he had said this, one of the officers standing by slapped Jesus with his hand, saying, "Do you answer the high priest like that?"

Matthew 26:67-68
Then they spit in his face and beat him with their fists, and some slapped him, saying, "Prophesy to us, you Christ! Who hit you?"

He was treated like some kind of cheap magician, when he was asked to perform a miracle before Herod. The king then dressed Christ up in a royal robe in utter mockery and returned the Lord to Pilate.

Luke 23:11-12
Herod with his soldiers humiliated him and mocked him. Dressing him in luxurious clothing, they sent him back to Pilate. Herod and Pilate became friends with each other that very day, for before that they were enemies with each other.

Pilate had Him scourged, crowned with thornes, and led away to His crucifixion.

John 19:1-2
Then Pilate therefore took Jesus and flogged him. The soldiers twisted thorns into a crown, and put it on his head, and dressed him in a purple garment.

Jesus was scorned, blasphemed, criticized, even laughed at, and humiliated before men on the cross until he breathed his last breath. Throughout all of it, He did not retaliate.

In 1 Peter 2, the apostle describes how Jesus never reviled or uttered threats in retaliation, but He entrusted Himself to God who judges. Jesus left all the judgment up to God and Peter exhorted Christians to do the same.

1 Peter 2:21-23
For to this you were called, because Christ also suffered for us, leaving you an example, that you should follow his steps, who did not sin, "neither was deceit found in his mouth." Who, when he [Jesus] was cursed, didn't curse back. When he suffered, didn't threaten, but committed himself to him who judges righteously.

Notice, Jesus relied on His Father to judge them rather than

Himself. Peter explains that we are to follow His example.

In Romans 12, Paul encouraged Christians in Rome to provide a place for God's wrath, rather than seek revenge. Christians must always remember that vengeance belongs to God and He will repay.

Romans 12:19-20
Don't seek revenge yourselves, beloved, but give place to God's wrath....it is written, "Vengeance belongs to me; I will repay, says the Lord." Therefore, "If your enemy is angry, feed him. If he is thirsty, give him a drink; for in doing so, you will heap coals of fire on his head."

This is difficult when suffering is afflicted on this Earth. All will be made right in the next life.

As we suffer persecution for the sake of Christ, we must remember that we should rely on God to avenge us rather than become bitter and vengeful ourselves. Once again, this does not negate self-defense.

A Greater Confidence in Hardship

Christians should meet persecution with the confidence that the Holy Spirit will provide the patient endurance they will need to glorify God. God will give them whatever they need to handle the situation. Often, believers will begin to anticipate some kind of persecution. They will begin to think that how they feel at the moment will be how they will react when the persecution is encountered. This simply is not true.

All suffering is fearful upon reflection but as the moment comes, God always provides His strength. Paul affirmed this when he suffered from his thorn in the flesh. He begged the

Lord three times to remove it, but the Lord refused to do it. He desired that Paul learn that in his weakness he would find God's strength.

2 Corinthians 12:810
Concerning this thing, I begged the Lord three times that it might depart from me. He has said to me, "My grace is sufficient for you, for my power [in you] is made perfect in weakness." Most gladly therefore will I rather glory in my weaknesses, that the power of Christ [in Spirit] may rest on me. Therefore I take pleasure in weaknesses, in injuries, in necessities, in persecutions, in distresses, for Christ's sake. For when I am weak, then am I strong.

When Stephen faced his own death by stoning, there was no pleading for his life. He did not beg for mercy or cry out in terror and fear. The Lord gave him a confidence in the suffering through a vision of Jesus Christ welcoming him to heaven. This vision was a message to all believers. Jesus will be there to welcome His saints home. In 2 Corinthians 5, the apostle Paul explains that to be absent from the human body means that Christians are at supernaturally at home with the Lord. What an assurance a believer has!

2 Corinthians 5:8
We are courageous, I say, and are willing rather to be absent from the body, and to be at home with the Lord.

In Acts 20, Paul met with his longtime friends, the elders of Ephesus, on his way to the city of Jerusalem. In verses 22-24, he explained to them, that the Spirit had testified of the terrible suffering that awaited him. There was no real fear or concern. He did not hold his life as dear to him. He desired to fulfill his ministry. Paul was a driven man. The suffering was a simple obstacle to overcome and keep going. He saw himself as running a race to win. And Paul ran with joy. He saw the goal in His mind's eye and would not depart from it

THE PERSECUTION OF THE SAINTS AND HOW TO OVERCOME IT

no matter who tried to stop him. His life was not important enough to end his ministry of the gospel. He desired to fully testify to all the people God brought his way, and the entire gospel was to be preached.

Acts 20:22-24
Now, behold, I go bound by the Spirit to Jerusalem, not knowing what will happen to me there; except that the Holy Spirit testifies in every city, saying that bonds and afflictions wait for me. But these things don't count; nor do I hold my life dear to myself, so that I may finish my race with joy, and the ministry which I received from the Lord Jesus, to fully testify to the gospel of the grace of God.

In Acts 21, Paul arrived in Caesarea and was about fifty or so miles from the city of Jerusalem. Again, a prophet warned him of the impending danger. The saints begged the apostle to turn back from his journey to the city of Jerusalem. Paul refused explaining that he was ready to not only be bound by them but even die for the gospel.

Acts 21:11-14
Coming to us, and taking Paul's belt, he bound his own feet and hands, and said, "Thus says the Holy Spirit: 'So will the Jews at Jerusalem bind the man who owns this belt, and will deliver him into the hands of the Gentiles.'" When we heard these things, both we and they of that place begged him not to go up to Jerusalem. Then Paul answered, "What are you doing, weeping and breaking my heart? For I am ready not only to be bound, but also to die...for the name of the Lord Jesus." When he would not be persuaded, we ceased, saying, "The Lord's will be done."

In Acts 13, when Paul was physically thrown out of city of Pisidian Antioch, he confidently went into Iconium. He had no fear and no terror. He was a man of determination to endure whatever came his way.

Acts 13:50
But the Jews urged on the devout women...and the chief men of the city, and stirred up a persecution against Paul and Barnabas, and threw them out of their borders.

In Acts 14, he was dragged out of Lystra, stoned, and left for dead. Afterward, He got up and entered the city of Derbe to continue his ministry.

Acts 14:19-20
But some Jews from Antioch and Iconium came there, and having persuaded the multitudes, they stoned Paul, and dragged him out of the city, supposing that he was dead. But as the disciples stood around him, he rose up, and entered into the city. On the next day he went out with Barnabas to Derbe.

This man, who is an example for all Christians, had a quiet, yet determined and fearless resolution to share the gospel. It did not matter what came his way.

Christians should have the exact same kind of confidence in suffering. As was previously discussed, the knowledge that their persecuted followers are filling up what is lacking in Christ's afflictions and bearing the marks of ownership by Him through the partnership of their suffering for Him, will increase their confidence. They knew they would be able to handle the persecution if it came. They are able to walk into the strife, mayhem, and chaos they might bring due to the proclaiming of the gospel with greater confidence. They will know that the Lord will provide the strength they need.

A Greater Joy in Suffering

In spite of the difficulty of persecution, Christians are to experience real joy in suffering. This appears to be exactly the opposite of what most people think would happen if one suffers for the gospel. Who has joy in suffering of any kind? With physical suffering one would expect to feel sad, angry, or depressed. This is not the case of suffering from general trials for believers, nor is it the case when suffering persecution for Christ's sake.

In 1 Thessalonians 1, the apostle Paul praised the church because these saints became imitators of Paul and the Lord in their tribulation. Why? In their affliction for the gospel, they not only received the Word and believed it, but they found the joy in the Holy Spirit. For the believer, when sharing the gospel, tribulation and joy will go hand in hand.

1 Thessalonians 1:6
You became imitators of us, and of the Lord, having received the word in much affliction, with joy of the Holy Spirit.

First, joy comes from the indwelling Holy Spirit. This is a joy that comes from deity itself. It is the true joy found in God.

Galatians 5:22-23
But the fruit [produced by] of the Spirit is love, joy, peace, patience, kindness, goodness, faith, gentleness, and self-control. Against such things there is no law.

The fruit of the Spirit is produced in a Christian's life as a response to being filled with the Holy Spirit not because of any kind of positive circumstances. The Christian's response to any of life's woes should be a reaction from the filling of the Spirit, not the deeds of the flesh. The Spirit will produce a true supernatural joy as we stand our ground.

The flesh will desire to be angry, grieved, and depressed at suffering for Christ, but the Spirit will provide joy.

Galatians 5:19-21
Now the deeds of the flesh [sin principle in our physical bodies] are obvious, which are: adultery, sexual immorality, uncleanness, lustfulness, idolatry, sorcery, hatred, strife, jealousies, outbursts of anger, rivalries, divisions, heresies, envy, murders, drunkenness, orgies, and things like these; of which I forewarn you...that those who practice such things will not inherit God's Kingdom.

Second, joy is a characteristic of the walk of Christians no matter what the Lord will allow life to bring their way. Paul, who had experienced much persecution, told the church at Philippi, who also had experienced much persecution, to be rejoicing in the Lord always. Then he repeats himself, just so he can make sure they fully understood its importance. He declared that they should be joyful in the Lord Jesus.

Philippians 4:4
Rejoice in the Lord always. Again I will say, Rejoice!

Third, Christians rejoice in the fact that standing firm in suffering is a clear proof of their faith in Christ. In 1 Peter 1, Peter told his readers that their faith is tested by fire.

1 Peter 1:7-9
That the proof of your faith, which is more precious than gold that perishes even though it is tested by fire, may be found to result in praise...glory and honor at the revelation of Jesus Christ - whom not having known you love; on whom, though now you don't see him, yet believing, you rejoice greatly with joy unspeakable and full of glory -- receiving the end of your faith, the salvation of your souls.

This produced real proof of their faith, which was more precious than gold. It would result in much praise, glory, and honor at the appearing of the Lord. He then praised them because though they had not seen Christ, they believed in Him. Also, they loved Him and greatly rejoiced in a joy that was inexpressible and full of glory.

Fourth, Christians are to find real joy in suffering because suffering is honorable. It glorifies our God, and it shows that He is highly valued.

In Acts 5, the apostles had been flogged and ordered not to preach publicly by the Sanhedrin. Then they went away rejoicing that they were worthy of suffering shame for Him.

Acts 5:41
They therefore departed from the presence of the council, rejoicing that they were counted worthy to suffer dishonor for Jesus' name.

Fifth, Christians rejoice because suffering tests their faith and produces endurance. This suffering leads to maturity in Christ. Paul explained to the Galatians that the goal of his ministry was for Christ to be formed in them and expressed the same goal to the Colossians but in different terminology.

Galatians 4:19
My little children, of whom I am again in travail until Christ is formed in you.

Colossians 1:22
Yet now he has reconciled in the body of his flesh through death, to present you [the church] holy and without blemish and blameless before him.

One of the ways in which the Father accomplishes this is through suffering. James told his many readers to consider it all joy when they encountered a wide variety of suffering. Why? It produced patient endurance which would result in making believers perfect and complete, lacking in nothing (in our service to God).

James 1:2-4
Count it all joy, my brothers, when you fall into various [varicolored] temptations, Knowing that the testing of your faith produces patience. Let patience have its perfect work, that you may be perfect and complete, lacking in nothing.

So, suffering aids in producing maturity in service.

Sixth, believers should rejoice in persecution because it results from sharing the gospel which brings people into His kingdom. In Philippians 2, Paul told the Philippians that he rejoiced as he was being poured out as a drink offering upon the sacrifice and service of their faith. The apostle Paul was willing to be a sacrifice for their souls.

Philippians 2:17
Yes, and if I am poured out on the sacrifice and service of your faith, I rejoice, and rejoice with you all.

He used a concept from the Old Testament to describe himself as a drink offering poured out on the altar for them.

Leviticus 23:37
These are the set feasts of Yahweh, which you shall proclaim to be holy convocations, to offer an offering made by fire to Yahweh, a burnt offering, and a meal-offering, a sacrifice, and drink-offerings, each on its own day.

The apostle Paul was being poured out in service to them as a sacrifice in suffering for them.

If Christians are to suffer, they should count it a privilege and joy to suffer for the sake of Christ. As was seen earlier, the knowledge that their persecuted followers are filling up what is lacking in Christ's afflictions, and bearing the marks of ownership by their Lord through the partnership of their suffering for Christ will increase their joy. These believers can walk into strife and proclaim the gospel with joy.

A Greater Endurance in Affliction

As we have seen, there are many reasons the Lord allows His own people to suffer persecution. As a result, we must endure it. This does not refer to a passive kind of suffering but a courageous active endurance. It's the attitude that we will never give in to any kind of torment in the name of Christ. We will withstand any circumstances that may be painful and difficult and will hold onto our faith, continue our ministry, and share the good news of Jesus Christ. This endurance will glorify Him. There are several aspects to this endurance that are found in the three words used to speak of endurance.

The first word focuses on our "holding on to our faith, ministry, and testimony amid trouble. The Greek word that is translated "endure" is derived from two words. The first is a preposition meaning "into the midst, in the midst, amid, among, or between" and the main verb meaning "to have or to hold." This "holding" can refer to "possessing, clinging or adhering to" something. As a result, this term carries the idea of holding onto one's faith, ministry, or testimony in the midst of trials and afflictions.

In his letter to the Thessalonians, the apostle Paul speaks of their adherence to these things in the persecutions that they faced.

2 Thessalonians 1:4
So that we ourselves boast about you in the assemblies of God for your perseverance and faith in all your persecutions and in the afflictions which you endure.

In the first letter to Corinth, he speaks of his adherence to his faith, ministry, and testimony in the midst of suffering for the name of Christ.

1 Corinthians 4:12
We toil, working with our own hands. When people curse us, we bless. Being persecuted, we endure.

Therefore, we must adhere, hold onto, and really cling to our faith, ministry, and testimony no matter what suffering we may encounter.

The second word focuses on "actively remaining" in our faith, ministry, and testimony. This term comes from two words. The first is a preposition meaning "by or under" and a verb meaning "to abide or remain" in a condition, state, or some other circumstance. In suffering for Christ, it would mean "remaining" in our faith, ministry, and continuing our testimony. This is not a passive "remaining" but an active "abiding."

In Matthew, the Lord Jesus uses the term to speak of the endurance of true believers throughout their entire lives on this earth.

Matthew 10:22
You will be hated by all men for my name's sake, but he who endures to the end will be saved.

In his letter to Timothy, Paul describes his total willingness to actively remain in his faith, ministry, and testimony.

2 Timothy 2:10
Therefore I endure all things for the chosen ones' sake, that they also may obtain the salvation which is in Christ Jesus with eternal glory.

Then, he adds one of the motivating factors for his continual endurance in his trials.

2 Timothy 2:12
If we endure, we will also reign with him. If we deny him, he also will deny us.

The author of Hebrews challenges them to remember their former suffering and how they actively retained their faith, ministry, and testimony.

Hebrews 10:32
But remember…former days, in which, after you were enlightened, you endured a great struggle with sufferings.

James, the half-brother of Jesus and brother of Jude, wrote of Job's great endurance. Even though Job was afflicted with great suffering, he never left his faith in God.

James 5:11
Behold, we call them blessed who endured. You have heard of the perseverance [same root] of Job, and have seen the Lord in the outcome, and how the Lord is full of compassion and mercy.

True believers face persecutions with a commitment to abide and remain in the faith, continue the ministry, and persist in preaching the gospel no matter what comes their way. They will continue in spite of the opposition.

The third term is also from two root words which mean "by or under" and "to carry or bear" a burden. This word focuses on the handling of persecution by carrying its weight no matter how heavy it is. It's the attitude that no matter how difficult or painful it is, we will handle it. Our faith, ministry, and testimony will continue with the weight of the suffering on our shoulders.

STANDING YOUR GROUND

Paul explains to his son in the faith, Timothy, how he had held the weight of sufferings that came his way because of the gospel of Christ.

2 Timothy 3:11
Persecutions, and sufferings: those things that happened to me.... I endured those persecutions. The Lord [Jesus] delivered me out of them all.

Peter speaks of slaves carrying the burden of suffering for their faith or righteousness and not retaliating.

1 Peter 2:19
For it is commendable [finds favor] if someone endures pain, suffering unjustly, because of conscience toward God.

Therefore, Christians will stand up for Christ by bearing the weight of the burden of persecution no matter what it is.

As we have seen, believers will face great persecution in a vigorous and active way. They will be willing to hold onto their faith, ministry, or testimony in the midst of trouble. No matter what suffering comes their way, they will never give up. Finally, the saints will continue in Jesus Christ, the Lord, and carry the burden of persecution His name brings.

As we discovered, the saints stood their ground against persecution in many different ways. Yet, once they came face to face with it, they responded with courageous persistence. As a result, the gospel of Christ was advanced, and the saints were protected. We must take this kind of stance.

Conclusion

As we conclude this book, I would like to leave us with some final thoughts about persecution and belief in Christ. First, if you have received Jesus as Savior and Lord, you now have the spiritual tools needed to stand your ground. If we follow the principles that we have discovered in the Holy Scriptures concerning persecution, then whatever we do we will glorify God.

Second, if you read this entire book and realized that you do not understand salvation or have never received Christ as Lord and Savior, then I would like to encourage you to seek Him. Please do not skip this critical section; it may be the most important in your life.

From all outward appearances, humans seem "good" and attempt to live decent lives. This is man's concept of himself. This is not God's concept. The Almighty's view is that people all over the world and throughout the ages sin, sin, and sin again (Romans 3:23). This is a terrible and utterly destructive condition. Yet, they have ramifications that are much worse. These sins condemn us to everlasting divine retribution. We will live for eternity without God in His condemnation. This means forever and ever and ever and ever.

Though described briefly in the Old Testament, the Lord Jesus Christ clearly announced and proclaimed the future punishment to come. Contrary to popular belief, Jesus did not only speak of love, grace, and mercy, He also spoke of the coming judgment for sin. He declared that the judgment of sin would be everlasting punishment in a place He called "Hell." The Lord portrayed this place as an eternal inferno (Matthew 18:8) where there would be the weeping (from the sorrow) and gnashing of teeth (from the agony and anguish of suffering) continually into eternity (Matthew 8:12; 13:42, 50; 22:13; 24:51; 25:30; Luke 13:28).

Why must people face this horrific punishment? Though God is a God of love, grace, and mercy, He is also a God of great holiness, righteousness, and justice (Psalm 89:14,18). These attributes are just as much a part of His divine nature as His love, grace, and mercy. You have broken God's law as we all have, and the penalty must be paid. This began with the first man Adam (Genesis 3:1-7). When this occurred, His love, grace, and mercy surfaced, and a provision was made. Someone else would have to take man's place and pay the penalty. Someone who had never transgressed Him, who would never deserve punishment, and would fulfill all of God's Laws, would be substituted in man's place. This was the Son of God, Jesus Christ.

As the God-Man, He would pay the penalty for our sins in His death on the cross. Once done, the Lord God made only one provision for people to appropriate what His Son had done on the cross for them. This provision is receiving Jesus Christ as Savior and Lord. Though I cannot possibly share with you this good news in the confines of this book, I would love for you to consider purchasing my book entitled **Finding the Light: The Kingdom of Heaven and How to Enter It.** It can be found on Amazon.com. It is inexpensive and contains the full gospel message for your consideration. This message is so important and extensive that it cannot be presented in a few pages at the end of a book. May you discover through the Lord Jesus Christ the joy only found in Him.

ABOUT THE AUTHOR

Dr. Donald Jones is currently a Christian Pastoral Counselor with thirty-eight years of experience in the fields of pastoral ministry, public education, and Christian counseling. He carries degrees and certificates from four major universities and from a variety of educational institutions. He has been a professor of Languages and Bible, a television commentator, and a featured speaker at a variety of events and seminars at churches, schools, and other organizations across the United States. He is a member in good standing of several secular and Christian professional organizations. Dr. Jones has been a published author since 1976. For further information view his website at www.donjonesphd.com.